Copyright
Law

The West Legal Studies Series

Your options keep growing with West Legal Studies

Each year our list continues to offer you more options for every area of the law to meet your course or on-the-job reference requirements. We now have over 140 titles from which to choose in the following areas:

Administrative Law	Family Law
Alternative Dispute Resolution	Federal Taxation
Bankruptcy	Intellectual Property
Business Organizations/Corporations	Introduction to Law
Civil Litigation and Procedure	Introduction to Paralegalism
CLA Exam Preparation	Law Office Management
Client Accounting	Law Office Procedures
Computer in the Law Office	Legal Research, Writing, and Analysis
Constitutional Law	Legal Terminology
Contract Law	Paralegal Employment
Criminal Law and Procedure	Real Estate Law
Document Preparation	Reference Materials
Environmental Law	Torts and Personal Injury Law
Ethics	Will, Trusts, and Estate Administration

You will find unparalleled, practical support

Each book is augmented by instructor and student supplements to ensure the best learning experience possible. We also offer custom publishing and other benefits such as West's Student Achievement Award. In addition, our sales representatives are ready to provide you with dependable service.

We want to hear from you

Our best contributions for improving the quality of our books and instructional materials is feedback from the people who use them. If you have a question, concern, or observation about any of our materials, or you have a product proposal or manuscript, we want to hear from you. Please contact your local representative or write us at the following address:

West Legal Studies, 3 Columbia Circle, P.O. Box 15015, Albany, NY 12212-5015

For additional information point your browser at

www.westlegalstudies.com

WEST LEGAL STUDIES
Thomson Learning™

Copyright Law

Richard Stim

WEST LEGAL STUDIES
Thomson Learning™

Africa • Australia • Canada • Denmark • Japan • Mexico • New Zealand • Philippines
Puerto Rico • Singapore • Spain • United Kingdom • United States

NOTICE TO THE READER

Publisher does not warrant or guarantee any of the products described herein or perform any independent analysis in connection with any of the product information contained herein. Publisher does not assume, and expressly disclaims, any obligation to obtain and include information other than that provided to it by the manufacturer.

The reader is expressly warned to consider and adopt all safety precautions that might be indicated by the activities herein and to avoid all potential hazards. By following the instructions contained herein, the reader willingly assumes all risks in connection with such instructions.

The Publisher makes no representation or warranties of any kind, including but not limited to, the warranties of fitness for particular purpose or merchantability, nor are any such representations implied with respect to the material set forth herein, and the publisher takes no responsibility with respect to such material. The publisher shall not be liable for any special, consequential, or exemplary damages resulting, in whole or part, from the readers' use of, or reliance upon, this material.

West Legal Studies Staff:

Business Unit Director: Susan Simpfenderfer
Executive Editor: Marlene McHugh Pratt
Acquisitions Editor: Joan Gill
Editorial Assistant: Lisa Flatley
Executive Marketing Manager: Donna Lewis
Executive Production Manager: Wendy Troeger
Production Editor: Betty L. Dickson
Cover Design: Connie McKinley

Library of Congress Cataloging-in-Publication Data

Stim, Richard.
    Copyright law / Richard Stim.
       p. cm.
    Includes bibliographical references and index.
    ISBN 0-8273-7988-9
    1. Copyright — United States. I. Title.
KF2995.S76 1999
346.7304'82 — dc21

99-38668
CIP

This book is dedicated to
Joseph D. Stim

Contents

Chapter 7   The Rights of the Public: First Sale and Fair Use

Chapter 8   Educational and Library Uses

Chapter 9   Artwork

Chapter 10   Musical Works and Sound Recordings

Chapter 11   Computers and the Internet

Chapter 12   Authorship and Ownership of Copyright

Chapter 13   Works Made for Hire

Chapter 14   Duration of Copyright

Chapter 15 Transfer of Copyright

Chapter 16 Copyright Research

Chapter 17 Copyright Notice

Chapter 18 Registration and Choosing Correct Application

Chapter 19 Preparing the Copyright Application

Chapter 20   Deposit Materials

Chapter 21   Processing, Correcting, and Canceling Registrations

Chapter 22   Copyright Infringement

Chapter 23   Defenses to Infringement

Chapter 24   Remedies for Copyright Infringement

Chapter 25   Resolving a Copyright Dispute Without Litigation

Chapter 26   Litigation

Chapter 27   International Copyright

Preface

Unlike other areas of law, copyright develops at a rapid pace. Propelled by technology and copyright owners, Congress amended the Copyright Act three times within a decade. Each revision redefined the copyright owner's monopoly while attempting to preserve the public's access to information. The Gatt Amendments harmonized United States copyright law with international laws; the Sonny Bono Copyright Term Extension Act extended copyright protection for twenty years; and the Digital Millenium Copyright Act modified rules relating to the Internet and computers. While Congress revised copyright law, the courts were engaged sorting out complex issues relating to copyright ownership, fair use, compilations, Internet infringement, and the rights relating to digital transfers of copyrighted works. The result has been a tidal wave of copyright changes.

Not long ago, keeping up with copyright law was only the responsibility of attorneys and judges. But that, too, has changed with the advent of the Internet and copying technology. Educators, artists, students, paralegals, and people in business now must stay current with copyright law. It is for these people that we have created this book—a modern plain language explanation of copyright principles and rules.

A MODERN GUIDE TO COPYRIGHT

The primary motivation in writing this book is to provide a compact modern copyright guide for nonlawyers. This book is intended to explain copyright law and to provide clear instructions for filing copyright applications, managing copyright portfolios, and answering common questions that arise when using copyrighted materials. In other words, this book fills the gap between lengthy legal treatises and rudimentary nutshell publications. Another motivation for creating this book has been Internet technology, which has made publishing more accessible but also brought potential copyright disputes to the masses. We hope we have anticipated most of the Internet issues and provided resources that will enable readers to stay current.

ORGANIZATION OF TEXT

By using a series of short chapters geared toward specific subjects, this book should serve as a convenient desktop reference. Chapters are organized into five categories: basic copyright principles; specific types of works; ownership issues; registration rules and procedures, and copyright disputes. The appendices provide helpful resources.

1. *Principles of copyright law:* The first seven chapters explain what is and is not protectible, fair use and first sale rules, the basics of derivative and compilation works, and the rights acquired by authors. In addition to these seven chapters, Chapter 27 also provides basic international copyright principles.

2. *Special categories of copyright protection:* Chapters 8 through 11 deal with specific applications of copyright law for educators, artists, musicians, and those who use computers and the Internet.

3. *Ownership issues:* Chapters 12 through 16 explain principles of ownership, including works made for hire, duration of copyright, transfer of ownership, and methods of researching copyright ownership.

4. *Registration rules and procedures:* Chapters 17 through 21 provide a comprehensive guide to copyright formalities and explain the use of notice of copyright, choosing copyright applications, preparing the application, deposit requirements, and processing, correcting, canceling, and expediting applications.

5. *Disputes:* Chapters 22 through 26 discuss copyright disputes including copyright infringement standards and liability, defenses to infringement, copyright remedies, resolving disputes prior to litigation, and the litigation process.

6. *Appendix resources:* The appendices add to the book's desktop features by including a website listing of common copyright resources; a glossary of terms; Copyright Office circulars and form letters; copyright forms; sample copyright agreements; a sample complaint and settlement agreement; a fee schedule; and information on international copyright.

FEATURES

In order to provide a readable and practical text, this book incorporates current trends in legal writing, particularly the dissection of complex material into readable outlines. Important rules and procedures are identified and isolated in comprehensible segments. In this manner, the reader is better able to find and digest complex rules and procedures. Many editorial features in this book are borrowed from website methodology. These include:

- bulleted lists and tables - presentation style graphics enable material, such as copyright termination rules, to be organized for easier explanation;
- FAQs—relevant frequently asked questions are covered in several chapters;
- sidebars—quotations taken from the *United States Code* are broken out in readable sidebars; and
- resource guides—website and contact information is provided at the end of appropriate chapters.

Copyright cases decided by Judge Learned Hand are summarized throughout the book. As any copyright lawyer will agree, Judge Hand had an unequaled influence on American copyright law, and his penetrating decisions make him the most cited source in copyright case law and treatises.

ROAD MAP OF TEXT/HOW TO USE THIS BOOK

The book is designed for ease of use, and there is extensive cross-referencing throughout the text. For example, those interested in Internet issues can find basic principles of Internet law in Chapter 11, information on resolving website disputes in Chapter 25, rules for registering websites in Chapter 18, and principles of getting permission for websites in Chapter 7.

ABOUT THE AUTHOR

Richard Stim is an attorney and adjunct professor at San Francisco State University. He is the author of four other books: *Intellectual Property: Patents, Trademarks and Copyrights* (West/ITP); *Music Law: How to Run Your Band's Business* (Nolo); *License Your Invention* (Nolo); and *Getting Permission: How to License & Clear Copyrighted Materials Online & Off* (Nolo).

ACKNOWLEDGMENTS

Thanks to Joan Gill, Lisa Flatley, the ITP West publishing team, and the reviewers:

Anthony M. Piazza
David N. Myers College

Ana M. Otero
Center for Advanced Legal Studies

Michael J. Cronen
Law Offices of Harris Zimmerman

FEEDBACK

As noted, copyright law changes at a rapid pace. A website (http://members.aol.com/rwstim/copyright/update.htm) has been created as a companion to this text. Accessing this web page will provide changes to copyright law that have occurred since publication of this book. In addition, the author can be contacted directly at rwstim@aol.com. Comments and suggestions for improving the text are appreciated.

CHAPTER 1
Copyrights and Intellectual Property

This chapter introduces and distinguishes:

- copyrights;
- trademarks;
- trade secrets; and
- patents.

It also includes an example of copyright law in real life—a profile of author Stephen King.

INTRODUCTION TO COPYRIGHT: STEPHEN KING

In 1710, the English government enacted the Statute of Anne, a law that allowed authors to prevent others from copying their books. It was this right to control copying that evolved into modern copyright law. Over the centuries copyright protection has extended beyond books to include works that are reproduced including drawings, photographs, music, motion pictures, architecture, and computer programs.

For the first three centuries of copyright law, a book could be reproduced only by printing it on paper. By the end of the twentieth century, books could be stored in a digital format and reproduced instantly over the Internet. Many commentators believed that the conversion to digital media would sound the death knell for printed books. Media guru Marshall McLuhan predicted the "death of print."

Are books headed for extinction? Not according to Stephen King, the world's best-selling author. Since 1973, King has earned his fortune from copyrights on dozens of books such as *Carrie, The Shining, Misery,* and *The Stand.* King's rights are protected under the same principles that have shielded authors since 1710.

When he completes a novel (considered a "literary work"), King acquires a bundle of rights. Included in this bundle is the exclusive right to publish the book. King can either sell this right to a publisher (known as an "assignment"), or he can license the publishing rights for a limited time. King acquires the same bundle of rights when he writes under the pseudonym Richard Bachman because copyright law protects pseudonymous and anonymous authors.

In order for his works to acquire copyright protection, King's writing must be original and fixed in a perceptible form. In 1994, he had an idea for a novel—he imagined that all the residents of a small desert town were killed by the sheriff. The work was not fixed until King put the words on paper or typed them into his computer and created the novel *Desperation.*

Copyright law also grants King the exclusive right to create new works based upon his books (known as "derivatives"). This derivative right allows him to carry characters from book to book, as in the serialization of his *Green Mile* series in 1996. This derivative right also allows him to sell filmmaking rights based upon his books. In fact, more films are derived from books by Stephen King than from books by any other writer except William Shakespeare, who died before copyright laws existed.

.When King's books and stories are sold in collections, the unique or creative way in which the material is selected and organized is protected as a compilation (known as a "collective work"). If excerpts of Stephen King books are read aloud for an audiobook, included in a multimedia CD-ROM, or provided at an Internet site (www.stephenking.com), these words are protected no matter whether they appear in print or digital format.

Like other successful copyright owners, King has been involved in legal disputes. In 1988, King won a lawsuit against an author who claimed King's book *Christine* was copied from (or "infringed") a ten-page manuscript entitled *Side Swiper.*[1]

How long will King's works be protected? The length of protection (or "duration") of copyright is for King's life plus seventy years after his death. King may transfer his copyright ownership through his will, enabling his estate to profit from his literary legacy through the twenty-first century and perhaps beyond.

INTELLECTUAL PROPERTY LAW

Writers, inventors, businesses, and artists transform ideas into tangible property. Because these creations are products of the mind, they are known as **intellectual property** (IP). In order for a product of the mind to achieve protection under intellectual property law, it must qualify under one of the forms of intellectual property:

- copyrights—protecting music, arts, movies, and writings;
- patents—protecting inventions, discoveries, product designs, and plants;
- trade secrets—protecting confidential business information;
- trademarks—protecting the words, symbols, or other identifiers of products and services; or
- right of publicity—protecting the commercial use of a person's name or image.

The rights and obligations of owners of intellectual property are similar to those of owners of other types of property such as an automobile or house. For example:

- the owner has the right to exclude others from using or taking the property;
- the owner can license, sell, or transfer the property; and
- the owner is subject to rules regarding government registration, recordation, abandonment, and forfeiture.

The various intellectual property rights are related and often mix in intellectual property lawsuits. For example, if without permission a photograph of Stephen King on his Harley Davidson motorcycle were used in an advertisement, the photographer could sue for copyright infringement based on the unauthorized use of the photograph; the Harley Davidson company could sue for trademark infringement based on the unauthorized use of the Harley Davidson trademark; and King could sue for infringement of his right of publicity. The following sections describe the different forms of intellectual property and the standards for protection.

Copyrights

What Is Protected.   Copyright law protects music, architecture, writing, computer programs, plays, movies, dance, or visual arts such as graphic arts, sculptures, photographs, or paintings. The person or entity that creates a copyrightable work is known as an author.

How Protection Is Acquired.   Copyright protection is acquired once an original work is fixed in a perceptible form. "Original" under copyright law means that the author did not copy it from another source. Registration of a copyright is *not* required for protection. However, registration is recommended because it enhances the value of copyright and provides rights in the event of litigation.

How Copyrights Are Regulated.   Copyright laws are created by Congress and interpreted by the federal courts. The Copyright Office, a division of the Library of Congress, administers the registration of copyrights.

How Long Copyright Protection Lasts.   Copyright protection begins once a work is created and generally lasts for the life of the author plus seventy years (for works created by a single author). Other works are protected for one hundred and twenty years from date of creation or ninety-five years from first publication, whichever is longer. Determining the duration of copyright depends upon many variables discussed in Chapter 14.

Patents

What Is Protected.   There are three types of patents—utility patents, design patents, and plant patents. The **utility patent** is the most common and will protect any new invention or discovery that is:

- within one of the classes described in the patent statute[2] (a machine, process, composition, article of manufacture, or new use of any of these);
- useful, that is, it has some purpose;

- novel, that is, it differs in some way from the publicly known or existing knowledge in the field. An invention is not novel if the application for the patent is made more than one year after sale, public disclosure, use, or offer of sale of the invention; and
- nonobvious, that is, persons working in the field would not consider the invention obvious.

Utility patents have been granted for the facsimile machine, the Scotchguard process, the hair-growth formula Rogaine, and the safety pin.

Designs and Plants.   The patent statute also protects designs and plants:

- A **design patent** protects new, original, and ornamental designs for useful objects. (The design patent protects only the appearance of an article and not its structure or utilitarian features.) Design patents have been granted for stained glass windows, Adidas shoes, and the shape of an electric guitar.
- A **plant patent** protects distinctive plants that are reproduced asexually (that is, by means other than seeds). Plant patents have been granted for new variations of tulips, roses, and tomatoes. Under some circumstances, a utility patent can cover sexually or asexually reproducible plants.

How Protection Is Acquired.   Unlike all other forms of intellectual property, protection does not exist for a patentable invention until a patent is issued by the United States Patent and Trademark Office (PTO). Without the issued patent (or "Letters Patent"), there are no rights under patent law. The application process is technical and requires the use of a special drafting language and drawings. Since the process is expensive and time-consuming, most applicants search the Patent Office records prior to filing an application in order to determine the likelihood of registration.

How Patents Are Regulated.   Patent laws are created by Congress and interpreted by the federal courts. The patent registration process is administered by the PTO, which is a division of the Department of Commerce.

How Long Patent Protection Lasts.   Plant and utility patents filed before June 8, 1995, enjoy patent protection for seventeen years from the date the patent is issued, provided that fees necessary to keep the patent in force are paid (maintenance fees). Patents filed after June 7, 1995, enjoy protection for twenty years from the date of filing, a change resulting from United States adoption of the GATT treaty (the General Agreement on Tariffs and Trades). A design patent is protected for a maximum of fourteen years. The owner of a patent may exclude others from making, using, or selling the patented subject matter (that is, the invention, design, or plant) throughout the United States. The length of United States patent rights in foreign countries depends upon foreign laws and international treaties.

Trade Secrets

What Is Protected.   A **trade secret** is any business information that is kept in confidence and that gives the business an advantage over competitors who do

not know it. Some examples of trade secrets are the Gatorade formula, survey methods used by professional pollsters, a new invention for which a patent application has not been filed, marketing strategies, manufacturing techniques, computer algorithms, recipes, and formulas. A trade secret has value because it is not published or publicly distributed. This is quite different from a copyright or a patent, the owner of which makes money from the publication and distribution of copies or objects embodying the copyrighted or patented material.

How Protection Is Acquired. Protection is acquired if the information is unknown to competitors and if the information is treated like a secret. The information cannot be shown to the public, and people who use the secret have an obligation to maintain secrecy. That is, they must have a confidential relationship or have signed a confidentiality agreement.

How Trade Secrets Are Regulated. Trade secrets are regulated by federal and state trade secret laws and by federal and state case law (or "common law") rulings. There is no registration process for trade secrets.

How Long Trade Secret Protection Lasts. Trade secret protection lasts for as long as the secret is kept confidential. Once a trade secret is made available to the public, trade secret protection ends. It is not a violation of trade secret law to analyze (or "reverse engineer") any lawfully obtained product and determine its trade secret.

Trademarks

What Is Protected. A **trademark** is any word, symbol, design, device, logo, or slogan that identifies and distinguishes one product or service from another. Trademarks inform consumers that a product comes from a particular source. For example, the Kodak trademark informs consumers that a box of film has a certain quality or reliability. This consumer connection, known as "goodwill," strengthens the value of all Kodak products. Examples of trademarks are Viking, the trademark for the publisher of Stephen King's books; Harley Davidson, the trademark for the manufacturer of King's motorcycle; and Castle Rock, the trademark for the movie company that produced two Stephen King movies.

A trademark does not have to be a word. It can be anything that identifies and distinguishes a product or service, for example, the yellow McDonald's arches, the color pink for Corning fiberglass, or the shape of the Absolut vodka bottle.

The owner of a trademark can exclude others from using a similar trademark on similar or related goods or services. In some cases, use of a similar trademark may be stopped if a court determines that the use of the similar mark dilutes or tarnishes the trademark. For example, the unauthorized use of the Adidas trademark made to look like a marijuana leaf would dilute or tarnish the shoemaker's image.

How Protection Is Acquired. Trademark protection is granted to the first person to sell a product using the mark. Rights are created only when the mark is used in commerce (or as one observer stated, "No trade, no trademark").

Trademark registration does not create trademark rights. However, registration offers special rights in the event of infringement.

How Trademarks Are Regulated.   Both the federal government and state governments have trademark laws.[3] A trademark owner can register the mark with the federal or state government. Federal registrations are administered by the PTO. State registrations are handled by the respective Secretary of State.

How Long Trademark Protection Lasts.   Trademark protection lasts for as long as a business continuously uses the trademark in connection with goods or services. Many valuable marks, such as Jell-O, have been in existence for over a century.

Right of Publicity

What Is Protected.   The right of publicity is the right to control the commercial exploitation of a person's name, image, or persona. This right is the "baby" of intellectual property law, a relatively new legal right developed over the past three decades. Although everyone has a right of publicity, the right is traditionally associated with celebrities because the name or image of a famous person is most often used to sell products or services. If a child's photograph is used to sell toys, that child could claim a misappropriation of the right of publicity. It is for this reason that all models or persons used in advertisements sign consent agreements.

How Protection Is Acquired.   The right of publicity exists without doing anything. However, this right only extends to commercial exploitation. The use of the name, likeness, or persona for news, information, or public interest purposes is not a violation of the right of publicity. For this reason, Madonna cannot prevent the use of a photo of her in a news story in the *National Enquirer.*

How Right of Publicity Is Regulated.   The right of publicity is a matter of state law. Some states have passed statutes regulating these rights,[4] while other states do not have right of publicity statutes but have established common law rights under case law. As of the writing of this book, approximately seventeen states have neither a statute nor case law regarding right of publicity.[5]

How Long Right of Publicity Protection Lasts.   The right of publicity exists for the lifetime of a person. Unlike other forms of intellectual property, the right of publicity is not always "descendible" (that is, it does not always survive the death of the person who owns the right). Only eleven states currently recognize that the right of publicity survives death.[6] Tennessee, the home of the late Elvis Presley, was one of the first states to recognize that the right of publicity could be passed to survivors.

OVERLAPPING INTELLECTUAL PROPERTY RIGHTS

There may be overlapping choices when choosing protection for new works or inventions. Some computer software programs can be protected under copyright law and patent law. The distinctive design of the Manischewitz wine bottle can be protected as a trademark and as a design patent. The appearance of a *Star Wars* toy can be protected by trademark, design patent, or copyright. How is the correct choice determined? An analysis is made that usually weighs the following factors:

- the cost of the various forms of protection (for example, trade secret protection is free while patent protection can cost thousands of dollars);
- the strength of the protection (for example, a patent owner can stop anyone manufacturing a similar invention, while a copyright owner must prove that the infringer *copied* the work); and
- the length of protection (for example, trademark protection begins when the mark is used in commerce and continues for as long as it is continuously used in commerce, while patent protection lasts less than twenty years).

EXAMPLE

Design Patents and Copyright. One example of overlapping rights occurs when a designer chooses between copyright and design patent protection. Both forms of intellectual property protect artistic design and visual imagery. For example, a three-dimensional cartoon character on a belt buckle could qualify for copyright protection. The same belt buckle also could qualify for a design patent because the design is new, original, and ornamental for an article of manufacture (that is, a belt buckle). Not all designs are protected under copyright *and* design patent law. The PTO will not issue design patents for surface ornamentation (that is, flat illustrations such as labels or drawings). Therefore, two-dimensional illustrations are protected *only* under copyright law and not as design patents.

JUDGE LEARNED HAND ON COPYRIGHT

Many of the chapters in this text include summaries of copyright cases decided by Judge Learned Hand. For over fifty years, Judge Hand served as a federal district and appellate court judge in New York. With the exception of Oliver Wendell Holmes, Judge Hand remains the most quoted jurist of the twentieth century. One reason for his impact and popularity is that he emphasized a simplicity of language. In copyright law, Judge Hand had an uncanny ability to size up the facts and make a determination with timeless implications. Some of his decisions predate changes in the copyright law, such as protection of computer programs, reform of copyright notice rules, analysis of infringement, separate protection for literary characters, and principles of co-ownership of copyright.

END NOTES

1. Glanzmann v. King, 887 F.2d 265 (6th Cir. 1989).
2. 35 U.S.C. § 1–376.
3. The federal statute is at 15 U.S.C. § 1051–1127.
4. California, Florida, Kentucky, Massachusetts, Nebraska, Nevada, New York, Oklahoma, Rhode Island, Tennessee, Texas, Utah, Virginia, and Wisconsin.
5. Alaska, Arizona, Colorado, Connecticut, Idaho, Illinois, Louisiana, Minnesota, Mississippi, New Hampshire, New Mexico, North Dakota, Oregon, South Carolina, South Dakota, Vermont, and Wyoming.
6. California, Florida, Georgia, Kentucky, Nebraska, Nevada, New Jersey, Oklahoma, Tennessee, Texas, and Virginia.

FOR MORE INFORMATION

The following resources may prove helpful for locating information about the topics discussed in this book. Websites are emphasized as a source of information, as they are current and free to use. Additional resources are provided in Appendix A.

Intellectual Property Resources

Yahoo Intellectual Property Directory
http://www.yahoo.com/Government/Law/Intellectual_Property/
   A thorough listing of IP resources on the Internet.

Legal Information Institute
http://www.law.cornell.edu/topics/topic2.html
   Intellectual property links and downloadable copies of statutes and cases.

Intellectual Property Mall
http://www.ipmall.fplc.edu
   Intellectual property links and information.

The American Intellectual Property Law Association
2001 Jefferson Davis Highway, Suite 203, Arlington VA 22202, (703) 415-0780
http://www.aipla.org
   Helpful links and information regarding IP attorneys.

Patents

The United States Patent and Trademark Office
Assistant Commissioner of Patents, Washington DC 20231
http://www.uspto.gov/
   The PTO offers a number of informational pamphlets, including an introduction to patents ("General Information About Patents") and an online

searchable database of patent abstracts (short summaries of patents). Most patent forms and publications, including the Manual of Patent Examining Procedures, Examination Guidelines for Computer-Related Inventions, and Disclosure Document Program, can be downloaded from the PTO website.

Patent Portal: Internet Patent Resources
http://www.law.vill.edu/~rgruner/patport.htm
Material on patent law, inventor assistance, and licensing.

Shadow Patent Office
http://www.spo.eds.com/patent.html
Information about recent patent filings and patent search services.

STO's Internet Patent Search System
http://www.sunsite.unc.edu/patents/intropat.html
Patent news, information about searching, and patent documents.

IBM Patent Site
http://www.patents.ibm.com
Access to IBM's in-house patent searching engine including some 1.4 million European patents.

Copyrights

United States Copyright Office
Publications Sections, LM-455, Copyright Office, Library of Congress, Washington DC 20559
http://www.loc.gov/copyright
The Copyright Office has numerous circulars, kits, and other publications that can help you, including one on searching copyright records. Frequently requested Copyright Office circulars and announcements are also available via the Copyright Office's fax-on-demand telephone line at (202) 707-9100.

Trade Secrets

Trade Secrets Home Page
http://execpc.com/~mhallign/
Case law, legislation, and current news regarding trade secret law.

Trademarks

Trademark Office
Assistant Commissioner for Trademarks, 2900 Crystal Drive, Arlington VA 22202-3515

http://www.uspto.gov

The Trademark Office website includes the relevant applications and forms and provides a method for searching registered marks.

CHAPTER 2
Sources of
Copyright Law

Copyright law is administered exclusively by the federal government. This chapter details the three ways in which the federal government oversees copyright:

■ drafting of federal copyright statutes;
■ interpretation of copyright statutes by the federal courts; and
■ administration of copyright regulations by the Copyright Office.

FEDERAL COPYRIGHT STATUTES

Article 1, section 8, of the Constitution authorizes the federal government to establish laws and regulations regarding copyright. Since 1790 there have been five major copyright acts, two of which are still effective:

■ the Copyright Act of 1909; and
■ the Copyright Act of 1976.

The Copyright Act of 1909

All works published between 1909 and 1978 are governed by the Copyright Act of 1909. For example, the song "(I'm) Chiquita Banana" was published in 1938 and is still protected under copyright law. If the owners of the song were to sue an infringer today, the federal court would interpret the Copyright Act of 1909 to determine the rights of the parties. The 1909 act protects:

■ works that are published with copyright notice; and
■ unpublished works that are registered with the Copyright Office.

Under the 1909 act, unpublished works that were not registered with the Copyright Office were protected by **common law copyright,** a collection of precedents established by court decisions. For more information on unpublished works, see Chapter 14.

The Copyright Act of 1976

The Copyright Act of 1976[1] protects works created on or after January 1, 1978. (Though enacted in 1976, the Copyright Act of 1976 did not go into effect until January 1, 1978.) The 1976 act also offers protection for certain unpublished works created before 1978. The act is distinguishable from previous copyright laws in that a work is protected once it is fixed in a tangible form, and copyright does not have to be renewed. Under the preceding Copyright Act, protection occurred only upon publication with notice, or upon registration of an unpublished work, and the copyright owner was required to file a renewal after a number of years. If the owner failed to renew, copyright protection was lost.

Although the Copyright Act of 1976 was intended to encompass new technologies, disputes arose about the issue of computer software programs under copyright law. In 1980, Congress amended the Copyright Act to specifically include computer programs as protected works. For more information on computers and copyright protection, see Chapter 11.

Berne Convention Implementation Act

Approximately eighty nations belong to the Berne Convention for the Protection of Literary and Artistic Works. These countries abide by a treaty that establishes common copyright rules. Portions of the Copyright Act of 1976 conflicted with the Berne rules, and the United States could not join the Berne Convention until it changed (or harmonized) its laws. Congress made several major amendments to the Copyright Act in 1989 and 1990, and as a result, the United States became a member of the Berne Convention. Among the changes are:

- the requirement of copyright notice is abolished. Works published on or after March 1, 1989, do not have to include copyright notice;
- protection is granted for architectural works; and
- special protection known as moral rights is granted to a work of fine art, that is, individual paintings or sculpture or limited editions of two hundred or less of prints or photographs.[2]

GATT Amendments

On December 8, 1994, President Clinton signed the Uruguay Round Agreements Act (URAA), which included the Uruguay Round General Agreement on Tariffs and Trade commonly known as GATT.[3] The GATT amendments[4] include a special treaty known as the Trade Related Aspects of Intellectual Property Rights (TRIPS) that:

- restores copyright for certain works first published outside the United States that have lost protection for technical reasons. For example, protection would be restored for a foreign author who lost copyright protection in the United States because of an omission of copyright notice;
- prohibits rental of computer programs; and
- prohibits bootlegging of live music performances and music videos.

The Sonny Bono Copyright Extension Term Act

In 1998, President Clinton signed the Sonny Bono Copyright Extension Term Act that extended the time period during which copyrighted works are protected. Extending copyright protection harmonizes our laws with European countries where copyright owners already enjoy longer protection. In summary:

- for works created on or after January 1, 1978, the copyright term is life of the author plus seventy years (instead of life plus fifty years);
- for works for hire and works published anonymously and pseudonomously, protection is extended from seventy-five to ninety-five years;
- for works in their renewal terms, protection is extended for an additional twenty years; and
- no new expired copyrights will enter the public domain until 2019.

For more information on the duration of copyright, see Chapter 14.

The Digital Millennium Copyright Act

In 1998, President Clinton signed the Digital Millennium Copyright Act (DMCA), which amended copyright law relating to the Internet and digital transmission of information. Among the DMCA's provisions are the following:

- prohibition of the circumvention of digital antipiracy devices;
- prohibition of the removal of secret codes known as digital watermarks from digital files;
- limitations on liability for Internet Service Providers (ISPs) in the event an infringing copy is offered online;
- protection for computer repair workers from certain claims of infringement;
- licensing standards by which Internet providers can webcast music (broadcast over the Internet); and
- a new form of intellectual property protection for the design of boat hulls.

The Code of Federal Regulations

Copyright Office Rules of Practice and related copyright regulations are located in the *Code of Federal Regulations* at title 37.[5] These regulations elaborate on the copyright statutes and provide standards for the copyright application and registration process.

THE FEDERAL COURTS

The federal courts interpret and enforce the copyright laws. The most common issue litigated in copyright cases is copyright **infringement.** Infringement occurs when a party with access to a work copies it without authorization or interferes with a right granted under copyright law.

Because the federal government has exclusive jurisdiction over copyright cases, lawsuits involving copyright law can be brought *only* in the federal courts. This is based on a principle known as **preemption,** which grants the federal government exclusive control over powers granted within the Constitution. If a copyright case is brought in a state court, it must be dismissed for lack of subject matter jurisdiction.

Even though state courts cannot hear federal copyright claims, federal courts *can* rule on state claims if related to the copyright activity. For example, a thief breaks into a movie studio, damages property, steals a film, and then makes video copies. The movie studio can sue the thief for copyright infringement, trespass, and property damage. Though trespass and property damage are state claims (not federal), the federal district court may hear all of the claims under a principle known as pendent jurisdiction. **Pendent jurisdiction** (also known as ancillary jurisdiction) permits a federal court to decide related claims arising under state law.

A copyright case is filed in the federal district court. There are ninety-four federal districts, and each state has at least one federal district court. If either party is unhappy with the federal district court opinion, this decision can be appealed to the appropriate United States Court of Appeals. There are thirteen federal appellate districts, including eleven numbered circuits (each having jurisdiction over three or more states), the District of Columbia, and the Court of Appeals for the Federal Circuit. If either party in a lawsuit is not satisfied with the court of appeals decision, that party may seek review by the United States Supreme Court. The Supreme Court's review is discretionary, that is, the Supreme Court does not have to hear the case. If the Supreme Court refuses to hear the case, the ruling of the court of appeals (or appellate court) is binding on the parties. If two courts of appeals have different decisions about the same facts, then the Supreme Court may agree to hear the case (or "grant certiorari"). This is what happened in the case of musician John Fogerty. A court of appeals ruled he should not receive attorneys' fees after winning a lawsuit. The Supreme Court agreed to hear the case and overruled the court of appeals.[6] The Supreme Court's decision takes precedent and establishes the standard for all federal courts.

Federal district court opinions are published in the United States *Patent Quarterly* and in the *Federal Supplement.* Courts of appeals decisions are published in the *Federal Reporter.* Supreme Court decisions are published in the *Supreme Court Reporter.* In addition, many decisions are now published online, either at Internet sites or through subscription services such as LEXIS and Westlaw.

THE COPYRIGHT OFFICE

The Copyright Office is a division of the Library of Congress. The responsibility of the Copyright Office is to determine if works meet copyright standards. If a work meets the legal standards for copyright, a Certificate of Registration is issued. A registration is not necessary to acquire protection, but it is recommended because it provides the author with rights in the event of infringement. If the work does not meet copyright standards, the work is rejected and the applicant is given the reason for copyright invalidity. If an applicant disagrees with the decision of the Copyright Office, the decision may be appealed to a federal court. The Copyright Office also issues numerous circulars and other publications, performs searches of Copyright Office information, records transfers of copyright ownership, and regulates certain compulsory licenses and royalties.

The Copyright Office does not advise on matters of infringement, assist in matters of publication, enforce rights of an author under copyright law, or grant permission to use a work. Some rules and regulations for Copyright Office activities are established in the Copyright Act of 1976 as well as in the *Code of Federal Regulations*. The director of the Copyright Office is the Register of Copyrights.

END NOTES

1. 17 U.S.C. § 101–810.
2. 17 U.S.C. § 106A.
3. The copyright aspects of the GATT amendments are also sometimes referred to as TRIPS amendments.
4. 17 U.S.C. § 104A.
5. 37 C.F.R. § 201.1 et seq.
6. Fogerty v. Fantasy, Inc., 510 U.S. 517 (1994).

FOR MORE INFORMATION

Copyright Office
http://www.loc.gov/copyright
> The Copyright Office site provides information regarding the Copyright Act of 1976, Copyright Office regulations, and rules including selected sections from the *Code of Federal Regulations.*

Legal Information Institute
http://www.law.cornell.edu/topics/copyright.html
> Read or download copies of the Copyright Act of 1976 and portions of the *Code of Federal Regulations*.

CHAPTER 3
What Is Protectible Under Copyright Law?

This chapter provides an examination of what is protectible under copyright law. The following subjects are discussed:

- the standards of originality and fixation;
- the distinction between a copyrightable work and a copy; and
- the eight categories of protectible works.

INTRODUCTION

Copyright protects the literary, musical, graphic, or other artistic form in which an author expresses intellectual concepts. If the author's creation meets the standards of copyright law, it is considered a **work of authorship.** When drafting the Copyright Law of 1976, Congress specifically chose not to limit the definition of a work of authorship, realizing that authors are continually finding new ways of expression. Section 102(a) of the Copyright Act provides guidance for what is protectible and sets two standards for protection: works must be **original** and must be **fixed** in a tangible form.

17 U.S.C. § 102(a) Subject matter of copyright

Copyright protection subsists, in accordance with this title, in original works of authorship fixed in any tangible medium of expression, now known or later developed, from which they can be perceived, reproduced, or otherwise communicated, either directly or with the aid of a machine or device.

17 U.S.C. § 101 Creation of a work

A work is "created" when it is fixed in a copy or phonorecord for the first time; where a work is prepared over a period of time, the portion of it that has been fixed at any particular time constitutes the work as of that time, and where the work has been prepared in different versions, each version constitutes a separate work.

Originality

Originality under copyright law does not mean aesthetic quality, uniqueness, novelty, or a high degree of creativity. It generally means that the work is original to the author. Originality requires only a modest degree of creative labor. A cruise ship photo or a child's finger-painting may not be outstanding art, but they are both copyrightable.

Unlike patent law, copyright is not based upon priority of creation. The order in which works are created does not automatically establish a superior right. That is, being *first* does not guarantee copyright protection or a right to sue someone. Being original (that is, creating without copying) is what triggers an author's rights.

JUDGE LEARNED HAND ON COPYRIGHT: A PLAGIARIST IS NOT AN AUTHOR

In *Sheldon v. Metro-Goldwyn Pictures Corporation*,[1] Judge Hand reviewed the standard for copyright originality by imagining if someone independently created the poem "Ode on a Grecian Urn" by John Keats. Judge Hand stated, "[I]f by some magic a man who had never known it were to compose anew Keats's 'Ode on a Grecian Urn,' he would be an 'author' and if he copyrighted it, others might not copy that poem though they might of course copy Keats's." This quotation expresses the principle that copyright law does not prevent the creation of identical works; it only prevents *copying*. Judge Hand's oft-quoted remark has become the standard for copyright originality.

Copyright Office Review of Originality.   Although the threshold for originality is very low, an examiner in the Copyright Office will still examine each work and make an initial determination on whether a work meets this threshold. If the Copyright Office determines that a work lacks originality and the applicant disagrees, the matter will be resolved by the federal courts. For example, when the Copyright Office refused to issue a copyright for the audiovisual display and sounds of a video game simulating paddle ball, the owner of the game appealed that decision to a federal district court.[2]

Lack of Originality as a Defense to Infringement.   The originality of a work is often challenged by the defendant in a copyright infringement lawsuit. The defendant attempts to prove that the plaintiff's work lacks originality and cannot be protected by copyright law.

EXAMPLE

The Greek Theater Masks. An artist manufactured clothing featuring classic Greek comedy and tragedy masks—one blank face with a smile, the other with a frown and tear rolling down the cheek. One of the artist's customers, a theater shop, manufactured shirts using the same mask images. The artist sued for copyright infringement. The theater shop argued that the mask images lacked sufficient originality because they were based upon public domain images. A federal court agreed, and since the masks were not protectible, the theater shop was free to copy the design.[3]

Fixation

A work is **fixed** when it is embodied in a *tangible* form that is perceptible by the human senses either directly or with the aid of a machine. The Copyright Act of 1976 requires that the work must be embodied in a form that is "sufficiently permanent or stable so as to permit it to be perceived, reproduced or otherwise communicated for a period of more than transitory duration."[4]

17 U.S.C. § 101 Fixation

A work is "fixed" in a tangible medium of expression when its embodiment in a copy or phonorecord, by or under the authority of the author, is sufficiently permanent or stable to permit it to be perceived, reproduced, or otherwise communicated for a period of more than transitory duration. A work consisting of sounds, images, or both, that are being transmitted, is "fixed" for purposes of this title if a fixation of the work is being made simultaneously with its transmission.

Examples of works that are fixed are a song that is recorded on audiotape, a story that is printed on paper, a visual image that is captured on photographic film, and an e-mail message that is stored in a computer. Works that are *not* fixed would include a speech that is not transcribed, and a live performance of a song or live broadcast of a television program that is not simultaneously recorded. For example, in a case involving the National Basketball Association, a federal court determined that a live basketball game (not the video broadcast) was unprotectible under copyright law.[5] However, the televised broadcasts of the underlying games are copyrightable as long as they are simultaneously recorded. The requirement of fixation does not mean that a work must be mass-produced or published. A handwritten diary is fixed and meets the requirement of copyrightability.

Prior to the 1976 act, a work would be protected only if it was fixed in a form that could be directly seen or read by the human eye. If the same rule were in effect today, the makers of motion pictures could not receive compensation for videotapes because the viewer cannot see the work by looking directly at the videotape. The drafters of the Copyright Act of 1976 found the requirement of visual perception to be unjustified and extended protection to works of authorship that can be perceived with the aid of a machine.

Is a Website Protectible Under Copyright Law? If the elements of the website—the text, graphics, audio, animation, film clips, or software programs—are original to the author of the website, they are copyrightable. If an element is not created by the author, it can be displayed and reproduced at the website if: (1) it is in the public domain; or (2) the copyright owner has granted permission for the use. More information about websites is provided in Chapter 11. Registration of websites is discussed in Chapter 18.

Separating the Work from the Copy. Whenever a work of authorship is fixed in a material object—for example, software programs on a disk or paint on a canvas—a copy is produced. This copy is a physical form in which the work is embodied. It is not the work. For instance, if a photographer takes a picture, the resulting image is the "work." The photograph is a **copy,** a tangible object that incorporates the image. This distinction is important when selling the photograph because selling the photograph is selling a print of the work, not the copyright to the work. For example, under copyright law, an oil painting is a copy. It may be the *only* copy of a visual image, but it is still a copy of the work. When a person buys the painting, that person is *not* acquiring the right to reproduce the image on the painting. The painter owns the image, which may be fixed on other items such as on a t-shirt, on a cup, or on the cover of a magazine, and each reproduction is a copy. There may be many copies, but only the underlying image, no matter how or where it is fixed, is protectible.

17 U.S.C. § 101 Copies

"Copies" are material objects, other than phonorecords, in which a work is fixed by any method now known or later developed, and from which the work can be perceived, reproduced, or otherwise communicated, either directly or with the aid of a machine or device. The term "copies" includes the material object, other than a phonorecord, in which the work is first fixed.

THE EIGHT CATEGORIES OF WORKS OF AUTHORSHIP

The first United States Copyright Act, enacted in 1790, granted protection to the creators of books, maps, and charts—all the necessary works of authorship for forging a new country. During the past two centuries, Congress has passed various copyright laws expanding the protection of copyright to include new technologies such as motion pictures, sound recordings, and computer programs. When the Copyright Act of 1976 was drafted, Congress listed seven broad categories of works. In 1990, the Copyright Act of 1976 was amended to include an eighth category, architectural works. The fact that a work does not fit into one of these categories does not disqualify it from protection. Congress intended that the act be "illustrative and not limitative." At issue in determining protectability is *not* whether a work falls into one of the categories, but whether it satisfies the requirements of section 102 of the Copyright Act of 1976.[6]

17 U.S.C. § 102 Works of authorship

Works of authorship include the following categories:

(1) literary works;
(2) musical works, including any accompanying words;
(3) dramatic works, including any accompanying music;
(4) pantomimes and choreographic works;
(5) pictorial, graphic, and sculptural works;
(6) motion pictures and other audiovisual works;
(7) sound recordings; and
(8) architectural works.

Literary Works

The book you are reading is a copy of a **literary work.** So is a Toyota Tercel repair manual, *The Onion* newspaper, and the novel *Milroy the Magician.* The Copyright Act of 1976 defines literary works as works "expressed in words, numbers, or other verbal or numerical symbols or markings, regardless of the nature of the material objects, such as books, periodicals, manuscripts, phonorecords, film, tapes, disks, or cards, in which they are embodied."[7]

Computer software programs such as Word Perfect and Netscape are considered literary works because they can be expressed in computer languages that use letters, words, or numbers. Certain works are not considered literary works, though expressed in words; lyrics for a song would be part of a musical work copyright, and the script for a play would be part of a dramatic work.

17 U.S.C. § 101 Literary works

"Literary works" are works, other than audiovisual works, expressed in words, numbers, or other verbal or numerical symbols or indicia, regardless of the nature of the material objects, such as books, periodicals, manuscripts, phonorecords, film, tapes, disks, or cards, in which they are embodied.

17 U.S.C. § 101 Computer program

A "computer program" is a set of statements or instructions to be used directly or indirectly in a computer in order to bring about a certain result.

Musical Works

A **musical work** is a musical composition. For example, the song "Happy Birthday" is a musical work published in 1935. The copyright for the musical composition protects both the words and music, and the copyright owner can control or limit the use of either element. For example, if someone were to print the words to the song "Do You Wanna Dance?" in a book, without permission of the songwriters, that would infringe copyright of the musical composition, even though only the lyrics were used. Certain music, such as music that accompanies a dramatic work or an audiovisual work, would not be protected in the musical works category. Instead such music would be protected and registered as a dramatic work or audiovisual work, respectively.

Dramatic Works

A **dramatic work** is usually a "play" (and any accompanying music) prepared for stage, cinema, radio, or television. Although a dramatic work does not have to have dialogue or plot, it is generally a narrative presented by means of dialogue and action. *Death of a Salesman, A Streetcar Named Desire, Rent,* and *A Chorus Line* are examples of dramatic works. A dramatic work provides directions for performance. That is, it explains how the play should be accomplished. A play can be embodied either in its manuscript form, or in video or other form of fixation.

Pantomimes and Choreographic Works

Choreography is the composition and arrangement of dance movement and patterns, often accompanied by music. A registrable choreographic work should be capable of being performed and usually includes direction for movement. Popular dance steps such as the Cha Cha and other simple routines are not copyrightable. **Pantomime** or "mime" is considered a mute performance with expressive communication. Since it is a form of acting that consists mostly of gestures, there is an overlap in the categorization of pantomime and dramatic works. Traditionally pantomime and choreographic works are fixed in a system of written notation, but the Copyright Act provides that they also may be fixed in any tangible medium including film, video, and photographs.

Pictorial, Graphic, and Sculptural Works

A pictorial, graphic, and sculptural work is any visual arts work. By their nature, pictorial, graphic, and sculptural works lend themselves to reproduction on many objects. Often these objects are functional, such as a pin, a shirt, a belt buckle, or a handbag. It is possible to protect a work (such as a picture or photograph) that is reproduced on a functional object, but it is never possible to protect the object itself. Under copyright law, such functional objects are referred to as "useful articles" and are not protected. A **useful article** is something that has some utilitarian function other than its appearance or ability to convey information. Useful articles may be protected under patent law.

17 U.S.C. § 101 Pictorial, graphic, and sculptural works

"Pictorial, graphic, and sculptural works" include two-dimensional and three-dimensional works of fine, graphic, and applied art, photographs, prints and art reproductions, maps, globes, charts, diagrams, models, and technical drawings, including architectural plans. Such works shall include works of artistic craftsmanship insofar as their form but not their mechanical or utilitarian aspects are concerned; the design of a useful article, as defined in this section, shall be considered a pictorial, graphic, or sculptural work only if, and only to the extent that, such design incorporates pictorial, graphic, or sculptural features that can be identified separately from, and are capable of existing independently of, the utilitarian aspects of the article.

When a work is incorporated on a useful article, copyright protection only extends to the pictorial, graphic, or sculptural features that can be identified separately from, and are capable of existing independently of, the utilitarian aspects of the article. In the case of a Swatch watch, for example, the visual image of the watch face may be protected, but not the mechanical or functional aspects of the watch.

Motion Pictures and Audiovisual Works

An image of a horse embodied on a photographic slide is considered to be a pictorial work. But when that same picture is presented as part of a slide show with a series of related slides (for example, the horse in stages of making a jump), the result is an audiovisual work. **Audiovisual works** are related images in a series (together with any accompanying sounds) that are shown by a machine or device. An audiovisual work does not have to have sounds (despite the use of the term *audio* in the name), and a silent film would be protectible as an audiovisual work.

The Copyright Act of 1909 did not initially protect motion pictures. To overcome this obstacle, the early film pioneers printed each reel of film on paper and registered their works as sheets of photographs. In 1912, after the United States Supreme Court had ruled on a case involving the silent film version of *Ben Hur,* the Copyright Act of 1909 was amended to include motion pictures.

17 U.S.C. § 101 Audiovisual works; motion pictures

"Audiovisual works" are works that consist of a series of related images which are intrinsically intended to be shown by the use of machines or devices such as projectors, viewers, or electronic equipment, together with accompanying sounds, if any, regardless of the nature of the material objects, such as films or tapes, in which the works are embodied.

"Motion pictures" are audiovisual works consisting of a series of related images which, when shown in succession, impart an impression of motion, together with accompanying sounds, if any.

Sound Recordings

A sound recording is a work resulting from the fixation of a series of musical or other sounds (including narration or spoken words). The performer, producer, or recording company usually claims copyright in the sound recording. Why is it necessary to have copyright protection for a musical work and a sound recording? A musical work copyright protects the musical composition. A sound recording copyright protects the way that the composition is performed and recorded.

For example, Frank Sinatra recorded the song "Yesterday" written by John Lennon and Paul McCartney. Sinatra did not write the song, so he is not entitled to claim copyright for the musical work. However, his unique arrangement and performance of "Yesterday" is entitled to sound recording copyright. Therefore, the compact disc containing Frank Sinatra's performance contains two copyrightable works: the Sinatra sound recording copyright, and the Lennon-McCartney musical work.

17 U.S.C. § 101 Sound recordings

"Sound recordings" are works that result from the fixation of a series of musical, spoken, or other sounds, but not including the sounds accompanying a motion picture or other audiovisual work, regardless of the nature of the material objects, such as disks, tapes, or other phonorecords, in which they are embodied.

Unlike other works of authorship, sound recordings are not embodied in copies, but are embodied in *phonorecords,* a term that can include records, cassettes, compact discs, DVDs, and other recording media. Because the method of recording and selling music is constantly evolving, a **phonorecord** is considered to be a material object in which sounds are fixed by any method, whether the method is now known or later developed. For instance, compact discs are considered phonorecords even though they were not available at the time the Copyright Act of 1976 was enacted. A movie or video that contains music, such as the film musical *Evita,* is *not* a phonorecord or sound recording. It is a copy of an audiovisual work.

Sound recordings were not protected under copyright law until 1972. Recordings embodied in a phonorecord on or after February 15, 1972, are eligible for protection under federal copyright law. If a sound recording was released on a phonorecord prior to this date, it would be protected only under state law (sometimes referred to as "state common law copyright"). That is, courts have determined that these recordings are protected, though not by federal law.[8] Some states, such as California, have passed specific laws regarding the protection of sound recordings fixed prior to February 15, 1972.[9]

In December 1993, section 104A was added to the Copyright Act. Among other things, this section provided that certain sound recordings fixed before

February 15, 1972, and first published in countries belonging to the Berne Convention (other than the United States) would receive protection under United States law. See Chapter 10 for information on music and copyright issues.

Architectural Works

In 1990, architectural works were added to the list of works protected under copyright law. An **architectural work** is the design of a building as embodied in any tangible medium of expression, including a building, architectural plans, or drawings. Although it may be hard to imagine, a building is a copy of an architectural work. That is, the building (or the plans or photographs) cannot be reproduced without the consent of the author of the work (usually the architect or developer). There are some exceptions for architectural works. For example, if the building is located in a place that is ordinarily visible to the public, photos or pictures of the building can be taken, distributed, or publicly displayed.

17 U.S.C. § 101 Architectural work

An "architectural work" is the design of a building as embodied in any tangible medium of expression, including a building, architectural plans, or drawings. The work includes the overall form as well as the arrangement and composition of spaces and elements in the design, but does not include individual standard features.

The owners of a building do not have to obtain consent of the copyright owner of the architectural work to make alterations or to authorize the destruction of the building. Note, however, if the interior of the building contains a work of visual art, such as a lobby mural, the unauthorized destruction of the mural may violate state fine art law or the moral rights provision of the United States Copyright Act.[10]

In a 1998 case,[11] the owner of an architectural copyright in a building design permitted replicas to be made of the buildings for use in the movie *Batman Forever*. An artist whose work was included in the architectural design claimed a separate copyright for his art and objected to the use in the movie. The court determined that the artwork was part of the architectural copyright and that the owner of the architectural copyright had the authority to permit the movie use.

END NOTES

1. 81 F.2d 49 (2d Cir. 1936).
2. Atari Games Corp. v. Oman, 693 F. Supp. 1204 (D. D.C. 1988), *rev'd on other grounds,* 888 F.2d 878 (2d Cir. 1989).
3. Bates v. Actors Heritage, Inc., 11 U.S.P.Q.2d 1732 (S.D.N.Y. 1989).
4. 17 U.S.C. § 101.

5. National Basketball Assoc. v. Sports Team Analysis & Tracking Sys., Inc., 939 F. Supp. 1071 (S.D.N.Y. 1996).

6. 17 U.S.C. § 102(a).

7. 17 U.S.C. § 101.

8. Goldstein v. California, 412 U.S. 546 (1973).

9. CAL. CIV. CODE § 980.

10. 17 U.S.C. § 106A.

11. Leicester v. Warner Bros., 47 U.S.P.Q.2d 1501 (C.D. Cal. 1998).

CHAPTER 4
Derivatives and Compilations

The previous chapter offered information about protectible works. This chapter discusses two special types of protectible works—derivatives and compilations. Information is provided about:

■ protecting derivative works;
■ protecting literary characters;
■ protecting compilations; and
■ the distinctions between a compilation and collective work.

INTRODUCTION

Derivative works and **compilations** are works that use preexisting works or materials. A preexisting work is a work that existed before the derivative or compilation was created. The author of a derivative work transforms or modifies the existing work, while the author of a compilation assembles, selects, or organizes preexisting materials. For example, when the song "Like a Virgin" was modified by Weird Al Yankovic to "Like a Surgeon," the result was a derivative work. When the song "Like a Virgin" is included on Madonna's greatest hits, "Immaculate Collection," the resulting collection of songs is a compilation. Copyright principles regarding derivatives and compilations are provided in section 103 of the Copyright Act.[1]

DERIVATIVE WORKS

The drafters of the Copyright Act of 1976 defined a **derivative work** as a work based upon one or more preexisting works such as a dramatization of a story, translation of a novel, or an upgrade of software. Some examples of derivative works and their sources include:

■ Office 2000 (computer program) derived from Office computer program;
■ *Frasier* (TV show) derived from *Cheers* (TV show);
■ *101 Dalmatians* (live action movie) derived from *101 Dalmatians* (animated movie); and
■ "I'll Be Missing You" (song written by Puff Daddy) derived from "Every Breath You Take" (song written by Sting).

One work can lead to numerous derivatives. For example, Robert Bloch's novel *Psycho* was the source for four films: Alfred Hitchcock's 1960 film *Psycho;* the 1983 sequel, *Psycho 2;* the 1986 sequel, *Psycho 3;* and *Psycho,* a 1998 re-creation of the Hitchcock film by director Gus Van Sant.

17 U.S.C. § 101 Derivative work

A "derivative work" is a work based upon one or more preexisting works, such as a translation, musical arrangement, dramatization, fictionalization, motion picture version, sound recording, art reproduction, abridgment, condensation, or any other form in which a work may be recast, transformed, or adapted. A work consisting of editorial revisions, annotations, elaborations, or other modifications which, as a whole, represent an original work of authorship, is a "derivative work."

Copyright for Derivative Work Protects Only New Elements

A derivative work is separately copyrightable. However, the copyright in the derivative will protect only new material that is sufficiently original. A derivative work does not *extend* the duration of the preexisting work. For example, the motion picture *Star Wars* was reissued in 1997 with additional scenes and a new soundtrack. This derivative version does not extend protection for the underlying film, originally published in 1977.

17 U.S.C. § 103(b) Compilations and derivative works

The copyright in a compilation or derivative work extends only to the material contributed by the author of such work, as distinguished from the preexisting material employed in the work, and does not imply any exclusive right in the preexisting material. The copyright in such work is independent of, and does not affect or enlarge the scope, duration, ownership, or subsistence of, any copyright protection in the preexisting material.

The Economics of Derivatives

During the twentieth century, the creation of derivative works proved to be a lucrative source of income. When director George Lucas completed the first *Star Wars* movie, he agreed to forego his payment as director and to take, instead, all revenue from succeeding *Star Wars* films, ventures, and merchandise. The film studio gave up these derivative rights because it did not believe that the movie would be very popular. As a result of the grant of derivative rights to *Star Wars,* Lucas has earned millions on books, video games, toys, and sequel films.

Derivatives Adapted from the Public Domain

Some derivative works are adapted from works that are not protected under copyright. For example, the song "Love Me Tender," written by Elvis Presley and Vera Matson, is derived from a public domain song, "Aura Lee," written in 1861. The authors of "Love Me Tender" cannot claim copyright to any elements borrowed from "Aura Lee," and they cannot stop others from creating a song based upon "Aura Lee." The authors' rights extend only to the new material added to "Aura Lee" to create the song "Love Me Tender." Similarly, if the derivative work is based upon a public domain work, copyright does not revive protection for the underlying work. For example, if an artist were to add color to black-and-white public domain drawings by William Blake, copyright would extend only to the additional color, not to the Blake drawings in the public domain.

Authorization

If a derivative is based upon a work protected under copyright, the author of the derivative should obtain authorization from the copyright owner of the underlying work. Authorization for such rights is commonly granted in return for a payment, a royalty, or a share of the profits of the derivative work. Clearance companies assist in the acquisition of rights. A listing of clearance companies is included in Appendix A. There is an exception to the requirement of authorization. Under fair use principles, portions of a work may be used without authorization, resulting in a protectible unauthorized derivative. Chapter 7 provides information about fair use.

17 U.S.C. § 103(a) Compilations and derivative works

The subject matter of copyright as specified by section 102 includes compilations and derivative works, but protection for a work employing preexisting material in which copyright subsists does not extend to any part of the work in which such material has been used unlawfully.

Translations as Derivative Works

Simply translating a list of words from English into another language would not constitute sufficient originality to make a copyrightable derivative work. However, the act of translating a novel from one language to another generally satisfies the minimum standard of originality because the translator must interpret and express the novel in a manner consistent with the second language. The importance of the translator's skill was demonstrated, for example, when two novels originally written in German by Franz Kafka, *The Trial* and *The Castle,* were published with new English language translations in 1998, sparking scholarly and critical debate.

EXAMPLE

Puppies On a Bench. In the case of *Rogers v. Koons,*[2] the photographer Art Rogers created the photograph entitled *Puppies,* which features a man and woman sitting on a bench and holding eight puppies. The artist Jeff Koons purchased two postcards of the image and, without obtaining Rogers's authorization, created a wood sculpture based on the image. Since the sculpture was substantially similar and was prepared without the authorization of Rogers, a court determined it was an infringement of Rogers's right to adapt the work. In other words, even though Koons had demonstrated sufficient originality in his statue, he could not sell his work because he failed to obtain permission from the photographer of the underlying copyrighted work.

Standards of Originality for Derivative Works

Sufficient Originality	Insufficient Originality
Addition of new routines or functions to a computer program	Correction of errors in a computer program
Translation of a book into a different language	Publication of a book with larger type to aid the vision-impaired
Addition of scenes and sequences to a previously released motion picture	Reproduction of a motion picture in videocassette format
Drawing created from a photograph	Duplication of a photograph on a lunchbox

Protection of Fictional Characters

Fictional literary or visual characters may become derivative works. For example, Walt Disney created the animated cartoon *Steamboat Willie,* in which the Mickey Mouse character first appeared. The character of Mickey Mouse is still widely recognized, while the original cartoon is remembered solely for its historical significance. Under copyright law, characters such as Mickey Mouse, Perry Mason, Wonder Woman, Snoopy, and Scarlett O'Hara may be protected, apart from the work from which they are derived. In the case of *Nichols v. Universal Pictures Corp.,*[3] Judge Learned Hand stated that "the less developed the characters, the less they can be copyrighted; that is the penalty an author must bear for marking them too indistinctly."

For example, a character who is alienated by modern life and becomes obsessed with assassinating a leader is too indistinct and not capable of copyright protection. But consider Travis Bickle, a tormented loner who drives a cab in New York, befriends a teen prostitute, and attempts to murder a presidential candidate in response to a thwarted love affair. This character, from the film *Taxi Driver,* is a protectible expression.

JUDGE LEARNED HAND ON COPYRIGHT: SAVING SUPERMAN

Judge Hand was one of the first to recognize that a character can be protected separately from the work. By applying this principle, Judge Hand saved Superman from being banished to the public domain in 1951. Several Superman comic strips had been published by a newspaper without copyright notice. The infringer argued that, as a result of these publications, the Superman character was in the public domain because under the Copyright Act of 1909, publication without copyright notice caused the loss of copyright. Judge Hand ruled that the absence of notice on one strip had no effect on the copyright of other protected strips.[4] Although several comic strips of Superman fell into the public domain, the Superman character was still protected.

When Characters Merge with Real People

As discussed in Chapter 1, laws known as the "right of publicity" protect individuals from unauthorized commercial use of their image or persona. For example, it is illegal to use a celebrity's name or image to endorse a product without authorization. Since celebrities portray characters in movies and on television, there are often two intertwined rights when a fictional character is used for commercial endorsement. For example, a company created robotic figures (that moved and talked) and licensed them for use in taverns. The robots were based upon two characters from the TV show *Cheers*. The robot company received permission from the TV company that owned *Cheers*. However, the company failed to get permission from the two actors who portrayed the characters in the TV series. These actors sued the robot company under the right of publicity.[5] When fictional characters are portrayed by real people, the use of these characters for commercial purposes requires two permissions: the copyright owner (for derivative copyright) and the actor (for right of publicity).

COMPILATIONS AND COLLECTIVE WORKS

Often an author creates a work by selecting various components and grouping them together in a unique manner. For example, the owners of copyright in *Bartlett's Familiar Quotations* have chosen famous quotes. The manner in which the authors of *Bartlett's* have selected and arranged the quotes is protectible as a **compilation.** A compilation is a work formed by the selective collection and assembling of preexisting materials or data.

17 U.S.C. § 101 Compilation

A "compilation" is a work formed by the collection and assembling of preexisting materials or of data that are selected, coordinated, or arranged in such a way that the resulting work as a whole constitutes an original work of authorship. The term "compilation" includes collective works.

Protecting the Manner and Arrangement: The *Feist* Case

Not all compilations are protectible. For example, anyone may copy a quote from *Bartlett's Familiar Quotations*. But the manner of arrangement and selection of the quotes, if they meet the standard of originality, are protectible. Similarly, a compilation will not be protected simply because an author has worked hard to gather information. In a 1991 case, *Feist Publications, Inc. v. Rural Telephone Service Co.*,[6] the United States Supreme Court reviewed a case in which one telephone book company copied the "white pages" of a competing telephone book publisher. The Supreme Court ruled that the names and telephone numbers in the directory were unprotectible facts and the method of arranging the names and numbers did not satisfy the minimum standards of copyright protection. Justice O'Connor labeled the telephone directory a "garden variety white pages directory, devoid of even the slightest trace of creativity."

What Is Protectible After *Feist?*

Under the *Feist* ruling, the owner of a compilation must demonstrate copyrightability by selection, coordination, and arrangement of the data. Although the *Feist* ruling effectively eliminated "white pages" phone books from protection under copyright, it did not eliminate "yellow pages" books. In one case, a court protected a business directory yellow pages because creating the directory required many instances of creative selection and judgment such as classifications of business, groupings based upon geography, or other categorization.[7]

The *Feist* guidelines have been applied in other instances of compilations. For example, a real estate title commitment (a document with facts about a parcel of real estate) was not sufficiently original and was considered unprotectible as a compilation.[8] In another decision, a compilation of shorthand numbered codes used on dental bills (for example, "00110" for "Initial oral examination") was considered to lack sufficient creativity.[9] In a 1996 case, a system of codes and formulas developed by a company rating workers' compensation claims was also considered to lack sufficient originality and was unprotectible under copyright law.[10]

In *Matthew Bender & Co. v. West Publishing Co.*,[11] a legal publisher incorporated another publisher's page numbering system on a CD-ROM product. That is, in order to cite public domain court opinions, Matthew Bender & Company used the page numbering system (known as "star pagination") developed by West Publishing Company. The court of appeals ruled that the use of star pagination was not protectible under the *Feist* ruling, and in any case, the page citation copying was permitted as a fair use.

When courts have protected compilations, the use of selective judgment by the authors is a strong factor. For example, a compilation of predicted used car values was protectible because the values were based upon the judgment and experience of the authors. By arranging the information by locales, equipment, and mileage, the authors of the compilation demonstrated adequate originality.[12] In another case, a computer company developed a list of "threshold values" that was used to anticipate the failure of computer hard drives. This compilation of values was protectible because the determination and the order involved creative judgment.[13]

COLLECTIVE WORKS

The term *compilation* includes **collective works.** A collective work is a work, such as a periodical issue (for example, a magazine), anthology, or encyclopedia, in which a number of contributions, constituting separate and independent works in themselves, are assembled into a collective whole. Unlike other compilations, such as a directory or book of quotes, the underlying elements assembled into a collective work can be separately protected. Examples would be a collection of short stories by John Updike or a collection of "greatest disco hits" recordings from the 1970s. Other examples of collective works would include a newspaper, a group of film clips, or a poetry anthology.

17 U.S.C. §101 Collective works

A "collective work" is a work, such as a periodical issue, anthology, or encyclopedia, in which a number of contributions, constituting separate and independent works in themselves, are assembled into a collective whole.

Collective works, like all compilations, must contain sufficient originality. For example, a selection of the *Best of Doonesbury* cartoons with a special introduction would be protectible because there is some creativity used in the choice of selection and the introduction. However, reprinting *Doonesbury* cartoons in chronological order does not demonstrate sufficient originality to be a separately copyrightable collective work.

END NOTES

1. 17 U.S.C. § 103.
2. 960 F.2d 301 (2d Cir. 1992).
3. 45 F.2d 119 (2d Cir. 1930).
4. National Comics Publications, Inc. v. Fawcett Publications, Inc., 191 F.2d 594 (2d Cir. 1951), *clarified,* 198 F.2d 927 (2d Cir. 1952).
5. Wendt v. Host Int'l, Inc., 125 F.3d 806 (9th Cir. 1996).
6. 111 S. Ct. 1282 (1991).
7. Bellsouth Advertising & Publishing Corp. v. Donnelly Info. Publishing, Inc., 933 F.2d 952 (11th Cir. 1991).

8. Mid Am. Title Co. v. Kirk, 59 F.3d 719 (7th Cir. 1995).
9. American Dental Ass'n v. Delta Dental Plan Ass'n, 39 U.S.P.Q.2d 1715 (E.D. Ill. 1996).
10. National Council on Compensation Ins., Inc. v. Insurance Data Resources, Inc., 40 U.S.P.Q.2d 1362 (S.D. Fla. 1996).
11. 158 F.3d 693 (2d Cir. 1998). *But see also* West Publishing Co. v. Mead Data, 799 F.2d 1219 (1986).
12. CCC Info. Servs. v MacLean Hunter Mkt. Reports, 44 F.3d 61 (2d Cir. 1994).
13. Compaq Computer Corp. v. Procom Technology, 908 F. Supp. 1409 (S.D. Tex. 1995).

CHAPTER 5
What Is Not Protectible Under Copyright Law?

The previous chapter described what is protectible under copyright law. This chapter provides an analysis of what is not protectible. The following subjects are discussed:

- the difference between an idea and expression;
- the lack of protection for useful objects, inventions, and short phrases;
- the public domain; and
- the distinction between expired, forfeited, and dedicated works.

INTRODUCTION

Copyright protection does not extend to ideas, only the manner in which the idea is expressed. Similarly, copyright does not extend to functional objects, although it may protect artistic expression included on the object. Copyright also does not protect names, titles, short phrases, blank forms, facts, and any works within the public domain. For more information on unprotectible elements, review 37 *Code of Federal Regulations* section 202.1.

17 U.S.C. § 102(b) What is not protectible

In no case does copyright protection for an original work of authorship extend to any idea, procedure, process, system, method of operation, concept, principle, or discovery, regardless of the form in which it is described, explained, illustrated, or embodied in such work.

Ideas

Copyright law does not protect ideas; it protects the expression of ideas. How can an idea be separated from its expression? One way is to summarize the plot or concept that is at the heart of a work. Consider this unprotectible idea—a brilliant criminal takes on a brilliant detective but is captured after making one fatal mistake. However, once this idea is embellished, as in the books of Agatha Christie or in movies such as *The Seven Percent Solution* or *Heat,* the expression of the idea becomes protectible.

In the case of narrative material, such as a literary, dramatic, or motion picture work, this approach is known as the "abstractions" test and was created by

Judge Learned Hand. Under his theory, every work starts with an abstract idea or plot upon which are built embellishments and expressions. Many works are based upon similar ideas or abstractions. Over the decades there have been numerous television comedies about space aliens living on earth (*My Favorite Martian, Mork and Mindy, 3rd Rock from the Sun*). Each of them is distinguishable by plot and incidents, but the underlying plot idea—an alien living on earth—is free for all to use.

JUDGE LEARNED HAND ON COPYRIGHT: THE ABSTRACTIONS TEST

In 1930, the author of the popular play *Abie's Irish Rose* sued the producers of a movie, *The Cohens and the Kellys*.[1] Both plots involved children of Irish and Jewish families who marry secretly because their parents are prejudiced. At the end of each work there is a reconciliation of the families, based upon the presence of a grandchild. Beyond that, the works had little in common except for ethnic clichés. Judge Hand established a standard to separate the idea from the expression. He used the term *abstraction*, which is a process of removing or separating something. He stated: "Upon any work, and especially upon a play, a great number of patterns of increasing generality will fit equally well, as more and more of the incident is left out." In other words, every narrative work is built around an underlying idea, in this case the basic plot summary. The idea may be similar to other plots, but the author's embellishments—the series of details and incidents that separate the idea from similar plots—trigger copyright protection. Copyright extends only to each author's unique expression, not to the underlying idea.

Applying the Abstractions Test.   Judge Hand's abstractions test is still in use. For example, in the case of *Litchfield v. Spielberg*,[2] a writer sued the makers of the movie *E.T.—The Extra Terrestrial*. The writer claimed that the film infringed her musical play, *Lokey from Maldemar,* a social satire designed to "illustrate the disunity of man, divided by egotism." The district court applied the abstractions test and determined that the only similarity in both works was the basic plot line—aliens with powers of levitation are stranded on earth, pursued by authoritarian characters, and finally bid their earthly friends farewell. These general similarities are ideas and are not protectible. The writer's expression of these ideas was not infringed by *E.T.*

This book is also an expression of an idea: to provide a text that will assist in learning and applying copyright law. The method of dividing the chapters into subject sections and the system of section headings are also ideas and are not protectible. Anyone is free to copy these ideas; but the unique textual expression of the author, the specific examples, and the system by which the information is collected and presented are protectible and may not be copied. The table accompanying this text gives examples of ideas and their expressions.

Ideas and Their Expression

Idea	Expression
Clever criminal plays dumb and manages to trick clever detective	*The Usual Suspects* (movie)
Clever detective plays dumb and manages to trick clever criminal	*Columbo* (TV series)
Dumb detective tries to be clever and miraculously manages to capture clever criminal	*The Pink Panther* (movie)

Useful Articles

A **useful article** is a functional object, like a lamp or a shoe, that has a purpose beyond portraying an appearance or conveying information. A useful article may be protected under patent or trademark laws, but it will not be protected under copyright. However, if there is an "artistic expression" included on the useful article and it is possible to separate the expression from the utility (or usefulness), that copyrightable expression will be protected.

17 U.S.C. § 101 Useful article

A "useful article" is an article having an intrinsic utilitarian function that is not merely to portray the appearance of the article or to convey information. An article that is normally a part of a useful article is considered a "useful article."

EXAMPLE

KOOSH Balls. Often it is difficult to separate the functional object from the artistic expression. For instance, the KOOSH ball is a spherical-shaped object with floppy, wiggly, elastic filaments radiating from a core. The Copyright Office denied copyright registration for the KOOSH ball because the ball's function could not be separated from any artistic expression.[3] Despite the lack of copyright protection, the KOOSH ball was still protected under patent and trademark laws.

EXAMPLE

Belt Buckles. In a 1980 case, Barry Kieselstein-Cord sued a company that copied his belt buckle designs.[4] Initially, the district court held that the belt buckles were not copyrightable because it was not possible to physically separate the sculptural work (the jewelry design) from the functional object (the belt buckle). However, the court of appeals reversed that decision and found that the artistic features of the belt buckle were *conceptually* separable. This was sufficient for protection under the Copyright Act of 1976.

EXAMPLE

Motorcycle Stands. In a 1995 case, the manufacturer of stylized chrome motorcycle parts attempted to register some of the company products (for example, kickstand mount, speedometer visor) as sculptural works. The Copyright Office refused to register these items, claiming that the function could not be separated from any claim of aesthetic worthiness. A district court upheld this decision, agreeing that the sculptural or artistic aspects were not conceptually separable.[5]

Why were the results different in the belt buckle and motorcycle cases? The courts are more likely to protect work on functional objects if the work can actually be viewed separately. The belt buckle designs could be "lifted" off the buckles and viewed as art. The stylish beauty of the motorcycle parts was inseparable from the function. As a general rule, the more minimal the aesthetic design, the *less likely* it will obtain copyright protection. The more ornate the design, the *more likely* it will be protected.

Inventions, Methods, and Processes

Copyright law will not protect methods, formulas, devices, or processes. For example, Albert Einstein's equation for the theory of relativity ($E = MC^2$), Paul Newman's formula for tomato sauce, Socrates's method of investigation, and Les Paul's electric guitar pickup would not be protected under copyright. Similarly, copyright law will not protect devices like slide rules, blank calendars, blank forms, scales, or other materials that are used to calculate measurements. Certain methods, systems, or inventions may be protected under patent or trade secrecy laws. Computer software programs are copyrightable because they are unique expressions in a computer language. Certain novel algorithms, methods, and formulas used within software programs also may be patentable.

EXAMPLE

The Unprotectible Cheeseball Recipe. A company published a book of recipes, all of which used yogurt as an ingredient. A court determined that the collection of recipes was protectible as a compilation; however, individual recipes such as "Swiss 'n' Cheddar Cheeseballs" and "Mediterranean Meatball Salad" were not protectible. In other words, a competitor could copy one or two recipes freely, but not the compilation of recipes. The court determined that each recipe was simply a collection of facts (for example, ingredients, measurements) and processes (for example, "broil for 20 minutes at 350 degrees"). Since facts and processes are unprotectible under copyright law, the author could not claim copyright protection for individual recipes.[6]

Facts and Theories

An author cannot obtain copyright protection for facts or theories. For example, the writer of a book on John Dillinger discovered certain facts about the gangster's death and concluded that Dillinger did not die in 1934 and that as of 1979, Dillinger was alive in California. A television series incorporated these facts and the theory into one of its episodes. The writer sued and a federal court determined that the television show could incorporate the facts and theories without infringing the copyright.[7] All that was protectible was the unique method by which the writer expressed the facts and theory.

Names, Titles, or Short Phrases

Phrases such as "Show me the money!" or "Beam me up" are not protected under copyright law. This is because short phrases, names, titles, or groups of words are considered common idioms of the English language and are free to all. Granting a copyright would, as one judge stated, "checkmate the public" and defeat the purpose of copyright—to encourage creativity. Therefore, titles of books or movies, slogans or mottoes, listings of ingredients, and names of products, services, or groups are not protected under copyright law. However, under appropriate conditions, names, titles, and short phrases may be protected under trademark, unfair competition, or false advertising laws. For example, the slogan "Just Do It" would not be protected under copyright law, but it is protectible as a trademark of the Nike company.

Typefaces

A typeface is a set of letters, numbers, or other symbolic characters whose forms are related by repeating design elements and whose function is for use in composing text. Congress deliberately excluded typeface designs from protection under the Copyright Act of 1976. The appearance of a typeface cannot be protected. Some computer programs create digitized typefaces. The appearance of the computer-created typeface will not be protected. However, protection will be granted for the underlying computer program that creates the typeface.

THE PUBLIC DOMAIN

Material that is not protected under copyright (or other proprietary laws) is free for the public to use and is considered to be in the **public domain.** Short phrases, facts, and ideas, for example, are in the public domain. There are several ways by which works of authorship may become public domain material.

Expired Copyright

Copyrights expire after a limited number of years. The period of copyright depends upon the nature of authorship and the year of creation or publication. Chapter 14 provides information about copyright duration. Once a work has expired, it falls into the public domain. Any work published in the United States before 1923 is in the public domain. The rules for determining the expiration of copyright changed in 1998 with the enactment of the Sonny Bono Copyright Term Extension Act, which extended copyright protection by twenty years. As a result of this law, no new expired copyrights will enter the public domain until 2019.

Forfeited Copyright

If an author fails to follow certain copyright formalities, the work may fall into the public domain (sometimes referred to as a "forefeiture"). Thousands of works have been placed in the public domain because of a failure to renew copyright or follow registration formality. These works can be reproduced without paying royalties. However, if a public domain work is modified, the modifications may be separately copyrightable, and copying these modifications may be an infringement.

Back from the Dead: Resuscitating Public Domain Works

When a film falls into the public domain, it does not cause separately protectible preexisting elements, such as the music or underlying story, to fall into the public domain.[8] Based on this principle, the status of public domain films such as *It's a Wonderful Life* and *McLintock* was altered in the 1990s. For example, Republic Pictures acquired rights to the music and story of the public domain film *It's A Wonderful Life,* and on that basis, Republic's attorneys now claim that no one can reproduce or broadcast the film without permission.

Another legal development that changed the status of public domain occurred when the United States amended copyright law to permit automatic restoration of copyright for certain foreign works in the public domain in the United States and protected by copyright in the respective country.[9] Information regarding automatic restoration is provided in Appendix F.

Dedicated Works

Sometimes an author deliberately chooses not to use copyright to protect a work. The author may dedicate the work to the public and place it in the public domain. The author must make this intention clear by including a statement with the work. For example, "This work is not protected under copyright and anyone is free to copy it and disseminate without authorization." However, do not assume that any work labeled "royalty-free" or "copyright-free" is in the public domain. Many companies incorrectly use this terminology when offering limited licenses to reproduce photographs or imagery. Always review any documentation accompanying such offers.

Works Created by United States Government Employees

Any work created by a United States government employee or officer is in the public domain provided that the work is created in that person's official capacity.[10] For example, anyone may reproduce the Starr Report or create derivative works from it, since it was produced by federal employees in their official capacity. This rule does not apply to state or local government employees and does not apply to personal letters or writings created by government employees. There are other exceptions to this rule, as provided in 15 *United States Code* section 290e.

Determining Public Domain Status

Determining whether a work is in the public domain requires research. The Copyright Office does not maintain a list of public domain works. However, private companies can perform searches and furnish public domain reports. Some of these companies even offer public domain compilations—that is, lists of works that are not protected by copyright. Information about these companies is included in Appendix A. For information on how to search Copyright Office records and companies that determine copyright status, see Chapter 16.

END NOTES

1. Nichols v. Universal Pictures Corp., 45 F.2d 119 (2d Cir. 1930).
2. 736 F.2d 1352 (9th Cir. 1984).
3. OddzOn Prods. v. Oman, 924 F.2d 346 (D.C. Cir. 1991).
4. Kieselstein-Cord v. Accessories by Pearl, Inc., 632 F.2d 989 (2d Cir. 1980).
5. Custom Chrome, Inc. v. Ringer, 35 U.S.P.Q.2d 1714 (D. D.C. 1995).
6. Publications Int'l, Ltd. v. Meredith Corp., 88 F.3d 473 (7th Cir. 1996).
7. Nash v. CBS, Inc., 691 F. Supp. 140 (N.D. Ill. 1988).
8. G. Ricordi & Co. v. Paramount Pictures, Inc., 189 F.2d 469 (2d Cir. 1951), *cert. denied,* 342 U.S. 849 (1951).
9. 17 U.S.C. § 104A.
10. 17 U.S.C. § 105.

CHAPTER 6
The Bundle
of Rights

This chapter provides a review of the rights granted under copyright law including the rights to:

- reproduce copies of the work;
- distribute copies of the work;
- adapt or create derivative works;
- perform the work publicly; and
- display the work publicly.

GRANT OF EXCLUSIVE RIGHTS

Section 106 of the Copyright Act of 1976 provides a bundle of exclusive rights to an author. This bundle includes the rights necessary to commercially exploit a work, including the rights to reproduce, adapt, publish, perform, and display the work. If one of these rights is exercised by someone without the authorization of the copyright owner, an infringement has occurred. Limitations to the rights granted under section 106 are discussed in the next chapter.

17 U.S.C. § 106 Exclusive rights in copyrighted works

Subject to sections 107 through 120, the owner of a copyright under this title has the exclusive rights to do and to authorize any of the following:

(1) to reproduce the copyrighted work in copies or phonorecords;
(2) to prepare derivative works based upon the copyrighted work;
(3) to distribute copies or phonorecords of the copyrighted work to the public by sale or other transfer of ownership, or by rental, lease, or lending;
(4) in the case of literary, musical, dramatic, and choreographic works, pantomimes, and motion pictures and other audiovisual works, to perform the copyrighted work publicly;
(5) in the case of literary, musical, dramatic, and choreographic works, pantomimes, and pictorial, graphic, or sculptural works, including the individual images of a motion picture or other audiovisual work, to display the copyrighted work publicly; and
(6) in the case of sound recordings, to perform the copyrighted work publicly by means of a digital audio transmission.

What If the Author Does Not Want to Sell the Work?

The grant of rights allows the author to earn money from the work or, if the author chooses, *not* to earn money from the work. For example, author J. D. Salinger has created new works but has chosen not to publish them. Copyright law grants Salinger the power to prevent others from copying or publishing these works.

RIGHT TO REPRODUCE THE WORK

A work is reproduced when it, or a substantial portion of it, is copied and fixed in a tangible form. If this book were photocopied, that would be a reproduction. If this book were scanned and placed on a computer file, that would also be a reproduction. To qualify as a reproduction, there must be fixation. For example, if the author John Grisham were to read from his book *The Firm,* and someone secretly taped the reading, that is, fixed it on audiotape, that would be a violation of Grisham's right to reproduce the book. Under copyright law, the unauthorized fixation of the words on the audiotape is as much of an infringement as an unauthorized photocopy of the book. Note, the audiotaping may also be a violation of Grisham's performance right—a new right established for performers discussed in Chapter 10.

RIGHT TO DISTRIBUTE THE WORK TO THE PUBLIC

The author controls distribution of the work to the public whether by sale, gift, loan, lease, or rental. This is also known as the *right to publish* the work or *publication right*. Although the Copyright Act of 1976 does not specifically define "distribution of the work to the public," it is generally considered to be circulation or dissemination either to a substantial number of persons or to a substantial portion of the market for the work. The distribution right is similar and related to the reproduction right in that publication must be in a fixed form (that is, copies or phonorecords). What is the difference between reproduction and distribution rights? If a person makes an unauthorized copy of the movie *Star Wars,* that is a violation of the reproduction right. If a person sells the unauthorized copy, that is an infringement of the distribution right.

RIGHT TO ADAPT THE WORK: RIGHT TO PREPARE DERIVATIVE WORKS

Prior to the twentieth century, authors had difficulty securing adaptation rights. For instance, a novelist could not stop a playwright from adapting the novel for stage. It was not until 1870 that Congress granted authors the right to control the dramatization or translation of their books. This was the origin of derivative rights, also known as *the right to adapt* a work. A *derivative work* is a work based upon one or more preexisting works. The right to adapt a work extends to all medias and includes adaptations, abridgments, translations, and any substantial modification of the preexisting work. For more information on derivative rights, see Chapter 4.

RIGHT OF PUBLIC PERFORMANCE

To perform a work publicly has a much broader meaning under copyright law than the common concept of a performance. The drafters of the Copyright Act of 1976 stated that "to perform a work means to recite, render, play, dance, or act it, either directly or by means of any device or process or, in the case of a motion picture or other audiovisual work, to show its images in any sequence or to make the sounds accompanying it audible."[1] Section 101 states that to perform a work "publicly" means that there is performance of the work where the public is gathered *or* the work is transmitted or otherwise communicated to the public.[2] Examples of public performance include:

- a disc jockey plays a phonorecord in a nightclub;
- a novelist reads aloud from her work at a bookstore;
- a dancer presents a performance during halftime at a football game;
- a motion picture company authorizes a showing of its latest film;
- a songwriter performs an original composition at a nightclub;
- a radio station plays a record containing a copyrighted song;
- a television station broadcasts a television show; and
- a cable TV company receives a television station broadcast and rebroadcasts it via cable transmission.

The performance right does not extend to pictorial, graphic, or sculptural works because these works cannot be *performed;* they can only be *displayed,* so these rights are covered by the display right. In 1994, the Copyright Act was amended to include digital performance rights for sound recordings and to prevent the bootlegging of live musical performances. These rights are discussed in Chapter 10.

Live Performances

Performing the work "where the public is gathered" refers to a performance at a place open to the public *or* at any place where a substantial number of persons outside of a normal circle of a family and its social acquaintances are gathered. For example, the song "Happy Birthday" is protected under copyright. When it is sung among a group of social acquaintances at a private party, there is no infringement of the performance right. However, when Marilyn Monroe sang it to President Kennedy at a public gathering, the work was performed publicly. Permission would have to be obtained from the copyright owners. The fact that a performance is not for profit does not affect the determination of whether a public performance has occurred. If you are making a public performance, how do you obtain permission from the copyright owners? Usually this is done through performing right societies. These organizations are discussed in Chapter 10.

Transmissions

To perform a work publicly also may mean that a performance of a work is transmitted to the public by means of a device or process. For example, it is considered a performance if a copyrighted song is played over a public address system or in a dance club. Similarly, any transmission of a work by a radio or television station is a performance. If the performance is transmitted, it does not matter if the public receives it at the same time or place as when it was transmitted. Therefore, if one station transmits a work and another station receives the broadcast and retransmits it later, that also would be a performance. Webcasting or "audiostreaming," the process of transmitting music over the Internet in real-time (that is, the music is heard as it is transmitted), is also considered a public performance.

Playing of Videotapes

If a business provided seating, charged admission, and played a motion picture for the public without authorization, that would violate the right to control public performance. But what if the business rented videotapes and provided viewing rooms for the public? According to court decisions, the showing of rented films in private booths is a public performance and permission must be acquired from the owner of the copyright.[3] The rental of videotapes for viewing in a hotel room, however, would not be an infringement of the public performance right. In that case, the hotel room rental is similar to home rental of the videotape.[4]

17 U.S.C. § 101 Perform or display a work publicly

To perform or display a work "publicly" means—

(1) to perform or display it at a place open to the public or at any place where a substantial number of persons outside of a normal circle of a family and its social acquaintances is gathered; or

(2) to transmit or otherwise communicate a performance or display of the work to a place specified by clause (1) or to the public, by means of any device or process, whether the members of the public capable of receiving the performance or display receive it in the same place or in separate places and at the same time or at different times.

RIGHT TO DISPLAY THE WORK

The right to display a work is similar to the right to perform a work. Both require a public gathering. The difference is in the nature of the work. A movie is performed because it is a sequence of images and sounds. A painting or sculpture is displayed because it is one image.

A painter has a right to control the public display of a work *prior to the sale* of that work. After the work is sold, the purchaser is permitted to display it publicly, such as in a public museum. However, the owner of the painting cannot broadcast the image of the painting outside of the museum. That right is still controlled by the artist. A person renting, leasing, or borrowing the painting does not have the right to publicly display it. Only the purchaser of the painting is allowed to do that.

Display Rights: Motion Pictures and Audiovisual Works

If individual images from the film *Sleeping Beauty* were projected at a public lecture, that showing would infringe the display right. If the complete film was shown in sequence, that would infringe the performance right. In both cases, the permission of the copyright owner should be acquired.

END NOTES

1. 17 U.S.C. § 101.
2. 17 U.S.C. § 101.
3. Columbia Pictures Indus., Inc. v. Redd Horne, Inc., 749 F.2d 154 (9th Cir. 1984); Columbia Pictures Indus., Inc. v. Aveco, Inc., 612 F. Supp. 315 (M.D. Pa. 1985), *aff'd,* 800 F.2d 59 (3d Cir. 1986).
4. Columbia Pictures Indus., Inc. v. Professional Real Estate Investors, Inc., 866 F.2d 278 (9th Cir. 1989).

CHAPTER 7
The Rights of the Public: First Sale and Fair Use

In the previous chapters, information was provided about the rights of the author. In this chapter, information is provided about the rights of the public, particularly the rights of the purchaser of a copy and the rights of a person who wants to use a portion of a copyrighted work. The following subjects are discussed:

- the rights of a purchaser of a copy;
- the criteria for determining if use of copyrighted material is a fair use; and
- the standards for deciding if a parody qualifies as a fair use.

THE FIRST SALE DOCTRINE

If you purchased this book, you are free to resell it without obtaining the permission of the copyright owner. You can also rent it, or even burn it if you wish (although please be careful if doing so). That is because once the *first* sale of a copy has occurred, the author's rights regarding that copy are limited by section 109 of the United States Copyright Act. This limitation is commonly known as the **first sale doctrine.** Every day, millions of consumers make use of this principle of copyright law. The rental of a videocassette, the display of a copyrighted painting, and the resale of a previously owned phonorecord are all permitted under the first sale doctrine. The basis of this doctrine is that the purchaser of a lawfully made copy or phonorecord has the right to dispose of it by sale, rental, or any other means without the authority of the author. The first sale doctrine also grants the purchaser of artwork the right to display it. The first sale doctrine is limited. Owning a copy does not grant rights to reproduce, adapt, or perform the work. For example, if you buy this book, you can sell or destroy it, but you cannot copy or adapt it.

First Sale: Exceptions

There are exceptions to the first sale doctrine. The first sale doctrine does not permit the rental of computer programs or sound recordings, and it does not permit the destruction of works of visual arts. These three exceptions are discussed in more detail in Chapters 9, 10, and 11. The purchaser's right to artwork is limited to displaying it where the artwork is located. In other words, under the first sale doctrine, you can display a lawfully purchased photograph in your home but you cannot broadcast it over a cable television channel.

The first sale doctrine only applies to the owner of the copy, not to a person who *possesses* the copy but does not own it. For example, a video store purchases a lawfully made videocassette copy of the movie *Fluke*. As the owner of that copy, the store can rent it to an individual. However, the person renting it cannot rent the copy to someone else. Only the owner of the copy has such rights.

Mounting and Resale of Art Prints: Conflict over First Sale

As with many areas of copyright law, there is some confusion about the boundaries of the first sale doctrine. Two cases involving the framing of artwork seem to have arrived at different results. In one case, a company purchased a book of prints by the painter Patrick Nagel, cut out the individual images in the book, and mounted them in frames for resale. The Ninth Circuit Court of Appeals in California held that this practice was an infringement and was *not* permitted under the first sale doctrine.[1] In a different case, however, a company purchased notecards and mounted them on tiles.[2] A federal court in Illinois determined that this practice was *not* an infringement and was permitted under the first sale doctrine. Under these rulings, a person in California cannot mount individual images from an art book, while a person in Illinois *can* mount individual notecards. Should it matter whether the object that is mounted is from an art book or from a notecard? In the California case, the justices felt that mounting the Nagel images separately created a derivative work. In the Illinois case, the judge did not believe that mounting an image on a tile created a derivative work, since the image was not altered or modified.

FAIR USE

Fair use is the right to use copyrighted material for limited purposes and without authorization of the author. When a music reviewer quotes lyrics from a song or a news commentator quotes from a candidate's speech, those are examples of fair use. Supreme Court Justice Blackmun wrote that the intent of fair use is "to encourage users to engage in activities the primary benefit of which accrues to others."[3] In other words, fair use is intended to promote a benefit to the public by permitting the borrowing of portions of a work. Traditionally, this has meant the right to comment upon, criticize, or parody copyrighted works. The application of fair use principles is also meant to incorporate and balance the right of free speech granted under the United States Constitution.

The Copyright Act of 1976 offers several examples of fair use such as copying for "purposes such as criticism, comment, news reporting, teaching (including multiple copies for classroom use), scholarship, or research." Other examples were presented in the legislative history of the Copyright Act of 1976 including:

- quotation of excerpts in a review or criticism for purposes of illustration or comment;

- use in a parody of some of the content of the work parodied;
- summary of an address or article, with brief quotations in a news report;
- reproduction by teacher or student of a small part of a work to illustrate a lesson; and
- reproduction of a work in legislative or judicial proceedings or reports.

Fair Use Is Always Asserted as a Defense

Fair use is an affirmative defense against infringement. A party accused of infringing argues that the copying is excused under the fair use doctrine. A court faced with this argument weighs several factors, and if the weight of the factors is in favor of the defendant, the unauthorized use of the material is permitted.

The Four Fair Use Factors

In order to guide judges in making determinations of fair use, the drafters of the Copyright Act of 1976 included four factors:[4]

1. the purpose and character of the use, including whether such use is of a commercial nature or is for nonprofit educational purposes;
2. the nature of the copyrighted work;
3. amount and substantiality of the portion taken in relation to the copyrighted work as a whole; and
4. the effect of the use upon the potential market for or value of the copyrighted work.

In addition to these fair use factors, a court may consider other factors, if relevant. The drafters of the Copyright Act of 1976 were careful to advise that the four fair use factors were intended only as a guideline, and the courts are free to adapt the doctrine to particular situations on a case-by-case basis.

When analyzing fair use, a court usually poses various questions in relation to each factor. The table accompanying this text provides examples of the types of questions that are asked, and in the following sections, these questions are reviewed in the context of actual examples of fair use.

Analysis of Fair Use Factors

Factor	Questions
Purpose and character of the use	Is the use transformative, that is, does it change the original by adding new expression or meaning? Is the use for educational, scientific, historical, or other purposes that further the dissemination of knowledge?

(Cont'd)

Analysis of Fair Use Factors (Cont'd)

Nature of the copyrighted work	Is the nature of the work that has been borrowed informational or entertaining? (for example, fact or fiction) Is the work that has been borrowed published or unpublished?
Amount and substantiality of the portion used	How much of the work is borrowed? How important is the portion borrowed to the work from which it was taken? (that is, is it the heart of the work?)
Effect of the use upon the potential market	Does the use deprive the copyright owner of income? Does the use undermine a new or potential market for the work?

Purpose and Character of the Use.   The first factor requires an analysis of whether the use is transformative. That is, did the defendant change the original by adding new expression or meaning? Did the defendant add value to the original by creating new information, new aesthetics, new insights and understandings? In a parody, for example, the parodist transforms the original by holding it up to ridicule.[5] The brief use of photographs in a film was considered to be transformative because the images were used in furtherance of the creation of a distinct aesthetic and overall mood.[6] The defendant's work does not have to transform the original work's expression as long as the purpose is transformative, for example, scholarship, research, education, or commentary.

Nature of the Copyrighted Work.   A court will generally consider whether the work being copied is informational or entertaining in nature. As the Supreme Court indicated,[7] "copying a news broadcast may have a stronger claim to fair use than copying a motion picture." Why? Because copying from informational works such as scholarly, scientific, or news journals encourages the free spread of ideas and encourages the creation of new scientific or educational works, all of which benefits the public.

In addition, a defendant has a stronger case of fair use if material is copied from a published work rather than an unpublished work. The scope of fair use is narrower with respect to unpublished works because of the author's right to control the first public appearance of his or her expression.[8] The impact of the unpublished status may also depend upon the amount and substantiality of the portion taken (the third fair use factor). In a case involving the novelist Richard Wright,[9] a court permitted a biographer to quote from six unpublished letters and ten of Wright's unpublished journal entries. The court determined that no more than one percent of Wright's unpublished letters and journal was copied.

EXAMPLE

How J. D. Salinger Rewrote Copyright Law. In *Salinger v. Random House*,[10] a biographer paraphrased portions of letters written by J. D. Salinger. Although the public could read these letters at a university library, Salinger had never authorized publication of the letters. Despite the scholarly purpose of the proposed Salinger biography, the court would not permit the unauthorized paraphrasing of Salinger's unpublished letters as a fair use. The Salinger case created concern among publishers, and in October 1992, section 107 of the Copyright Act was amended by the addition of the following sentence: "The fact that a work is not published shall not itself bar a finding of fair use if such finding is made upon consideration of all the above [fair use] factors." That is, the court must base its fair use decisions upon the four factors, not simply upon whether the work is published or unpublished.

EXAMPLE

Politics and Fair Use. In a 1978 case, *Keep Thomson Governor Committee v. Citizens for Gallen Committee*,[11] a person running for political office used fifteen seconds of his opponent's copyrighted campaign song in a political ad. A federal court excused the copying as a fair use, taking into consideration that the use of the song was part of the political message of the advertisement. However, it is unlikely that the borrowing of a whole song would be excused. During the 1996 presidential campaign, the staff of Republican candidate Bob Dole modified the song "Soul Man" so that it was performed as "Dole Man." The owner of the song threatened a lawsuit, and the Republicans halted their unauthorized use.

Amount and Substantiality of Portion Used. The more that is taken from a work, the more difficult it becomes to justify it as a fair use. In a 1989 case, *Love v. Kwitny*,[12] the defendant copied more than half of an unpublished manuscript to demonstrate that the plaintiff was involved in the overthrow of the Iranian government. The copying was not justified by fair use. When considering the amount and substantiality of the portion taken, the court considers not just the quantity of the material but the quality of the material taken. Determinations regarding "quality" or "substantiality" are subjective and may be difficult to reconcile. For example, the copying of one minute and fifteen seconds of a seventy-two-minute Charlie Chaplin film, used in a news report about the comedian's death, was considered substantial and not a fair use.[13] However, in 1996, another court determined that copying forty-one seconds from a boxing match film was not substantial and permitted it as a fair use in a movie biography of Muhammed Ali.[14]

In certain rare cases, copying of a complete work may be considered as a fair use. For example, in the *Sony*[15] case discussed in the following text, the Supreme Court permitted the off-the-air copying of complete television programs.

Effect of the Use on the Potential Market.   The fourth factor in a fair use determination is the effect of the use on the potential market for the work that was copied. One court stated that consideration of this factor is intended to strike a balance "between the benefit that the public will derive if the use is permitted and the personal gain that the copyright owner will receive if the use is denied."[16]

A judge must consider the effect on the *potential* market for the copyrighted work. This consideration goes beyond the past intentions of the author or the means by which the author is currently exploiting the work. For example, in *Rogers v. Koons,*[17] a photograph was adapted into a wood sculpture without the authorization of the photographer. The fact that the photographer never considered converting the photograph into a statue was irrelevant. What mattered was that the *potential* market existed as demonstrated by the fact that the defendant earned hundreds of thousands of dollars selling such statues.

Some uses are not considered to undermine the potential market. Copying a magazine cover for purposes of a comparative advertisement is a fair use because the comparative advertisement does not undermine the sales or need for the featured magazine. Similarly, the appearance of a poster in the background of a television series for less than thirty seconds was not considered to harm the potential market for the poster.[18]

Effect of Acknowledgment of Source Material

Many people believe that it is permissible to use a work (or portion of it) if acknowledgment is made—that is, that it would be okay to use a photograph in a magazine as long as one printed the name of the photographer. This is not true. Acknowledgment of the source material (such as citing the photographer) may be a consideration in a fair use determination, but it will not protect against a claim of infringement. In some cases, such as advertisements, acknowledgments can backfire and create additional legal claims such as misappropriation of the right of publicity. When in doubt about the right to use or acknowledge a source, the most prudent course is to seek permission of the copyright owner.

The best method of understanding the flexible principle of fair use is to review the case law and consider some specific examples.

EXAMPLE

The Hidden Fair Use Factor: Are You a Good Guy or a Bad Guy? You may find that the results in fair use cases seem to contradict one another or conflict with the rules expressed in preceding paragraphs. That is, they seem to have similar facts but different results. This is because fair use cases involve subjective judgment and the outcomes are affected by factors such as a judge or jury's personal sense of right or wrong. A judge's sense of fairness may be offended by a defendant's actions. For example, in *Harper & Row v. Nation Enterprises,*[19] the Supreme Court, ruling against a defense of fair use, criticized the defendant for "knowingly exploit[ing] a purloined manuscript." The interpretation of fair use is often shaped by such feelings.

EXAMPLE

In a 1984 case, *Universal City Studios, Inc. v. Sony Corp. of America*[20] (commonly known as the *Betamax* or *Sony* case), the Supreme Court weighed the four fair use factors and determined that the home videotaping of a television broadcast was a fair use. However, the taping must be off-the-air and for personal use, not for commercial purposes. Since evidence indicated that most viewers were "time-shifting" (taping in order to watch later) and not "library-building" (collecting the videos in order to build a video library), the court reasoned that this "delayed" system of viewing did not deprive the copyright owners of revenue and was permitted as a fair use.

EXAMPLE

In *Religious Technology Center v. Lerma*,[21] the defendants argued that posting complete publications of the Church of Scientology on the Internet was similar to the off-the-air taping permitted in the *Sony* case. The federal court disagreed and noted that in *Sony*, the owners of copyright in the television shows had broadcast the shows and the taping was merely for the convenience of later viewing of this "free programming." In the case of the Scientology documents, however, permission had not been given by the owners of copyright to "broadcast" the information over the Internet. In a related case, the *Washington Post* used three brief quotations from the Scientology texts posted on the Internet. This was permitted as a fair use because only a small portion of the work was excerpted and the purpose was for news commentary.[22]

EXAMPLE

In a 1985 case, *Harper & Row v. Nation Enterprises*,[23] the *Nation* magazine was accused of infringing the rights of ex-president Gerald Ford by publishing excerpts from his unpublished memoirs. The publication in the *Nation* was made several weeks prior to the date of serialization of Ford's book in another magazine. The Supreme Court weighed the four fair use factors. The first factor weighed in favor of the *Nation*. Clearly, the purpose of the use was informational and scholarly. The second factor weighed in favor of Ford because fair use is narrowly interpreted for unpublished works. As for the third factor, the actual portion borrowed from President Ford's work was small, consisting of approximately three hundred to four hundred words. However, the fact that the *Nation*'s work was timed to scoop Ford's publication seriously damaged the marketability of serialization rights. The Supreme Court would not excuse the *Nation*'s use of the material as a fair use.

EXAMPLE

In a 1993 case, *Twin Peaks v. Publications International, Ltd.*,[24] the publisher of a book entitled *Welcome to Twin Peaks—A Complete Guide to Who's Who and What's What* was sued by the owner of the *Twin Peaks* television show. The book contained direct quotations and paraphrases from the show, as well as detailed descriptions of plot, character, and setting. The publisher argued that the use of these materials was educational and excused under the fair use doctrine. The court disagreed and determined that: the purpose of the use was commercial; the nature of the work taken was creative and fictional; the amount of the material taken was substantial; and the publication of the book adversely affected the potential market for the books about the program that were authorized by the owners of copyright in the *Twin Peaks* television shows.

EXAMPLE

In a 1998 case, *Castle Rock Entertainment, Inc. v. Carol Publishing Group,*[25] the copyright owner of the *Seinfeld* TV show sued a company that published the *Seinfeld Aptitude Test,* a trivia book that asked questions such as "What candy does Kramer snack on while observing a surgical procedure from an operating-room balcony?" As to the first factor, a court of appeals determined the work did not serve a critical or otherwise transformative purpose. The *Seinfeld Aptitude Test's* purpose was only to "satiate *Seinfeld* fans' passion for the 'nothingness' that *Seinfeld* has elevated into the realm of protectable creative expression." The second and third factors weighed against the publisher because *Seinfeld* was fictional and the *Seinfeld Aptitude Test* had taken extensively from the TV show. As for the fourth factor, even though *Seinfeld's* owner had no intention of releasing a trivia book, the court of appeals ruled that the decision not to saturate the market with *Seinfeld* derivatives should be respected. On that basis, the book was not a fair use.

EXAMPLE

In *Hustler Magazine, Inc. v. Moral Majority, Inc.,*[26] the publisher of *Hustler* magazine, Larry Flynt, unsuccessfully sued the Reverend Falwell for copyright infringement. Flynt's magazine, *Hustler,* had printed a parody that included unflattering comments about Falwell, and Falwell reproduced hundreds of thousands of copies of the *Hustler* parody as part of a fundraising drive. A federal court in California determined that the copying was a fair use. Falwell's use was for a combination of purposes—political, personal, and financial. As for the second factor, the article was copied not for its creative efforts but for the information contained in it about Falwell. As for the third factor, only one page was taken from the magazine. Finally, as to the fourth factor, the court determined that Falwell's use would not diminish the sales of the magazine, since it was already off the market, and would not affect the marketability of back issues.

EXAMPLE

In *Los Angeles News Service v. KCAL-TV Channel 9*,[27] a 1997 case, a Los Angeles television station broadcast a copy of a videotape of truck driver Reginald Denny's beating following the Rodney King verdict. The television station had previously been denied the right to broadcast the videotape but obtained a copy from another station and broadcast a portion on several occasions. The station claimed its broadcast of this newsworthy event was a fair use. As for the first factor, the Ninth Circuit Court of Appeals said that the use was not transformative because the station had simply superimposed its logo and used the tape for the same purpose as it was initially intended. The second factor weighed in favor of the defendant, since the videotape was published and informational. The third factor weighed against the defendant because the most important part, or the "heart," of the videotape was broadcast. The fourth factor also weighed against the defendant because the defendant was in the business of licensing news tapes, and the use of the tape for free affected the market for the work. Therefore, the TV station's use of the tape was not excused as a fair use.

PARODY AS FAIR USE

In order to parody something, it is necessary to borrow a portion of the work. It would be difficult to parody the movie *Gone with the Wind* without using the names Rhett and Scarlett. Generally, a court views the use of materials in a parody in terms of the fair use factors. However, the parody defense has acquired some of its own characteristics. Judges understand that by its nature, parody demands some taking from an original work, and a more extensive use of a copyrighted work is permitted, therefore, in order to "conjure up" the original. When analyzing the four fair use factors, two issues become especially important: whether the use is transformative, that is, whether the parodist has created something new; and the effect on the potential market—or as it is sometimes phrased, whether the parodist's result had the intent or the effect of fulfilling a demand for the original work.

The Difference Between Parody and Satire

Not every humorous use of a work is a parody. In *Campbell v. Acuff-Rose Music*,[28] the Supreme Court defined parody as the use of an existing work to create a new one that, at least in part, comments on the earlier work. In a parody, the copyrighted work is the target. For that reason, the parody needs to mimic the work to make its point. In a satire, the copyrighted work is merely a medium by which to poke fun at something else. A satire is not a transformative use and may not be as likely to qualify as a fair use. For example, in one case[29] involving a book entitled *The Cat NOT in the Hat! A Parody by Dr. Juice,* a publisher had mimicked the style of a Dr. Seuss book while retelling the facts of the O. J. Simpson murder trial. The Ninth Circuit Court of Appeals determined that the book was a satire, not a parody, because the book did not poke fun at or ridicule Dr. Seuss, but merely used the Dr. Seuss characters and style to tell the story of the murder. Because the defendant's work was nontransformative and commercial, it was not excused as a fair use.

Following are summaries of parody cases. As with the fair use cases, you may find that some of the cases have similar facts but different results. Decisions in copyright cases, particularly in regard to subjective factors such as parody and fair use, often reflect a merger of law and the judge or jury's personal views.

EXAMPLE

In *Campbell v. Acuff-Rose Music*,[30] the rap group 2 Live Crew parodied some of the lyrics to the song "Pretty Woman." The rap group borrowed only the opening guitar riff and the words (but not the melody) from the first line of the song ("Oh pretty woman walking down the street"). The rest of the lyrics and the music were different. For example, the 2 Live Crew song featured rhymes such as "Big hairy woman all that hair it ain't legit/Cause you look like 'Cousin It'/Big hairy woman." The Supreme Court acknowledged that the guitar riff and opening line were the "heart" of the original composition but stated, "the heart is also what most readily conjures up the song for parody, and it is the heart at which parody takes aim." The Supreme Court determined that the fact that the purpose was commercial did not prevent a fair use determination because of the "transformative" nature of the parody. In other words, a parody can be a fair use, even if its purpose is to make money for the parody artist. One interesting aspect of this case was that the rap group had initially sought to pay for the right to use portions of the song but was rebuffed by the publisher, who did not want "Pretty Woman" used in a rap song.

EXAMPLE

In *Fisher v. Dees*,[31] the composers of the song "When Sunny Gets Blue" claimed that their song was infringed by "When Sonny Sniffs Glue," a twenty-nine-second parody that altered the original lyric line and borrowed six bars of the plaintiff's music. The plaintiff argued that the parody reflected negatively on the original song and therefore affected its marketability. The court responded that: "[T]he economic effect of a parody with which we are concerned is not its potential to destroy or diminish the market for the original—any bad review can have that effect—but whether it *fulfills the demand* for the original." The court weighed the fair use factors and determined that the balance tipped in favor of the parodist and permitted the brief parody as a fair use. Note, however, the borrowing of a complete song (not merely twenty-nine seconds) and modifying the lyrics is unlikely to be excused as fair use or parody. Performers such as Weird Al Yankovic who earn a living by humorously modifying hit songs seek permission from the song owners before recording their parodies. See Chapter 10 for more information on music rights.

EXAMPLE

In *Elsmere Music, Inc. v. National Broadcasting Co.*,[32] the late-night TV comedy show *Saturday Night Live* parodied the song "I Love New York" using the words "I Love Sodom." Only the words "I Love" and four musical notes were taken from the plaintiff's work, yet the court recognized the musical-lyrical phrase as being substantial (that is, the "heart of the composition"). However, emphasizing the fourth fair use factor (the economic impact), the court determined that "the defendant's version of the jingle did not compete with or detract from the plaintiff's work" and excused it under a fair use analysis.

EXAMPLE

In *Original Appalachian Artworks, Inc. v. Topps Chewing Gum, Inc.*,[33] a manufacturer of novelty cards parodied the successful children's dolls known as the Cabbage Patch Kids. The parody card series was entitled the "Garbage Pail Kids" and used gruesome and grotesque names and characters to poke fun at the wholesome Cabbage Patch image. In a decision that surprised some copyright experts, a federal court considered the parody an infringement, not a fair use because the novelty cards were meant to capitalize on demand for the successful children's toys—that is, to make money from imitating the dolls.

EXAMPLE

A Tale of Two Movie Posters. In a 1998 case, *Leibovitz v. Paramount Pictures Corp.*,[34] a movie company used a photo of a naked pregnant woman and superimposed the head of actor Leslie Nielsen. The photo was a parody, using similar lighting and body positioning, of a famous photograph taken by Annie Leibovitz of the actress Demi Moore for the cover of *Vanity Fair* magazine. Leibovitz sued the movie company, and the court of appeals determined that the movie company's copying was excusable as a fair use parody. Although a large amount had been borrowed from the original and the use of the parody was commercial, the "transformative" nature of the parody was considered to be a form of commentary. The court stated, "Like all parodies, it relies for its comic effect on the contrast between the original—a serious portrayal of a beautiful woman taking great pride in the majesty of her pregnant body—and the new work—a ridiculous image of a smirking, foolish-looking pregnant man. It thus fits squarely within the definition of parody as a 'literary or artistic work that imitates the characteristic style of an author or a work for comic effect or ridicule."

In a 1987 case, *Steinberg v. Columbia Pictures Industries, Inc.*,[35] the plaintiff-artist created a cover for the *New Yorker* magazine that presented a humorous view of geography through the eyes of a New York City resident. Steinberg's skewered map presented the typical New York City resident's geographical viewpoint (that is, that New York City is the center of the world).

Features of Manhattan and neighboring areas were prominent, while the rest of the country receded on the horizon.

The defendant's movie poster advertised the film *Moscow on the Hudson* using a similar piece of artwork with similar elements—that is, a humorous map skewered so that it prominently featured elements of New York City. The federal court considered the movie company's commercial purpose and determined that the poster was an infringement, not an excusable parody.

How is the *Steinberg* case distinguishable from the *Leibovitz* case? In *Leibovitz*, the plaintiff's photograph was a serious work and the defendant's poster mocked it by superimposing a ridiculous image. It was a true parody, characterized by a juxtaposition of imagery that actually commented on or criticized the original. In the *Steinberg* case, the plaintiff's work already was a parody. The defendant's movie poster merely took the humorous aspects and style of the original work and used them for a commercial purpose. In other words, in *Steinberg,* the defendant did not actually create a "parody" but simply borrowed the plaintiff's viewpoint.

EDUCATIONAL AND LIBRARY FAIR USE ISSUES

Fair use guidelines have been developed for libraries and educational institutions. Although these guidelines are not part of copyright law, they provide standards for avoiding liability and have been adopted by some courts. A summary of the guidelines is provided in Chapter 8.

END NOTES

1. Mirage Editions, Inc. v. Albuquerque A.R.T. Co., 856 F.2d 1341 (1988). A similar result was reached in *Greenwich Workshop, Inc. v. Timber Creations, Inc.,* 932 F. Supp. 1210 (C.D. Cal. 1996).
2. Lee v. Deck the Walls, Inc. 925 F. Supp. 576 (N.D. Ill. 1996). The same result occurred in C. M. Paula Co. v. Logan, 355 F. Supp. 189 (D.C. Tex. 1973).
3. Universal City Studios v. Sony Corp., 464 U.S. 417 (1984).
4. 17 U.S.C. § 107.
5. Dr. Seuss Enters., L.P. v. Penguin Books USA, Inc., 109 F.3d 1394 (9th Cir. 1997).
6. Sandoval v. New Line Cinema Corp., 973 F. Supp. 409 (S.D.N.Y. 1997).
7. Universal City Studios v. Sony Corp., 464 U.S. 417 (1984).
8. Harper & Row v. Nation Enters., 471 U.S. 539 (1985).
9. Wright v. Warner Books, Inc., 953 F.2d 731 (2d Cir. 1991).
10. 811 F.2d 90 (2d Cir. 1987).
11. 457 F. Supp. 957 (D. N.H. 1978).
12. 772 F. Supp. 1367 (S.D.N.Y. 1989).
13. Roy Export Co. Estab. of Vaduz v. Columbia Broadcasting Sys., Inc., 672 F.2d 1095, 1100 (2d Cir. 1982).
14. Monster Communications, Inc. v. Turner Broadcasting Sys., Inc., 935 F. Supp. 490 (S.D.N.Y. 1996).
15. Universal City Studios v. Sony Corp., 464 U.S. 417 (1984).

16. MCA, Inc. v. Wilson, 677 F.2d 180 (2d Cir. 1981).

17. 960 F.2d 301 (2d Cir. 1992).

18. Ringgold v. Black Entertainment Television, Inc., 40 U.S.P.Q.2d 1299 (S.D.N.Y. 1996).

19. 471 U.S. 539 (1985).

20. 464 U.S. 417 (1984).

21. 40 U.S.P.Q.2d 1569 (E.D. Va. 1996).

22. Religious Technology Ctr. v. Pagliarina, 908 F. Supp 1353 (E.D. Va. 1995).

23. 471 U.S. 539 (1985).

24. 996 F.2d 1366 (2d Cir. 1993).

25. 150 F.3d 132 (2d Cir. 1998).

26. 606 F. Supp. 1526 (C.D. Cal. 1985).

27. 108 F.3d 1119 (9th Cir. 1997).

28. 510 U.S. 569 (1994).

29. Dr. Seuss Enters., L.P. v. Penguin Books USA, Inc., 109 F.3d 1394 (9th Cir. 1997).

30. 510 U.S. 569 (1994).

31. 794 F.2d 432 (9th Cir. 1986).

32. 482 F. Supp. 741 (S.D.N.Y.), *aff'd* 632 F.2d 252 (2d Cir. 1980).

33. 642 F. Supp. 1031 (N.D. Ga. 1986).

34. 137 F.3d 109 (2d Cir. 1998).

35. 663 F. Supp. 706 (S.D.N.Y. 1987).

FOR MORE INFORMATION

For excellent fair use information, review Stanford University's fair use website at http://fairuse.stanford.edu

CHAPTER 8
Educational and Library Uses

In the previous chapter information was provided regarding the fair use defense. In this chapter information is offered about specific exceptions to copyright law for educational and library uses. The following subjects are discussed:

- the rights of a library to reproduce copies;
- fair use principles as applied to education;
- the use of copyrighted materials in "face-to-face" teaching; and
- the fair use of digital materials in education.

EDUCATIONAL FAIR USE GUIDELINES

Fair use is the right to use copyrighted material for limited purposes and without authorization of the author. When the Copyright Act of 1976 was drafted, publishers and scholars established a set of fair use guidelines for educational copying. These guidelines were not adopted as law; that is, they are not part of the Copyright Act. However, the rules establish the minimum standards for fair use in education, and many judges look to them when making a fair use determination.[1] A teacher or pupil following the rules can feel comfortable that the use is permissible and not an infringement.

Obtaining the Guidelines

The educational fair use guidelines, as well as other regulations and rules regarding libraries, are available in Copyright Office Circular 21, *Reproduction of Copyrighted Works by Educators and Librarians.* You can obtain this circular by writing to the Copyright Office or by visiting the Copyright Office website where the complete text of the guidelines is available. Information about copyright circulars and contacting the Copyright Office is in Chapter 16.

What Are "Educational Purposes"?

The guidelines define "educational purposes" as: (a) noncommercial instruction or curriculum-based teaching by educators to students at nonprofit educational institutions, or (b) research and scholarly activities, such as planned noncommercial study, investigation directed toward making a contribution to a field of knowledge, and noncommercial presentation of research findings at peer conferences, workshops, or seminars.

Rules for Photocopying Material Used in Teaching

The guidelines permit that a teacher preparing to teach a class may make one copy of any of the following: a chapter from a book; an article from a periodical or newspaper; a short story, short essay, or short poem; or a chart, graph, diagram, drawing, cartoon, or picture from a book, periodical, or newspaper.

A teacher can photocopy articles to hand out in class, but there are restrictions. Classroom copying cannot be used to replace texts or workbooks used in the classroom. Pupils cannot be charged more than the actual cost of photocopying. When multiple copies are made, they cannot exceed more than one copy per pupil. A notice of copyright should be affixed on each copy. The instructor may have to affix the notice if it is absent from the copy. Chapter 17 contains information regarding notice. Some examples of what can be copied and distributed in class are:

- a complete poem if less than 250 words or an excerpt of not more than 250 words from a longer poem;
- a complete article, story, or essay of less than 2,500 words, or an excerpt from any prose work of not more than 1,000 words or ten percent of the work, whichever is less; and
- one chart, graph, diagram, drawing, cartoon, or picture per book or per periodical issue. In addition, not more than one short poem, article, story, essay, or two excerpts may be copied from the same author, nor more than three from the same collective work or periodical volume during one class term.

As a general rule, a teacher has more freedom to copy from newspapers or other periodicals if the copying is related to current newsworthy events. Copies must come from the teacher, not from school administrators. In addition, the idea to make copies and their actual use must be so close together in time that it would be unreasonable to expect a timely reply to a permission request. Also, there may be only nine instances of such copying for one course during one term.

Educational publishers *do not* consider it a fair use if the copying provides replacements or substitutes for the purchase of books, reprints, periodicals, tests, workbooks, anthologies, compilations, or collective works.

Coursepacks and Copy Shops.   An academic coursepack is a collection of photocopied materials used in the classroom. It may be bound like a book or in the form of class handouts. It is usually offered for sale in the campus bookstore, although professors may arrange to sell coursepacks in class. For many years, photocopies were made without the authorization of the copyright owners. However, in 1991, a federal court determined that a Kinko's copy shop had infringed copyright of a book company by reprinting portions of books in a coursepack. The copying was not excused as a fair use.[2] The owner of a copying service in Michigan believed that the *Kinko's* case was wrongly decided and continued to copy course materials for students and professors. As a result he was sued by several book publishers.[3] A court of appeals reviewed the classroom guidelines for copying and determined that the Michigan copy shop's uses were "light years away" from the educational guidelines. For example, one professor's coursepack included six excerpts of copyrighted works, containing from five to thirty percent of the original works. The magnitude of the copying and the commercial motivation weighed heavily against a fair use determination, and the court ruled that the photocopy shop must pay damages.

Rules for Using Sound Recordings and Audiovisual Works for Educational Purposes

If a teacher or educational institution owns a sound recording, a single copy (such as a tape, disc, or cassette) of copyrighted music may be made for the purpose of constructing aural exercises or examinations. For example, if the class is studying jazz history, the instructor may make a cassette of one of his jazz recordings and play it for the class. If students are performing copyrighted songs, a single copy of a student recording may be made for evaluation or rehearsal purposes.

It is not an infringement for sound recordings or audiovisual works such as movies to be played by instructors or pupils in the course of systematic face-to-face instruction (see the next section) in a nonprofit educational institution. *Nonprofit* refers to the corporate status of the institution. That is, it is registered with the state as a nonprofit institution. (This is not a guideline—it is an exemption specifically written into the Copyright Act at 17 *United States Code* section 110.) The exemption does not permit the reproduction of copies. In other words, a teacher can play a recording but cannot copy it unless it is for the educational purposes listed previously. Motion pictures are included within the teaching exemption, but the teacher or pupil must use a lawfully made copy (a copy produced under license of the movie company, not a homemade duplication).

Face-to-Face Teaching Activity

A face-to-face teaching activity is any teacher-pupil exchange within an educational institution including transmitting the material to a place where students are present. For example, a system hooking up several television monitors within a school is a face-to-face teaching activity. In order to qualify as a face-to-face teaching activity, the audience must be composed of pupils. A performance at a school event mixing pupils and nonstudents, such as a parent-student meeting, would not qualify as face-to-face teaching. It is also not a face-to-face activity to broadcast from a location *outside* a school into a classroom.

Using Digital Photos and Multimedia Projects

In 1996, guidelines were proposed for digital photo reproductions and educational multimedia projects. (As of the writing of this book, these guidelines have not yet been adopted.) A digital reproduction occurs when a picture is converted (or scanned) to a digital code, usually for use on a computer. Under the proposed guidelines, educators can digitize a lawfully acquired image for educational use unless the image is readily available in usable digital form at a fair price. An educator may display digital images for educational purposes, including face-to-face teaching and research at a nonprofit educational institution.

A multimedia project refers to a work that combines various medias such as sound and text or pictures and film clips. Under the proposed guidelines, students and educators may incorporate digital portions of legitimately purchased copies for their own educational multimedia projects, subject to certain limitations. The student or teacher may claim fair use for the following media:

- a clip of motion media (animation, motion pictures, and so on)—up to ten percent or three minutes, whichever is less;
- a portion of a text—up to ten percent or one thousand words, whichever is less; and
- music and lyrics—up to ten percent but no more than thirty seconds of a song.

The educator or student cannot sell or distribute the works (unless, of course, permission is obtained from the copyright holder). The student can retain the work as part of the student's portfolio for purposes such as applying for jobs or admission to graduate school.

These proposed guidelines may be downloaded at the Copyright Office website or may be obtained, free of charge, by mailing or faxing a written request to: CONFU Report, Office of Public Affairs, United States Patent and Trademark Office, Washington, DC 20231.

Exceptions Available to Educational Broadcasters

Certain educational institutions rely on televised teaching systems. Literary and musical works (and only these types of works) may be broadcast without authorization if the broadcast is (1) part of a regular instructional activity, (2) directly related to the teaching content of the broadcast, and (3) made primarily for reception in places of instruction (or to persons unable to attend places of instruction). This and other musical exemptions are discussed in Chapter 10.

RIGHTS OF LIBRARIES AND ARCHIVES TO REPRODUCE COPIES

Libraries and archives are granted rights to make copies under section 108 of the Copyright Act of 1976.[4] In addition, there are guidelines for photocopying and for digital copying of copyrighted materials. These rules are presented in the following text.

Can a Library Make Copies of Works?

Section 108 of the Copyright Act of 1976 provides that nonprofit libraries or archives open to the public may prepare single copyrighted copies or phonorecords of works. These copies and phonorecords must bear the copyright notice (see Chapter 17). Libraries may make copies for the preservation or replacement of a work in the collection when it is not possible to purchase a replacement at fair price; or upon request from another library, one article from a periodical or a small part of any other copyrighted work may be copied and distributed to that library. The rights of reproduction and distribution under section 108 do not apply to a musical work; a pictorial, graphic, or sculptural work; or a motion picture or other audiovisual work.

Must a Library Supervise Use of Its Photocopy Machines?

A library or archive will not be liable for copyright infringement for the unsupervised use of photocopying machines provided that there is a notice on the photocopy machine that making copies may be subject to copyright law. This is not true, however, if the library is aware or has reason to believe that multiple copies are being made of a single work.

When copies of text works are requested (the library is making the copies), the warning notice must be printed within a box located prominently on the order form, either on the front side of the form or immediately adjacent to the space for the name and signature of the user. The copying, whether performed by the library or whether performed unsupervised by the library patron, cannot be for a commercial advantage (the library or a copying service hired by the library cannot profit from the copying).

If a library or educational institution makes a copy of a work for a patron, the actual copyright notice (for example, © 1999 Ashbury Press) from the material being copied must be included. If the material contains no copyright notice, the material should be stamped with the notice "This material may be protected by copyright law (Title 17 U.S.C. Code)."[5]

Warning Required on Library Photocopy Machines

In order to comply with the Copyright Act, the following warning should be placed prominently on all photocopy machines and wherever orders for copying are accepted. If the warning is on or near a photocopy machine, it should be printed on heavy paper or other durable material in at least 18-point type size. If the warning is on a photocopy order form, it should also be located prominently and printed in the same type size throughout the form.

NOTICE
WARNING CONCERNING COPYRIGHT RESTRICTIONS

Fair Use Rules Regarding a Library's Right to Rent Digital Copies

A nonprofit library can, under certain circumstances, rent computer programs to patrons. These guidelines are discussed in Chapter 11, which deals exclusively with computer programs and digital works. As of the date of writing of this book, formal digital guidelines for nonprofit libraries have not yet been adopted. Check the Copyright Office website for more up-to-date information.

Effect of Extension of Copyright Term on Library Copying

In 1998, the Sonny Bono Copyright Term Extension Act extended the period of copyright protection for an additional twenty years. Congress provided that during the last twenty years of any term of copyright of a published work, a library or archives may reproduce a copy of the work for purposes of preservation, scholarship, or research provided that: the work is not being commercially distributed; the work cannot be obtained at a reasonable price; or the copyright owner or its agent provides notice that either of these conditions applies.

END NOTES

1. Encyclopedia Britannica Educ. Corp. v. Crooks, 447 F. Supp. 243 (W.D.N.Y. 1978); and Basic Books, Inc. v. Kinko's Graphics Corp., 758 F. Supp. 1522 (S.D.N.Y. 1991).
2. Basic Books, Inc. v. Kinko's Graphics Corp., 758 F. Supp. 1522 (S.D.N.Y. 1991).
3. Princeton Univ. v. Michigan Document Servs., 99 F.3d 1381 (6th Cir. 1996).
4. 17 U.S.C. § 108.
5. 17 U.S.C. § 108(a).

FOR MORE INFORMATION

Information about established and proposed guidelines can also be found in the extensive list of links regarding educational uses of copyrighted material at Christine Sundt's Art and Copyright website: http://oregon.uoregon. edu/~csundt/cweb.htm

CHAPTER 9
Artwork

In this chapter information is presented about the rights of graphic artists, painters, sculptors, and other artists who create visual arts works. The following subjects are discussed:

- the difference between copyrighted art and "works of visual art";
- the special rights granted to an artist who creates a work of visual art;
- the rights related to art on useful objects;
- the rights of persons who commission artwork; and
- the rights of persons who purchase copies of the artwork.

COPYRIGHT AND WORKS OF VISUAL ART: MORAL RIGHTS

Artwork such as drawings, paintings, computer-generated images, sculptures, and photographs are all protectible under copyright law, and an artist can stop infringements of these works. However, some artists receive *more* rights than normally granted under copyright law. Artists who create a painting, drawing, print, photograph, or sculpture in a single copy or limited edition of two hundred copies or fewer (that are signed and consecutively numbered) receive protection under the Visual Artists Rights Act (VARA).[1]

17 U.S.C. § 101 Work of visual art

A "work of visual art" is—
(1) a painting, drawing, print, or sculpture, existing in a single copy, in a limited edition of 200 copies or fewer that are signed and consecutively numbered by the author, or, in the case of a sculpture, in multiple cast, carved, or fabricated sculptures of 200 or fewer that are consecutively numbered by the author and bear the signature or other identifying mark of the author; or
(2) a still photographic image produced for exhibition purposes only, existing in a single copy that is signed by the author, or in a limited edition of 200 copies or fewer that are signed and consecutively numbered by the author.
A work of visual art does not include—
(A)(i) any poster, map, globe, chart, technical drawing, diagram, model, applied art, motion picture or other audiovisual work, book, magazine, newspaper, periodical, data base, electronic information service, electronic publication, or similar publication;

(ii) any merchandising item or advertising, promotional, descriptive, covering, or packaging material or container;

(iii) any portion or part of any item described in clause (i) or (ii);

(B) any work made for hire; or

(C) any work not subject to copyright protection under this title.

VARA incorporates certain rules developed in Europe to protect the **moral rights** of artists. European law grants certain rights to artists based upon moral principles. For example, the creator of a work of fine art (or the artist's heirs) can share in subsequent sales of the work and can prevent the destruction or mutilation of a work. Under these principles, known as *droit de moral,* the artist's rights continue after the sale of the art. An unknown artist who sold a work inexpensively could share in revenues if the work later appreciated in value.

The United States refused to recognize moral rights for most of the twentieth century. However, in order to join in an international treaty known as the Berne Convention, Congress amended the Copyright Act in 1990 to include VARA. The Visual Artists Rights Act incorporates two of the features of European *droit de moral*—**attribution** and **integrity.** Attribution is the right to claim or disclaim authorship of a work. That is, the artist has a right to demand that credit be given for, or to have credit removed from, an artwork. The right of integrity is the right to prevent distortion, mutilation, or other modification of the work. These rights are independent of the other rights granted under copyright law. In other words, all artworks (photos, paintings, and so on) are protected under copyright. But art that is produced in a single copy or limited edition of two hundred copies or fewer, signed and numbered, is protected under VARA as **works of visual art.**

What Is and What Is Not Protected by VARA

Protected by VARA	Not Protected by VARA
A limited edition of ten copies of a photograph, numbered and signed by the photographer	A photograph reprinted on one thousand postcards
A religious sculpture of the Ten Commandments	Miniature replicas of the Ten Commandments sculpture sold by a religious mail order company

What happens if an oil painting is reproduced in a museum booklet or in a magazine review? Does that mass production remove the work from VARA status? No, the artist could still exert VARA rights over the single oil painting. However, the artist could not prevent destruction or mutilation of the reprints in the booklet, as these would not be covered by VARA, although they would still be covered under normal copyright principles.

VARA: No Destruction of Fine Arts Works

If you are the owner of this book, you can destroy it if you wish. However, if you purchase a painting, you do not have the same freedom. A painting is considered a **work of visual art,** and the artist, under section 106A, can prevent the "intentional distortion, mutilation, or other modification of that work which would be prejudicial to his or her honor or reputation." This is the most powerful right granted under the VARA provisions. For example, if you buy a limited edition photograph (that is, less than two hundred prints were made), you cannot destroy it without permission from the artist. If the work is destroyed, the artist can sue under VARA and recover damages.

The rule regarding destruction does not apply if: (1) the work was created prior to enactment of the VARA provisions on December 1, 1990; (2) the artist specifically waives the rights in a written statement signed by the artist and owner of the artwork; or (3) the destruction or modification results from the passage of time or because of the materials used to construct the work. For example, certain works such as ice sculptures and sand sculptures self-destruct, and the owner would have no obligation to affirmatively prevent such destruction.

17 U.S.C. § 106A(e) Transfer and waiver of VARA rights

The rights conferred . . . may not be transferred, but those rights may be waived if the author expressly agrees to such waiver in a written instrument signed by the author. Such instrument shall specifically identify the work, and uses of that work, to which the waiver applies, and the waiver shall apply only to the work and uses so identified. In the case of a joint work prepared by two or more authors, a waiver of rights under this paragraph made by one such author waives such rights for all such authors.

EXAMPLE

The Statue in the Parking Garage. In 1963, the sculptor Philip Pavia created a work for the lobby of the Hilton Hotel in New York. The work, *The Ides of March,* consisted of three large, diamond-shaped standing forms and a smaller form lying on its side. In 1988, the owners of the sculpture contracted to display the work at a parking garage in New York. The work was divided, and only two of the four forms were displayed. The artist sued under VARA (and also under New York state laws). A federal court would not enforce the VARA rights because the work was separated prior to the enactment of VARA.[2] The court determined it would be unfair to impose the VARA restrictions retroactively, since the owners were not violating the law at the time the work was separated. However, the artist was able to enforce certain rights under state law, as discussed in the following text.

VARA: No Rights If Work Made for Hire

Under certain circumstances, the person who employs an artist or commissions artwork acquires copyright ownership. This principle is known as "work made for hire" and is discussed in Chapter 13. If artwork is created as work made for hire, there are no VARA rights. That is, although normal copyright law applies to the work, neither the artist nor the person commissioning the work can claim rights of integrity or attribution under VARA.

EXAMPLE

The Walk-Through Sculpture. Three artists were hired to create a walk-through sculpture for the lobby of an office building in New York City. The sculpture addressed environmental concerns and included materials such as recycled glass. The company that contracted for the sculpture fired the artists one day and indicated that the work would be removed or altered. The artists sued under the VARA provisions, but the court of appeals determined that the sculpture was a work made for hire and was not protected under VARA. That is, under work for hire principles, the company that hired the artists owned the work and could remove it or alter it.[3]

VARA: No Registration Required

One interesting feature of the VARA provision is that the artist does not have to file a registration with the Copyright Office before filing an infringement lawsuit. Every other creator of a work must file a registration prior to suing for infringement. However, registration of a pictorial, graphic, or sculptural work is still recommended, as discussed in Chapter 18.

VARA: No Transfer of Rights

The rights granted under VARA—attribution and integrity—are not transferable. Only the artist can exert these rights. This makes sense because these rights are personal and relate to the artist's moral view of the work. Even though the rights cannot be transferred, they can be waived, meaning that the artist will not enforce the rights. For example, a patron pays a large sum of money to commission a painted portrait. However, the patron wants the right to destroy the portrait if he does not like it. He pays the artist an extra payment if the artist agrees in writing to waive his right to prevent mutilation or destruction. The artist, in return for the extra payment, agrees to waive moral rights.

VARA: Rights Last for Life of the Author

Although copyright protection normally lasts for the life of the author plus seventy years, the rights granted under VARA only last for the life of the artist.

That is, once the artist has died, the work can be destroyed, under VARA, without seeking consent from the artist's estate. In this manner, American moral rights differ from European moral rights, which are descendible (that is, they pass to the estate of the artist). However, certain state laws, as explained in the text that follows, may provide longer duration of artists' rights.

VARA: When Art Is Incorporated in a Building

Special rules[4] apply if a VARA work is incorporated in a building. If removing the work from the building will cause the destruction or other modification of the work, the owner of the building must either provide notice or make a good faith attempt to notify the artist of the owner's intentions affecting the work. The artist has the option to either remove the work or to pay for its removal. The owner of the building does not have to bother with these requirements if the artist consented to the installation of the work before December 1, 1990, or executed a written agreement after that date specifying that installation of the work may subject the work to destruction or modification by reason of its removal. In order to guarantee receipt of notice by the artist, the Register of Copyrights has established a system whereby the artist may record his or her identity and address with the Copyright Office.

VARA: State Art Statutes

Some states such as California have passed more comprehensive statutes regarding art preservation and resale. Under the California statute,[5] for example, an artist is entitled to five percent of the resale of a work of fine art. These rights survive for twenty years after the death of the artist. New York and eight other states also have laws that grant certain rights to artists.[6]

LIMITATIONS FOR PICTORIAL, GRAPHIC, AND SCULPTURAL WORKS

The previous sections have been devoted to works protected under the Visual Artists Rights Act (VARA). These VARA works are part of a larger group of works protected under copyright law. That is, they are a subset of works protected as pictorial, graphic, or sculptural works. The following sections deal with some important rights and limitations related to copyrightable artworks regardless of their status under VARA.

Works Made for Hire

The most contentious and litigated issue regarding artwork is whether the work is a "work made for hire." If the work is made for hire, the employer, not the artist, claims copyright in the work. The works made for hire rules are complex. For example, even if an artist signs a statement saying that the work will be work made for hire, *that is not enough* to create a work made for hire. Chapter 13 provides more information on works made for hire.

Digitizing and Modifying Artwork on the Computer

Many computer users scan or download images and modify them with programs such as Adobe Photoshop. Modification or reproduction of a copyrighted image, including posting it to or downloading it from the Internet, is a copyright violation unless the use is authorized by the copyright owner or excused under fair use principles.

Clip Art and the Public Domain

"Clip art" refers to line art drawings and graphics that are contained in electronic files and can be displayed on a computer. Occasionally artwork is supplied as part of a computer program and labeled "copyright-free" or "royalty-free." Never assume that such artwork is in the public domain or free to use without limitation. Read the shrink-wrap agreement on the program envelope, the "click-wrap" agreement posted at the website, or the "readme" text file that accompanies the clip art files. Even if the clip art agreement permits unrestricted usage of individual images, this is not a license to copy the complete collection.[7]

Limitations on the Display Right

As discussed in Chapter 6, an artist has the right to control the public display of a work *prior to the sale* of that work. For example, if an artist lends an unsold painting to a friend, the work cannot be displayed publicly without the consent of the artist. After the work is sold, the purchaser is permitted to display it publicly, such as in a museum. The definition of "publicly display" means that the showing is for more than a gathering of social friends and acquaintances.

The owner of a painting (or other pictorial, graphic, or sculptural work) can display it publicly but cannot broadcast the image. That right is still controlled by the artist. A person renting, leasing, or borrowing the painting does not have the right to publicly display it. Only the purchaser of the painting is allowed to do that.

Limitations on the Reproduction Right: Art on Useful Objects

An artist in some cases will license rights of an artwork to a company for use on a product. A license is the limited right to use the artwork, in return for which the artist receives a fee or royalty payment. Licenses are discussed in Chapter 15. When an artist licenses use of artwork on a useful object, it is *not* an infringement to reproduce the artwork in an advertisement or a review for the product. For example, if an artist's drawing is used on a T-shirt, the artist cannot prevent the use of the drawing in a catalog advertisement for the T-shirt.[8]

EXAMPLE

Is a Photograph of the Mona Lisa in the Public Domain? The Bridgeman Art Library specializes in high-quality photo reproductions of public domain artwork such as the Mona Lisa. Companies pay Bridgeman for the right to use these high-quality reproductions. In 1998, Bridgeman sued the Corel Corporation, alleging that Corel had copied several Bridgeman photographs of public domain works.[9] Bridgeman claimed that its photographer's creative choices of lighting, camera angle, and lens justified its copyright in photos of public domain works. A federal judge ruled there was insufficient originality in the photograph to claim copyright. How can it be original, the judge asked, when the photographer is trying to create a perfect copy? Therefore, the photo was not protected under copyright law and Corel was free to copy the unprotected public domain images.

END NOTES

1. 17 U.S.C. § 106A.
2. Pavia v. 1120 Ave. of the Americas Assocs., 901 F. Supp. 620 (S.D.N.Y. 1995).
3. Carter v. Helmsley-Spear, Inc., 71 F.3d 77 (2d Cir. 1995).
4. 17 U.S.C. § 113(d).
5. CAL. CIV. CODE §§ 986–989.
6. CONN. GEN. STAT. ANN. § 42-116t (1989); LA. REV. STAT. ANN. §§ 51:2151–2156 (1987); ME. REV. STAT. ANN. tit. 27, § 303 (Supp. 1987–1988); MASS. GEN. LAWS ANN. ch. 231, § 85s (1988); N.J. STAT. ANN. §§ 2a:24a-1 to -8 (1987); N.M. STAT. ANN. § 13-4b-3 (1987) N.Y. ARTS & CULT. AFF. LAW §§ 14.10–.03 (1984); PA. STAT. ANN. tit. 73, §§ 2101–2110 (1987); R.I. GEN. LAWS § 5-62-2 *et seq.* (1987).
7. Marobie-Fl v. National Assoc. of Fire Equip. Distribs., 983 F. Supp. 1167 (N.D. Ill. 1997).
8. 17 U.S.C. § 113.
9. Bridgeman Art Library, Ltd. v. Corel Corp., 25 F. Supp. 2d 421 (S.D.N.Y. 1998).

CHAPTER 10
Musical Works and Sound Recordings

This chapter contains information about the rights of musicians, record companies, music broadcasters, and businesses that play music. The following subjects are discussed:

- how songwriting income is computed and collected;
- an explanation of compulsory licensing;
- the difference between mechanical, performance, and synchronization rights;
- the rights of record companies and recording artists;
- antibootlegging laws;
- laws protecting digital rights in music; and
- exemptions for businesses or persons using music.

INTRODUCTION

There are two types of copyrights for music: musical works copyrights, which protect songs; and sound recording copyrights, which protect the manner in which music is arranged and recorded, that is, the sounds fixed on the recording. These forms of copyright protection create two overlapping sources of income. Songwriters earn income from the exploitation of songs. Recording artists and record companies earn money from the sale of recordings. The same person or business can own both types of copyrights, but the musical works copyright is usually owned by the songwriter or a music publisher, and the sound recording copyright is usually owned by a record company.

SONGS: THE RIGHTS OF COMPOSERS AND MUSIC PUBLISHERS

A great deal of wealth in the music business is centered around the ownership of musical works copyrights (that is, songs). **Music publishers** own song copyrights and collect revenue, handle business formalities, sue infringers, and look for new ways to exploit songs. Music publishers acquire ownership of song copyrights when the songwriter transfers copyright ownership in exchange for payments or an ongoing royalty. Most music publishers offer an upfront sum or "advance" to the songwriter and share the revenue with the songwriter as the song earns money. That is, the songwriter continues to earn a percentage of the revenue through the life of the copyright. For example, even though Paul McCartney does not own the copyright in the Beatles songs, he still receives revenue from the music publisher that does own the copyright. Sometimes, a music publisher may act unfairly. A publisher may take advantage of a songwriter and pay a marginal amount for copyright. For example, the composer of the song "Louie, Louie" sold all rights for $750. The song went on to earn millions.[1]

What Does a Music Publisher *Publish?*

In the early 1900s, a songwriter's primary source of income was the publication of sheet music, and the term *publisher* was used to describe the owner of the copyright. Today, sheet music is a small fraction of income earned by music publishers. Some publishers are also known as administrators because they "administer" copyrights. That is, they may not own the copyright but they earn revenue from managing the business for the songwriter.

EXAMPLE

How the Owner of a Song Earns Money: "Stand by Me." The owner of a song earns money in three ways: sales of recordings, performance on the radio, and use in motion pictures or television. The song "Stand by Me," written by Ben E. King, Mike Stoller, and Jerry Lieber, was a hit as performed by Ben E. King in 1961, and the songwriters earned money from sales of records and radio play. Six years later, the songwriters earned more money when the song was recorded by Spyder Turner and became a hit again. And in 1975 and 1980, the song was a hit two more times when recorded by John Lennon and Mickey Gilley, respectively. In 1986, Rob Reiner made the movie *Stand by Me,* based upon a story by Stephen King. Reiner used the song "Stand by Me" (re-recorded by Ben E. King), and it became a hit again when the soundtrack for the movie sold millions of copies. The songwriters earned money from the use of the song in the movie, record sales of the soundtrack, radio play, and when the movie was later broadcast on television.

Mechanical Rights: Recording a Song

At the beginning of the twentieth century, songwriters earned the right to collect money when their songs were reproduced on piano rolls. To distinguish this new source of income from sheet music publishing, songwriters referred to the piano roll payments as "mechanical income" or "mechanical royalties" (because the rolls were produced and played on machines.) Today, those terms refer to the *reproduction* of musical work on phonorecords—that is, the "pressing" of the song onto a vinyl recording or the transfer to audiotape, compact disc, or DVD. Broadcasting a song over the radio or TV is not considered a mechanical reproduction and mechanical royalties would not apply.

Every time a song is "pressed" (or fixed) on a phonorecord, the songwriter is entitled to a mechanical royalty. The rates are constantly changing; for example, it was common in the 1970s for a songwriter to receive two cents for every song pressed on a recording. The table accompanying this text gives the rates expected through the year 2006. The current mechanical rate can be determined by calling the Copyright Office Licensing Division at (202) 707-8150 or by consulting 37 *Code of Federal Regulations* section 255. Two rates are provided: per song and per minute. The songwriter is paid whichever rate is higher.

Mechanical Royalty Rates

Years	Per Song	Per Minute
January 1, 1998 to January 1, 2000	7.1 cents	1.35 cents
January 1, 2000 to January 1, 2002	7.55 cents	1.45 cents
January 1, 2002 to January 1, 2004	8 cents	1.55 cents
January 1, 2004 to January 1, 2006	8.5 cents	1.65 cents
After January 1, 2006	9.1 cents	1.75 cents

Sometimes, a songwriter or music publisher will agree to accept a rate lower than the rate set by Congress. It is quite common for a songwriter to accept three-quarters of the mechanical royalty rate (sometimes referred to as a three-quarter rate). Why would a songwriter accept less than what the law provides? Usually the songwriter has no choice, since the record company may refuse to make a deal unless the songwriter accepts the lower rate.

Determining Mechanical Royalties.   A songwriter is paid the mechanical royalty rate multiplied by the number of songs on a recording. If a songwriter wrote one song on a recording released in the year 2000 and 100,000 copies of the recording were pressed, the songwriter (or publisher) would be entitled to $7,550 (100,000 copies times the rate of .0755). If a songwriter wrote ten songs on a recording, he or she would be entitled to $75,500 (100,000 copies times the rate of .0755 times 10). Who pays this money? The record company that is pressing the record pays the fee.

Compulsory Licenses to "Cover" a Song.   A **compulsory license** (sometimes known as a "statutory license") is a system established under the Copyright Act[2] that permits the use of copyrighted works under certain circumstances, provided fees are paid. In the case of musical works, the advantage of compulsory licensing is that the recording artist does not have to negotiate directly with the copyright owner for permission to record the work. That is, the songwriter *must* allow the recording of the song if four requirements are met:

1.   the song must have been previously recorded and distributed to the public;
2.   the purpose of the recording is to make phonorecords, not to record the song in a movie or TV show or for some purpose other than normal retail record sales;

3.   the recording artist must send a notice to the copyright owner of the song within thirty days of making the recording and prior to distributing it. After that, payments based upon the mechanical royalty rate must be made every month; and

4.   the lyrics, basic melody, or fundamental character of the work cannot be altered without permission of the copyright owner.

Obtaining a compulsory license does not also grant the right to reproduce the lyrics,3 for example, on the screen of a karaoke machine. In that case, synchronization rights (as explained in the following text) must be obtained from the owner of copyright in the song.

Negotiating and Collecting Mechanical Royalties: Harry Fox.   Arrangements for mechanical royalties can be negotiated directly with the song owner. In addition, one agency will negotiate or collect mechanical royalty payments on behalf of songwriters or record companies: Harry Fox Agency, 205 East 42nd Street, New York, NY 10017. (http://www.harryfox.com)

Performance Rights: Broadcasting and Playing a Song

The composer of a song controls the right to publicly perform it (known as the **performance right**). The "performance" of a song has a broad meaning, encompassing live concerts, playing of a recording at a club, and transmission of a song via radio, television, cable, or digital signals. Songwriters earn money whenever their song is performed (known as "performance royalties").

It would be impractical if the proprietors of radio and TV stations or nightclubs had to contact each songwriter for permission each time a song was publicly performed. Performing rights societies were established in order to negotiate and collect these fees. These societies, most of which are nonprofit, act as agents for songwriters, surveying radio stations on a regular basis and using the surveys as a basis for payments to songwriters. Television stations furnish logs of music played, and agreements are also made with club owners where phonorecords are played and with concert halls where live music is performed.

Sync Rights: Use of Songs in Motion Pictures or Television Shows

The third major source of income for songwriters is when a song is used in a motion picture or television show (known as the **synchronization right**). The technical definition is "the right to record music in timed relation to visual images and to reproduce, perform and distribute the musical work in connection with an audiovisual work." Basically, it means playing a song in conjunction with the movie, for example, so that the song is heard during a love scene or when the credits roll. Synchronization rights are negotiated directly with the music publisher. This synchronization payment is independent of payments earned from having the song included on the soundtrack recording.

Copying Portions of a Song in Another Song

There is a myth among musicians that a songwriter can use four bars of music from any song without an infringement occurring. The criteria is not the *amount* taken, but the *importance* of the portion taken. If the copied portion of a song is quantitatively small, the court will determine the importance of that portion to the plaintiff's work. For example, the copying of two bars of music in one song was held to be an infringement, while the copying of six bars of music in another song was not an infringement. The same standards apply for lyrics. For more information on infringement, see Chapter 22.

Two Songs Based on the Same Source

A defendant in an infringement action may argue that both songs at issue are based upon common musical notation and language. Blues, rock, and country songs, for example, are based on traditional chord patterns and changes. The use of these common musical forms is considered public domain. For example, when accused of infringement, songwriter John Fogerty demonstrated that many elements in his songs are common to many rock and roll songs and therefore are unprotectible.[4] Similarly, the use of a common phrase such as "got my mojo working" is considered to be in the public domain and is unprotectible.[5]

Jukebox Play

It would be impractical and expensive for a restaurant with a jukebox to negotiate performance royalties with song owners. Therefore, section 116 of the Copyright Act permits such businesses to obtain a compulsory license—that is, to pay a fee established by law—if:

- the patrons, not the employees, choose and pay for the songs played on the jukebox;
- a list of all song titles is displayed prominently on the jukebox; and
- the business makes no direct or indirect charge for admission.[6]

A jukebox kept behind a bar and operated by the owner of the tavern would not qualify for the compulsory license fee. The proprietor would have to negotiate performance rights.

Broadcasting and Downloading over the Internet

There are two ways that songs are transmitted on the Internet: songs are broadcast in real-time (known as "webcasting" or "audiostreaming"); and songs are made available to be digitally downloaded—that is, a copy is delivered via phone lines to the user's computer. In webcasting, the listener hears the song at the same time it is played by the Internet site. When downloading, the user obtains a copy, usually in a file format known as MP3. The performance rights societies—the American Society of Composers, Authors, and Publishers

(ASCAP) and Broadcast Music Incorporated (BMI)—have taken the position that both webcasting and downloading are forms of public performance and require licenses. This position may be modified by litigation or legislation over the coming years. Information about these licenses can be obtained by visiting the performance rights websites listed in Appendix A. A statutory license is required from the owner of a sound recording copyright when digital music is transmitted over the Internet. This license is discussed in the following text.

Using a Song to Promote Products or Services

Microsoft reportedly paid one million dollars for the use of the Rolling Stones's song "Start Me Up" to advertise the launch of a new version of Windows software. The use of a pop song to promote a product or service requires a grant of rights from the owner of copyright of the song and the sound recording. It also requires permission from the performer on the sound recording because the unauthorized use may infringe a principle known as the "right of publicity." If the company creating the advertisement re-records the song, that is, makes a new version, permission is not needed from the record company or the performer unless the re-recorded version of the song imitates the style of the performer.

MUSICIANS AND RECORDING COMPANIES

The copyright owner of the sound recording is usually the record company. When radio stations in the United States play copyrighted sound recordings, they do not have to pay record companies, although they do have to pay performance royalties, as discussed earlier, to the songwriter or music publisher. Many countries provide performing rights for sound recordings, and in those countries, the owner of a sound recording copyright receives payment whenever the recording is played over the radio or in a club. American record companies whose recordings are played abroad do not share in foreign performance royalties.

Digital Performance of Sound Recordings

Some website subscription services permit a user to download recordings from the Internet. In light of these developments and the ease with which such music can be copied, legislation was passed in 1995 granting sound recording owners the right to control the digital performance or digital delivery of such sound recordings (the Digital Performance Right in Sound Recordings Act). This entitled record companies to get payments when a subscription digital broadcaster (such as a cable radio service) played a digital recording. However, technology changed quickly, and in addition to downloading music, some Internet sites began real-time digital broadcasts of music (known as "webcasting").

In 1998, legislation was passed[7] that modified the law. Webcasters can transmit performances if they pay a fee to the record company. The fee is fixed by law, so the webcaster does not have to negotiate with the record company for permission. The webcaster must also pay a fee to the song owner. Webcasters are allowed to make single copies of songs necessary in webcasting (known as "ephemeral recordings"). The rules to qualify for the statutory license can be obtained from the Copyright Office website. Local radio stations simulcasting their signal online are required to follow a similar set of rules and pay a licensing fee.

Sampling

The digital recording process has made it possible to "sample" a portion of a sound recording. These digital samples can be manipulated to replay once or twice or repeated as a "loop" throughout a new recording. The use of a musical sample may infringe both the musical works and sound recording copyrights. Whether the use qualifies as an infringement depends upon the portion sampled and its qualitative or quantitative importance to the copyrighted work. Initially, the courts took a rigid approach,[8] prohibiting any use of digital samples. However, in a 1997 case, a court determined that the rap group Run DMC's use of a drum sample from a 1973 recording was not infringing.[9]

Sound recordings were not protected by copyright law until 1972. The use of a musical sample from a work created prior to 1972 would not be an infringement of a sound recording copyright, although it may be a violation of applicable state laws. In order to avoid claims of infringement, recording artists seek sample clearance from copyright owners.

What Is an MP3?

As of the writing of this book, the most common system for music downloads is via a system known as MPEG 1 Layer 3, or "MP3" for short. This technology compresses sound files so that approximately sixty minutes of music can be stored on thirty-two megabytes of computer memory. The distribution of MP3 files is an infringement unless authorized by the respective copyright owners. In 1998, the Rio appeared, the first handheld MP3 storage device. The music industry attempted to halt sales of the Rio, arguing that the Rio failed to meet standards established in the Audio Home Recording Act (AHRA). In 1998, a judge refused to issue an injunction halting the sale.[10]

Record Companies and Performers' Rights—Antibootlegging

In 1994, as part of the implementation of the GATT agreement, the United States passed legislation that allows a performer or record company to prevent "bootlegging."[11] Bootlegging is the unauthorized recording of a live performance. Even though a singer may not own a copyright in any of the songs she is performing, she can still prevent a fan from recording her show. The singer can also prevent anyone from "trafficking" in bootlegs from the show. "Trafficking" is the transportation or transfer of unauthorized copies.

Why do record companies have a right to prevent a bootleg recording of a performer? Because record companies enter into exclusive recording agreements with performers giving the company the exclusive right to release that performer's recordings. Under the antibootlegging law, performers or record companies do not have to register with the Copyright Office in order to receive protection, and there is no time limit on how long the protection lasts. In other words, even though this law is part of the Copyright Act, it does not have the same formal requirements for protection as other works (for example, literary, musical, or audiovisual) previously discussed.

JUDGE LEARNED HAND ON COPYRIGHT: SOUND RECORDINGS AND PERFORMERS' RIGHTS

It took a great effort by record companies and musical performers to obtain protection for sound recordings. Until 1972, federal law protected songs but not sound recordings. The only exception to this rule was Judge Learned Hand who believed that both sound recordings and performers' rights should be protected by copyright. In a 1955 decision, *Capitol Records, Inc. v. Mercury Records Corp.*,[12] Judge Hand stated the arrangement and performance of a song were often quite as original as the song itself and "[t]here should be no doubt this is within the Copyright Clause of the Constitution." The majority of the circuit court overruled Judge Hand, but two decades later, in 1972, Congress finally granted protection to sound recordings.

Making a Copy of Recorded Music for Personal Use

It is generally considered to be excusable as a fair use to make a copy of legitimately acquired music for personal use. However, making more than one copy or making a copy from an unauthorized copy would be an infringement.

LIMITATIONS ON MUSICAL WORKS AND SOUND RECORDINGS

The rights of songwriters and record companies are limited by principles of fair use and the first sale doctrine, as discussed in Chapter 7. There are also various "special" limitations created as a result of lobbying efforts of various business interests. These limitations are discussed in the following text.

Playing the Radio or Television at Stores, Bars, or Restaurants

Performing rights societies collect fees from establishments where music is played, such as clothing stores, bars, and restaurants. In 1998, legislation was passed[13] that expanded the exemptions depending upon the size of the establishment or the number of speakers or televisions. Businesses that play the radio or television do not have to pay performances fees if they meet the following criteria:

- the business is a restaurant or bar under 3,750 square feet;
- the business is a retail establishment under 2,000 square feet; or
- the business, regardless of size, has no more than six external speakers, but not more than four per room, or four televisions measuring 55 inches or less, but not more than one per room.

These exemptions apply only to establishments that play radio and television. Establishments playing prerecorded music, such as compact discs, are still subject to licenses. No permission is required to play a song in a record store or if the song is played via licensed jukebox.

Right to Play Songs in Record Stores.   The Copyright Act permits the playing of musical works at businesses that "sell and promote the sale of copies or phonorecords of musical works."[14] In other words, it is not an infringement for a business such as Tower Records to play musical works in the store. This applies only if the business is open to the public, does not charge admission, and the musical performance is not transmitted outside the establishment.

Right of Radio Station to Make Copies: Ephemeral Recordings

Radio stations often need to make copies of musical works for purposes of later transmission. These copies (or phonorecords) are referred to as ephemeral recordings. The Copyright Act permits a broadcaster, under certain circumstances, to make ephemeral recordings.[15] The conditions may vary, based upon the nature of the intended use, the nature of the work, and the type of broadcaster.

Nonprofit Performances

No fees must be paid for performances of musical and nondramatic literary works[16] if the performance is not for "commercial advantage" and before a live audience. This means that the performers are not paid and that admission is not charged. If a fee is charged, the net proceeds must be used exclusively for educational, religious, or charitable purposes, and the song owner must be notified. This no-fee rule does not apply to the transmission of a work.

Religious Services.   No fees must be paid if a musical work is performed in the course of religious services at a place of religious assembly. This no-fee rule is only for religious worship, not for social activities, and does not extend to religious broadcasts, even when the broadcasts are from a place of worship.

Agricultural Fairs.   No fee must be paid if a musical work is performed by a nonprofit agricultural or horticultural organization at annual fairs or other exhibitions.[17] This no-fee rule does not apply to private contractors, such as a food contractor, who play music at the gatherings.

Veteran and Fraternal Organizations. Nonprofit veteran organizations or nonprofit fraternal organizations do not have to pay a fee for performing literary or musical works in the course of a social function. This no-fee rule applies only if the general public is not invited and the proceeds, after deducting reasonable costs, are used exclusively for charitable purposes. The rule does not apply to the social functions of any university fraternity or sorority unless the social function is held solely to raise funds for a specific charitable purpose.

Instructional Broadcasting

Musical works may be publicly broadcast without authorization of the copyright owner to nonprofit educational institutions or to government bodies if the broadcast is: (1) part of a regular instructional activity; (2) directly related to the teaching content of the broadcast; and (3) made primarily for reception in places of instruction (or to persons unable to attend places of instruction) or to government employees as part of their official duties. This exemption is intended to permit, for example, the performance of a song as part of a televised teaching program.

Secondary Transmissions: Compulsory License for Cable Systems

Sometimes a broadcast is received and then retransmitted. For example, a cable television company receives broadcasts and retransmits the broadcasts to its subscribers, or a hotel receives cable channels and retransmits them to rooms in the hotel. The Copyright Act of 1976 breaks down the series of transmissions into primary and secondary transmissions and provides complex definitions. Regulations regarding these transmissions are established in the Copyright Act[18] and can be found at the Copyright Office website.

END NOTES

1. In 1986, Richard Berry, the songwriter of "Louie, Louie," won a court battle over income from the song and was awarded over $2 million.
2. 17 U.S.C. § 115.
3. Abkco Music, Inc. v. Stellar Records, Inc., 96 F.3d 60 (2d Cir. 1996).
4. Fantasy, Inc. v. Fogerty, 510 U.S. 517 (1994).
5. Stratchborneo v. Arc Music Corp., 357 F. Supp. 1393 (S.D.N.Y. 1973).
6. 17 U.S.C. § 116.
7. Title IV of the Digital Millennium Copyright Act.
8. *See* Grand Upright Music, Ltd. v. Warner Bros. Records, 780 F. Supp. 182 (S.D.N.Y. 1995), in which the court stated, "The conduct of the defendants herein, violates not only the Seventh Commandment [Thous shalt not steal], but also the copyright laws of this country."

9. Ruff 'N' Rumble Management v. Profile Records, Inc., 42 U.S.P.Q.2d 1398 (S.D.N.Y. 1997).

10. Recording Indus. Ass'n of Am., Inc. v. Diamond Multimedia Sys., Inc., No. 98-8247 (D. Cal. 1998).

11. 17 U.S.C. § 1101.

12. 221 F.2d 657 (2d Cir. 1955).

13. The legislation, entitled "The Fairness in Music Licensing Bill," was added to the Sonny Bono Copyright Term Extension Act. For a copyright owner's view of this law, review the ASCAP commentary at http://www.ascap.com/legislative/legislative.html.

14. 17 U.S.C. § 110(7).

15. 17 U.S.C. § 112.

16. 17 U.S.C. § 110(4).

17. 17 U.S.C. § 110(6).

18. 17 U.S.C. § 111.

FOR MORE INFORMATION

Organizations

Broadcast Music Incorporated (BMI)
320 West 57th Street, New York, NY 10019, (212) 586-2000
http://bmi.com

American Society of Composers, Authors, and Publishers (ASCAP)
One Lincoln Plaza, New York, NY 10023, (212) 621-6000
http://www.ascap.com

SESAC
421 West 54th Street, 4th Floor, New York, NY 10036, (212) 586-3450
http://www.sesac.com

The Harry Fox Agency
711 Third Avenue, 8th Floor, New York, NY 10017, (212) 370-5330
http://www.harryfox.com

Registering Musical and Sound Recording Works
See Chapters 18 and 19.

Infringement of Musical Works and Sound Recordings
See Chapter 22.

CHAPTER 11
Computers and the Internet

This chapter provides information about:

- the rights of software manufacturers;
- the rights of software and Internet users;
- issues relating to protection of software programs;
- principles of shrink-wrap agreements;
- rights of Internet users and website owners; and
- protection available for semiconductor chips.

SOFTWARE PROTECTION

Computer software programs are protected under copyright law as literary works. Why are computer programs placed in the same classification as books? Because software programs are written in computer codes that, if printed on paper, are combinations of letters and numbers. The Copyright Act defines literary works as works that are expressed in words, numbers, and other identifying markings such as grammatical symbols (that is, "indicia"). Therefore, though computer programs may include visual, audio, or other qualities, the underlying software code is protected as a literary work.

Though software is registered as a literary work, the audiovisual aspects of the program are still protectible. For example, it is possible to infringe the audiovisual aspects without copying any of the computer code.[1] For information on registration of computer programs, see Chapter 18.

17 U.S.C. § 101 Software program

A "computer program" is a set of statements or instructions to be used directly or indirectly in a computer in order to bring about a certain result.

Are Menus and Icons Protectible Under Copyright Law?

Most programs feature menus. That is, by clicking on a word such as "File," a series of choices appear or "drop down," such as "Open" or "Close." Menus usually lack sufficient originality to be protectible. For example, the menu structure of an engineering computer program was considered to be an uncopyrightable process.[2] In another case, a federal court determined that the menu hierarchy in Lotus 1-2-3 was an uncopyrightable method of operation.[3]

Many of the images known as icons that indicate different activities or programs are also unprotectible under copyright law. For example, a court of appeals determined that the "garbage can" icon (used to signify "delete") was, by itself, an unprotectible element.[4] As a general rule, if there is a limited number of ways to express a menu or icon, for example, an image of an envelope to signify e-mail, the courts will permit copying under the merger doctrine explained in Chapter 23. Icons may be protectible under design patent laws (see the next section) or under trademark laws.

Computer Programs and Patent Protection

As a result of a 1981 Supreme Court case,[5] software programs that qualify as software-based inventions are eligible for patent protection. In 1996, the United States Patent and Trademark Office issued "Examination Guidelines for Computer Related Inventions," a publication that provides assistance on software patents. Although the costs of registration and maintenance for utility patent protection are higher than for copyright protection, patent rights are stronger. Under patent law, unlike copyright law, it is not necessary to prove that an infringer copied the work. The registration of a software patent requires a higher level of scrutiny than when seeking a copyright. Not all software programs are protectible under patent law. For example, patent law will not protect mathematical expressions that have no practical purpose. In the competitive world of software programming, an applicant may have difficulty meeting patent requirements, and the one-year bar (a work must be patented within one year of sale or offer for sale) may pose problems. In addition, the patent application process takes longer than the copyright registration process. Despite these drawbacks, there is a trend among attorneys to seek patent protection because the protection is so broad. In addition, computer-created icons, if they meet the requirements, can be protected as design patents.

Works Created by Users of Copyrighted Software Programs

An author can acquire protection for a work created using a copyrighted software program—for example, artwork created using a drawing program. However, when copying a work requires reproducing a copyrighted program— for example, a user must copy a music program in order to hear computer-created music—a license is required from the copyright owner of the software program.

EXAMPLE

Game Genies, Duke Nukem, and Derivatives. Is a program that enhances or modifies a video game a derivative work? That depends whether you are playing with a Game Genie or Duke Nukem 3D. The Game Genie is a program that allows Nintendo players to change specific features of a game without altering the data stored in the Nintendo cartridge. In 1992, the Ninth Circuit Court of Appeals determined that the Game Genie was not derivative of the Nintendo program because it did not incorporate any Nintendo software code.[6] However, in a 1998 case, the same court of appeals determined that a CD-ROM containing programs adding new levels of game play infringed the derivative right of the Duke Nukem game owner.[7] The court of appeals distinguished the cases, stating that the Duke Nukem CD-ROM created new story lines using the same characters, whereas the Game Genie did not.

JUDGE LEARNED HAND ON COPYRIGHT: CODE WORDS AND COMPUTERS

In *Reiss v. National Quotation Bureau, Inc.*,[8] the author of a book of nonsense words used to create secret codes sued a publisher who had copied his work. The publisher argued that copyright could not protect the writing because it had no "meaning." Judge Hand stated that copyright law did not impose a standard of comprehension on works of authorship and that the code words were like "an empty pitcher," in that they had a prospective meaning, but as yet had not received it. The underlying principle of this case—that a copyrighted work does not have to be comprehensible—is now an established rule of copyright. A half-century after the decision, opponents of legal protection for computer programs argued that software could not be protected under copyright because the computer code was incomprehensible. A national commission disagreed and used the *Reiss* case as the basis for protecting computer software.

Is E-Mail Protected by Copyright?

E-mail correspondence is no different than a handwritten letter. If the e-mail meets the standards of copyright protection (originality and fixation), the author has a right to prevent copying. However, as a practical matter, it is difficult to control the distribution of e-mail, and copying of some e-mail may be excused as a fair use.

Protection for Compilations (Electronic Databases)

Electronic works, particularly those on the Internet, combine two features: a collection of data and a program (known as a **search engine**) used to sift through the data. Referred to as **electronic databases** (or automated databases), the search engine and the data can be protected separately. The search engine may be protected as a computer program while the data is protectible as a compilation. Copyright protection for the data depends upon the creativity and originality involved in the selection, coordination, and arrangement of the data. For more information, see the discussion about the *Feist* case in Chapter 4.

Limited Right to Make Copies of Computer Programs

In 1984, Congress amended section 117 of the Copyright Act to permit the purchaser of a computer program to make a copy of that program provided either:

- that the copy is created in order to utilize the computer program (and not for purposes of sale, and so on); or
- that the new copy is for archival (or backup) purposes only and that the copy is destroyed in the event that the owner sells or transfers the program.

In a 1988 case, a court of appeals ruled that the archival copy permitted under section 117 can be created in order to guard against all types of risks, including physical and human mishap as well as mechanical and electrical risks.[9] The shrink-wrap agreement, discussed in the next section, restates the rights expressed in the Copyright Act and adds additional limitations.

17 U.S.C. § 117 Limitations on exclusive rights: Computer programs

Notwithstanding the provisions of section 106 [17 U.S.C. § 106], it is not an infringement for the owner of a copy of a computer program to make or authorize the making of another copy or adaptation of that computer program provided:

(1) that such a new copy or adaptation is created as an essential step in the utilization of the computer program in conjunction with a machine and that it is used in no other manner, or

(2) that such new copy or adaptation is for archival purposes only and that all archival copies are destroyed in the event that continued possession of the computer program should cease to be rightful.

Any exact copies prepared in accordance with the provisions of this section may be leased, sold, or otherwise transferred, along with the copy from which such copies were prepared, only as part of the lease, sale, or other transfer of all rights in the program. Adaptations so prepared may be transferred only with the authorization of the copyright owner.

Right of a Computer Repair Person to Make a Copy

In the early 1990s, a computer repair firm was sued by Mai Systems, a software company. The repair company had fixed a client's computer and, in the process, had activated operating and diagnostic software created by Mai Systems. Mai argued that the repair company, since it was not the owner or lessee of the computers, had no right to activate the software, even for purposes of repair. A federal appeals court agreed and ruled that the computer repair company had infringed Mai's software.[10] The ruling made computer repair companies liable anytime they turned on a client's computer.

In order to avoid this result, Congress passed the Digital Millennium Copyright Act in 1998, ensuring that lawful owners or lessees of a computer program may authorize an independent service provider—a person unaffiliated with either the owner or lessee of the machine—to activate the machine for the sole purpose of servicing its hardware components. In other words, a computer repair company is no longer liable for infringement simply by turning on a client's computer.

The Shrink-Wrap Agreement: When You Buy Software, You Are Not Buying Software

Anyone who has used a personal computer is aware of the ease with which programs can be copied from disk to disk. In the 1970s, the manufacturers of computer software were concerned about the loss of revenue from unlawfully made copies. They were also concerned because the first sale doctrine (explained in Chapter 7) permitted the purchaser of software to rent copies.

Copyright lawyers created a solution. Instead of *selling* the program, software products would be *licensed*. A **license** is a contract that grants rights or permission to do something under certain conditions. Anyone who purchases the software (the licensee) and violates the terms of the license agreement can be sued for breach of contract. Since the software would now be licensed and not sold, no *first sale* would occur and the first sale doctrine would not be triggered. This is known as a **shrink-wrap agreement,** because the consumer enters into the agreement by breaking the shrink-wrapped plastic that seals the disks. In the case of software that is downloaded, the agreement is referred to as a click-wrap agreement because the user clicks on the mouse button to accept the terms. Shrink-wrap and click-wrap agreements take away most of the rights granted under the copyright law and replace them with restrictions.

How does a consumer enter into a shrink-wrap agreement? Sometimes the consumer must answer "yes" or "no" questions before using the program. If the shrink-wrap is on an envelope or the outside packaging, there is usually a warning to the effect that by opening the envelope or package, the consumer agrees to be bound by the terms and conditions set forth in the agreement. If the consumer does not wish to enter into the shrink-wrap agreement, the program can be returned for a full refund. Although there has been some debate about whether these agreements are enforceable, a court of appeals held in 1996 that a shrink-wrap agreement was valid and enforceable.[11] In addition, software companies have lobbied for passage of legislation under state commercial codes (known as Uniform Commercial Codes) that would codify shrink-wrap licenses.

Are Shareware and Freeware Protected Under Copyright Law?

Shareware is a system of marketing software. It is distributed at no charge on a trial basis, and if the recipient likes the software and intends to use it, a fee is paid. Shareware is also distributed in a form with a "lock" feature built into the software, disabling portions of the program. The user can try the unlocked portion at no charge and, if the user likes what he or she sees, can buy the "key" in the form of a floppy disk and registration number that enables the user to use the whole program.

Freeware is software that is made available to the public for free. That is, unlike shareware, there are no fees. Both of these forms of software are protected under copyright law, and you cannot reproduce or distribute these programs unless authorized by the copyright owners—even if you got them for free. For example, in one case, a company gathered various shareware programs and offered them in a CD-ROM collection, despite warnings on the shareware prohibiting such use. A court ruled that the shareware, originally placed on the Internet for free distribution, was entitled to federal copyright protection.[12]

Can a Purchaser Modify a Software Program for a Particular Purpose?

Customizing or adapting a program is permitted only to the extent that such rights are granted in the shrink-wrap agreement. Many programs permit adaptation for business use. For example, an accounting program may be customized for use in a mortuary. Even if customizing of the program is permitted, distributing the customized copies (without permission of the copyright owner) would be an infringement.

Is It Permissible to Share a Software Program over a Network?

A user cannot share a software program over a network unless the program is licensed for network use (sometimes referred to as a "site license"). Information about network licensing is available on the packaging or from the vendor. The use cannot exceed the permitted network license number. For example, if a site license is for five users, it cannot be used by more than five.

Is It Permissible to Rent a Computer Program?

Congress amended the Copyright Act in 1990 and prohibited the rental of computer programs.[13] Under this amendment, any business renting software is infringing copyright. Businesses have attempted to circumvent this rule, for example, one store offered a conditional sales arrangement whereby a purchaser of software could return it within several days for a partial refund. This attempt was considered to be a violation of the no-rental rule for software.[14]

Nonprofit libraries, however, are permitted to rent or lend software without authorization. In addition, renting or lending of computer programs is permitted:

(1) if the program is embodied in a machine that does not permit copying (for example, an exercise machine or handheld dictionary); or (2) if the software is intended for "limited purpose" computers designed for playing video games (for example, cartridge styled software used in Nintendo games, but not disk style software games used in personal computers). Finally, under a provision that went into effect December 1, 1991, the owner of an authorized arcade (coin-operated) video game can display or perform the game publicly without the copyright owner's consent.

THE INTERNET: NEW ISSUES FOR COPYRIGHT PROTECTION

The Internet allows computer users to access a worldwide database of copyrighted works and make near-perfect digital copies of everything they encounter. For this reason, Congress and copyright owners have been busy sorting out novel issues related to the Internet. Large corporations are policing cyberspace for websites that permit users to download (or copy) unauthorized copyrighted materials. Copyright owners from the Church of Scientology[15] to *Playboy* magazine[16] pursue websites that provide unauthorized materials.

Is It a Violation of Copyright Law to Download an Image or Text from the Internet?

If material is copyrighted and has been posted without authorization, downloading is an infringement because the user is making an unauthorized copy. If the posting is authorized by the copyright owner, downloading material is an infringement unless permitted by the copyright owner or excused as a fair use. For more information on fair use, see Chapter 7.

Giving It Away—Liability for Free Downloads.   In a 1994 case, *United States v. La Macchia,*[17] the operator of a computer bulletin board escaped prosecution under federal law for distributing copyrighted software because he *gave* the works away rather than *selling* them. This so-called *La Macchia* loophole was closed in 1998 when President Clinton signed the "No Electronic Theft Act," which created stiff criminal penalties for Internet infringement.[18]

Framed Links as Infringing Works

Websites can be linked to one another by clicking on highlighted text or images. Some sites, however, make use of a deceptive linking practice by reproducing someone else's website within a frame. For example, site A offers information on dental hygiene and gum disease. The user clicks on the button for gum disease, and site B, another dental site, appears—except it is framed by information from site A and the user is not aware that he or she is looking at a new site. The user believes he or she is only viewing site A. In this situation, the use of framed links is an infringement because it creates a derivative work without authorization.[19]

DMCA Provides a Method for Internet Service Providers to Avoid Liability

Under the Digital Millennium Copyright Act of 1998 (DMCA), an internet service provider (ISP) can avoid liability in the event an infringing copy is offered online. Among the conditions that must be met are the following:

- the ISP obtains no financial benefit from the infringement;
- the ISP does not have actual knowledge or awareness of facts indicating infringing transmissions; and
- upon learning of infringing transmission, the ISP acts quickly to remove or disable access to the infringing transmission.

In addition to these and other requirements, the ISP must establish an agent for receiving notice of infringement. The ISP requirements and the rules for establishing an agent are available from the Copyright Office website.

How Will Copyright Owners Protect Rights on the Internet?

In order to transact commerce in the "digital environment," businesses will rely on anticopying systems that scramble digital signals or prevent second generation copying (that is, a work can be copied once, but not twice). In addition, copyright owners are planning to implement a system of embedded copyright management information (CMI, or "digital watermarks") that will identify the copyright owner and provide information about the work. The Digital Millennium Copyright Act (DMCA) prohibits the removal of these digital watermarks.

To prevent the circumvention of these systems, the DMCA outlaws "little black box" technology. A little black box is any program or device that "undoes" the copy protection systems installed by the copyright owner. Or, as it is officially described, it is any technology that exists primarily to "avoid, bypass, remove, deactivate, or impair a technological measure, without the authority of the copyright owner." There are criminal and civil penalties for those who make and market this technology. Under certain conditions, law enforcement agencies are exempt from these restrictions.

How Does a Website Owner Obtain Permission to Use or Display Copyrighted Material?

Each component used in a website, such as music, photographs, or film clips, must be authorized by the copyright owner. Music can be licensed from the music publisher and record company (see Chapter 10). Photographs must be licensed from the owner of copyright. For information about companies offering photographic licensing services and copyright clearing houses that can help, see Appendix C. Motion picture clips are licensed from the motion picture production companies or from "clipmedia" services that license stock film imagery.

SEMICONDUCTOR CHIP PROTECTION

Semiconductor chips are tiny transistor-looking plastic and ceramic devices that transmit information inside computers and other devices. In 1984, Congress passed the Semiconductor Chip Protection Act, which protects "mask works" (the integrated circuit patterns encoded on semiconductor chips). These patterns are protected for a limited time (ten years) provided that the mask work is registered within two years after the mask work is first "commercially exploited" (that is, when the work is distributed to the public or when a written offer is made to sell it). The Copyright Office administers the Semiconductor Chip Protection Act, and mask works are registered by using the Copyright Office's Form MW. Information about statutory protection can be acquired from the Public Information Office, Copyright Office, Library of Congress, Washington, DC 20559, (202) 707-3000. Circular 100, distributed by the Copyright Office, contains information regarding mask work protection. This is also available at the Copyright Office website.

END NOTES

1. Stern Elecs., Inc. v. Kaufman, 559 F.2d 852 (2d Cir. 1981).
2. MiTek Holdings, Inc. v. Arce Eng'g Co., 89 F. 3d 1548 (11 Cir. 1996).
3. Lotus Dev. Corp. v. Arce Eng'g Inc., 49 F.3d 807 (1st Cir. 1995). The Supreme Court agreed to hear the case but failed to resolve this issue when it deadlocked 4-4.
4. Apple Computer, Inc. v. Microsoft Corp., 35 F.3d 1435 (9th Cir. 1994).
5. Diamond v. Diehr, 450 U.S. 171 (1981).
6. Lewis Galoob Toys, Inc. v. Nintendo of Am., Inc., 964 F.2d 965 (9th Cir. 1992).
7. Micro Star v. FormGen, Inc., 154 F.2d 1107 (9th Cir. 1998).
8. 276 F. 717 (S.D.N.Y. 1921).
9. Vault Corp. v. Quaid Software, Ltd., 847 F.2d 255, 268–70 (5th Cir. 1988).
10. MAI Sys. Corp. v. Peak Computer, 991 F.2d 511 (9th Cir. 1993).
11. ProCD, Inc. v. Zeidenberg, 86 F.3d 1447 (7th Cir. 1996).
12. Storm Impact, Inc. v. Software of the Month Club, 13 F. Supp. 2d 782 (N.D. Ill. 1998).
13. 17 U.S.C. § 109.
14. Central Point Software v. Global Software & Accessories, 34 U.S.P.Q.2d 1627 (E.D.N.Y. 1995).
15. Religious Technology Center v. Lerma, 40 U.S.P.Q.2d 1569 (E.D. Va. 1996); Religious Technology Center v. Pagliarina, 908 F. Supp. 1353 (E.D. Va. 1995).
16. Playboy Enters., Inc. v. Frena, 839 F. Supp. 1552 (M.D. Fla. 1993).
17. 871 F. Supp. 535 (D. Mass. 1994).
18. 17 U.S.C. § 506(a).
19. Futuredontics, Inc. v. Applied Anagramic, Inc., 45 U.S.P.Q.2d 2005 (C.D. Cal. 1998).

CHAPTER 12
Authorship and Ownership of Copyright

This chapter provides the basic principles and rules regarding ownership of copyright. Information is furnished regarding:

- principles of copyright ownership;
- joint authorship and co-ownership;
- responsibilities and rights of co-owners of copyright; and
- principles of copyright ownership in a collective work.

INTRODUCTION

The author is the original owner of copyright. That is, the author is the first person to own the copyright. Under copyright law, an author can be either the creator of the work or, under some circumstances, the person who employs the creator or the person who commissions the work. It may seem unusual that an employer or person who commissions a work can be considered the author, but this rule (known as **works made for hire**) is designed to guarantee that businesses own copyright in employee-created works. For example, Microsoft is the author of computer programs created by its employees. Not every employee-created or commissioned work is a work made for hire; these principles are discussed in Chapter 13.

Not all owners of copyright are authors, since the author may transfer rights, or rights may be transferred under operation of the law. The **owner of copyright** holds *title* to the work. "Title" is a legal concept associated with real and personal property. The copyright owner can sell, transfer, license, or grant rights to another person.

Disputes often arise between people who both believe they have acquired copyright ownership. Usually these matters are settled by a court. In one case, a daughter of Hank Williams, born out of wedlock, battled a music publisher over rights to songs by her father.[1] Proving ownership requires evidence documenting the creation of the work or documenting the transfer of the title of copyright.

Registration Does Not Prove Ownership

Registration of copyright by the Copyright Office does not prove ownership; it creates a presumption of ownership (or what is known in law as *prima facie* proof). Like all legal presumptions, it can be defeated in a court case by a sufficient showing of proof to the contrary (that is, it is *rebuttable*). For example, a company registers copyright for a software program, but a programmer later proves to a court that he is the copyright owner. In that event, the company's registration would be canceled and a new registration would be issued to the programmer. How could the company acquire registration if it were not the owner? It might accidentally or deliberately falsify information on the application. Fraudulent representation in a copyright application may be punishable by a criminal fine of up to $2,500.[2]

Ownership of a Copy Does Not Establish Rights

Ownership of a material object, like a painting, is distinct from the ownership of copyright. For example, in the 1980s, a woman in Tennessee bought a box of master tape recordings by musical performers Paul Simon and Johnny Cash that had accidentally been discarded by the Columbia Record Company. Since she had only acquired ownership of a material object (the reels of tape) and had not acquired ownership of copyright, the woman could not authorize copying of the musical works or the sound recordings embodied on the tape.

JOINT AUTHOR SHIP AND CO-OWNERSHIP

When two people create a work together, they are referred to as co-authors or joint authors, and the result of the collaboration is a **joint work.** Joint authors are co-owners of copyright. Examples of joint works would be the book *All the President's Men,* written by Bob Woodward and Carl Bernstein; a series of paintings created by Andy Warhol and Jean Michel Basquiat; and the song "Satisfaction," written by Mick Jagger and Keith Richards.

To qualify as joint authors, three requirements must be met:

1. each author must intend that his or her contribution will be merged with that of the other author(s);
2. each author must intend to be a joint author at the time he or she makes the contribution; and
3. each author must contribute copyrightable subject matter.[3]

In the midst of collaboration, it is sometimes difficult to determine if each author has contributed something copyrightable. In the following situations, the contributions were not considered to be copyrightable:

- an editor advised a writer on how to modify a book;[4]
- a writer supplied a 1 1/2-page introduction to a 546-page manual;[5] and
- an actor improvised lines during a play's performance.[6]

17 U.S.C. § 101 Joint work

A "joint work" is a work prepared by two or more authors with the intention that their contributions be merged into inseparable or interdependent parts of a unitary whole.

Determining the Value of Each Author's Contribution

If one author writes lyrics and one writes music, what percentage of income should be given to each joint author? Are the lyrics worth more than the music? If there is no agreement, a court will presume that each joint author has an equal interest in relation to the total number of joint authors. For example, if three authors write a song and there is no written agreement, the presumption is that each is entitled to one-third of the revenues.

When authors enter into an agreement, they may divide revenues from the work in any manner they choose. The authors may divide different sources of revenues in different ways. For example, two software programmers may agree to one method of dividing revenue from retail sales, and another method of dividing revenue from foreign licensing. A **collaboration agreement** (sometimes known as a **co-authorship** agreement) is a contract in which joint authors specify the rights, obligations, and percentage of copyright ownership and revenues attributable to each author. Collaboration agreements are common in the creation of works such as books (for example, where an illustrator and writer collaborate), songs, software programs, and screenplays.

Other Forms of Copyright Co-Ownership

Co-ownership of copyright can result from the transfer of ownership, death of the author, or community property laws. For example, one of two joint authors may transfer his or her interest to another person or an author's will may provide that copyright ownership shall be split between two children. These methods of transferring rights are discussed in Chapter 15.

How to Determine If Co-Ownership Exists

If the answer is "yes" to any of the following questions, a co-ownership arrangement probably exists:

- Is the work a joint work, created by two or more authors?
- If the work was created by one author, has the author transferred copyright ownership jointly to several persons?
- If the work was created by one author, has the author transferred a portion of the copyright interest and retained the remaining interest?
- Has the author died and has copyright ownership passed to two or more heirs?

■ Is the work subject to community property laws?

■ Do renewal rights in the work belong to two or more persons? (Renewal rights are discussed in Chapter 14.)

Co-Owners Are Tenants in Common

Co-owners are **tenants in common.** A **tenancy in common** is a legal principle by which a co-owner has an independent right to use or license the work, provided that he or she accounts to the other co-owners for any profits. For example, any co-owner of the work may grant a nonexclusive license for the work or, if necessary, sue infringers of the work, provided that the other co-owners receive a fair share of the profits or judgment. This rule of co-ownership, memorialized in the Copyright Act of 1976, was adopted from a 1944 court decision by Judge Learned Hand.

JUDGE LEARNED HAND ON COPYRIGHT: CO-OWNERSHIP RIGHTS

In *Edward B. Marks Music Corp. v. Jerry Vogel Music,*[7] one of the co-authors of a song entitled "The Bird on Nellie's Hat" sued the writer of an infringing song. The author of the infringing song argued that both co-owners of "The Bird on Nellie's Hat" must sue in order for the case to go forward. Judge Hand established the legal principle that either co-owner of copyright may bargain for or litigate rights regarding the copyright, provided that the other co-owner receives a fair share of the results. In this case, and in a case he decided earlier,[8] Judge Hand formulated the boundaries of joint authorship that were adopted in the definitions of the Copyright Act of 1976.

All Co-Owners Must Consent to First Use of a Song or Any Exclusive License or Transfer

There are a few exceptions to the rules regarding co-ownership. All co-owners of copyright in a song must consent to the first publicly distributed recording of the song. In addition, all co-owners of any work must consent to any exclusive license. An **exclusive license** is an agreement to grant proprietary rights solely to one person. For example, two programmers create a software program. A company wants an exclusive license to distribute the program (that is, it is the *only* company that can distribute the program). The consent of both programmers must be obtained. In addition to these rules, some countries require consent of all co-owners even for nonexclusive uses.

Death of a Co-Owner of Copyright

If a co-owner dies, his or her share goes to beneficiaries or heirs. For example, John Lennon and Paul McCartney jointly created the song "Yesterday." After Lennon's death, his rights in the song passed to his estate, not to McCartney.

What If Co-Owners Negotiate Deals Conflicting with Agreements Negotiated by Other Co-Owners?

Unless prohibited by a co-ownership agreement, any co-owner is permitted to grant nonexclusive rights without the consent of another co-owner. Conflicts develop when one co-owner grants *exclusive* rights without the consent of *all* co-owners. If the situation does occur, it is resolved by litigation or alternate dispute resolution, as discussed in Chapters 25 and 26.

What Happens If a Co-Owner Recovers Money in an Infringement Lawsuit?

Any co-owner may litigate or be sued regarding the copyright. If any co-owner recovers damages in a lawsuit, that co-owner is only entitled to damages equal to his or her equitable interest in the copyright.

What If a Co-Owner Dies Without a Will?

Each state has rules regarding what happens to property when there is no will. These rules are known as intestate succession, and they commonly provide for transfer to spouses and children. For example, a state law may provide that property shall be divided equally between a surviving spouse and child.

OWNERSHIP OF COPYRIGHT IN COLLECTIVE WORKS

A collective work is a form of compilation in which separate and independent works are assembled into a collective whole. Chapter 4 provides information on compilations and collective works. The person selecting and assembling the works is the author and copyright owner of the collective work. For example, the editor who assembles various poems for a poetry anthology is the author of the collective work. As copyright owner, that person controls the right to duplicate the collection as a group, that is, to reproduce all of the poems together, but none separately. In addition, the owner of copyright in the collective work can revise the collection. For example, Nancy, a poet, permits the use of her poem in *Splendor,* a poetry magazine. The owner of *Splendor* (unless there is a written agreement to the contrary) acquires only the right to use the poem in the magazine. The magazine acquires no right to revise the poem or to use it in a different collection. In some circumstances, the owner of the collection may also acquire the right to reproduce the collection in digital format.[9]

Contribution to a Collective Work

The author of each contribution to a collective work can acquire copyright for his or her contribution.[10] That is, each contribution acquires a separate copyright. These separate copyrights are distinct from copyright in the collective work as a whole. This rule guarantees that a poet owns the copyright of his or her poem, despite publication in a collective work. The contributor to a collective work, however, can agree to transfer his or her copyright ownership in the separate work. For example, freelance writers or graphic artists may transfer their copyright to a collective work such as a magazine. Why do these writers and artists give up copyright? Often, it is because they will not be paid unless all rights to the contribution are transferred to the magazine. Rules regarding transfers are discussed in Chapter 15.

Distinguishing Between a Contribution to a Collective Work and Joint Authorship

What is the difference between creating a contribution for a collective work and being a joint author? The primary difference is that the author of a contribution to a collective work intends to create a separate work. The creator of a joint work intends to create a work that is a merger with another artist or author. Consider the following example: Nancy is a poet. Her poem, "Spring" is selected for use in a poetry collection. Nancy has copyright ownership of her poem, but she has no copyright ownership or control over the collection (the collective work). A musician asks Nancy to write lyrics for a song called "Winter." The resulting song is a joint work, and Nancy and the musician are co-owners. The difference between the two is that Nancy never intended to merge "Spring" with another work when she wrote it. However, when writing "Winter," she intended that her words would be merged with music to create a song.

Can a Contributor to a Collective Work Use the Same Contribution in a Different Collection?

Unless there is a written agreement to the contrary, the author of a contribution to a collective work owns copyright in the individual work and controls the right to reproduce it.

END NOTES

1. Stone v. Williams, 970 F.2d 1043 (2d Cir. 1992).
2. 17 U.S.C. § 506(e).
3. Childress v. Taylor, 945 F.2d 500 (2d Cir. 1991).
4. *Id.*
5. Rubloff, Inc. v. Donahue, 31 U.P.S.Q.2d 1046 (D.C. Ill. 1994).
6. Erickson v. Trinity Theatre, Inc., 13 F.3d 1-61 (7th Cir. 1994).
7. 140 F.2d 268 (2d Cir. 1944).

8. Maurel v. Smith, 220 F. 195 (D.C.N.Y. 1915).
9. Tasini v. New York Times, 981 F. Supp. 841 (S.D.N.Y. 1997).
10. 17 U.S.C. § 201(c).

CHAPTER 13
Works Made for Hire

This chapter presents the basic principles for determining if a work is "made for hire." Information is provided regarding:

- distinction between the two types of works made for hire;
- factors for determining if an artist is an employee or independent contractor; and
- standards for a work made for hire agreement.

WHAT IS A WORK MADE FOR HIRE?

Under some circumstances, the author of a work is the person who pays for it, not the person who creates it. The premise of this principle (known as **works made for hire**) is that a business that authorizes and pays for a work owns the rights to the work. There are two distinct ways that a work will be classified as "made for hire":

1. the work was created by an employee within the scope of employment; or
2. it is a commissioned work that is the subject of a written agreement that falls within a special group of categories.

If the work qualifies under one of these two methods, the person paying for the work (the hiring party) is the author and copyright owner. The hiring party will be named as the author on the application for registration. The work made for hire status of a work affects the length of copyright protection and termination rights. Most of this chapter is devoted to the rules under the Copyright Act of 1976. However, at the end of the chapter, information is provided about works under the 1909 act.

How to Determine If a Work Is Made for Hire

There are two types of works made for hire: those created under an employer-employee relationship, and those commissioned with a written contract. How do you determine if a work qualifies as either type? The first step would be to determine if an employer-employee relationship exists. If an employer-employee relationship does not exist, an analysis should be made as to whether the work falls into the second category ("commissioned work"). Why should the analysis be done in this order? Because if an employer-employee relationship exists and the work is created within the scope of the employment, the analysis is over. Every copyrightable work created by an employee within the scope of employment is a work made for hire. There are no other requirements—no review of the special categories and no need for a written agreement. It is for this reason that courts, when sorting out ownership issues, first analyze whether an employer-employee relationship exists.

WORKS PREPARED BY AN EMPLOYEE WITHIN THE SCOPE OF EMPLOYMENT

There are two requirements to qualify as an employer-employee work made for hire. First, the work must be created "within the scope" of employment; and second, the person creating the work must be an employee.

Scope of Employment

The term *scope of employment* does not refer to whether the work was created during business hours or at home. It refers to whether the work is within the "scope" or range of activities expected from the employee—or, as one court stated, whether it is "the kind of work [the employee] was employed to perform."[1] For example, if a music publisher hires an employee to write songs, the publisher will own the songs created by the employee, even if they are created during a lunchbreak.[2] However, if a gas station hires an employee to pump gas, the gas station will not own a song created by the employee while he is pumping gas. Writing songs is not within the scope of working in a gas station.

Defining an Employee-Employer Relationship

An artist paid to create a work is either an employee or an independent contractor. Works created by an employee are *automatically* classified as works made for hire. This is not true for independent contractors. There is no definition of "employee" in the Copyright Act of 1976, and distinguishing between an employee and an independent contractor requires an analysis of several factors established by the Supreme Court in a 1989 case entitled *Community for Creative Non-Violence v. Reid.*[3] In that case, the Supreme Court narrowed the traditional definition of an employee and established a list of factors to be used in determining if an employer-employee relationship exists.

Employment Factors: *Community for Creative Non-Violence v. Reid.*   The Community for Creative Non-Violence (CCNV) is a nonprofit organization dedicated to eliminating homelessness in America. In 1985, a CCNV director conceived of a Christmas pageant display—a homeless family huddled over a steam grate (an analogy to the nativity scene). The CCNV hired a sculptor named Reid who prepared a sketch. The CCNV requested some changes; Reid agreed to create the sculpture and received a $3,000 advance. The CCNV constructed the steam grate portion of the exhibit. On December 24, 1985, twelve days after the due date, Reid delivered the sculpture and was paid the final $15,000. After the pageant and a month on display, the CCNV wanted to take the sculpture to other cities. Reid, who now had possession of the sculpture, objected, claiming it was too fragile, and proposed taking it on a less demanding exhibition tour. Both parties claimed copyright in the work.

The Supreme Court held that the sculpture was *not* a work made for hire because Reid was not an employee, as defined under law. To determine whether Reid was an employee or independent contractor, the Supreme Court created a list of factors (many of which were borrowed from Internal Revenue Service rules):

- the hiring party's right to control the manner and means by which the product is accomplished. If the hiring party exercises control, this factor weighs in favor of an employment relationship;
- the skill required in the particular occupation. If the work to be performed requires a unique skill, for example, sculpting, this factor weighs against an employment relationship;
- whether the employer or the worker supplies the instrumentalities and tools of the trade. If the person performing the work supplies the tools, this factor weighs against an employment relationship;
- the location of the work. If the hiring party determines the location of the work, this factor weighs in favor of an employment relationship;
- the length of time for which the person is employed. The longer the period of work, the more this factor weighs in favor of an employment relationship;
- whether the hiring party has the right to assign additional work projects to the worker. If the hiring party can assign additional tasks, including tasks that do not result in copyrightable works, this factor weighs in favor of an employment relationship;
- the extent of the worker's discretion over when and how long to work. If the hiring party controls the working times, particularly if it is a regular workweek, this factor weighs in favor of an employment relationship;
- the method of payment. If the payment is per job, not per day or week, this factor weighs against an employment relationship;
- the hired party's role in hiring and paying assistants. If the person doing the work cannot hire and pay assistants, this factor weighs in favor of an employment relationship;
- whether the work is part of the regular business of the hiring party. If the hiring party does not regularly perform this type of work, for example, creating a sculpture, this factor weighs against an employment relationship;
- whether the person performing the work is in business. If the person doing the work has his or her own business, this factor weighs against an employment relationship;
- the provision of employee benefits. If vacation or health benefits are granted to the person performing the work, this factor weighs in favor of an employment relationship; and

- the tax treatment of the hired party. If payroll and employment taxes are paid by the hiring party, this factor weighs in favor of an employment relationship.

Reid was involved in a skilled occupation as a sculptor and supplied his own tools. He did the work at his own location and was treated as an independent contractor for purposes of payment, benefits, and taxes. The creation of sculptures was not part of the regular business of the CCNV, and the CCNV had little discretion over Reid's working hours or his performance of further work. However, the CCNV did some supervision of Reid's work and contributed a portion of the work (the steam grate).

Applying these factors, the Supreme Court determined that Reid was not an employee under the Copyright Act of 1976. The case was sent back to a lower court for a determination if the CCNV and Reid were joint authors of the work. That is, did the parties have the intention that their contributions be merged into inseparable parts of a whole? A lower court later determined that the sculpture was a joint work and that Reid and the CCNV were joint authors and co-owners of copyright.

Which *CCNV* Factors Are the Most Important? The Supreme Court stated that not all of the *CCNV* factors are applicable in each case and no single factor is determinative. The factors are to be weighed based upon the particular facts of each case. However, case law since the *CCNV* case has demonstrated that certain factors generally have more weight than others. Particularly important seem to be the economic factors, such as the method of payment (weekly or per job), whether employee taxes are withheld, and whether the artist receives employee benefits.

For example, in a New York case,[4] several artists argued they were independent contractors when they created artwork in the lobby of a building. A federal court determined, however, that they were employees because they were paid a weekly salary, worked a forty-hour week, and received employee benefits such as paid vacation and life, health, and liability insurance. In addition, employee taxes were taken from their paychecks. In fact, two of the artists filed for unemployment benefits after they were terminated, and they listed the hiring company as a former employer. The hiring party could also assign additional projects to the artists, and the artists could not hire assistants without getting approval from the hiring party. Under those circumstances, the artists were considered employees, and as a result, all work they created during their employment was work made for hire.

In a Michigan case,[5] a video production company produced a "video postcard" about Mackinac Island. The photographers and scriptwriter/narrator argued they were the authors of the video, not the video production company. The video production company disagreed and stated that the photographers and scriptwriter were employees. The court of appeals did not find an employer-employee relationship, noting, among other factors, that no payroll taxes were withheld and no benefits were provided.

Employment Agreement Is Not Controlling

Occasionally a hiring party will ask that a written agreement be signed stating that the worker performing the services is an employee and that any works resulting are works made for hire. This agreement may be a factor in determining if an employer-employee relationship exists, and it also may be a factor in the second method of determining a work made for hire (that is, a commissioned work). But an agreement, even if it is titled "Work Made for Hire," does not, by itself, prove that an employment relationship exists or that a work is made for hire. The only method of *proving* an employer-employee relationship is to make an analysis of the factors in the *CCNV* case. Therefore, when assessing whether a work is made for hire under an employer-employee relationship, an employer should not assume that a signed agreement confirms ownership of the copyrighted work.

Effect of State Employment Law

Some states, such as California, require that employers who claim copyright ownership through employer-employee work made for hire relationships must pay employee benefits, including workers' compensation, unemployment insurance, and disability insurance.[6] That is, if a California employer wants to claim works made for hire, the business must pay payroll taxes, workers' compensation, and unemployment insurance.

What If an Employee Desires to Retain Control of Works?

It is possible for an employee to retain control of a specific work created during the scope of employment. This can be done by executing an agreement with the employer confirming the ownership arrangement. The letter agreement in the following example would enable an employee to retain control over a specific manual.

EXAMPLE
LETTER AGREEMENT CONFIRMING EMPLOYEE OWNERSHIP OF WORK.

Dear Employer:

This confirms the agreement between ElectroCo and myself that I shall own exclusive rights to the manual commonly known as *Managing Multiple Electrical Outlets*. The manual comprises approximately 68 pages and includes tips for homeowners and businesses regarding management of electrical outlets. A copy of the manual is attached to this agreement. Although I created *Managing Multiple Electrical Outlets* within the scope of my employment at ElectroCo, ElectroCo now agrees that I shall be the owner of all rights, under copyright law, to *Managing Multiple Electrical Outlets*. You represent and warrant that you have the power to grant these rights on behalf of ElectroCo and that if required, a representative of ElectroCo will furnish any other necessary documents required to demonstrate my ownership. If this letter accurately reflects our agreement, please sign and return one copy to me.

[signed by both parties]

COMMISSIONED WORKS

A work created by an independent contractor (unlike a work created by an employee) is not automatically classified as a work made for hire. To qualify as a commissioned work made for hire, three requirements must be met:

1.   the work is specially ordered or commissioned;
2.   the work is used in one of a group of specially enumerated categories; and
3.   there is a written agreement signed by both parties indicating it is a work made for hire.

In order to meet the standards of a commissioned work, *all* of these criteria must be met.

Specially Ordered or Commissioned

A work is "specially ordered or commissioned" when the commissioning party is the motivating factor in the creation of the work. For example, consider an artist's painting of a beach. Even if the artist allows a calendar company to use the painting, it will not be a commissioned work because the calendar company was not the motivating force behind its creation. Often a court will find that the "motivation" for the creation of a commissioned work is payment or the promise of payment. When an ongoing payment relationship exists between the parties, a court may presume that the series of works is commissioned. For example, if a magazine regularly buys cartoons from an artist, the cartoons will be presumed to be "commissioned" even though the artist may not have been specifically motivated to create a particular cartoon by the magazine. The commissioning party does not have to exercise artistic control over the work in order for it to qualify as a commissioned work.

Enumerated Categories

To qualify as a commissioned work made for hire, the work must be used in one of the following categories:

1.   as a contribution to a collective work;
2.   as a part of a motion picture or other audiovisual work;
3.   as a translation;
4.   as a supplementary work (that is, a work prepared for publication as a supplement to a work by another author for the purpose of introducing,

concluding, illustrating, explaining, revising, commenting upon, or assisting in the use of the other work, such as forewords, afterwards, pictorial illustrations, maps, charts, tables, editorial notes, musical arrangements, answer material for tests, bibliographies, appendixes, and indexes);

5.   as a compilation;

6.   as an instructional text. (An instructional text is a literary, pictorial, or graphic work prepared for use in day-to-day instructional activities. For example, a textbook would be an instructional text, but a novel used in a literature class would not);

7.   as a test or as answer material for a test; or

8.   as an atlas.

These enumerated categories apply *only* to works created by independent contractors. Any work created by an employee (as defined in the preceding sections) is a work made for hire, regardless of the category. If an artist is not an employee and if the use of the commissioned work does not fall into one of the enumerated categories, the result will not be a work made for hire. It does not matter if the parties have signed a written agreement stating that the work is made for hire. For example, a painter is commissioned to create a mural for a school. The painter signs an agreement entitled "Work Made for Hire." The painting is owned by the painter (not the school) because paintings are not included in the list of categories.

Timing of Signed Agreements

To qualify as commissioned work made for hire, the parties must sign an agreement. For many years, it was believed that a work made for hire agreement must state that it is a "work is made for hire" agreement and that it be executed *prior* to creation of the work. However, a case involving the artist Patrick Nagel indicated that the agreement may be executed after the creation of the work.

In *Playboy Enterprises v. Dumas,*[7] a court of appeals held that an agreement signed by the parties *after* a work was completed was valid as a work made for hire agreement. In that case, the artist, Patrick Nagel, furnished drawings for *Playboy* magazine over a seven-year period. The magazine paid Nagel by check, and on the back of each check was a statement that indicated the drawings were works made for hire. Nagel endorsed the checks. Later, when Nagel's widow sued for ownership of the drawings, *Playboy* argued that Nagel's check signatures constituted a written works made for hire agreement.

The court of appeals ruled that a work made for hire agreement can be executed after the work is completed provided that, at the time the work was created, the parties intended to enter into such an agreement. In other words, if Nagel and *Playboy* intended to create works made for hire, the written agreement could be executed later. The court of appeals determined that Nagel intended to enter into a work made for hire agreement. Why? Because Nagel's continued signature on the checks over a seven-year period demonstrated that he did not object and accepted the arrangement.

Use of the Words *Made for Hire* in the Agreement

The Copyright Act states that a commissioned work can be a work made for hire only if there is "a written instrument signed by [the parties] that the work shall be considered a work made for hire." In the case of *Playboy Enterprises v. Dumas,* discussed in the preceding section, *Playboy* magazine had used two different styles of check agreements with the artist. On one group of checks, *Playboy* used the term *works made for hire.* On the other, *Playboy* only stated it acquired "all right, title and interest." The artist's estate was able to claim ownership of the works that were paid for by checks lacking the "works made for hire" language. The court of appeals held that it was necessary for *Playboy* to use "works made for hire" language in order to obtain rights.

However, in a subsequent North Carolina case,[8] a federal court ruled that the term *work made for hire* need not be used in a written contract to establish a commissioning party's copyright ownership. In the North Carolina case, an artist sued a company called Laser Images for copyright ownership of illustrations for a map. The written agreement stated that the illustrations would "remain the sole property of Laser Images, and cannot be reproduced or used for any other purpose." Even though the agreement did not use the words *copyright* or *works made for hire,* the court ruled that it fulfilled the written agreement requirement of a work made for hire. Since this case conflicts with the *Playboy* case, the issue may eventually be resolved on appeal or by the Supreme Court. To preserve their rights, commissioning parties should continue to use the term *work made for hire* in their agreements.

An example of a work made for hire agreement is included in Appendix E.

CHECKLIST FOR DETERMINING IF A WORK IS MADE FOR HIRE UNDER COPYRIGHT ACT OF 1976

The rules regarding works made for hire are complex. There are two methods for creating a work made for hire, and the examination should begin with the first method, the employer-employee relationship.

Method One: Works Created as an Employee

If the answer is "yes" to both of the following questions, the work is owned by the hiring party:

1. Is the work created within the scope of employment?
2. Do the parties have an employer-employee relationship?

The employment relationship is determined by weighing the following factors:

- Does the hiring party control the manner and means by which the work is created?
- What is the level of skill required in the particular occupation?

- Does the employer supply the instrumentalities and tools of the trade?
- Where is the location of the work?
- What is the length of time for which the worker is employed?
- Does the hiring party have the right to assign additional work projects to the worker?
- What is the extent of the worker's discretion over when and how long to work?
- What is the method of payment (that is, by the job, by the hour, and so on)?
- What is the worker's role in hiring and paying assistants?
- Is the work part of the regular business of the hiring party?
- Is the worker in business?
- Is there any provision of employee benefits?
- What is the tax treatment of the worker?

Method Two: Commissioned Works

If there is no employment relationship, the person creating the work is an independent contractor. The work will qualify as a work made for hire only if all three of the following questions are answered affirmatively:

1. Is the work specially ordered or commissioned?
2. Is there a signed agreement stating that it is a work made for hire?
3. Does the work fall within one of the enumerated categories? [(1) a contribution to a collective work; (2) as a part of a motion picture or other audiovisual work; (3) as a translation; (4) as a supplementary work; (5) as a compilation; (6) as an instructional text; (7) as a test or as answer material for a test; or (8) as an atlas]

WORKS MADE FOR HIRE UNDER THE 1909 ACT

A work created prior to January 1, 1978, is subject to the rules regarding the Copyright Act of 1909. The work made for hire principles under the 1909 act did not divide the work into categories of employee-created and commissioned works. Instead, a party was considered to own a work as a work made for hire if three elements were present:

1. the hiring party instigated the creation of the work, either under an employment arrangement or by commissioning the work;
2. the hiring party paid the artist to create the work; and
3. the hiring party exercised control over the creation of the work.

This test was referred to as the "instance and expense" test, and its final element, the exercise of control, increased in importance during the final years of the 1909 act. "Control" referred to the hiring party's ability to affect the work performed. For example, if the hiring party could affect the content of the work, request modifications, or establish standards that the work had to fulfill, then the hiring party exercised control. These rules are still important because ownership battles over works created under the 1909 act are still occurring. For example, the *Playboy* case cited earlier involved works under both the 1909 and 1976 acts.

EXAMPLE

A Nun's Work Is Not "Made for Hire" Under the 1909 Act. In a 1984 case,[9] a manufacturer argued that ceramic figures (known as Hummel figurines) based upon the drawings of Sister Hummel were works made for hire. After Sister Hummel's death, there was a dispute about whether her relatives could claim rights for the figurines created under the 1909 act. The manufacturer argued that since the nun had taken a vow of poverty and renounced all worldly goods, she had intended that all the "fruits" of her labors pass to the convent. Therefore, the manufacturer maintained, the nun was "employed" by the convent and the drawings were works made for hire. A federal court disagreed, applying the most important factor under the 1909 act, whether the convent had exercised any control or authority over the creation of the work. Since Sister Hummel had created and controlled the drawings and supervised the creation of the ceramic figures, the works were not made for hire.

END NOTES

1. Avtec Sys., Inc. v. Peiffer, 21 F.3d 568 (4th Cir. 1994).
2. When works are created during an employee's off-hours, a court may inquire as to whether the work was motivated by the employee's desire to further the company's goals. *See* Avtec Sys., Inc. v. Peiffer, 21 F.3d 568 (4th Cir. 1994).
3. 490 U.S. 730 (1989).
4. Carter v. Helmsley-Spear, Inc., 71 F.3d 77 (2d Cir. 1995).
5. Hi-Tech Video Prods., Inc., v. Capital Cities, 58 F.3d 1093 (6th Cir. 1995).
6. *See* CAL. LAB. CODE § 3251.5; CAL. UNEMP. INS. CODE §§ 621(d), 686.
7. 53 F.3d 549 (2d Cir. 1995).
8. Armento v. Laser Image, Inc., 40 U.S.P.Q.2d 1874 (D.C.N.C. 1996).
9. Schmid Bros., Inc. v. Goebel, 589 F. Supp. 497 (E.D.N.Y. 1984).

CHAPTER 14
Duration of Copyright

How long does copyright protection last? This chapter provides information regarding the length (or "term") of copyright protection. Information is furnished regarding:

- the duration of copyright under the 1909 Copyright Act;
- the principles of renewal under the 1909 act;
- the extended renewal period under the 1909 act;
- the restoration of copyright protection for foreign works;
- the duration of copyright for works under the 1976 act; and
- the Sonny Bono Copyright Term Extension Act (1998).

THE COPYRIGHT ACT OF 1909

In order to determine how long copyright lasts, it is necessary to determine when copyright protection begins (or "vests"). Under the Copyright Act of 1909, rights did not vest until either the author published the work with notice or the unpublished work was registered. If a songwriter created a song, wrote it down, but never published it or registered it, it would not be protected under the Copyright Act of 1909. The Copyright Act of 1976 and subsequent amendments created rules regarding the length of protection offered for unpublished works, and we discuss those rules later in this chapter.

Under the 1909 act, unpublished, unregistered works were protected under **common law copyright.** Common law copyright is a system of protection based upon the rules and principles established by court decisions. Unlike federal copyright law, which is based upon written statutes and regulations, common law copyright is based upon rules of law developed solely by judges.

Duration Under the Copyright Act of 1909

Under the 1909 act, protection lasts for an initial term of twenty-eight years from the date that copyright vested. Copyright vested on the date of first publication or on the date when the work was registered (if unpublished). If the copyright was renewed during the last year of the term (that is, the twenty-eighth year), copyright protection would continue for an additional twenty-eight-year period. The second twenty-eight-year period of copyright term is known as the **renewal term.** If renewed, the total time for protection was fifty-six years. If the copyright was not renewed, protection ended after twenty-eight years, and the work fell into the public domain. Many well-known works fell into the public domain because the proprietors failed to renew copyright. If an author died before the renewal period, the author's estate could renew, although this often required application of rules regarding probate (laws affecting transfer of property after death).

Effect of the Copyright Act of 1976

It appeared unfair that authors under the 1909 act received fifty-six years of protection while authors under the 1976 act received seventy-five years or more. Therefore, the drafters of the 1976 act offered a bonus to works protected under the 1909 act. These older works could extend the total length of copyright to seventy-five years. If a 1909 work was in its renewal term when the Copyright Act of 1976 went into effect, the renewal term was extended from twenty-eight to forty-seven years (granting a total of seventy-five years). Alternatively, a work registered under the Copyright Act of 1909 in its first term on January 1, 1978, could be renewed for a period of forty-seven years. This forty-seven-year period is known as the **extended renewal term.** For example, if a work was first published in 1940 and renewed in 1968, the duration of copyright would automatically be extended to 2015 (forty-seven-year renewal term). This period was extended further by passage of the Sonny Bono Copyright Term Extension Act in 1998, as described in the following section.

Twenty More Years! The Sonny Bono Copyright Term Extension Act

The passage of the Sonny Bono Copyright Term Extension Act in 1998 extended the time period during which copyrighted works are protected. Works in their extended renewal terms were granted an additional twenty years—a total of ninety-five years of copyright protection. For example, if a work was first published in 1950 and renewed in 1978, the duration of copyright would automatically be extended to 2045 (sixty-seven-year renewal term). The Term Extension Act saved many 1909 act works, such as early animated features of Mickey Mouse and Winnie the Pooh and the music of George Gershwin, from falling into the public domain.

Works Not in Their Renewal Term as of January 1, 1978

If a work protected under the Copyright Act of 1909 was not in its renewal term on January 1, 1978 (the date the Copyright Act of 1976 went into effect), the owner was required to renew copyright for an extended renewal term. Failure to renew resulted in loss of copyright protection. For example, if a work was published in 1962 and the owner did not renew in 1990, the work fell into the public domain. It is estimated that over ninety percent of published works were not renewed. Since this system resulted in many unfair losses of copyright protection, Congress amended the Copyright Act in 1991 and provided for *automatic* renewal. Owners of copyright for works protected under the Copyright Act of 1909 no longer have to renew copyright. The protection is automatically extended for an additional sixty-seven-year period. However, certain incentives are offered to authors who voluntarily register for renewal during the twenty-eighth year.

Restoring Protection to Public Domain Works

Until 1994, there was no provision under the Copyright Act of 1976 or its amendments to restore copyright protection for a work that had fallen into the public domain. In other words, if an author failed to renew, copyright protection could not be revived. However in 1994, in order to conform to international copyright treaties, the Copyright Act was amended to permit certain public domain works to be restored. A work can be restored if:

- it is in the public domain because the author failed to follow certain formalities, such as renewal or use of copyright notice as explained in Chapter 17;
- at the time the work was created, at least one author was a national or domiciliary of an "eligible country." An eligible country is a country, other than the United States, that is a member of the Berne Convention, the World Trade Organization (WTO), or is subject to a presidential proclamation that extends restored copyright protection to that country (see Chapter 27);
- if published, the work must have first been published in an eligible country and must not have been published in the United States during the thirty-day period following its first publication in that eligible country; and
- copyright protection still exists in the country where the work was created (the "eligible country").

For example, many works by the Dutch artist M. C. Escher lost copyright protection because they were published without notice in the United States. The works were created in Holland (the eligible country) where they are still protected under Dutch copyright law.

Eligible copyrights are restored automatically. However, if an author or the author's estate wants to enforce rights against a person who relied on the public domain status of the work to reproduce it ("reliance parties"), the author of a restored work must file a notice of intent with the Copyright Office and with the "reliance parties." A copy of the notice is provided in Chapter 27. This notice informs the reliance parties that the work is being restored and to halt future reproductions. For more information, consult Circular 38B. Copies of Circular 38B and the notice of intent can be downloaded from the Copyright Office website, as explained in Chapter 16.

If copyright is restored, protection lasts for the remainder of the term of copyright that the work would have enjoyed if the work had never entered the public domain in the United States. For example, a French short story that was first published without copyright notice in 1935 will be treated as if it had been both published with a proper notice and properly renewed, meaning that its restored copyright will expire on December 31, 2030 (ninety-five years after the United States copyright would have come into existence).

THE COPYRIGHT ACT OF 1976

The Copyright Act of 1976 eliminated the concept of copyright renewal and replaced it with a simpler system involving fixed time periods.

Date of Vesting of Copyright Under the Copyright Act of 1976

The Copyright Act of 1976 went into effect January 1, 1978. After that date, an author acquires copyright the moment a work is created. This "moment" occurs when the work is fixed, that is, when an artist places paint on a canvas, when a musician records a song on an audiotape, or when a choreographer notates the steps of a ballet. The date of creation is the date when copyright protection begins. For example, if a songwriter has a melody in her head and sings it aloud, rights are not vested until she writes it down or records it.

One Author

The length of protection under the Copyright Act of 1976 depends on the type of authorship. If a work is created by one author, the term of protection is for the life of the author plus seventy years. For example, a musician writes a song in 1980 and dies in 1990. Protection will extend to 2060—seventy years from the date of the author's death. This timetable will not apply if the work is published anonymously or if the work is made for hire, as explained in the following sections. If a work was unpublished and unregistered before 1978, but published after 1978, special rules apply (see the section entitled "Unpublished Works" in the following text).

Joint Authors

If a work is created by two or more authors, protection will extend for the life of the author who lives the longest (the surviving author) plus seventy years. For example, if two songwriters collaborate and one dies in 1980 and the other dies in 1990, the work will be protected until 2060 (seventy years from the date of the surviving author's death).

Works Made for Hire

Works made for hire are protected for a period of ninety-five years from first publication or one hundred and twenty years from creation, whichever is shorter. Therefore, if a publishing company created a work made for hire in 1990 but did not publish it until 2000, copyright protection would extend to 2095 (ninety-five years from the date of publication).

Anonymous and Pseudonymous Works

An author's contribution to a work is **anonymous** if that author is not identified on the copies or phonorecords of the work. For example, the bestseller, *Primary Colors* listed its author as Anonymous. An author's contribution is **pseudonymous** if the author is identified by a fictitious name. For example, the author Stephen King used the pseudonym Richard Bachman for several novels. Copyright protection for anonymous and pseudonymous works is ninety-five years from the date of publication or one hundred and twenty years from creation, whichever is shorter. However, if the name of the author is disclosed in the records of the Copyright Office, the disclosure will convert the term to life plus seventy years. For example, consider the bestseller *Primary Colors,* published anonymously in 1995. The media eventually determined that the author was Joe Klein, a writer for *Newsweek* magazine. If Klein were to die in 2030 without disclosing his name to the Copyright Office, the term of copyright for *Primary Colors* would end in 2090 (ninety-five years from publication); however, if Klein were to disclose his name, protection would extend until 2100 (seventy years from his death).

Year-End Expiration of Copyright Terms

The length of copyright protection, regardless of whether under the copyright acts of 1909 or 1976, runs *through the end* of the calendar year. In other words, the last day of copyright protection for any work is December 31. For example, if an author died in 1990, protection of the works would continue through December 31, 2060.

The Sonny Bono Copyright Term Extension Act

In 1993, European countries extended the term of copyright protection to the life of the author plus seventy years. In order to harmonize United States copyright law with European law, the Sonny Bono Copyright Term Extension Act was passed in 1998. The act extended United States copyright protection for an additional twenty years and established rules regarding the protection of unpublished and unregistered works.[1]

Unpublished Works

Unpublished works created after January 1, 1978, are protected for the life of the author plus seventy years. Unpublished work created after January 1, 1978, that are works made for hire, pseudonymous, or anonymous are protected ninety-five years from first publication or one hundred and twenty years from creation, whichever is less.

Some additional rules regarding works that were unpublished and not registered with the Copyright Office before 1978 are:

- copyright expires seventy years after the death of the author—*unless* the author has already been dead more than seventy years. In that case, protection expires on January 1, 2003; and
- regardless of when the author died, the copyright in an unpublished work created before 1978 but published before January 1, 2003, will not expire before December 31, 2047.

For example, Jane Austen died in 1817, but an unpublished Austen manuscript was located and published in the 1990s. The book will be protected through December 31, 2047—230 years after her death!

Determining Length of Protection

Works published in the United States before 1923	Copyright has expired and these works are in the public domain
Works published from 1923 through 1963	Initial term of twenty-eight years. If renewed during the twenty-eighth year, copyright is extended for an additional sixty-seven-year period
Works published from 1964 through 1977	Protection is ninety-five years from date of first publication
Works created on or after January 1, 1978, whether published or unpublished	One author: life of author plus seventy years Joint authors: life of surviving author plus seventy years Works made for hire: ninety-five years from first publication or one hundred and twenty years from creation, whichever is less Anonymous and pseudonymous works: ninety-five years from first publication or one hundred and twenty years from creation, whichever is less. If author's name is disclosed to copyright office, life of author plus seventy years
Works created before 1978 and unpublished as of December 31, 2002	Copyright expires seventy years after death of author unless the author has already been dead more than seventy years, in which case protection ends on January 1, 2003. (The work must not have been registered prior to 1978.)
Works unpublished and not registered as of 1978 but published between January 1, 1978, and January 1, 2003	Copyright expires seventy years after death of author, but no earlier than December 31, 2047

END NOTE

1. The Sonny Bono Copyright Term Extension Act can be downloaded from the Copyright Office website at http://www.loc.gov/copyright/legislation/s505.pdf.

CHAPTER 15
Transfer of
Copyright

This chapter provides information regarding the transfer of copyright including:

- distinctions between assignment and license;
- use of copyrights as security interests and mortgages;
- transfers resulting from death of an author;
- involuntary transfers;
- methods of terminating transfers; and
- the impact of the proposed twenty-year extension of copyright.

LICENSES AND ASSIGNMENTS

Each right granted under copyright is separate and divisible. This means that each right (such as the right to publish a work) can be treated separately, and each right can be divided and transferred to different people. For example, Anne Rice can divide her right to publish *Interview with a Vampire* between a hardback publisher, a softcover publisher, and a third publisher for audiobook rights. She can divide the right to adapt the work among a movie company, a TV company, and a video game company. The right to use copyrightable elements of "Interview with a Vampire" on merchandise can be divided among a T-shirt company, a poster company, and a company that sells garlic.

In order to transfer rights, an author uses one of three methods:

1. a nonexclusive license;
2. an exclusive license; or
3. an assignment.

17 U.S.C. § 101 Transfer of copyright ownership

A **"transfer of copyright ownership"** is an assignment, mortgage, exclusive license, or any other conveyance, alienation, or hypothecation of a copyright or of any of the exclusive rights comprised in a copyright, whether or not it is limited in time or place of effect, but not including a nonexclusive license.

Nonexclusive License

A **nonexclusive license** allows one or several companies to publish or perform a work for a period of time, and in return, the author receives periodic payments (known as "royalties") that are usually tied to the sales or number of performances of the work. The person granting the rights, usually the author, is the *licensor.* The person paying for the license is the *licensee.* When a license is nonexclusive, more than one licensee may acquire the same right. For example, a software developer may create a program that allows a user to post photographs on the Internet. Several companies may want to incorporate this program into their products, so they execute nonexclusive licenses with the developer. Under a nonexclusive license, the author remains the owner of copyright even though others may have a license to publish or perform the work. The situation is more complex in the case of an exclusive license.

Exclusive License

Under an **exclusive license,** only one party acquires a right. That is, no other company or person is granted a similar right. The arrangement may be limited in regard to time or location. For example, a company may acquire the exclusive right to publish a book in the United States for a period of five years. Under an exclusive license, the rights may revert (or return) to the licensor after the license period is over. An example of an exclusive license agreement is provided in Appendix D.

Assignment

An **assignment** is a transfer of ownership rights (sometimes referred to as the "title" to the work). The person assigning the rights, usually the author, is the *assignor,* and the person paying for the rights is the *assignee.* The assignee owns copyright under the assignment agreement and the author retains no rights. However, the assignor may receive periodic payments based on the terms of the assignment agreement. In addition, an assignment agreement may provide for a method whereby the rights are assigned back to the assignor in the event of a certain condition, for example, the assignee stops selling the work.

Under copyright law, the heirs of an author (the assignor) may recapture rights granted under an assignment. This principle is discussed later in this chapter. Some assignments are often referred to as being perpetual, that is, forever. This is not accurate because the longest an assignment can last is for the length of the copyright.

EXAMPLE

Distinguishing Between Licenses and Assignments. In order to compare the three forms of transfer (exclusive license, nonexclusive license, and assignment), consider a TV show called *Luna:*

- if a company wanted to acquire *all* rights and become the copyright owner for the full term of copyright of *Luna* (including all derivatives and sequels), it would acquire an assignment of all rights;
- if a company wanted to be the only distributor of *Luna*, but only sought that right for a period of ten years, it would acquire an exclusive license; and
- if a company did not mind if other companies could distribute or perform *Luna*, it would acquire a nonexclusive license.

Two examples of copyright assignments are provided in Appendix E.

Spousal Signatures. The Copyright Act of 1976 requires that only the assignor (usually the author) sign the agreement. Some attorneys consider it prudent for the spouse of a copyright owner to also sign the assignment. One court has held that a spouse has a community property interest in the other spouse's copyrighted work.[1]

When Unclear, the Courts Decide

The type of agreement—license or assignment—can have an impact on the parties. For example, the Internal Revenue Service categorizes income from an assignment in a different manner than income from a license. Depending on how it is written, an exclusive license can be interpreted to have the same effect as an assignment. Sometimes confusion arises because an exclusive license can have the same effect as a transfer of ownership, or it can transfer exclusive ownership of *one* of the rights under copyright law. Because these two forms of transfer overlap and because lawyers may misstate or miscategorize these transfers, courts always examine the conditions and obligations of the agreement rather than simply relying on terms such as *assignment* and *exclusive license.*

Assignments and Exclusive Licenses: Get It In Writing

The Copyright Act of 1976[2] states that any assignment or exclusive license must be in writing and signed by the person granting the rights. There are exceptions to this rule, for example, when a person dies without a will or when bankruptcy is declared. These exceptions will be discussed later.

17 U.S.C. § 204(a) Transfers of copyright ownership

A transfer of copyright ownership, other than by operation of law, is not valid unless an instrument of conveyance, or a note or memorandum of the transfer, is in writing and signed by the owner of the rights conveyed or such owner's duly authorized agent.

MORTGAGES AND SECURITY INTERESTS

A homeowner may mortgage the home or use the home as security for a loan. In both cases, money is paid to a party and the property is held as collateral.

If the money is not repaid, the person loaning the money keeps the property. Similarly, a copyright owner may mortgage a copyrightable work or use it as security for repayment of a debt. For example, the author Stephen King assigned certain motion picture rights to his book *The Shining* to Warner Brothers, the motion picture company. In 1983, Warner Brothers mortgaged and assigned copyright ownership to a bank, as security for a debt that the movie company had incurred. If Warner Brothers repaid the debt, the mortgage would terminate, and ownership of the movie *The Shining* would revert to Warner Brothers. If Warner Brothers failed to pay the debt, the bank would acquire ownership of the motion picture rights.

EXAMPLE

David Bowie Bonds: Creative Copyright Transfers. Copyright owners are constantly developing new methods of earning money from the transfer of rights. In 1997, David Bowie marketed asset-backed bonds that pay interest from royalties on his songs. The bonds allowed Bowie to collect $55 million upfront instead of waiting for the royalty checks to arrive over a period of years. The royalty payments will go, instead, to the purchasers of the bonds. The bonds were expected to provide the purchaser with a 7.9 percent return on the investment over ten years.

A Transfer of Payment Rights Is Not a Transfer of Ownership

Many licensing agreements provide for continuing payments to the author. Under state law, an author can sign an agreement that transfers the payments from the author to someone else. This transfer of money is also referred to as an assignment, although it is not the same as a copyright assignment. It is an assignment of payments, not rights.

EXAMPLE

The Songwriter Who Owed Money. A songwriter licensed rights to his songs to BMI, a performance rights organization. Twice a year, BMI sent the songwriter payments. The songwriter later assigned all future BMI payments to two people to whom he owed money. The songwriter informed BMI of the arrangement, and the organization made future payments to these people. Later, the Internal Revenue Service (IRS) sued the songwriter to obtain back taxes and demanded the money from BMI, arguing that the songwriter failed to record his assignment of payments with the Copyright Office. A federal court determined that the assignment of payments was not a transfer of ownership and was not a mortgage or security interest because the songwriter retained copyright ownership. Therefore, the arrangement with the creditors did not have to be recorded with the Copyright Office, and the IRS was not entitled to the BMI money.[3]

TRANSFERS OTHER THAN BY WRITTEN AGREEMENT

A transfer of copyright ownership may occur other than by written agreement. The three most common examples are:

1. transfer upon death;
2. transfer of ownership by operation of law; or
3. involuntary transfer.

Transfer upon Death

If an owner of copyright dies, the copyright will be transferred to the beneficiary or beneficiaries designated in the will. If an owner of copyright dies without a will, transfer of ownership will occur according to the rules of intestate succession. Each state has its own rules regarding such transfers. For example, in most states, the immediate family—the spouse and children—inherit property according to a formula. Transfers resulting from the death of the copyright owner commonly result in co-ownership of copyright, as the author's family may divide the copyright interests. Often these transfers result in conflicts among the beneficiaries, particularly when an author transfers property to an organization such as a university or foundation rather than to family members.

JUDGE LEARNED HAND ON COPYRIGHT: AN AUTHOR'S INTENT

The author Kahil Gibran died in 1931 and left only a handwritten will that stated, "The royalties on my copyrights which copyrights I understand can be extended upon request of my heirs for an additional period of 28 years after my death, are to go to my hometown." The hometown was later referred to in the will as Bechari, Republic of Lebanon.

After Gibran's death, a lawsuit was brought to determine who had the right to renew copyright to Gibran's works: Gibran's sister, Mary, or the National Committee of Gibran, a foundation created by Gibran's hometown.[4] According to Judge Hand, when an author is deceased, renewal rights under the 1909 copyright vest in the author's estate, that is, the beneficiary named in the will, which in Gibran's case was his hometown. Despite Gibran's failure to name an executor and his use of the term *heir* in his will, Judge Hand fashioned a decision that honored Gibran's intent as well as the language of the Copyright Act of 1909.

Involuntary Transfers

Under certain circumstances, copyright ownership can be transferred without the consent of an author. These involuntary transfers (sometimes referred to as "operation of law") can occur in a bankruptcy proceeding, when a court transfers copyright ownership to pay creditors. In a divorce proceeding, the court may order the copyright owner to divide the ownership interest with a spouse. A court may also transfer copyright ownership when a creditor forecloses on a security or mortgage in which the copyright is held as collateral.

Methods of Transferring Ownership of Copyright

Assignment or exclusive license	An assignment is a transfer of ownership interest. An exclusive license is a grant of one or all of the rights comprising copyright in such a manner that no other party will be granted a similar right. Assignments and exclusive licenses require a written agreement evidencing the transfer signed by the party transferring rights.
Mortgage or security	A copyright may be mortgaged or used as security for an obligation. Mortgages and security interest transfers require written agreement evidencing the transfer signed by the party transferring rights.
Transfer upon death	If an owner of copyright dies with a valid will, the copyright will be transferred to a designated beneficiary. If an owner of copyright dies without a will, transfer of ownership will occur according to the rules of intestate succession.
Involuntary transfers	Under certain circumstances (for example, bankruptcy, mortgage foreclosure, divorce), a court can order the transfer of copyright.

RECORDING COPYRIGHT TRANSFERS

It is not a requirement of copyright law that all transfers of ownership be recorded with the Copyright Office. However, recordation provides constructive notice of the transfer (which is important in the case of creditors), and the recordation may also be necessary to establish jurisdiction in a copyright infringement action. A transfer of ownership (transfer of exclusive rights, assignments, mortgage, and so on) must be in writing, and notarization is recommended (see the text that follows). Nonexclusive licenses or other documents pertaining to copyright also may be recorded. In fact, licenses and assignments for works that have not yet been created can also be recorded, for example, a songwriting agreement in which a musician assigns all rights for future songs. Recordation:

- may be required to allow a transferee to file an infringement suit;
- establishes a priority between conflicting transfers or nonexclusive licenses;
- establishes a public record of the contents of the transfer or document; and
- provides constructive notice to the public of the facts in the recorded document.

17 U.S.C. § 205(a) Conditions for recordation

Any transfer of copyright ownership or other document pertaining to a copyright may be recorded in the Copyright Office if the document filed for recordation bears the actual signature of the person who executed it, or if it is accompanied by a sworn or official certification that it is a true copy of the original, signed document.

Must the Transfer Be Notarized?

The Copyright Office does not require that recorded documents be notarized. However, if a transfer is properly notarized or accompanied by a certificate of acknowledgment, this creates prima facie evidence of the execution of the transfer. That is, notarization creates a presumption that the transfer is valid. This presumption may be rebutted, but the burden of proof is on the party trying to prove the transfer is invalid. Certain transfers, such as mortgages or security interests, may have to be notarized under state laws. For this reason, it is prudent to notarize all documents to be recorded.

Document Must Bear Signature of Person Granting Rights

Any grant, transfer, license, or assignment must be signed by the party giving up the rights. If a photocopy is furnished, not the original signed document, a certification must be included stating that the photocopy is a true reproduction of the original document (that is, "I swear under penalty of perjury under the laws of the United States that the attached document is a true and correct copy of the original"). If the document is notarized or accompanied by a certificate of acknowledgment, it is considered to create a legal presumption or prima facie evidence of the execution of the transfer.

Document Must Be Complete and Legible

All of the required information to be recorded must be in the document. If, for example, a reference is made to an exhibit, schedule, or attachment, that should be recorded as well. The document must be of such quality and readability that it can be reproduced in legible microfilmed copies.

Fee and Cover Letter

The current fee for recording documents pursuant to section 205 can be determined by calling the Public Information Office at (202) 679-0700 or Certification and Documents at (202) 707-6850. The documents and fee should be mailed to Documents Unit LM-462, Cataloging Office, Library of Congress, Washington, DC 20559.

Document Cover Sheet

The Copyright Office provides a Document Cover Sheet, a copy of which is included in Appendix D. This cover sheet contains the necessary affirmation and certification statements so the party requesting the filing does not have to type this information. A cover letter should also be included (for example, "Enclosed please find an original and one copy of the [*insert name of document*] for recording pursuant to section 205 of the Copyright Act. Please return a copy of the document as it is recorded to this office."). If you are recording the document on behalf of a third party or client, a copy of the Document Cover Sheet and letter should be sent to the client or transferee, and a review should be calendared for eight weeks from the mailing to check on the recording of the document. For more information about the recordation of transfers and other documents, the Copyright Office provides Circular 12. (See also Circular 96, section 201.4.) The fees for recording documents are listed in Appendix G.

Unacceptable Documents

Documents will be returned unrecorded if:

- the document purports to be a transfer but does not bear a signature of the transferor;
- the capacity of the person signing for the transferor is unclear;
- the date of certification or notarization is earlier than the date of execution;
- the date of receipt is earlier than the date of execution;
- the document submitted is not capable of being reproduced legibly;
- the transferor/transferee is not clearly identified in the document;
- the titles are listed in a cover letter but not in the document itself;
- the document is incomplete by its own terms;
- the document is marked as an exhibit;
- the document purports to be a notice of termination but does not meet the formal requirements;
- the complete recordation fee is not submitted; or
- it is unclear whether the document is to be recorded.

TERMINATING TRANSFERS

Artists and authors often enter agreements at a time when they cannot fully appreciate the value of their works. Vincent Van Gogh never sold a painting in his lifetime, but today his work is valued in the millions. Many songwriters signed away copyright to their songs for a small amount of money, and later those songs appreciated in value. Both the Copyright Act of 1909 and the Copyright Act of 1976 provide a means for the author or the author's estate to recapture the copyright after certain types of transfers.

The business community is generally opposed to the termination of lucrative licenses and assignments. Therefore, when drafting these termination rights,

Congress sought to satisfy authors and the business community by requiring strict procedures and limiting the period of time when transfers could be terminated. As a result, the rules regarding terminations of transfers are complex.

Grants Made on or After January 1, 1978

Section 203 of the Copyright Act of 1976 provides that an author, or the author's immediate family, may, in certain circumstances, terminate a grant of rights made on or after January 1, 1978.[5] In other words, certain types of transfers may be canceled and the author or the author's family may reclaim those rights. This right of termination cannot be waived in advance or contracted away. For example, an author licenses his book to a publisher for seventy years. After thirty-five years from publication, the author may automatically terminate that transfer and renegotiate those rights at a better price.

Only Certain Grants May Be Terminated

Section 203 provides only for termination of transfers executed by the author on or after January 1, 1978. This right to terminate *does not* include the following:

- *transfers made prior to 1978.* Section 203 is not retroactive and does not permit termination of earlier grants. However, earlier grants may be terminated pursuant to the provisions of 17 *United States Code* section 304, discussed in the text that follows.
- *works made for hire.* Grants or transfers of works made for hire may not be terminated under Section 203.
- *works protected under foreign copyright law.* Congress did not intend to interfere with agreements made under foreign copyright laws. Therefore, if an author licenses a foreign publisher to publish a translation of his book, the right to terminate would not extend to the foreign publication.
- *grants made in an author's will.* A grant made by an author in a will cannot be terminated. For example, if an author, in her will, grants a license to publish to an organization or company, that grant may not be terminated.

In addition, the right to terminate does not include related trademark and character licensing rights and ownership rights in the material object in which the work is first fixed. Finally, the owners of derivative works prepared from the work can continue to distribute the derivative works.

Who May Terminate a Grant

Under section 203, the author may terminate the grant or, if the author dies prior to exercising the right to terminate, that right may be exercised as follows:

- the widow or widower owns the author's entire termination interest unless there are any surviving children or grandchildren of the author, in which case the widow or widower owns one-half of the author's interest;

- the author's surviving children, and the surviving children of any dead child of the author, own the author's entire termination interest unless there is a widow or widower, in which case the ownership of one-half of the author's interest is divided among them;
- in the event that the author's widow or widower, children, and grandchildren are not living, the author's executor, administrator, personal representative, or trustee shall own the author's entire termination interest.

Transfer Termination Rules for Transfers Executed on or After January 1, 1978

Termination rights do not apply to	Transfers made prior to 1978. (However, earlier grants may be terminated pursuant to renewal procedures of section 304, discussed in text in section entitled "Terminating Grants Made Prior to 1978.") Works made for hire Works protected under foreign copyright law Grants made in an author's will
Work published before the date of a grant	The transfer may be terminated any time during a five-year period that starts at the end of thirty-five years from the execution of the grant. For example, John publishes a book in 1990. He assigns rights to the book in 1992. The grant may be terminated between January 1, 2028, and December 31, 2032.
Work has not been published prior to the grant	The transfer may be terminated any time during a five-year period beginning either: at the end of thirty-five years from the date of publication under the grant, or at the end of forty years from the date the grant was executed, whichever term ends earlier. For example, John assigns a license for his book in 1992. The company publishes the book in 1994. The applicable five-year period would be thirty-five years from the date of publication under the grant (that is, January 1, 2028), as that is the *earlier* period. If the grant does not involve publication, termination may occur within a five-year period beginning thirty-five years from the grant.
Method of terminating transfer	Review procedures in Copyright Act (17 *United States Code* section 203) and in *Code of Federal Regulations*.
Office action: What should be done if administering or managing a copyright	At time license or grant is executed: - determine if transfer is exempt from termination rights; - if not exempt, calendar the period when termination may occur and document termination period in copyright administration files; - notify the author or heirs (by letter) of termination period.

As for joint authors, termination of a grant may be made by a majority of authors who executed the grant. If any such joint author is dead, that author's right to terminate may be exercised by the surviving spouse, children, grandchildren, or the executor, as the case may be.

TERMINATING GRANTS MADE PRIOR TO 1978

As noted previously, the Copyright Act of 1909 provided an initial term of twenty-eight years and a renewal term of twenty-eight years. The renewal term was subsequently lengthened, first to forty-seven years and eventually to sixty-seven years. Two methods exist whereby transfers are terminated for works registered under the Copyright Act of 1909.

Works in Their Initial Twenty-Eight-Year Term

Consider the following example: An author assigns all rights to her novel to a publisher in 1961. The assignment agreement states that the publisher will own copyright for the initial and renewal term of copyright. The novel is published in 1962. The author dies in 1980. Will the publisher own copyright in the book during the renewal term? Not necessarily. During the last year of the initial twenty-eight-year term of copyright, the author's estate may renew copyright. By renewing copyright, the author's estate effectively terminates all prior grants, even if the author had promised the renewal rights to the publisher. The estate could grant rights for the renewal period to another party. However, if the author were alive at the time of renewal, she would be bound by the terms of the assignment. Note that under the 1909 act, the term *estate* does not refer specifically to family members of the author. The estate can also be an institution or a foundation, as in the case of Kahil Gibran mentioned previously, or the *Rear Window* case that follows.

Derivative Rights: The *Rear Window* Case

In 1942, the author Cornell Woolrich published a story entitled "It Had to Be Murder." He assigned the motion picture rights to a movie company that adapted the story into the film *Rear Window*. Woolrich agreed to renew the copyright and to assign the renewal rights to the film company. However, he died in 1968 before he could renew the copyright. The executor for his estate renewed copyright in the story in 1969 and assigned the rights to Abend, who sued to prevent any further distribution of the movie *Rear Window*. Abend believed he owned all rights to control derivatives from the story. The United States Supreme Court agreed,[6] stating that if an author dies before the renewal term has occurred, any promise to assign renewal rights is ineffective. Therefore, the movie company, even if they had been making, selling, and distributing the film for many years, must renegotiate with the owner of the renewal rights. The underlying principle is the same as for the termination of all grants—the renewal term gives the author's family or estate the opportunity to renegotiate any previously negotiated rights.

Automatic Renewal and Termination of Derivative Transfers

In 1991, Congress amended the Copyright Act to provide automatic renewal, meaning that owners of works in the last year of the renewal period no longer had to renew copyright. Protection would be automatically renewed without filing. However, the law provided certain incentives for authors to continue to voluntarily file for renewal of copyright during the twenty-eighth year. One incentive is that by filing a renewal, the author can prevent the continued use of the work in derivative works. For example, an author publishes a novel in 1965, which is adapted for a movie produced in 1970. The first renewal period for the novel ends in 1993. The owner of copyright does not have to do anything to maintain protection. The work is automatically protected for an additional sixty-seven-year period. However, if the work is voluntarily renewed by filing with the Copyright Office, the owners of copyright in the movie may not continue to distribute or perform the film without the permission of the novel's author.

Works in Their Extended Renewal Term

Congress added further protection for works published under the 1909 act. Section 304 of the Copyright Act of 1976[7] provides that for works in the extended renewal term (the sixty-seven-year period following the initial twenty-eight-year term), a transfer may be terminated at two different times: fifty-six or seventy-five years after first publication of the work.

For example, for a work published in 1970, the heirs will have two termination periods: one beginning in 2026 (fifty-six years from when copyright vested), and a second in 2045 (the start of the proposed twenty-year extension). Notices of termination of transfers may be effected at any time during a period of five years beginning at the end of fifty-six years or seventy-five years from the date copyright was originally secured. For example, John published and registered his book in 1974 and assigned rights to the book in 1982. The book was published in 1994. John may terminate rights at any time during January 1, 2030, through December 31, 2034 (the five-year period beginning fifty-six years after the date protection was secured) or at any time during January 1, 2049, through December 31, 2054 (the five-year period beginning seventy-five years after the date protection was secured).

With a few exceptions, the rules regarding section 203, which pertain to terminating transfers, also apply to grants for works in the extended renewal period under the 1909 act. One exception is that under section 203, only grants made by the author may be terminated. Under section 304, however, grants may be terminated that were made by the author or the author's beneficiaries during the renewal period. Grants for derivative rights may not be terminated during the extended renewal period. Section 201.10 of the *Code of Federal Regulations*[8] provides the system by which a notice of termination for works in an extended term is accomplished.

Rules for Terminating Transfers Made Prior to January 1, 1978

Work in its initial twenty-eight-year term	The work is automatically protected for an additional sixty-seven-year period. However, if the work is voluntarily renewed by filing with the Copyright Office, the author or heirs may terminate grants such as derivative rights made during the initial term. For voluntary renewal procedures, *United States Code* section 304 as amended in 1992.
Work in its extended renewal term of sixty-seven years	If the work is not (a) a work made for hire; (b) a work protected under foreign copyright law; or (c) a grant made in an author's will, the author, heirs, or executor (if there are no surviving heirs) may terminate a transfer at two different points: during a five-year period beginning at the end of fifty-six years from the date protection was first granted, or any time during a period beginning on January 1, 1978, whichever is later; or at the end of seventy-five years from date protection was first granted.
Terminating a transfer	Review procedures in *Code of Federal Regulations* section 201.10.
Office action: What should be done if administering or managing a copyright	▪ Calendar the period when termination may occur and include the information in the appropriate copyright files. ▪ If client is author, assignee, or licensee, notify by letter of possible termination rights and period of termination.

Failure to Give Notice of Termination

If notice of termination is not given or properly recorded with the Copyright Office, there is no change in the grant of rights. For example, if an author granted a right of publication to a publisher and the author failed to terminate the grant in a timely manner, the publisher will continue to have the right to publish the work under the original agreement.

Exercising Recovered Rights

Rights that are recovered by the termination process can be granted again. All persons alive on the effective date of the notice of termination are entitled to recover rights whether they joined in signing the notice or not. That is, if three persons are entitled to terminate and two of them sign and serve the notice of termination, the third party will be bound. A sole beneficiary may make future grants without restriction. However, if there are multiple beneficiaries or co-owners, the same number and proportion of owners who can terminate also may grant the new right. It does not matter if it is the same persons who terminated the grant; it only matters that the same *number* of persons and proportion of interest make the new grant. An agreement to transfer these rights must be executed after the date of termination.

END NOTES

1. *In re* Marriage of Worth, 195 Cal. App. 3d 768, 241 Cal. Rptr. 185 (1987). *Cf.* Rodrique v. Rodrique, 50 U.S.P.Q.2d 1278 (E.D. La. 1999).
2. 17 U.S.C. § 204(a).
3. Broadcast Music, Inc. v. Hirsch, 104 F.3d 1163 (9th Cir. 1997).
4. Gibran v. National Comm. of Gibran, 255 F.2d 121 (2d Cir. 1958).
5. 17 U.S.C. § 203.
6. Stewart v. Abend, 495 U.S. 207 (1990).
7. 17 U.S.C. § 304.
8. 37 C.F.R. § 201.10.

CHAPTER 16

Copyright Research

This chapter provides methods for performing copyright research and obtaining copyright rules and procedures. Information is furnished regarding:

- obtaining information and records from the Copyright Office;
- researching the copyright status of a work;
- using the Internet to locate copyright information; and
- contacting the Licensing Division of the Copyright Office.

It may take weeks to receive Copyright Office documents by mail. The same documents can be retrieved in minutes over the Internet. For this reason, use of the Internet is strongly recommended for most copyright research activities.

OBTAINING INFORMATION FROM THE COPYRIGHT OFFICE

The Copyright Office is the best source of easy-to-understand information on copyright law and procedures. The Copyright Office publishes:

- information circulars;
- answers to common questions;
- announcements of changes in federal regulations;
- compulsory licensing guidelines; and
- information on pending legislation.

These materials can be obtained by writing to the Copyright Office or by accessing the Copyright Office website. Circulars and publications can also be ordered by calling the Forms and Publications twenty-four-hour Hotline. An index of circulars is provided in Appendix C.

- **Copyright Office:** http://lcweb.loc.gov/copyright or write to Library of Congress, Washington, DC 20559-6000. (For publications, write to Publications Section, LM-455.) Information: (202) 707-3000. Fax-on-Demand: (202) 707-2600.

Additional phone numbers and websites are provided in Appendix A.

Fax-on-Demand Service

Frequently requested Copyright Office circulars and announcements are also available via the Copyright Office's fax-on-demand telephone line. The procedure is simple. Call the fax-on-demand number at (202) 707-2600. Follow instructions to obtain an index of document numbers. Key in the phone number where the documents should be faxed. Up to three items can be ordered at one time. The documents are usually faxed within minutes of the phone call. Copyright application forms are not available by fax.

RESEARCHING COPYRIGHT STATUS

Copyright research may be necessary when trying to determine the public domain status of a work, the ownership of a work, or issues related to infringement. The first step is to investigate the basic facts surrounding the work at issue (that is, the name of the author, copyright owner, year of publication, and so on). In addition, it may be necessary to locate information about the *status* of the copyrighted work. For example, has ownership been transferred? There are several methods of researching a copyrighted work, and various combinations of these methods are often necessary:

- examine copies of the work;
- search records at the Copyright Office in person;
- search the Copyright Office files over the Internet;
- hire the Copyright Office to perform searches;
- search the Internet; or
- hire private companies to perform searches.

Examining the Work

Begin any copyright investigation by examining the work. Looking at a book, computer program, or compact disc may provide information such as the date of publication, copyright claimant, and author. In addition, review the copyright notice. You can be fairly certain that the name in the copyright notice is accurate as of the date of publication. However, it is possible that ownership may have been transferred since then. In any case, the name in the notice provides a starting point for identifying the owner. If the work was published in the United States before 1923, it is in the public domain. If published between 1923 and before 1964, it is in the public domain if the work was not renewed. If the work was first published before March 1, 1989, and did not include copyright notice, the work may be in the public domain. For more information on omission of notice, see Chapter 17. In addition to the notice, identifying codes such as ISBN and ISSN numbers (see the next section) and sound recording tracking numbers (such as ALMOCD004) can be helpful in learning about copyright ownership and status.

ISBNs and ISSNs.   All literary publications have a standardized numbering system: ISBNs (International Standard Book Numbers) are used for books, and ISSNs (International Standard Serial Numbers) are used for magazines, journals, newsletters, and other serialized publications. These numbers can be found on or near the title or copyright page or near the publication's UPC bar code. Since several numbers may be printed on the bar code, make sure the number is preceded either by ISSN or ISBN. For information about obtaining an ISSN or ISBN, call the Copyright Office at (202) 707-6372.

Searching Records at the Copyright Office

It is possible to inspect Copyright Office records by visiting the Library of Congress in Washington, DC, located at 101 Independence Avenue, S.E., on the fourth floor of the James Madison Memorial Building, between the hours of 8:30 A.M. and 5 P.M. weekdays (except holidays). There is an extensive card catalog in room 459. Alternatively, a person may ask the Reference and Bibliography section in room 450 to conduct a search for an hourly fee. Extensive information on the Copyright Office card catalog can be obtained by visiting the Copyright Office website and downloading Circular 23 or by using fax-on-demand, discussed earlier. A listing of copyright search fees is provided in Appendix G.

Catalog of Copyright Entries (CCE).   The Catalog of Copyright Entries (CCE) is divided according to the classes of works registered. The CCE contains the same information as the card catalog, but is in book form (and is actually more complete than the card catalog). Portions of the CCE are available only in microfiche form (a photographic format requiring a special viewer). The CCE contains essential facts about registrations but does not include verbatim reproductions of the registration record. There is a time lag, so more recent registrations may not be included. Finally, the CCE cannot be used for researching the transfer of rights, since it does not include entries for assignments or other recorded documents. The CCE is available not only at the Copyright Office but also in many libraries throughout the country—typically university research libraries and large libraries such as the New York Public Library.

Day of the LOCIS: Searching Copyright Office Files over the Internet

Searchers can connect to the Library of Congress Information System (LOCIS) through use of an Internet system known as Telnet. Telnet is an online text-only system, which means there are no images. Telnet is more challenging to use than a typical Internet connection and requires special software that can be obtained for free from an Internet service provider. Telnet usually works in one of two ways. One way is to have a Telnet account and run the software by itself connected to the Telnet system via telephone. The other, more common, way is to "piggy-back" the program on an Internet connection. Using this method, a user would start an Internet program (for example, Netscape) and then, once connected to the Internet, start the Telnet program.

If unable to connect to LOCIS, a user should contact his or her Internet service provider. The Copyright Office does not offer search assistance to users of LOCIS and also does not offer assistance with software, hardware, or other computer-related problems.

- **LOCIS Telnet address:** Once connected via Telnet, go to: LOCIS.LOC.GOV (the numeric address is 140.147.254.3). Note: these addresses will not work if typed into a web browser. A Telnet connection must be used.

LOCIS contains a series of copyright files. It is possible to search multiple files at one time, following the instructions in the Search Guide, a description of which follows. All copyright information is located in the following three directories:

1. **COHM:** Contains information about works registered since January 1978. Included are published and unpublished text, maps, motion pictures, music, sound recordings, works of the performing and visual arts, graphic arts works, games, mask works, and so on. Also included are renewals of previous registrations. You can search by author, claimant, title, and registration number. COHM is updated weekly. Note: the renewal information available on LOCIS is available only for works published after 1949.
2. **COHS:** Contains information about serial publications (magazine or other periodic publications). COHS is updated twice yearly.
3. **COHD:** Contains copyright registrations and other documents including assignments and other transfers. COHD is updated weekly.

LOCIS Guide. The Library of Congress has prepared the LOCIS Quick Search Guide, a thirty-page publication intended for users of the LOCIS file. The Quick Search Guide is available in three versions for downloading. It can be acquired using file transfer protocol (FTP). Every Internet service provider provides a method for FTP transfers. Go to FTP.LOC.GOV and get the documents from the directory/pub/lc.online. Printed copies of the Quick Search Guide are also available from the Library of Congress Cataloging Distribution Service. Call (202) 707-6100, or fax to (202) 707-1334.

LOCIS Commands and Prompts. LOCIS searching is built around a series of commands, prompts, and abbreviations. For example, to display a record in full (not an abbreviated form), the user must type "d full" along with the number of the record; to go to the next record, the user must type "n." For copyright purposes, the following abbreviations are especially important:

- AUTH (author)
- DREG (date of registration)
- CLNA (name of copyright claimant or owner)
- DCRE (date of creation)
- DPUB (date of publication)
- OREG (original date of registration, or in the case of renewals, original registration number)

■ ODAT (original date of publication)
The following is an example of a renewal record from the COHM file:

> RE-438-737
> TITL: Franny and Zooey. By Jerome David Salinger.
> CLNA: J. D. Salinger (A)
> DREG: 10Oct89
> ODAT: 23Aug61
> OREG: A591015
> LINM: NM: author's note
> XREF: acJ. D. Salinger. SEE Jerome David Salinger, 1919-

Searching Performed by the Copyright Office

The Copyright Office will search the Copyright Office records for an hourly fee (or fraction of an hour). A search is usually initiated by submission of a Search Request Form (see form included here) or by calling (202) 707-6850. The Copyright Office will quote a fee for such services. A search may be expedited, but the fees are higher—as much as $125 for the first hour and $75 per hour (or fraction of an hour) after that. See Appendix G for fee information. For more information, consult the Copyright Office website, Copyright Circular 22, or 37 *Code of Federal Regulations* section 201 *et seq.*

Search Request Form. The following is an example of the Copyright Office's special "Search Request Form."

SEARCH REQUEST FORM

TYPE OF WORK:

___ Book ___ Music ___ Motion Picture ___ Drama ___ Sound Recording
___ Photograph/Artwork ___ Map ___ Periodical ___ Contribution
___ Computer Program ___ Mask Work

SEARCH INFORMATION YOU REQUIRE:

___ Registration ___ Renewal ___ Assignment ___ Address

SPECIFICS OF WORK TO BE SEARCHED:
TITLE: _____
AUTHOR: _____
COPYRIGHT CLAIMANT (if known): _____ (name in copyright notice)
APPROXIMATE YEAR DATE OF PUBLICATION/CREATION: _____
REGISTRATION NUMBER (if known): _____
OTHER IDENTIFYING INFORMATION: _____

(Cont'd)

Search Request Form (Cont'd)

If you need more space please attach additional pages.

YOUR NAME: _____ DATE: _____

ADDRESS: _____

_____

DAYTIME TELEPHONE NO. (____) _____

Convey results of estimate/search by telephone? ____ yes ____ no

Fee Enclosed? ____ yes Amount $_____ ____no

Good Faith Searching

The records in the Copyright Office may not always provide all of the information needed to research ownership because registration of copyright and the filing of copyright assignments are not mandatory. However, even if records of ownership cannot be found, the act of searching demonstrates good faith in the event that the searcher is later sued over an unauthorized use.

Searching the Internet

The Internet is a good source of information about copyrighted works. Performing rights organizations such as ASCAP and BMI allow users to search catalogs containing millions of songs online. Information about books can be located at online bookstores such as amazon.com or barnesandnoble.com. Out-of-print books can be researched at the R.R. Bowker site. Information about authors can be obtained from the Author's Registry. The Software Publishers Association (SPA) can provide information about owners of computer programs. These and other websites are listed in Appendix A.

Private Search Companies

Companies provide searches of Copyright Office records for a fee. These companies provide additional information such as tracing the copyright history of a fictional character or locating similarly titled works. Some companies provide information regarding copyright clearance. That is, they can determine if a work is in the public domain or whether rights can be obtained in relation to the work. Clearance and search companies are listed in Appendix A.

OBTAINING COPIES OF COPYRIGHT OFFICE RECORDS

If basic information is known about a work (that is, name of author, title of work, year of publication), copies of registrations and records can be acquired directly from the Copyright Office.

Seeking a Certified Registration

If an additional certificate of registration is required, the following should be furnished to the Copyright Office:

- title;
- type of work involved (that is, novel, lyrics, and so on);
- registration number including the preceding letters (for example, TX000-000);
- year of registration or publication;
- author(s) name including any pseudonym by which the author may be known;
- any other information needed to identify the registration; and
- the appropriate fee should accompany the request, in the form of a check or money order payable to the Register of Copyrights. A listing of copyright fees is provided in Appendix G.

Certification of copyright records is often necessary for litigation or other activities and requires an additional fee.

Seeking Other Forms of Documentation

If documentation other than registration is required, a request for copies should clearly identify the records to be copied. The request should include the following information, if possible:

- type of work involved (that is, novel, lyrics, and so on);
- registration number including the preceding letters (for example, TX000-000);
- year date or approximate year date of registration (for example, 1985);
- complete title of the work;
- author(s) names including any pseudonym by which the author may be known;
- claimant(s) name;
- if the requested copy is of an assignment, license, contract, or other recorded document, the volume and page number of the recorded document.
- specify whether certified or uncertified copies are required (see the next section);
- comply with any special requirements that are outlined in the following text for obtaining copies of certain types of documents; and
- include telephone number and address.

Certification of Documents

A certified copy of a public record includes a statement under the seal of the Copyright Office attesting that the document is a true copy of the record in question. Certified copies are often requested as evidence of the authenticity of documents when litigation is involved. The Certification and Documents section will review requests for other copies and quote fees for each document. A list of copyright certification fees is provided in Appendix G.

Obtaining Copies of Deposits

In some cases, a person may need a copy of a work, not just the registration. For example, an attorney may want to view a copy of the work as it was registered with the Copyright Office. The Copyright Office will provide certified or uncertified reproductions of works if one of the following conditions is met:

- written authorization is received from the copyright claimant, his or her agent, or the owner of any exclusive right (as demonstrated by written documentation of the ownership transfer);
- written request is received from the attorney for a plaintiff or defendant in copyright litigation involving the copyrighted work. Such a request must include (a) names of all parties and nature of the controversy; (b) name of the court where the case is pending; and (c) satisfactory assurance that reproduction will only be used in connection with the litigation;[1] or
- a court order is received for a reproduction of a deposited article, facsimile, or identifying portion of a work that is the subject of litigation in its jurisdiction.

The Copyright Office will review each request and quote a fee. Write to Certifications and Documents Section, LM-402, Copyright Office, Library of Congress, Washington, DC 20559.

Where to Send Requests

All requests for certified or uncertified copies of Copyright Office records or deposits should be made to the Certifications and Documents Section, LM-402, Copyright Office, Library of Congress, Washington, DC 20559, (202) 707-6787. It is also possible to walk into the Copyright Office Certifications Department on the fourth floor of the James Madison Memorial Building in Washington, DC, between the hours of 8:30 A.M. and 5 P.M. weekdays (except holidays). For more information, see Copyright Office Circular 6.

LICENSING DIVISION

In several of the preceding chapters, information is provided about compulsory licensing procedures for cable TV, jukeboxes, and commercial and noncommercial broadcasting. To locate information about existing licenses or procedures for obtaining a license, contact the Licensing Division of the Copyright Office, LM-458, Copyright Office, Library of Congress, Washington, DC 20559, (202) 707-8150.

END NOTE

1. *See* 37 C.F.R. § 201.2(d).

CHAPTER 17
Copyright Notice

This chapter deals with copyright notice. Information is provided regarding:

- form of copyright notice;
- placement of notice;
- effect of notice omission under the 1909 and 1976 acts;
- reform of notice omission law; and
- restoration of copyright for foreign works published without notice.

NOTICE OF COPYRIGHT

The most visible sign of copyright ownership is the copyright notice—the © symbol or the word *copyright* followed by the year of first publication and the name of the copyright claimant. For most of the twentieth century, Congress required that every visually perceptible published copy contain a notice of copyright ownership. If the notice was omitted, there were drastic penalties. Many works fell into the public domain simply because the owner failed to include the proper copyright notice. The rationale for requiring copyright notice was that it informed the public that the work was protected.

The law regarding copyright notice changed with the passage of the Berne Convention Implementation Act of 1988. In order to affiliate with the Berne Convention, an international copyright treaty, the United States amended the Copyright Act so that works first published on or after March 1, 1989, do not have to include notice. Despite this change, the voluntary use of copyright notice is recommended, and certain incentives exist for its continued use.

Notice Required on Visually Perceptible Copies

Copyright notice is only required on visually perceptible copies. A visually perceptible copy is a copy that can be seen directly or with the aid of a device. For example, books, paintings, drawings, films, architectural plans, and computer programs are all visually perceptible. Some copies of works are not visually perceptible. When a book is recorded on audiotape, the literary work is not visually perceptible. A listener can hear it, but not *see* it, so copyright notice is not required on the cassette. Similarly, a song on a compact disc is not visually perceptible. However, copyright notice would be required on sheet music because the words and music notation are visible.

17 U.S.C. § 401(a) Notice of copyright: Visually perceptible copies

Whenever a work protected under this title is published in the United States or elsewhere by authority of the copyright owner, a notice of copyright as provided by this section may be placed on publicly distributed copies from which the work can be visually perceived, either directly or with the aid of a machine or device.

FORM OF COPYRIGHT NOTICE

The copyright notice has three elements: the symbol © or word "Copyright"; the year of first publication; and the name or abbreviation of the owner of copyright. Although the order is not set forth in the Copyright Act of 1976, the elements are traditionally presented as follows:

© 1998 Microsoft Corporation *or*
Copyright 1998 Microsoft Corporation

The only exception to this is for phonorecords, discussed later in this chapter.

17 U.S.C. § 401(b) Form of notice

If a notice appears on the copies, it shall consist of the following three elements:
(1) the symbol © (the letter C in a circle), or the word "Copyright," or the abbreviation "Copr."; and
(2) the year of first publication of the work; in the case of compilations or derivative works incorporating previously published material, the year date of first publication of the compilation or derivative work is sufficient. The year date may be omitted where a pictorial, graphic, or sculptural work, with accompanying text matter, if any, is reproduced in or on greeting cards, postcards, stationery, jewelry, dolls, toys, or any useful articles; and
(3) the name of the owner of copyright in the work, or an abbreviation by which the name can be recognized, or a generally known alternative designation of the owner.

The Copyright Symbol

The copyright symbol ©, the word "Copyright," or the abbreviation "Copr." are all acceptable notice. However, it is preferable to use the © symbol because the Universal Copyright Convention, an international treaty, has adopted the © symbol as the *only* accepted symbol of copyright protection. Therefore, to guarantee protection for works that may be placed in international commerce, it is advisable to use the © symbol. As for phonorecords of sound recordings, the symbol ℗ should be used (the letter "p" in a circle).

Copyright Symbols on a Word Processor. Most computer users can access the © symbol on word processing programs even though the symbol is not identified on the keyboard. Look for "Insert Symbol" or look in the Help file of the program or in the index of the program manual under "Special Characters" or "Symbols" or "ASCII Characters." Not all programs include the ℗ symbol.

Year of First Publication

The copyright notice must include the year when the work is *first* published. This date would either be the year:

- when copies are first distributed to the public; or
- when the author first offered the work for distribution, public performance, or public display.

It is *not* a publication to:

- make copies of a work if the copies are not distributed;
- publicly perform a work;
- display a work; or
- send copies of the work to the Copyright Office.

A musical work is not published if the work was recorded and the recording was distributed to the public prior to 1978. However, a musical work is considered to be published if recorded and the recording is distributed after January 1, 1978.

A "limited publication"—that is, distribution of copies limited in number and purpose—is also not a publication. For example, previewing a movie to a select group[1] or distributing architectural plans to building authorities[2] are both limited publications.

17 U.S.C. § 101 Publication

"Publication" is the distribution of copies or phonorecords of a work to the public by sale or other transfer of ownership, or by rental, lease, or lending. The offering to distribute copies or phonorecords to a group of persons for purposes of further distribution, public performance, or public display, constitutes publication. A public performance or display of a work does not of itself constitute publication.

There is no required form for presenting the year of first publication. For example, the year 1995 may be presented as 1995, Nineteen Ninety Five, Nineteen Hundred & Ninety Five, or MCMLXXXXV. Altering the date of publication on the notice could adversely affect the rights of the copyright owner. However, if a new version of the work is published, the date should be changed to reflect publication of the new version. To qualify as a new version (for example, a derivative), there must be more than editing or correction of errors. For example, a new version is created when an author adds a new chapter to a book or additional program code is added to computer software.

No Requirement to Include the Year: Greeting Cards and Useful Articles. Certain industries successfully lobbied Congress for the right to omit the year on copyright notice, and as a result, the date can be omitted on greeting cards, stationery, jewelry, toys, or useful articles on which a pictorial, graphic, or sculptural work (and accompanying text) is included.[3] For example, in 1997, Bob Smith published a greeting card with an original cartoon. He may use the notice: © Bob Smith.

Name of Copyright Owner

The owner of copyright is the "name" that should be used in the copyright notice. Since the author may transfer various rights to different people, the name in the copyright notice depends upon the version of the work. For example, Mario Puzo is the author of the novel *The Godfather* and the original owner of copyright. Paramount is the exclusive owner of the rights to the motion picture *The Godfather.* Paramount is the name that should be used on the copyright notice for the motion picture.

An abbreviation or a generally known alternative for the owner's name also can be used. For example, © 2000 ABC can be used for the American Broadcasting Company. If there is more than one owner of a work, the names of all of the copyright owners should appear on the notice. For example, if George Earth and Joan Sunn jointly own a work, the notice would read © 2001 George Earth & Joan Sunn.

Error in Name.   If the person named in the notice is not the owner of copyright, this error can be corrected by either:

- recording a statement in the Copyright Office (signed by the person named in the notice) that states the correct ownership; or
- registering the work in the name of the true owner or owners.

For example, if copyright notice incorrectly listed Bill Jones as the owner, instead of Tom Smith, Bill Jones could correct the error by recording a document with the Copyright Office, stating that Tom Smith is the owner. Alternatively, Tom Smith could correct the error by registering the work in his own name.

Derivative Works

Copyright notice for derivative works should express the owner of the derivative and year of first publication of the derivative. For example, the Alfred Hitchcock film *Psycho* was released in 1960. The copyright in the 1960 film was owned by Alfred Hitchcock's company, Shamley. In 1998, director Gus Van Sant released his version of *Psycho,* a shot-by-shot recreation of the 1960 film. The

1998 film is a derivative work owned by Imagine Entertainment, and the copyright notice for this film should be: © 1998 Imagine Entertainment.

Although it is not required by law, many copyright owners indicate a range of years for a work. For example, on the introductory screen of a computer program, it is common to see a copyright notice expressed as © 1994–2000 or © 1994, 1995, 1998, 2000 to encompass the original and derivative versions.

It is also acceptable to specify new and old copyrighted materials by separate dates. For example, Jane McLear published a book in 1996. In 2000, the book is published with a new introduction by Mimi Snow. The notice may read: © 1996 Jane McLear; introduction © 2000 Mimi Snow.

Collective Works and Contributions to Collective Works

Generally, copyright notice for a collective work protects all works included within the collection. For example, if Bookco selects and groups several articles about baseball into a book entitled *Great Baseball Stories* and publishes the collection in 2001, the copyright notice for the book would be: © 2001 Bookco.

This notice provides the legal requirement for notice for each individual work. However, it is advisable for the owner of each story to have a separate copyright notice. This gives warning to potential infringers of the work and prevents an infringer from arguing that the copying was "innocent."

Advertisements Appearing in Collective Works. Under the Copyright Act of 1976, copyright notice for a collective work does not extend to advertisements. For example, copyright notice in a newspaper will protect the editorial content such as the stories and news photos, but it will not extend to any portion of an advertisement. Therefore, the owner of copyright of an advertisement should *always* include a separate notice.

Sound Recordings

Two copyrights coexist in a recording—a sound recording copyright (for example, protection of the particular arrangement of recorded sounds), and the underlying musical work copyright (protection for a song) or underlying literary or dramatic work copyright. Sound recordings embodied on phonorecords are required to include a special notice—the symbol ℗ (the letter "P" in a circle) followed by the year of first publication of the sound recording and the name of the copyright holder, for example: ℗ 1998 RossCo.

There is no word or substitute symbol for the sound recording symbol ℗. The notice should appear on the compact disc or packaging. The symbol ℗ is *only* used for sound recordings. All other copyrightable works embodied on phonorecords (such as a song, spoken word recordings, or motion picture soundtrack) are not required to have a notice because they are not visually perceptible. In other words, the song or literary work cannot be *seen*.

Often, a compact disc or cassette tape will have two notices, such as: ℗ 2000 Pretend Records and © 2000 Pretend Records. The ℗ notice indicates protection of the sound recording. The © notice indicates protection of the artwork and accompanying text used on the cover, booklet, or label. No copyright notice is required for musical works embodied on the sound recordings unless the lyrics are printed.

Works Using United States Government Publications

Any work published before March 1, 1989, that includes works of the United States government must include a special notice indicating portions of the work consist of United States Government publications. For example, if, in 1987, Bookco published a book about the army that incorporates a United States military manual, the notice should state:

> © 1987 Bookco. Copyright is not claimed to the U.S. Government military manual excerpted in Chapter Twelve.

This government notice requirement is optional for works first published on or after March 1, 1989. However, use of the notice is recommended because it can prevent an infringer from arguing that the copying was "innocent."

Unpublished Works

Copyright notice is not required on unpublished works. However, since issues may arise as to whether a work is published or unpublished, it is advisable to include a notice. For example:

> Unpublished © 1990 Artie Rimshot.

General Rules About Form for Copyright Notice

The following is a summary of the rules of notice for different types of works:

- *General rule for most works.* Apply © or "Copyright" or "Copr." (although © is recommended for international publication) with year of first publication and name (or abbreviation) of copyright owner on all visually perceptible copies.
- *Derivatives.* Apply © or "Copyright" or "Copr." with year of first publication of derivative and name of copyright owner of derivative on all visually perceptible copies.
- *Compilations.* Apply © or "Copyright" or "Copr." with year of first publication of compilation or collective work and name of copyright owner of compilation or collective work on all visually perceptible copies. This copyright notice will protect authors of separately copyrightable contributions (except advertisements). However, it is recommended that a separate copyright notice be used by each author for separately copyrightable works within the compilation.

- *Sound recordings.* Apply ℗ with year of first publication and name (or abbreviation) of copyright owner of the sound recording. Apply to disc or packaging. Use © or "Copyright" or "Copr." to protect cover art, printed lyrics, or other materials included on the packaging.

PLACEMENT OF COPYRIGHT NOTICE

Where should the copyright notice be placed? Section 401 of the Copyright Act of 1976[4] states that notice shall be affixed to the copies "in such manner and location as to give reasonable notice of the claim of copyright." Regulations regarding notice placement are located at 37 *Code of Federal Regulations* section 201.20. The complete regulations may be obtained from the Copyright Office by requesting Circular 96. In addition, Circular 3 explains the basics of copyright notice. The following list indicates some acceptable placements for copyright notice:

- *Books.* Place notice on title page or on page immediately following the title page; or on either side of the front cover or back cover; or, if no title page or cover, on first or last page of the work.
- *Single leaf* (two-sided work such as a single sheet). Place notice on front or back.
- *Periodicals or serials.* Follow the same rule as for books; or place it adjacent to the masthead or on the page containing the masthead; or adjacent to a prominent heading (near the front of the issue) containing the title, volume, and date of the issue.
- *Separate contributions to collective works.* Place the notice under the title, near the beginning of the separate contribution; on the first page of the contribution; or immediately following the end of the contribution.
- *Software programs and other machine-readable copies.* Notice can be displayed on the screen when the program begins (for example, when the user signs on); or the notice can be continuously displayed as the program runs. The notice can also be placed on a gummed label securely affixed to the copies (disks or tape), box, or other permanent packaging for the copies. If the computer code for the software program is printed out when copies are deposited, notice can be placed on the printout—usually included within the first or last twenty-five pages.
- *Motion pictures and other audiovisual works.* Notice should be placed either: near the title, or with the cast, credits, and similar information; immediately following the beginning of the work or immediately preceding the end of the work. If the work is sixty seconds or less, the notice should also be placed on the leader of the film. If the work is distributed to the public for private use (for example, videocassettes), the notice should appear on the cassette shell or container.
- *Pictorial, graphic, and sculptural works.* For two-dimensional copies, notice should be affixed permanently to: the front or back of the copies; or

on backing, mounting, framing, or other material. For three-dimensional copies, notice should be affixed permanently to: any visible portion of the work; or on a base, mounting, framing, or other material on which the copies are attached. For works on which it is impractical to affix a notice to copies, even by a durable label (for example, jewelry), notice is acceptable if it appears on a tag or label attached to the copy so that it will remain with it as it passes through commerce, for example a hanging tag. For sheetlike or strip material bearing multiple reproductions (for example, fabrics or wallpaper), notice may be applied: to the margin (known as "selvage") or reverse side of the material at frequent and regular intervals; or if the material has no reverse side or selvage, on labels or tags attached to the copies and to any spools, reels, or containers for the fabric so that the notice is visible as it passes through commerce.

■ *Websites.* Although the Copyright Office has not, as of the writing of this book, provided guidelines for placement of notice on websites, it is advisable to place notice on all displayed pages, not just the "index" or "home" page.

OMISSION OF COPYRIGHT NOTICE

Under certain circumstances, omission of copyright can have a disastrous effect and result in the loss of copyright ownership. The effect of an omission depends upon the date of first publication of the work. As explained in this chapter, the omission of notice has little effect on works first published on or after March 1, 1989. However, regardless of the date of first publication, it is important to know if an omission has occurred. An omission of copyright notice can occur if:

■ notice does not contain the copyright symbol, the word *copyright,* or the appropriate abbreviation;

■ notice is dated more than one year later than the date of first publication;

■ location of the notice is such that it does not give reasonable notice of the claim of copyright, for example, the notice on the back of a painting has been sealed over with backing materials and is no longer visible;

■ notice lacks the statement required for works consisting preponderately of United States government material; or

■ notice lacks name or date (unless the date is not required).

Works Published Under the Copyright Act of 1909

Copyright protection could be secured under the Copyright Act of 1909 only if the owner had published the work with copyright notice. If an authorized copy of a work was published without notice, the work would be placed permanently in the public domain. For example, if a computer chess game was published without notice, the author would lose all rights to the game, and anyone would be free to copy it.[5] Omission of notice was excused only if it resulted from accident or mistake. However, lack of knowledge or the law or negligence is not an excuse.

The issue of omission generally arises when a copyright owner sues an infringer. For example, an artist sued a merchandise company for infringement. The merchandise company located a copy of the artist's work published without notice, and the infringement lawsuit was dismissed. Why? Because the lack of notice placed the work in the public domain. This was what happened in 1970 when the cartoonist Robert Crumb permitted a comic book publisher to use his drawing *Keep on Truckin'* on a business card. When authorizing the use, Crumb did not require notice on the card. Later, when Crumb sued an infringer, the district court declared the cartoon to be in the public domain because it had been published without notice on the business card.[6]

JUDGE LEARNED HAND ON COPYRIGHT: PETER PAN FABRICS

In a 1960 case,[7] Peter Pan Fabrics sued a company that copied its fabrics. In defense, the infringer claimed that Peter Pan Fabrics' copyright was invalid because copies had been published without notice. Peter Pan Fabrics admitted that it *had* removed copyright notice from some of its fabrics because customers complained that the notice (on the edge of the fabric) interfered with clothing production. Judge Hand reasoned that Peter Pan Fabrics would have lost sales if it complied with the statute and the infringer was not misled by the lack of notice. Therefore, Judge Hand refused to invalidate the copyright and place the fabric design in the public domain. This decision predated the changes brought about by the Berne Convention Implementation Act—that an infringer who was not misled by the lack of notice should not be able to profit by such copying.

Restored Works—Foreign Works Published Without Notice Under the 1909 Act. Certain works that are in the public domain because of notice omission can be restored. A work is eligible if it meets *all* of the following requirements:

- the work is in the public domain in the United States because the author failed to follow certain formalities (such as a failure to include notice on published copies or failure to renew);
- at the time the work was created, at least one author must have been a national or domiciliary of an "eligible country." An eligible country is a country, other than the United States, that is a member of the Berne Convention, the World Trade Organization (WTO), or is subject to a presidential proclamation that extends restored copyright protection to that country;

- if published, the work must have first been published in an eligible country and must not have been published in the United States within thirty days following its first publication; and
- copyright protection still exists in the country where the work was created (the "eligible country").

Eligible copyrights are restored automatically. However, if an author or the author's estate wants to enforce rights against persons who relied on the public domain status of the work to reproduce it ("reliance parties"), then the author of a restored work must file a notice of intent with the Copyright Office and with the reliance parties. This notice informs the reliance parties that the work is being restored and to halt future reproductions. For more information, consult Circular 38b. Copies of Circular 38b and the notice of intent are in Chapter 27 and can be downloaded from the Copyright Office website, as explained in Chapter 16.

The "restored copyrights" law became effective on January 1, 1996, and the owner of a restored work cannot sue for infringements that occurred before this date. If restored, the work will be protected for the remainder of the copyright term—that is, the period of protection if the work had never entered the public domain. For example, a Spanish book is first published in Spain in January 1965. In June 1965, it is published without notice in the United States. When copyright is restored, protection will expire on December 31, 2060 (ninety-five years after the United States copyright would have come into existence).

Works Published Between January 1, 1978, and March 1, 1989

The drafters of the Copyright Act of 1976 attempted to alleviate some of the unfairness of the notice requirements of the Copyright Act of 1909. Under the provisions of section 405, omission of notice is excused if:

- the notice was omitted from no more than a relatively small number of copies or phonorecords;
- a reasonable effort is made to add notice to all copies or phonorecords that are distributed after the omission has been discovered and registration of the work is made before or within five years of discovery of the omissions; or
- the notice is omitted in violation of a written agreement, for example, as a condition of licensing the work.

Despite this "savings clause," numerous works published under the Copyright Act of 1976 have fallen into the public domain. Therefore, copyright owners should carefully police all authorized copies to guarantee that the notice is properly affixed. If a work first published before March 1, 1989, is licensed by another company, it is important to determine if notice has been omitted from any of the licensed copies. If notice is omitted and such omission is not corrected, an infringer will be able to argue that copyright is invalid.

The obligation to cure an omitted copyright notice can haunt a copyright owner after March 1, 1989. For example, in 1994, a federal court ruled that the copyright owner of a jewelry design failed to make the required "reasonable effort" to cure the defective notice for a work first published in 1988.[8]

Works Published on or After March 1, 1989

By the 1980s, the United States was the only country that terminated copyright ownership as a result of the omission of notice. In order to affiliate with the international Berne Convention, the United States passed the Berne Implementation Act of 1988, which became effective on March 1, 1989. If copyright is omitted from works first published on or after this date, the owner will not suffer a loss of copyright protection.

Despite the change in the law regarding notice requirements, there are still incentives for the continued use of copyright notice for works published after March 1, 1989. The notice informs the public that the work is protected and identifies the owner. In addition, if the owner has been using the proper notice and there is an infringement, the infringer will not be able to claim that the infringement was "innocent." This determination may affect the amount of damages awarded to the copyright owner. In addition, use of the copyright symbol, ©, may eliminate certain formal requirements in countries that belong to the Universal Copyright Convention (see Chapter 27).

WHAT TO DO WHEN AN OMISSION OF COPYRIGHT NOTICE IS DISCOVERED

The following table summarizes the appropriate course of action to take when a work is published without notice.

Responding to Omission of Copyright Notice

Work is published before 1978	Determine if omission was an accident or mistake as interpreted under section 21 of the Copyright Act of 1909.
Work is published between 1978 and March 1, 1989	Determine if omission can be corrected under section 405 of the Copyright Act of 1976. Consider the following questions: Was the notice omitted from a small number of copies? Can reasonable effort be made to add notice to copies that were distributed? Has the work been registered? Was the publication with the omitted notice done by a licensee or other transferee who was required by written agreement to include the notice as a condition of the agreement?
Work is published after March 1, 1989	Is this a derivative or has the work been published in an earlier form without notice prior to March 1, 1989? Review methods of correcting omission under section 405.

(Cont'd)

Responding to Omission of Copyright Notice (Cont'd)

Work was first published outside the United States	Review the rules on restored copyrights (see Circular 38b), and the section on restored copyrights presented earlier. If applicable, prepare a notice of intent for any person who has relied on the lack of notice.

END NOTES

1. American Vitagraph, Inc. v. Levy, 659 F.2d 1023 (9th Cir. 1981).
2. Schuchart & Assocs., Professional Eng'rs, Inc. v. Solo Serve Corp., 220 U.S.P.Q. 170 (W.D. Tex. 1983).
3. 17 U.S.C. § 401(b)(2).
4. 17 U.S.C. § 401.
5. Data Cash Sys., Inc. v. JS&A Group, 628 F.2d 1038 (7th Cir. 1980).
6. Crumb v. A.A. Sales, 188 U.S.P.Q. 447 (N.D. Cal. 1975). The case was later reversed on appeal. Settlement by the parties precluded a new trial.
7. Peter Pan Fabrics, Inc. v. Martin Weiner Corp., 274 F.2d 487 (2d Cir. 1960).
8. Garnier v. Andin Int'l, Inc., 36 F.3d 1214 (1st Cir. 1994).

CHAPTER 18
Registration and Choosing Correct Application

This chapter and the following three chapters offer information on the copyright application and registration process. Information is provided in this chapter regarding:

- principles and advantages of copyright registration; and
- choice of correct application form.

THE REGISTRATION PROCESS

Registration of copyright is an administrative process. The applicant submits an application, a fee, and deposit materials. An examiner at the Copyright Office determines whether:

- the material deposited constitutes copyrightable subject matter; and
- the legal and formal requirements of copyright law have been met.

If these standards are met, the Register of Copyrights issues a Certificate of Registration to the applicant. The certificate contains the information provided in the application, together with the number and effective date of the registration. If the Copyright Office determines that material deposited does not constitute copyrightable subject matter or that the claim is invalid for any other reason, the Register of Copyrights will refuse registration and notify the applicant in writing of the reasons for the refusal.

Basic Registration

The Copyright Office permits one basic registration to be made for each version of a particular work. This is known as the "single registration rule." For example, one basic registration would be filed for the book *Eight Weeks to Optimum Health,* written by Dr. Andrew Weil. This basic registration serves as the primary copyright record.

Each version of a work is entitled to its own basic registration. For example, if the book *Eight Weeks to Optimum Health* was revised along with a new introduction and additional text, a basic registration would be made for this new version. Similarly, if a motion picture was adapted from the book, a basic registration would be made for the film.

If a basic registration must be corrected or amplified, Form CA would be filed, as explained in the next chapter. If ownership is transferred, a new basic registration would *not* be made. Instead documents or records regarding this transfer of ownership would be filed separately.

Exceptions: More Than One Basic Registration Permitted

There are two exceptions to the general rule of one basic registration per work. In the following situations, the Copyright Office will permit more than one basic registration:

- *Previously registered as unpublished work.* If a work has been previously registered in unpublished form, a second registration can be made to cover the published version. For example, John registers an unpublished computer program. Later, he publishes the computer program in virtually the same format as the unpublished version. Even though there are no substantial changes between the published and unpublished version, John should file a separate registration for the published version.
- *Someone other than the author is identified as copyright claimant.* In cases where someone other than the author is named as the copyright claimant (that is, the owner of copyright), the Copyright Office will later accept an application from the author. For example, John creates a computer program and assigns copyright to WebFunk. WebFunk registers the work, lists John as author, and lists WebFunk as copyright claimant. Later, John reacquires the rights to the program. He may now register the work a second time in his name.

REASONS TO APPLY FOR REGISTRATION

Registration is not mandatory in order to secure copyright protection. However, there are three important reasons to obtain a copyright registration:

1. registration creates a presumption of ownership and validity;
2. if a work has been registered prior to an infringement, the copyright owner may be entitled to statutory damages and attorney fees; and
3. registration is required to file a copyright infringement lawsuit.

Presumption of Ownership and Validity

Registration within five years of first publication creates a legal presumption of ownership and validity. A presumption is an inference as to the truth or validity of an allegation. A presumption of validity shifts the burden to the defendant—the party accused of infringement—to disprove the fact at issue, that is, ownership of the copyright.

For example, Bob registers a claim to copyright to his hand-tinted photographs. He sues Andrea for selling similar photos without his permission. Andrea maintains that she is the owner of copyright and that Bob has stolen the works from her. Because of Bob's registration, the court presumes that Bob is the owner of copyright and that his registration is valid. Andrea has the burden of proving that Bob's registration is not valid and that Bob is not the owner. If she can furnish sufficient evidence regarding either of these allegations, she will have overcome the presumption, and the court will rule in her favor. This legal presumption is also known as *prima facie* (that is, "on first appearance") proof of copyright ownership. The presumptions created by registration are helpful in enforcing copyright, although they do not conclusively prove ownership.

Owner May Recover Statutory Damages and Attorney Fees If Work Is Registered Prior to Infringement

If a copyright owner prevails in an infringement lawsuit, the court determines an amount that will compensate the copyright owner. For example, if an infringer had profits of $10,000 from the infringing activity, the copyright owner would be awarded $10,000. Often it is difficult to prove the extent of the profits or damages. The Copyright Act of 1976 provides that the court, in its discretion, may award damages of between $500 and $20,000 per infringement. In cases of willful infringement, an award up to $100,000 may be granted. These enumerated awards are known as statutory damages. The copyright statute provides for these sums to be awarded and does not require proof of the copyright owner's monetary loss or the infringer's profit.

However, statutory damages will be awarded in a copyright infringement lawsuit only if the work at issue has been registered either (a) prior to the infringement, or (b) within three months of the first publication of the work. For example, WebFunk publishes a new video game, They Came from Within, on May 1, 2000. Diskco infringes the game on June 1, 2000. If WebFunk registers the work within three months of May 1, 2000, WebFunk will be able to obtain statutory damages.

The same rules apply for attorney fees. If a registration has been made within three months of publication or prior to an infringing activity, the copyright owner may be awarded attorney fees incurred in enforcing the copyright. This award is at the discretion of the court. This means that if the court determines fees should be awarded, the infringer may have to pay his own attorney fees *and* the attorney fees for the copyright owner. This can be a substantial deterrent to an accused infringer who is undecided about whether to fight a copyright infringement lawsuit.

Registration Is Required to File an Infringement Lawsuit

An action for infringement cannot be filed until registration of the copyright claim has been made. For example, Sasha discovers that Tom has been selling unauthorized copies of her book *Chihuahua Training Tips*. Sasha has not registered her work. As a condition of filing a lawsuit against Tom, it is mandatory that Sasha register her work. The Certificate of Registration will be referenced in the lawsuit and attached to the lawsuit as an exhibit.

Exception: When Registration Is Not Necessary Prior to Filing an Infringement Suit.   Registration is not required to file an infringement lawsuit in the following situations:

- If registration has been refused by the Copyright Office even though it was in the correct form, the copyright owner can still institute a lawsuit, provided that a copy of the lawsuit is also served on the Register of Copyrights. For example, WebFunk creates a video game, Wall Banger. The Copyright Office refuses to register the work, claiming that the game does not possess sufficient originality. Diskco illegally copies the Wall Banger game. Although the Copyright Office has refused to register the work, WebFunk can still sue for copyright infringement, *provided* that a copy of the infringement lawsuit is also served on the Register of Copyrights.
- Non–United States works that meet the definition of Berne Convention works (the author is a national of a Berne Convention country and the work was first published in a Berne Convention country—see 17 *United States Code* section 101).
- Works of visual art (fine art limited editions of two hundred or fewer copies as defined in 17 *United States Code* sections 101 and 106A).
- If a work is embodied in a physical object simultaneously with its transmission, the owner of that work can institute an infringement lawsuit provided that the owner serves a notice of intent to register and then registers the work within three months of first transmission. For example, the National Football League (NFL) broadcasts the *Super Bowl* football game. The NFL fixes the game on a videotape as the game is broadcast. At the time of the broadcast, Tom videotapes the game and makes copies for sale. The NFL can sue for infringement provided that a notice is served on Tom between ten and thirty days from the date of the game—the date when it was embodied on videotape by the NFL—and that the notice contains certain information including an intent to register. The NFL must register the work within three months after the initial transmission.

REGISTRATION IS NOT MANDATORY FOR COPYRIGHT PROTECTION

Copyright registration is not mandatory under the 1976 Copyright Act, although it is recommended for the reasons explained in this chapter. There is one exception to this rule that applies to works first published on or after January 1, 1978, but before March 1, 1989. If a relatively small number of copies of the work is published without copyright notice, one of the requirements of correcting the omission of notice, according to section 405(a)(2), is to register the work within five years after the publication without a notice. In addition, a reasonable effort must be made to add notice to all copies or phonorecords distributed to the public after the omission is discovered. See Chapter 17 for more information on omission of notice.

---

17 U.S.C. § 408 (a) Registration permissive

At any time during the subsistence of the first term of copyright in any published or unpublished work in which the copyright was secured before January 1, 1978, and during the subsistence of any copyright secured on or after that date, the owner of copyright or of any exclusive right in the work may obtain registration of the copyright claim by delivering to the Copyright Office the deposit specified by this section, together with the application and fee specified by sections 409 and 708. Such registration is not a condition of copyright protection.

COPYRIGHT APPLICATION FORMS

Examples of the various application forms are provided in Appendix D. A summary of each form follows here:

- *Form TX:* For published or unpublished nondramatic literary works (works expressed in words or numbers such as a novel, nonfiction book, short story, poetry, textbook, reference work, directory, catalog, advertising copy, article, or computer software program).
- *Short Form TX:* Simplified version of Form TX.
- *Form PA:* For published or unpublished works of the performing arts (works intended to be performed before an audience such as a play, musical composition, song, choreography, opera, motion picture, or audiovisual work).
- *Short Form PA:* Simplified version of Form PA.
- *Form SR:* For published or unpublished sound recordings such as a record, cassette recording, or compact disc, but not the audio portion of an audiovisual work such as a motion picture soundtrack or an audiocassette accompanying a filmstrip. In addition, Form SR would be used if the author also wishes to simultaneously register the sound recording and underlying musical, dramatic, or literary work embodied on the sound recording.
- *Form VA:* For published or unpublished works of the visual arts. These include two-dimensional and three-dimensional visual arts works such as an advertisement, label, artwork applied to useful articles, bumper sticker, cartoon, collage, doll, toy, drawing, painting, mural, fabric, wallpaper, greeting card, game, puzzle, hologram, computer artwork (other than audiovisual artwork used in a computer program), jewelry, map, logo, mask, engraving, silkscreen, sewing pattern, poster, needlework, print, sculpture, stained glass, technical drawing, weaving, tapestry, or artwork such as a record cover or book jacket. Form VA is also used for an architectural work.

- *Short Form VA:* Simplified version of Form VA.
- *Form SE:* For serials such as an individual issue of a periodical, newspaper, journal, magazine, proceeding, annual edition, or serialized publication that is intended to be issued in successive parts bearing numerical or chronological designations, but not an individual contribution to a serial publication.
- *Short Form SE:* Simplified version of Form SE.
- *Form SE/Group:* For registration of a group of serials.
- *Form G/DN:* For registration of a group of daily newspapers.
- *Form RE:* For claims to renewal of copyright.
- *Form RE/CON:* Continuation form to be used in conjunction with Form RE.
- *Addendum to Form RE:* For all works published between January 1, 1964, and December 31, 1977, not registered during their first twenty-eight-year term.
- *Form GATT:* For restored works under the GATT provisions (see Chapter 27).
- *Form GATT/GRP:* GATT group registration form.
- *Form GATT/CON:* Continuation form to be used in conjunction with Form GATT.
- *Form MW with instructions:* For registration of a mask work fixed in a semiconductor chip product (see Chapter 11).
- *Form MW/CON:* Continuation sheet to be used in conjunction with Form MW.
- *Form CA:* To correct an error or amplify the information given in an application.
- *Form CON:* Continuation sheet to be used in conjunction with basic application Forms CA, PA, SE, SR, TX, and VA only.
- *Form GR/CP:* An adjunct application to be used for a group of contributions to periodicals in addition to an application Form TX, PA, or VA, such as a series of columns or articles in which all of the works are by the same author, have the same copyright claimant, and were published as contributions to periodicals within a twelve-month period.
- *Document Cover Sheet:* For use when submitting a document (for example, a transfer of ownership, security interest) for recordation in the Copyright Office.

Short Forms

In the mid-1990s, the Copyright Office began using Short Forms TX, PA, and VA. These short forms are only one page and very simple to fill out. Examples are in Appendix D. These forms also provide an opportunity to list who should be contacted when permission is sought to use the work. Short forms can be used when:

- the applicant is the only author and is the copyright owner of the work;
- the work was not made for hire; or

- the work is completely new—that is, it is not a derivative or compilation and does not contain material previously published or registered or in the public domain.

OBTAINING COPYRIGHT APPLICATION FORMS

The three most common methods of acquiring copyright application forms are:

1. by mail from the Copyright Office;
2. downloaded from the Copyright Office website; and
3. via interactive copyright software sold by private companies.

The forms can also often be obtained at local government bookstores.

Obtaining Forms by Mail

Forms can be obtained by writing to the Publications Section (LM-455) of the Copyright Office. Delivery takes approximately two to four weeks. Only one copy of each form will be furnished. You may photocopy the forms, as long as the copies conform to the Copyright Office requirements:

- on paper measuring 8.5 by 11 inches;
- printed back to back; and
- not "shrunk" or scaled to a smaller size on the page.

Downloading Forms from the Internet

Copyright application forms can be downloaded from the Copyright Office website. These application forms are available in a computer format known as "PDF." Word processing software cannot "read" these forms. The Adobe Acrobat Reader, a software program available for free from Adobe Systems, must be used in order to view and print the forms. The Adobe website address is provided in Appendix A and is also "linked" to the Copyright Office website. When visiting the Copyright Office website, click on "Adobe Acrobat Reader" to be directed to the free software.

After downloading and installing the Adobe Acrobat Reader, the forms can be viewed and printed. The forms should be printed back to back using both sides of a single sheet of paper. Short forms are one-sided. Dot matrix printer copies of the forms are not acceptable, and inkjet printer copies of the forms may require enlarging (if using the "shrink to fit page" option). To achieve the best quality copies of the application forms, the Copyright Office recommends a laser printer. Printers should have memory capability of at least 1 megabyte. Older printers may require more memory.

The forms submitted to the Copyright Office must be clear, legible, and on a good grade of 8.5-inch by 11-inch white paper. The Copyright Office produces completed registration certificates through an optical scanning system that utilizes an image scanned from the original application submitted. Therefore, a sloppy application results in a sloppy registration.

At the time of writing of this book, downloaded forms are not interactive. That is, you cannot use your computer to enter information on the form. You must print the form and then type or write the information on the printed copy. Some software programs such as advanced versions of Adobe Acrobat and Delrina Form Flow allow a user to enter information on forms. See the following section on interactive forms.

Interactive Copyright Application Forms

Interactive copyright application forms allow applicants to enter information directly onto a form on the computer screen and then print out the completed form. These programs also offer other documents such as cover letters and special handling documentation. Companies that supply such forms are listed in Appendix A.

CHOOSING THE CORRECT APPLICATION FORM

In order to choose the correct application form, the applicant must determine the nature of the work. What *is* the work? As explained in the previous chapters, the form in which the work is embodied does not determine the nature of the work. For example, the play *A Streetcar Named Desire* is printed in a book, along with photos from the original Broadway cast presentation. The fact that the play is printed in a book does not make *A Streetcar Named Desire* a literary work. It is a dramatic work that is intended to be performed before an audience. Similarly, the fact that the photos are printed in the book does not change the nature of the photographs. The photos are a pictorial work (that is, a work of the visual arts). The play should be registered by using Form PA, and the photographs should be registered by using Form VA.

Derivatives and Compilations

There are no application forms specifically for derivative works and compilations. A derivative or compilation is registered within one of the eight categories of works of authorship discussed in Chapter 3. For example, *The Addams Family* television series and film would be registered as an audiovisual work using Form PA. The same rules apply to compilations and collective works. For example, the collected stories of J. D. Salinger, even if they were presented on audiotape, would be registered as a literary work using Form TX.

Mixed Works and Multimedia Works

One of the most common sources of confusion in the registration process is what form to choose if a work consists of two or more forms of authorship. For example, a book is published with illustrations or a filmstrip is published in conjunction with an audiocassette. Such works are considered "mixed" works, "mixed class" works, or **multimedia works.** A multimedia work is defined as a work that combines authorship in two or more media.

A single application may be used for multimedia work provided that:

- the copyright claimant is the same for each element of the work; and
- the elements of the work are unpublished or, if published, are published together as a single unit.

The applicant must identify all of the copyrightable elements of the mixed work. For example, consider an instructional exercise program on videotape. There are several copyrightable elements: the audiovisual work and accompanying sounds, and the visual arts work embodied in the packaging of the tape including photographs and graphic design. If the person claiming ownership is the same for all of these elements and the work is published as a unit, one application (Form PA) should be used. If the copyright claimant for the packaging is different than the claimant for the audiovisual work, two applications would be made using Form PA for the audiovisual work and Form VA for the visual arts work.

The Copyright Office has established a procedure for selecting the appropriate application to use in the case of a mixed work. The following list indicates the preference for the application form. Regardless of the form chosen, the application will include a claim for all of the original authorship in the work. An applicant should examine this list, and choose the *first* form on the list that pertains to the work:

- Use Form PA if the work contains an audiovisual element (for example, a filmstrip, slides, film, or videotape) regardless of whether there are any sounds.
- Use Form SR if the work does *not* contain an audiovisual element, but contains a sound recording, for example, an audiotape, compact disc, or MP3 music file. Sounds that accompany an audiovisual work are not considered a sound recording.
- Use Form VA if the work does *not* contain an audiovisual element or a sound recording, but does contain a visual works element such as a pictorial, graphic, or sculptural work.
- Use Form SE if the work is a nondramatic literary work intended to be published in serial form (for example, a journal, newspaper, or newsletter.)
- Use Form TX if the work contains only text, such as a manual and computer program that produces a textual screen display.

Websites

For information regarding registration for websites and online works, read Copyright Circular 66. Generally, a single registration can be used for all the elements that are displayed on the web page. Software downloaded from the site should be registered in a separate application. Copyright protection for a website does not extend to the layout, "look and feel," or design of the site. In other words, the website's style cannot be protected under copyright law. Style may be protectible under trademark law as a form of trade dress.

Form SR must be used if the website contains a sound recording (sounds or music that do not accompany a series of images). Otherwise, the applicant can use Form TX if it is primarily text, Form VA if it is primarily imagery, or Form PA if the work contains audiovisual elements. Most website registrants use Form TX.

Since a website changes periodically, it may be more economical (if one of the following is applicable) to register using a group registration for:

- updates to an automated database—read Copyright Circular 65;
- serials—read Copyright Circular 62; or
- daily newsletter—read Copyright Circular 62c.

There are rules for each of these group registrations, and it is possible that a website may not qualify for any of the three. For example, a website may not qualify as a serial if it is revised more than once a week. Rules for these group applications are provided in the following sections.

Software Programs

Form TX is generally used when applying for registration of a computer program. The Copyright Office believes that a single basic registration is sufficient to protect the copyright in a computer program including related screen displays, without a separate registration for screen displays. Computer programs often include a manual or booklet that helps the user understand and use the computer program. The manual may be registered separately as textual work; however, the Copyright Office also will permit the applicant to include the manual as part of the program application, provided that the copyright claimant is the same for the manual and the program and manual are published together as a single unit.

Automated Databases

Form TX is used in an application for registration of an automated database. An automated database is a compilation of facts, data, or other information assembled into an organized format suitable for use in a computer. The collection of judicial opinions on a legal database such as Westlaw or LEXIS would be an example of an automated database. Often, an automated database is a collection of facts, such as a directory of pharmaceutical compounds. Copyright protection only extends to the original expression of the compilation, not the underlying facts. Chapter 4 offers more information on compilations.

Group Applications for Automated Database Revisions. Many automated databases are updated regularly. In this way, an automated database may be a combined derivative and compilation. For example, an automated database of "Baseball Pitching Statistics" would be a compilation, but if the database were updated with new statistics, the subsequent version would be both a derivative and a compilation. Special provisions exist for the registration of an automated database and its updates or other revisions. An automated database and its updates or revisions may be registered using a single Form TX if the following conditions are met:

- all of the updates or revisions must be fixed only in machine-readable copies. If the work is fixed or published in a form other than machine-readable copies (for example, a book), group registration is *not* possible;
- all of the updates or revisions were created or (if published) were first published within a three-month period, all within the same calendar year;
- all of the updates or revisions are owned by the same copyright claimant and have the same title, general content, and organization; and
- the updates or revisions, if published before March 1, 1989, bear a copyright notice naming the owner of the copyright, and that name is the same in each notice.

Serials

A serial is a work like a magazine or a newsletter intended to be issued in successive parts bearing numerical or chronological designations (for example, Volume 1, Number 2) and intended to be continued indefinitely. Examples of serials include periodicals, newspapers, magazines, bulletins, newsletters, annuals, journals, proceedings of societies, and similar works. There are three forms that can be used for registering serials: Form SE, Short Form SE, and Form SE/Group. Form SE is the standard form and is appropriate for any serial.

Short Form SE is one page and can be used if *all* the following criteria are met:

- the claim is in the entire collective work;
- the collective work is essentially all new;
- the author is a United States citizen or domiciliary;
- the work is a work made for hire;
- the author(s) and claimant(s) are the same; and
- the work is first published in the United States.

For example, WebFunk publishes *End User,* a monthly newsletter for purchasers of its computer programs. The newsletter is created by WebFunk employees, is first published in the United States, and is essentially all new each month. Therefore, Short Form SE may be used. If any of the criteria listed here do not apply, or if the applicant is in doubt about using Short Form SE, then standard Form SE should be used. The Copyright Office provides specific information about serial registrations in Circular 62.

Group Registration of Serials.   Rather than registering each issue separately, the Copyright Office permits the registration of a group of issues using Form SE/Group if the following criteria apply:

- a complimentary subscription for two copies of the serial has been given to the Library of Congress, confirmed by letter to the General Counsel, Copyright Office. Subscription copies must be mailed separately to: Library of Congress, Group Periodicals Registration, Washington, DC 20540;
- the claim must be in the collective works and the collective works must be new;
- the author is a United States citizen or domiciliary;
- each issue must be a work made for hire;
- the author(s) and claimant(s) are the same;
- each issue must have been created no more than one year prior to publication; and
- all issues must have been published within the same calendar year.

Contribution to a Serial.   A claim for a serial does not include individual contributions to the serial publication. Any individual contribution should be registered separately. For example, Josephine writes an article on copyright for a law school journal. If the law school seeks to register the issue, Form SE would be used. If Josephine applies to register her work, she would use Form TX.

Group Contributions to Periodicals

John is a cartoonist who creates a comic strip for a monthly magazine. He has retained copyright in the comic strips. Does he have to file twelve separate registrations for his monthly comic strips? No, a single copyright registration can be used for a group of works if *all* the following conditions are met:

- all of the works must be published on or after March 1, 1989;
- all of the works are by the same author (an individual);
- all of the works are first published as contributions to periodicals (including newspapers) within a twelve-month period;
- all of the works have the same copyright claimant;
- one copy of the entire periodical issue or newspaper section in which each contribution is first published is deposited with the application; and
- the application identifies each contribution separately, including the periodical containing it and the date of its first publication.

In order to apply for a single registration to cover a group of contributions to periodicals, *two* application forms must be submitted. A basic application on either Form TX, Form PA, or Form VA must be completed. *The title and dates of publication should be left blank.* For example, a cartoonist such as John would use Form VA, leave the title and date of publication blank, and complete the remainder of Form VA. A columnist, such as Ann Landers or Dave Barry, would use Form TX. When completing the basic application form, the year of creation is the year that the last of the contributions was completed.

In addition to this basic application, the applicant also must submit Form GR/CP that consists of two parts, Part A (Identification of Application) and Part B (Registration for Group of Contributions). Part A requires that the applicant identify the type of form (TX, VA, or PA) that is submitted, as well as identifying the author and copyright claimant. Part B requires specific information about the title of each contribution, title of the periodical, date of first publication, volume, number, issue date, and nation of first publication. The two forms are submitted together with deposit materials and the appropriate fee.

Proposed Regulation: Group Registration of Photographs

The Copyright Office has proposed regulations permitting the group registration of photographs. Form VA should be used for the group registration, and the proposed regulations would apply if *all* the following requirements are met:

- a single photographer owns copyrights in all of the photographs;
- the photographs must have been created on or after March 1, 1989; and
- if unpublished, the photographs were taken within one calendar year; or if published, the photographs were taken within a three-month period.

As of the writing of this book, these regulations have not been adopted. Consult 37 *Code of Federal Regulations* section 202.3(b)(9)(i).

Music

Applicants are sometimes confused when registering a sound recording because of the relationship between sound recordings and the underlying musical or textual works. For example, a musician writes a song, records it, and then releases an audiocassette containing the recording. Is it necessary to register the song and the sound recording as two separate works? Should Form PA or Form SR be used?

If the author of the sound recording and the author of the musical work are the same, both would be registered with one Form SR. The table accompanying this text, prepared by the Copyright Office, demonstrates the appropriate copyright form to use in various sound recording situations. For more information about registration of sound recordings, the Copyright Office provides Circular 56.

Choosing an Application for Music Works

What Is Being Registered	Form
Author writes a song (no words) and wishes to claim copyright in the song	PA

(Cont'd)

Choosing an Application for Music Works (Cont'd)

Author writes a song (music and words) and wishes to claim copyright in the song	PA
Vocalist performs and records a song and wishes to claim copyright in the recorded performance only	SR
Author/performer writes a song, performs and records it, and wishes to claim copyright both in the music and the recording	SR
Author writes a poem and records it and wishes to claim copyright only in the poem itself, not in the recorded performance	TX
Author writes a play and records it and wishes to claim copyright only in the play itself, not in the recorded performance	PA
Author writes a poem or narrative and records it and wishes to claim copyright in both the text and the recorded performance	SR
Author writes a musical composition in machine-readable copy (computer disk) and wishes to claim copyright only in the musical composition	PA
Author writes a musical composition in machine-readable copy (computer disk) and wishes to claim copyright in both the composition and the performance	SR

Motion Pictures and Video Recordings

Form PA is used in an application for registration of a motion picture or video recording. Creating a motion picture or video recording is a collaborative effort. A screenplay or script is created, performers recite the material, photographers capture the activity, and editors and directors cut and splice the final result. Numerous technical contributions are made including lighting, sound recording, set designs, and costume creation. All these contributions merge into one work.

The screenplay is the script of the motion picture. Once the motion picture is made or fixed, the screenplay, to the extent that it is embodied in the motion picture, is considered to be an integral and protectible part of the motion picture. However, if the motion picture has not been made, the screenplay would be protectible as a performing arts work and would be registered using Form PA, intended for works that are to be performed before an audience or with the aid of a machine or device. Form TX would *not* be used to register the screenplay because that form is intended for use only for *nondramatic* textual material.

Architectural Works

Form VA is used in an application for registration of an architectural work. An architectural work is an original design of a building embodied in any tangible medium of expression including a building, architectural plans, or drawings.

An architectural work includes the overall form as well as the arrangement and composition of spaces and elements in the design, but does not include individual standard features such as windows, doors, and other staple features.

Only architectural works created on or after December 1, 1990, or any architectural work that is unconstructed and embodied in unpublished plans or drawings on that date, are eligible for protection. Protection for any work that is unconstructed and embodied in unpublished plans or drawings prior to December 1, 1990, will terminate on December 31, 2002, unless the work is constructed by that date.

Secure Tests

What happens when a national testing service wants to register an examination such as the Scholastic Achievement Test (SAT)? The Copyright Office cannot guarantee the security or confidentiality of text materials mailed to the office. However, if the examination is a secure test, the Copyright Office provides a procedure to register the work. A secure test is a nonmarketed test administered under supervision at specified centers on specific dates, all copies of which are accounted for and either destroyed or returned to restricted locked storage following each administration. A test is "nonmarketed" if copies are not sold and the test is distributed and used in such a manner that ownership and control of copies remain with the test sponsor or publisher. The Copyright Office offers a special procedure to hand-carry Form TX and secure test material through the application procedure. For more information about registration of secure tests, the Copyright Office provides Circular 64, or contact Copyright Office, Information Section, LM-401, Library of Congress, Washington, DC 20559.

FOR MORE INFORMATION

Preparation of Application Form
See Chapter 19.

Deposit Materials
See Chapter 20.

Processing Applications; Correcting and Canceling Registrations
See Chapter 21.

CHAPTER 19
Preparing the Copyright Application

The previous chapter provided information on registration and choosing the correct application for registration. This chapter deals with preparing a copyright application including special requirements for:

- software;
- motion pictures;
- architecture; and
- mixed media.

INTRODUCTION

The Copyright Office receives over 600,000 applications for copyright each year. In order to proceed effectively through the application process, knowledge of the copyright application is essential. The copyright application has been designed for laypersons and often includes information that can help guide the applicant through the process.

Many of the decisions that must be made by an applicant can have a serious effect on the protection of the work. The person preparing the application must avoid the use of any statement or representation that may prove to be untrue or fraudulent.[1] The Copyright Office provides guides for filling out each application as well as circulars dealing with the registration of a particular work. These are all downloadable from the Copyright Office website as described in Chapter 18. In the following sections, elements of the copyright application are analyzed. Examples of copyright applications are included in Appendix D.

SPACE 1: TITLE AND NATURE OF THE WORK

Space 1 of each application requires that the applicant provide the title and alternate or previous title of the work. Every work must be given a title in order to be registered because the title is used to index the work in Copyright Office records. The title should be exactly as it appears on the work. Nondescriptive titles such as "Work Without a Title" can be used. Titles not presented in alphanumeric format cannot be used. For example, if the title of a work is "☺," the work should be registered as "Happy Face" or a similar title. Titles in a foreign language should be presented in the Roman alphabet.

Title

Architectural Works. In the case of works of architecture, the applicant should indicate the title of the building *and* its date of construction. If the building has not yet been constructed, the applicant should note after the title, "not yet constructed."

Websites. In the case of website registrations, the title may be the domain name, for example, "bandbusiness.com." If the applicant is registering the code for the site (as source code), then the title could be "HTML code for bandbusiness.com."

Alternate or Previous Title. The alternate or previous title is any additional title under which someone searching for the registration might look. For example, the song "Everybody's Talkin' " is also known by an alternate title, "Theme from Midnight Cowboy." The title of a different version of the work (such as a derivative work) is *not* an alternate or previous title. For example, the application for the motion picture *The Godfather III* should not list *The Godfather II* as a previous or alternate title.

Nature of Work

Space 1 of Forms VA, PA, and SR require information about the "nature of the work." In the case of Form SR, the applicant must check a box indicating the nature of the material recorded (that is, musical, dramatic, literary, and so on). In the case of Form VA, the applicant must provide a brief description such as "pen and ink drawing," "photographs," or "architectural work." Similarly, for Form PA, the applicant should state whether the work is a "drama," "musical play," "choreography," "motion picture," or other performing arts work. In the case of motion pictures, the applicant should provide a statement of the nature of the work such as "motion picture." In the event the motion picture is included as part of a multimedia kit, state "multimedia kit including motion picture and textual material." If further assistance is needed in determining the nature of the work, consult the line-by-line instructions provided by the Copyright Office for each application form. Examples are included in Appendix D.

Publication as a Contribution. Forms TX and VA require information regarding whether the work was published as a contribution to a periodical. If the work was published as part of a serial publication or as part of a collective work, information should be presented regarding the serial publication. For example, Julie Feldman is the author of a short story called "Cello Lovers." The story was first printed on pages 55 to 60 of a magazine, *Female Trouble* (Volume 21, Number 2, Issue Date May 1, 1999). Space 1 would read as follows:

> *Title of This Work:* Cello Lovers
> *Previous or Alternative Titles:* (Blank)
> *Publication as a Contribution/Title of Collective Work:* Female Trouble
> *Volume:* 21 *Number:* 2 *Issue Date* 5/1/99 *Pages* 55–60

In an application to register serials, such as magazines or newspapers, Form SE requires information about the volume and number of the serial, as well as the frequency of publication.

SPACE 2: THE AUTHOR

Space 2 of the copyright application requires that the applicant provide information about the author or authors. In order to fill out this space, the applicant must determine the manner in which the author is identified and the nature of the author's contribution. In the event that the work is a derivative work, the applicant should only provide the name of the author of the *new* material, not the author of underlying work. For example, Joyce Maynard is the author of the novel *To Die For*. Buck Henry is the author of the derivative screenplay of *To Die For*. When registering the screenplay, Buck Henry would be listed as the author; when registering the novel, Joyce Maynard would be listed as the author.

Anonymous and Pseudonymous

An author is anonymous if that author is not identified on the copies or phonorecords of the work. For anonymous works, the Copyright Office offers three choices to the applicant:

1. leave the author space blank;
2. state "Anonymous" in the space; or
3. reveal the author's identity.

An author is pseudonymous if the author is identified by a fictitious name. For pseudonymous works, the Copyright Office offers three choices to the applicant:

1. leave the author space blank;
2. give the pseudonym and identify it as such (for example, Mark Twain, pseudonym); or
3. reveal the author's name, making it clear that it is a pseudonym (for example, Samuel Clemens whose pseudonym is Mark Twain).

Works Made for Hire

If the work is made for hire, the full name of the hiring party should be used. Works such as motion pictures are almost always works made for hire, either because the individual contributions are made by employees within the scope of their employment or because the contribution is for a specially commissioned motion picture work. In either case, the applicant should confirm the work for hire status of all contributions. If it is unclear whether the work is made for hire, refer to the checklist, "Determining If a Work Is Made for Hire," in Chapter 13.

Nature of Authorship

Provide a short statement of the nature of each author's contribution. For example, if Bob wrote the words and music to a song, the nature of authorship would be "words and music." If Bob wrote the music and Sally wrote the words, the nature of Bob's authorship would be "music" and the nature of Sally's authorship would be "words" or "lyrics." If in doubt about a sufficient phrase that describes the nature of authorship, refer to the specific line-by-line instructions provided by the Copyright Office for each application form. If the work is a derivative, the nature of authorship would describe only the new material added to the work. For example, if an author writes a screenplay of a novel, the nature of authorship would be "dramatization." If the work is a compilation and all of the material in the compilation has been previously published or is in the public domain, the nature of authorship is "compilation." If the compilation contains some material being registered or published for the first time, the nature of authorship would be "additional text and compilation."

Special Situations

Music. If an author claims copyright in a song, the nature of authorship is "music and words" or "music." If claiming copyright only in a recorded performance, the nature of authorship is "performance and sound recording." If claiming copyright both in the music and the recording, the nature of authorship is "music and performance" or "music, words, performance."

Websites. The applicant should list the elements of the site, for example, "text, photographs, and graphics" or "text and audiovisual material." If the applicant is registering the code for the site, state "text of HTML code." Elements of style, such as "layout" or "overall design," should not be listed, as these look-and-feel elements are unregistrable.

Software Programs. Generally, the nature of authorship for a software program is "entire work" or "entire computer program." If the applicant is primarily concerned with the program and not the audiovisual aspect, "entire program text," "program text," or a similar statement will suffice for nature of authorship. However, if the statement given by the applicant is "entire computer program including screen displays" or "entire computer program including audiovisual material," the applicant *must* deposit identifying material for the screens or audiovisual aspects, as explained in Chapter 20. If a manual is being registered with the program, nature of authorship should state "entire text of computer program and user's manual." For more information regarding the registration of computer programs, see Circular 61.

Mixed Works. The nature of authorship for a mixed media or multimedia work depends on the configuration of the work. The table accompanying this text provides some examples of types of multimedia and the suggested nature of authorship.

Movies. If the entire work was made for hire, the hiring party would be listed as the author, and the nature of authorship would be "entire motion picture."

Multimedia Authorship

Type of Media	Nature of Authorship
Slides and a booklet	"Entire work" or "text and photography"
Film strip, booklet, and audiocassette	"Entire work" or "text as printed and recorded photography and sounds"
Videocassette and manual with text and pictorial illustrations	"Entire work" or "cinematography, text, and illustrations"
Audiocassettes and a manual	"Text as printed and recorded, and sound recording." Note: *Do not use the term "entire work" for Form SR*
Compact discs, sheet music, and manual *work"*	"Text, music, and sound recording." Note: *Do not use the term "entire* *for Form SR*
Posters and manual	"Entire work" or "artwork and text"
Manual and identifying materials for computer program on machine-readable diskette (or cassette) that	"Text of manual and computer program"

If contributions were not works made for hire, each author would be listed separately, along with his or her contribution, for example:

> 2a *Name of Author:* Mary Smith
> *Nature of Authorship:* Script
> 2b *Name of Author:* John Jones
> *Nature of Authorship:* Director, producer
> 2c *Name of Author:* William Johnson
> *Nature of Authorship:* Camera work

Architecture. The nature of authorship is "architectural work" or "building design."

Automated Databases. If the material in the database has been previously published, previously registered, or is in the public domain, the nature of authorship would be "compilation." Where all, or a substantial portion, of the material represents copyrightable expression and is being published or registered for the first time, the nature of authorship would be "text," "revised text," or "additional text."

Serials. Completing Space 2 for serials requires knowledge as to the ownership of the various contributions. For example, Angelco publishes *End User,* a monthly newsletter for purchasers of its computer programs. All of the material is created by Angelco employees, it is first published in the United States, and the newsletter is essentially all new each month. The author would be Angelco, the nature of authorship is "entire text" or "entire text and illustrations," and the box marked "Collective Work" would be checked. If John Jones contributed an article to *End User* and assigned rights, he would be listed as an author in Space 2b. Under nature of authorship for John Jones, the application would state "text of one article."

Dates of Birth and Death

If an author is deceased, the year of death should be provided. Although it is not mandatory, the date of birth of each author should be provided. In the case of a work made for hire, this section of Space 2 should remain blank.

Nationality

The author's nationality may have an effect on the registrability of the work. An unpublished work may be registered regardless of the author's nationality; however, a published work is subject to United States copyright laws only if the work is published in a foreign nation that, on the date of first publication, is a member of the Universal Copyright Convention *or* if the work is published in a nation that comes within the scope of a presidential proclamation extending copyright protection.

SPACE 3: CREATION AND PUBLICATION

Space 3 of the copyright application requires that the applicant provide information about the dates of creation and first publication of the work. As indicated in previous chapters, creation and publication have two very different meanings under copyright law.

A work is **created** when it is fixed in a tangible form for the first time. As a general rule, the date of creation is the date of completion of the work being registered. For example, if an author's novel is revised with an editor, the date of the final revisions would be the date of creation. If a computer company creates a program, tests it among users, and revises it before publication, the date of the final revisions would be the date of creation. The date of creation for an unpublished work is the date when the latest version was completed.

A work is **published** if copies or phonorecords, in the case of sound recordings, are distributed to the public by sale or other transfer of ownership, or by rental, lease, or lending. A work is also published if an offer is made to distribute copies or phonorecords to a group of persons for purposes of further distribution, public performance, or public display. As indicated in Chapter 17, it is *not* a publication to:

- make copies of a work if the copies are not distributed;
- publicly perform a work;
- display a work;
- send copies of the work to the Copyright Office; or
- distribute a small number of copies for a limited purpose.

To help sort out the issue of publication, some examples are provided.

EXAMPLE

The News Broadcast. A TV station telecasts and simultaneously videotapes a nightly newscast. The newscast is a copyrightable audiovisual work. However, it has not been published. Why? Because multiple copies have not been made and the work has not been offered to a group for further distribution. All that has happened is a public performance of the work, and that, by itself, does not constitute publication under copyright law. The work may be registered as an unpublished audiovisual work.

EXAMPLE

The TV Commercial. An advertising agency creates a commercial promoting Angelco computer products. The agency contacts several television stations and offers to purchase time to broadcast the commercial. The work has been published because multiple copies have been offered for public performance.

EXAMPLE

The Portrait. A painter sells a portrait to a museum. The museum displays the work. The work has not been published.

EXAMPLE

The Website. George creates a website for fans of the *Gong Show* called "Chuçkie! Chuckie! Chuckie!" A viewer who accesses "Chuckie! Chuckie Chuckie!" receives a copy of the site on his or her own computer. Is this a publication of the site? The Copyright Office leaves it up to the applicant to decide (see Copyright Circular 66). Approximately ninety-nine percent of website applicants register their sites as published works.

Date and Nation of First Publication

The applicant should give the full date (that is, month, day, and year) when the work is published. If the applicant is unsure, it is acceptable to state "approximately" (that is, approximately June 4, 1998). If the work is first published in the United States, the initials "U.S.A." may be used. If the work is simultaneously published (that is, within thirty days) in two countries, for example, the United States and Canada, it is acceptable to state "U.S.A." If the work is first published in a foreign country, the foreign edition constitutes this first publication.

Special Situations

Architecture. For works of architecture, the year of creation is the year in which architectural plans or drawings for the building were completed. The date of publication is the first date of sale, or the first date of an offering for sale or public distribution of copies of the design embodied in blueprints, design plans, drawings, photographs, or models. The first date of sale may also be the first date of an offer to distribute copies to a group of persons for further distribution or public display. By way of example, the sale of copies of architectural plans or distribution of blueprint copies to contractors may be regarded as publication.

SPACE 4: THE COPYRIGHT CLAIMANT

Space 4 of the copyright application requires that the applicant provide information about the copyright claimant. The claimant is either the author of the work or a person or organization to whom the copyright has been transferred. In the case of a work made for hire, the copyright claimant is the hiring party. For example, Jim, an employee of Angelco, creates a computer program within the scope of his employment at Angelco. The program is a work made for hire, and the copyright claimant would be Angelco. Generally, the person who owns all rights to the work is the claimant. However, if the applicant has acquired one of the exclusive rights granted under copyright law, the applicant may be listed as the copyright claimant.

If Ownership Is Limited

In certain instances, a claimant may own the rights to the work for a limited period of time. For example, the computer company Diskco may exclusively license a work for a period of five years. Diskco may state in Space 4, "Diskco, Inc., by written agreement for a period of five years" or "Diskco, Inc., by written agreement terminating April 15, 2002."

Claimant Must Be Living

The applicant should not name a deceased person as the copyright claimant. For example, a deceased author's estate wishes to register copyright in a book that is to be published posthumously. The executor or administrator of the estate should be named as claimant, or, if known, the party who has inherited the ownership of the author's copyright.

Name and Address

The copyright claimant should be clearly identified using the full legal name of the claimant. An abbreviation is acceptable if it identifies the claimant. The address for the claimant also should be included.

Transfer

If the person named as claimant is not the same as the person in Space 2 (the "Author"), the applicant must provide a brief statement of how the claimant acquired copyright. For example, any of the following statements are acceptable:

- by written contract;
- by transfer of all rights by author;
- by operation of state community property law;
- by assignment; or
- by will.

The applicant should *not* attach the transfer documents (that is, the assignment, will, or contract) to the application. Transfers should be recorded separately or at a later date with the Copyright Office. The procedure for recording such documents is presented in Chapter 15.

SPACE 5: PREVIOUS REGISTRATION

Space 5 of the copyright application requires that the applicant provide information about any previous copyright registrations for this work or earlier versions of the work. The Copyright Office is only concerned with whether this work or a previous version have been *registered*. If the work has not been previously registered, check the "no" box.

In Space 5, the Copyright Office is only seeking information about earlier registrations of the work. For example, the author Stan Soocher may register his book *They Fought the Law* as a literary work. If a revised version of the book is published that includes new material, he would check the "yes" box. However, if a movie was made based upon the book *They Fought the Law,* the application for the motion picture would *not* list the book as a previous registration because the motion picture is considered to be an original work, distinct and separate from the book. Assuming there were no other registrations for the motion picture or underlying screenplay, the box marked "no" would be checked. If the motion picture was revised, additional scenes were later added, and it was released on video, the application for that subsequent motion picture would indicate that an earlier registration was issued.

Basis for Seeking New Registration

If the applicant checked the "yes" box on Space 5, a new registration will be issued provided that the work meets any one of the following conditions:

- *previously unpublished*—the work has been registered in unpublished form and a second registration is now being sought to cover the first published edition;
- *author seeking registration as claimant*—someone other than the author is identified as a copyright claimant in the earlier registration, and the author is now seeking registration in his or her own name; or

- *changed version*—the work has been changed and the applicant now seeks registration to cover the additions or revisions.

Previous Registration Number and Year of Registration

The registration number of a previous registration is listed on the upper right-hand corner of the registration and usually begins with the letters of the form (for example, TX 113-800 or PA 334-821). Space 5 also should include the year that the previous registration was issued. If unsure whether the work has been previously registered, a search of the Copyright Office records may be initiated as explained in Chapter 15.

SPACE 6: DERIVATIVE WORK OR COMPILATION

Space 6 of the application requires the applicant to determine if the work being registered is a derivative work or a compilation. Space 6 has two parts, and the following rule is applied:

- for derivative works, the applicant completes 6a and 6b; and
- for compilations, the applicant completes 6b.

The author of a derivative work has transformed, recast, or adapted the preexisting material, while the author of a compilation has assembled, selected, or organized the preexisting materials without transforming them. (For more explanation, review Chapter 4.) The motion picture *The Addams Family* is a derivative work because it is derived from the cartoons of Charles Addams. The author of the motion picture would complete the form as follows:

6a (*preexisting material*): original cartoons by Charles Addams
6b (*material added*): dramatization for motion picture

The use of selected cartoons by Charles Addams in a book, *Great Cartoons from the New Yorker,* would be a collective work constituting a compilation. Space 6 would be completed as follows:

6a (*preexisting material*): (leave space blank)
6b (*material added*): compilation of cartoons, additional text, and introduction

Derivative Works

For some applicants, Space 6 creates confusion because it may be difficult to differentiate the preexisting material and the new material. Following are some examples of how Space 6 would be completed for a derivative work:

***First Blood* (movie)**
6a (*preexisting material*): original novel (*First Blood*)
6b (*material added*): dramatization for motion picture

"Chipmunks Macarena" (performance of song by the Chipmunks group)

6a (*preexisting material*): words and music

6b (*material added*): musical and vocal arrangement

"Understanding Macbeth" (student guide to Macbeth)

6a (*preexisting material*): Shakespeare's *Macbeth*

6b (*material added*): introduction, foreword, and additional text

Map of mountain bike routes in Northern California

6a (*preexisting material*): United States Geological Survey map of northern California

6b (*material added*): additional cartographic authorship and text

New version of previously registered video swimming lessons

6a (*preexisting material*): previously registered video production

6b (*material added*): revisions and new cinematographic material

Television documentary about recycling

6a (*preexisting material*): previously published footage and photographs

6b (*material added*): editing, narration, and new footage

Website for fans of the Vox Guitar

6a (*preexisting material*): previously published text, photographs, and graphics

6b (*material added*): additional text and photographs

Compilations and Collective Works

When completing Space 6, an applicant may be confused about whether the work is a compilation. When an author creates a work by selecting various components and grouping them together in a unique manner, the result is a compilation. Copyright will protect a compilation only if the manner in which the work has been assembled is original and constitutes separately protectible authorship. (See Chapter 4 for more information.) Following are some examples of how to complete Space 6 when applying for registration of a compilation:

Videocassette of baseball bloopers

6a (*preexisting material*): leave space blank

6b (*material added*): compilation of various baseball motion picture and videotape sequences; introduction and accompanying soundtrack

Directory of former child stars

6a (*preexisting material*): leave space blank

6b (*material added*): foreword and compilation of names, addresses, and list of films or TV shows of former child stars

Encyclopedia of home brewing tips

6a (*preexisting material*): leave space blank

6b (*material added*): compilation of articles, index, and foreword

Sound recording of Marvin Gaye's greatest hits

6a (*preexisting material*): leave space blank

6b (*material added*): compilation of Marvin Gaye sound recordings

Mixtures of Derivatives and Compilations

Some works are compilations *and* derivatives, for example, a French translation of O. Henry stories. In such a case, Space 6a (preexisting material) would list the existing material (that is, "original stories by O. Henry"), and Space 6b (material added) would indicate the compilation and new material (that is, "translation in French and compilation").

Special Situations

Automated Database. If the material in an automated database contains previously published information, Space 6a would be completed "previously published data" or "public domain data." Space 6b would be completed "compilation." If material contained in the database is entirely new and never before registered or published, Space 6a would be left blank. If the database is revised or periodically updated, Space 6 would be completed as follows: Space 6a, "previously registered database"; Space 6b, "revised and updated text; revised compilation."

SPACE 7: DEPOSIT ACCOUNTS AND CORRESPONDENCE

Space 7 on the copyright application (except Form TX where it is Space 9), requires information about whether the registration fee is to be charged to a deposit account and where correspondence regarding the application should be mailed.

Deposit Accounts

The Copyright Office maintains deposit accounts for applicants registering works on a regular basis. If the applicant maintains a deposit account, the registration fee can be charged against the balance. Information about establishing a deposit account is provided in Chapter 21.

Correspondence

Space 7 requires the name, address, area code, and telephone number of the person to be consulted if correspondence about the application becomes necessary. (Note: This information is located in Space 9 in Form TX.) If the copyright examiner has a question regarding the application, the person named in this space will be contacted. If this space is not completed, the copyright examiner may attempt to contact the person named as copyright claimant.

SPACE 8: CERTIFICATION

The person preparing the application may not be the applicant for copyright. For example, this person could be an attorney, executor of an estate, or even a friend. According to the Copyright Office, Space 8 "speaks directly" to the person filling out the application. The person must check one of the four boxes in Space 8 as either the author, other copyright claimant, owner of exclusive rights, or authorized agent. (Note: This information is in Space 10 on Form TX.)

- *Author.* Check this box if the person filling out the form is the person (or one of the persons) named in Space 2 of the application. This box would not be checked if the applicant is *not* a person named in Space 2.
- *Other copyright claimant.* Check this box if the person filling out the application has obtained ownership of all rights under the copyright initially belonging to the author. Generally this box is checked if the person filling out the application is not the author, but is listed as the copyright claimant in Space 4 (along with an explanation of how the copyright was transferred).
- *Owner of exclusive right(s).* Check this box if the person filling out the application is not the author and is not the copyright claimant, but does own a limited right (for example, the exclusive right to reproduce the work for a period of years).
- *Authorized agent.* Check this box if the person filling out the application is the authorized representative of the author, claimant, or owner of exclusive rights. For example, if the application has been prepared by an attorney or a friend.

Signature

After checking the appropriate box, the person completing the application should type or print his or her name and date and sign the application where marked. Note that the person who signs the application is certifying to the Copyright Office that the information contained in the application is correct to the best of his or her knowledge. Section 506(e) of the Copyright Act of 1976 provides that a "false representation of a material fact" in a copyright application may result in a fine of up to $2,500. It is in the best interest of the person signing the application to review the material and be sure of its accuracy. An application for registration of a published work will not be accepted if the date in the certification box is earlier than the date of publication given in Space 3 of the application.

SPACE 9: MAILING INFORMATION

Space 9 of the copyright application (or Space 11 on Form TX) becomes the mailing label when the certified registration is mailed back to the applicant. That is, after the application has been processed, it will be mailed back in a window envelope, and Space 9 ("Mailing Information") is the mailing address.

THE FEE

A filing fee is required along with the application and deposit material. At the time of writing this book, the fee is $30 per application except for Forms

G/DN and SE/Group. See Appendix G for fee information. A check or money order, made payable to *Register of Copyrights,* should be enclosed with the application. If the application is rejected or if the applicant withdraws it, the fee will not be refunded. If the check is drawn against insufficient funds, the Copyright Office will not proceed with registration or will revoke the registration if it has already been issued.

WHEN WILL THE COPYRIGHT OFFICE ACCEPT ELECTRONIC REGISTRATIONS?

As of the writing of this book, the Copyright Office is in the second phase of its CORDS project, the goal of which is to develop and test a system for copyright registration and recordation with copyright applications, copies of works, and copyright-related documents transmitted in digital form over communications networks such as the Internet. No date has been established for the implementation of the CORDS project. The Copyright Office website provides information on the current status of the project.

END NOTE

1. 17 U.S.C. § 506(e).

FOR MORE INFORMATION

Deposit Requirements for Copyright Registration
See Chapter 20.

Application Process; Correcting and Canceling Registrations
See Chapter 21.

Contacting the Copyright Office
See Appendix A.

CHAPTER 20
Deposit Materials

The previous chapter discussed registrations and copyright applications. This chapter deals with deposit requirements including:

- standard deposit requirements for literary, visual arts, sound recording, and performing arts works; and
- special deposit requirements for multimedia, software, websites, motion pictures, automated databases, serials, and secure tests.

INTRODUCTION

An applicant must supply two complete copies of the best edition of the work along with the copyright application. These deposit materials are a requirement for registration, and the Copyright Office will not process the application without them.

There is a mandatory requirement that two complete copies of the work be deposited with the Library of Congress within three months of publication of the work even if an application is *not* filed. In other words, even if an author does not register a work, the author must deposit copies of the work.

What happens if an author does not file an application and does not abide by this mandatory deposit law? Nothing. Failure to provide deposit materials (except in conjunction with a copyright application) will have no effect on copyright protection. The mandatory deposit law is essentially "toothless" and usually disregarded by copyright owners who do not register their works. The owner will be penalized only if, at some point, the Copyright Office specifically *requests* the deposit materials and the copyright owner fails to supply the materials within three months of the request. The fines for failing to respond to the request cannot exceed $350 per work but may rise to $2,500 if the copyright owner willfully or repeatedly fails to comply with the Copyright Office demands. Certain works—greeting cards, postcards, stationery, three-dimensional sculptural works, and works published on jewelry, textiles, or any useful article—are exempt from this mandatory deposit requirement. The Copyright Office cannot request these deposit materials under the mandatory deposit rules.

Complete Copies

An applicant must provide two complete copies of the best edition of the work (with some exceptions, as explained in the following text). A complete copy includes all elements comprising the publication of the best edition of the work, including elements that, if considered separately, would not be copyrightable or would be exempt from mandatory deposit requirements. In the case of a sound recording, for example, the deposit materials would include textual or pictorial matter embodied on the record sleeve or cover of the compact disc. In the case of a motion picture, a copy is complete only if it is clean, undeteriorated, and free of any splices or defects.

Best Edition

The rules regarding best editions are set forth in 37 *Code of Federal Regulations* section 202.19(b) and can be obtained by acquiring Copyright Circular 7b. Best edition rules are based upon commonsense principles. For example, a hard cover version of a book is preferred to a soft cover; an illustrated book is better than an unillustrated work; a larger photograph is preferred to a smaller. These rules are the same for mandatory deposit or copyright registration except for computer software programs.

Determining the Number of Copies to Deposit

In most cases, two complete copies of the best edition of published works must be deposited. As for unpublished works, only one copy should be deposited. There are numerous exceptions in which only one copy of a work needs to be deposited. These exceptions are set forth in 37 *Code of Federal Regulations* section 202.19(b).

Special Relief

The Copyright Office has the discretion to relieve the copyright owner of deposit requirements. For example, under certain circumstances, the Copyright Office may permit the deposit of one copy of a work, instead of two. In other situations, it may not be necessary for *any* copy of the work to be deposited. An applicant's request for relief from the deposit requirements should be made to Chief, Examining Division, Copyright Office, Library of Congress, Washington, DC 20559.

MULTIMEDIA AND MIXED WORKS

The deposit requirement for a multimedia work varies according to the type of work being registered and whether the work has been published. In most cases, one complete multimedia work (or kit) containing all elements should be provided for unpublished works. All elements should bear the title of the work. For published works, one complete copy of the best *published* edition should be provided. The complete copy must include all of the elements in the kit or work. For more information on copyright registration for multimedia works, consult Copyright Office Circular R55.

COMPUTER PROGRAMS

Preparing deposit materials for a computer program requires knowledge of the programming process. A program is usually written in one of various computer languages, sometimes collectively referred to as *source code*. Source code can be expressed in letters and numbers and printed on paper. The source code is eventually assembled into a very simple computer language called *object code* or *machine language* that consists of a series of "0" and "1" symbols that set in motion "on" and "off" electrical impulses in the central processing unit of the computer. The software can be embodied or stored on disks, although video game programs are often stored on chips inside cartridges.

Since the copyrightable aspects of a computer program are its code, the Copyright Office will not accept disks or machine-readable copies of the computer program as suitable identifying materials. Instead, the Copyright Office prefers identifying materials that consist of source code of the program.

- For unpublished or published software programs, the applicant should deposit the first twenty-five pages and last twenty-five pages of the program in source code form (along with the page containing the copyright notice, if any).
- If the software program is less than fifty pages of source code, the entire source code should be deposited. The printouts for these deposit materials should be consecutively numbered.
- If the application is for a revised version of a computer program, the same rules regarding identifying material will apply unless the revisions are not located in the first twenty-five and last twenty-five pages of source code, in which case, any fifty pages representative of the revised material may be used (along with the page containing the copyright notice, if any).
- If the applicant is registering the user manual with the program, a copy of the published user's manual or other printed documentation should accompany the other identifying material.
- The applicant also may deposit identifying materials for the screens. These identifying materials consist of printouts, photographs, or drawings clearly revealing the screens. However, if the "nature of authorship" statement in Space 2 of the application is "entire computer program including screen displays," the applicant *must* deposit identifying material for the screens.
- If the work is predominantly audiovisual, such as a video game, a half-inch VHS videotape of the audiovisual video game screen is acceptable. If the applicant listed "audiovisual material" in the "nature of authorship" section of Space 2, this deposit requirement regarding screen displays is mandatory.

Programs Containing Subprograms

Many computer programs are actually collections of programs that perform different functions. For example, the America Online program contains subprograms that identify modems, send e-mail, browse the Internet, and so on. Even though these subprograms could stand alone as separate working modules, they can all be registered as one program. A court of appeals ruled in 1997 that given the structure of computer programs, the various modules and subprograms may be registered as a single work.[1]

Programs Containing Trade Secrets

Some computer programs contain valuable trade secrets. A trade secret is information that is not generally known and that gives the owner an advantage over competitors. In such cases, the copyright owner may not wish to disclose source code to the Copyright Office, as that information will be available to the public. When a computer program contains trade secrets, the applicant may deposit any of the following:

- first twenty-five pages and last twenty-five pages of source code with some portions blocked out, provided that the blocked out portions are proportionately less than the material still remaining;
- first ten pages and last ten pages of source code alone (with no blocked out portions);
- first twenty-five pages and last twenty-five pages of object code plus any ten or more consecutive pages of source code with no blocked out portions; or
- for programs fifty pages or less in length, the entire source code with trade secret portions blocked out.

If the work is revised and contains trade secrets, these deposit requirements apply unless the revisions are not present in the first and last twenty-five pages, in which case the applicant can furnish:

- twenty pages of source code containing the revisions with no portions blocked out; or
- any fifty pages of source code containing the revisions with some portions blocked out.

Rule of Doubt

If the applicant for registration of a computer program desires to protect trade secrets, the identifying deposit materials may not be sufficient for the copyright examiner to verify originality. When the Copyright Office has a reasonable doubt about the application, it will be processed under the **rule of doubt.** This means that the office is processing the registration but has a doubt about whether the requirements of the Copyright Act have been met or whether the deposit materials constitute protectible subject matter. If a dispute arises in regard to these issues, the final determination will be made by a federal court.

AUTOMATED DATABASES

If the automated database is fixed or published only in machine-readable copies, the deposit requirements are the same for published and unpublished databases *except* that, if the database is first published prior to March 1, 1989, the deposit material also must include a copy of the page containing the copyright notice. The deposit material consists of two types of identifying material, depending on whether the work is a **single file database** or a **multiple file database.** A single file database is a database that consists of data records pertaining to a single common subject matter, for example, a database of *Academy Award Winners.* A multiple file database consists of separate and distinct groups of data records, for example, a database consisting of *Grammy Awards, Academy Awards,* and *Emmy Awards.*

The identifying material for automated databases consists of one copy of the identifying portions reproduced in a form visually perceptible without the aid of a computer, usually either paper or microfilm. In the case of a single file database, the first twenty-five pages and last twenty-five pages must be deposited. In the case of a multiple file database, the requirement is to deposit a representative portion of each file (either fifty data records or the entire file, whichever is less). If the database has been revised, representative portions of the added or modified material (fifty pages or the entire revised portions, whichever is less) must be deposited. If the deposit is encoded (that is, not written in a natural language), the deposit should include a key or explanation of the code. If the examiner is unable to determine the presence of copyrightable material, a rule of doubt registration (see previous section) may issue. Special relief may be granted for trade secrets, as explained earlier in the section regarding computer program applications.

Websites

The Copyright Office considers a website to be an "online work" and offers two choices for deposit materials:

- a computer disk containing the website along with either a printout of at least five pages of representative portions or a videocassette of representative portions; or
- a printout or videocassette of the entire website (without a computer disk).

If the site consists of complex graphics and links, submission of the HTML code also may be appropriate. If the site changes, a new application should be filed to protect new material. If the website owner is registering the website as an automated database, the deposit material rules for group registrations for automated databases will apply (see the next section).

Group Registrations for Automated Databases

For group registrations of automated databases, the identifying deposit material required includes fifty representative pages from a single file database or fifty records from each updated data file. In addition, the deposit material must include a brief, typed or printed descriptive statement indicating the title of the database, the name and address of the claimants, and certain information regarding the content, subject, origins, approximate number of data records, and nature, location, and frequency of changes. For specific information about registration of automated databases, see Copyright Office Circular 65.

SOUND RECORDINGS

Generally, the deposit requirements for a claim in a sound recording are one or two phonorecords, depending on whether the work is published or unpublished. If the work is published on or after January 1, 1978, two complete copies of the best edition along with any printed or other visually perceptible material such as record sleeves and jackets must be deposited. If the work was first published prior to 1978, two complete phonorecords of the work as first published must be deposited. (Note: copyright protection did not extend to sound recordings until 1972.) For sound recordings first published outside of the United States, one complete phonorecord of the work as first published must be deposited. For sound recordings created in machine-readable form (for example, computer disk), the Copyright Office will not accept the computer disk as a deposit material. The author must deposit an audiocassette of the work.

MOTION PICTURES

The deposit materials for motion pictures are different than for other works. For unpublished or published motion pictures, the Copyright Office requires a separate description of the work. This description should be as complete as possible. If the work is a theatrical film or major television production, a shooting script or a press book is sufficient. In addition to the separate description, deposit materials for a published motion picture must include a complete copy, clear and undamaged, free of splices and defects that would interfere with viewing the work. (This copy will be returned to the owner by a procedure explained in the next section.) If the work is first published in the United States, the copy must be a complete copy of the best edition. If the work is first published outside the United States, the applicant should furnish one complete copy as first published. If the work is unpublished, a complete copy of the work containing all the visual and aural elements should be deposited.

An alternative deposit system is available for unpublished motion pictures. A motion picture is *unpublished* when:

- no copies of the film have been made or are ready for distribution or have been offered for distribution; or
- no copies of the film are distributed to the public by sale, rental, lease, or lending.

Performance or broadcast of a motion picture does not, by itself, constitute publication. The applicant for an unpublished motion picture may send either a recording of the complete soundtrack or reproductions of images from each ten-minute segment of the work. The written description for such alternative deposit must include the title, summary of the work, date the work was fixed, first tele-cast (if applicable) and whether the telecast was fixed simultaneous with trans-mission, running time, and the credits. For more information about copyright registration for motion pictures including video recordings, see Copyright Office Circular 45.

Special Rules: Return of Motion Pictures Deposits

Special rules regarding the return of motion pictures have been implement-ed by the Library of Congress. These rules permit the owner of copyright in a motion picture to sign a Motion Picture Agreement, whereby the depositor of a motion picture may have the motion picture returned under certain conditions. For more information, contact the Motion Picture Section, Motion Picture Broadcasting and Recorded Sound Division, Library of Congress, Washington DC 20540.

ARCHITECTURE

The deposit materials required for an architectural work (whether or not the building has been constructed) consist of one complete copy of the architectural blueprints or drawings in visually perceptible form showing the overall form of the building and any interior arrangement of spaces, or design elements, in which copyright is claimed. If the claim covers a building that has been constructed, the deposit materials also should include photographs of the completed structure clearly revealing the design elements on which the claim is based. In each case, the Copyright Office requires that the deposit must be marked to show the date of publication, if any, and the date of completion of construction of the architectur-al work. For more information about copyright claims in architectural works, see Copyright Office Circular 41.

END NOTE

1. Fonar Corp. v. Domenick, 105 F.3d 99 (2d Cir. 1997).

CHAPTER 21
Processing, Correcting and Canceling Registrations

This chapter offers information about Copyright Office procedures and the processing of copyright applications including:

- expediting the registration process;
- responding to Copyright Office inquiries;
- correcting a Certificate of Registration;
- the cancellation process; and
- establishing a deposit account.

MAILING THE APPLICATION AND DEPOSIT MATERIALS

An applicant seeking copyright registration should mail a package to the Copyright Office containing:

- the *completed application;*
- *deposit materials;*
- the *fee* (payment in check or money order made payable to the Register of Copyrights); and
- a *cover letter* detailing the contents of the package and referencing the name of the work and the applicant.

This package should be mailed to the Register of Copyrights, Library of Congress, Washington, DC 20559-6000.

The applicant does *not* receive an acknowledgment of receipt from the Copyright Office, and the Copyright Office will not respond to queries about whether an application has been received. Receipt can be verified by sending the application by registered or certified mail and requesting a return receipt from the United States Postal Service. The applicant can also enclose a self-addressed postcard to verify receipt.

EXPEDITING REGISTRATION

It is sometimes necessary for the applicant to expedite the registration process. For a handling fee of $500 (plus the $30 filing fee), the Copyright Office will process an application within five working days. This ser-vice is not for convenience; it is allowed only in urgent cases. The Copyright Office has prepared a form for "Request for Special Handling," an example of which is included in

Copyright Circular 10. As an alternative to using this form, an applicant can prepare a cover letter answering the following questions:

- Why is there an urgent need for special handling? (for example, litigation, customs matter, contractual or publishing deadline, or other reasons as specified)
- If the action is requested in order to go forward with litigation: (a) Is the litigation actual (the suit will definitely be filed) or prospective (the suit *may* be filed)? (b) Is the party requesting the expedited action the plaintiff or defendant in the action? (c) What are the names of the parties and what is the name of the court where the action is pending or expected?

The person requesting the expedited action must certify that the statements are correct to the best of his or her knowledge and must provide a mailing address and phone number for contact. The letter and the envelope should be addressed to Special Handling, Library of Congress, Department 100, Washington, DC 20540. Money orders or cashiers checks are recommended for the fee. A personal check will be accepted, but if the check bounces, the registration will be revoked. Expedited registrations can be sent by Federal Express or other overnight courier. It is wise to include a prepaid return envelope (for example, FedEx, Express Mail) for overnight mailing of the Certificate of Registration.

RECEIPT BY THE COPYRIGHT OFFICE: THE EFFECTIVE DATE

When an application (other than for expedited processing) is received, the Copyright Office records the date of receipt. After that, the application may sit for weeks or months before it is assigned to a copyright examiner who specializes in that particular class of works. The examiner reviews the package and determines whether it is complete (that is, whether it contains a properly prepared application, fee, and deposit materials). If the application is complete, a Certificate of Registration will be issued, and the effective date of the registration will be the date that the application was received by the Copyright Office (the date of receipt).

If the application is missing an element (for example, the application is missing the name of the claimant), the examiner may telephone the applicant and obtain the name of the claimant. The date of the telephone call will become the effective date of registration. That is, the effective date of registration is the date when *all* information and materials are received by the Copyright Office.

17 U.S.C. § 410(d) Effective date of registration of claim

The effective date of a copyright registration is the day on which an application, deposit, and fee, which are later determined by the Register of Copyrights or by a court of competent jurisdiction to be acceptable for registration, have all been received in the Copyright Office.

The effective date of registration has an impact on whether certain remedies are available to a copyright owner. For example, if the effective date is prior to an infringement, the copyright owner can seek statutory damages and attorney fees. As explained in Chapter 18, the registration does not affect copyright protection. The work is protected regardless of the registration.

RESOLVING ISSUES WITH THE COPYRIGHT OFFICE

A copyright examiner relies on regulations established in the Copyright Act and the *Code of Federal Regulations.* The examiner uses special Copyright Office rules and procedures. Most of these regulations and rules are summarized in the *Compendium of Copyright Office Practices,* a manual prepared by the Copyright Office. To obtain a copy, contact the Government Printing Office, Superintendent of Documents, P.O. Box 371954, Pittsburgh, PA 15250-7954.

If the examiner has a question or requires changes in the application, the applicant will receive a letter or phone call. Generally, if the matter is small (for example, supplying a date or name), the examiner telephones. If the matter is more complex (for example, an issue of copyrightability), a letter is sent. The applicant has 120 days to respond. Failure to respond to the examiner's letter will result in closing of the file at the Copyright Office, and the applicant will be required to submit a new application, fee, and deposit materials.

If the registration is granted, a copy of the Certificate of Registration is mailed to the address located in the final space of the application. Once the Certificate of Registration is received by the applicant, copies should be made, and the registration number and date should be recorded in a separate file. If the certificate is mailed to a law office or agent representing the applicant, the applicant should be furnished the original Certificate of Registration with instructions regarding its safekeeping.

If the examiner refuses registration, the applicant can request a re-examination. If, after re-examination, the application is again refused, the applicant receives a notice of refusal by the head of the Examining Division. Refusal is not final, however, until the Chief of the Examining Division furnishes a final decision. This document (the Final Refusal) is necessary to appeal the Copyright Office decision in federal court.

What If the Copyright Application Disappears?

If no response is received from the Copyright Office within six months of mailing an application, contact the "Material Controls" department at (202) 707-8239. If the office cannot track your application—that is, it is lost—you will be given another chance to apply. Assuming there is evidence of your earlier date of mailing, such as a return receipt card, this earlier date will become your effective date when the registration is issued.

FORM CA: CORRECTING OR SUPPLEMENTING THE COPYRIGHT REGISTRATION

A copyright owner may want to correct information in a basic registration (for example, the author's name is misspelled) or may wish to add information, facts, or explanations necessary to protect the work. In that case, a supplementary application (Form CA) is filed to correct an error in copyright registration or to add information.

For example, the Certificate of Registration for the book *Rain Dance*, incorrectly names Sam and Jane as the authors. The real authors are Sam and Joan. Form CA would be filed listing the correct authors. A supplementary application should *not* be used if there is a change in ownership rights. For example, if the book *Rain Dance* is sold to Macmillan Publishing, Form CA would not be used. That transfer should be recorded separately in the Copyright Office using the procedures for recording transfers explained in Chapter 15.

Supplementary Registration

Form CA is not an application form. It is intended solely to correct or add information to a basic registration. The filing of a supplementary application does not void the underlying basic registration; it merely expands the information.

Space A: Basic Instructions

Space A of Form CA ("Basic Instructions") requests information regarding the title of the work, name of authors, registration number of basic registration, year of basic registration, and names of copyright claimants. All information in this space should match the information in the basic registration.

Space B: Corrections

Corrections should be provided in Space B. If there is no correction, this section should be left blank. Space B requires the following information:

- the line number of the incorrect information on the basic registration;
- the line heading of the incorrect information on the basic registration;
- the incorrect information as it appears in the basic registration; and
- the corrected information.

The "line number" refers to the large gray numeral on the left side of the basic registration (for example, referred to in this book as Space 1, Space 2, and so on). The "line heading" is where the incorrect information is located (for example, "date of first publication").

Space B on Form CA also provides an area for an "Explanation of Correction." This portion is optional; the applicant has no obligation to complete it. A lack of explanation will not prevent the processing of Form CA. If there is any confusion about the correction, a copyright examiner will contact the applicant by letter or telephone.

Space C: Amplification

If the applicant intends to amplify, expand, or augment information in a basic registration, Space C is completed. If there is no amplification, this section should be left blank. If more than one portion is to be augmented, the line number and heading for a second or third portion would be marked in Space C (or in Space D—a space provided for continuation of material). For example, if a song was first registered under the title "Computer Vampire" but has been become known by the title, "I Byte Your Neck," the registrant would augment the basic registration by completing Space C as follows:

Line number: 1
Line heading or description: previous or alternative title
Amplified information: "I Byte Your Neck."

Space C on Form CA also provides an area for an "Explanation of Amplified Information." As with Space B, this portion is optional. A lack of explanation will not prevent the processing of Form CA.

Space D

If more room is needed for corrections and amplifications, Space D is used as a "continuation" section.

Spaces E through G

The remaining sections of Form CA (E—Deposit Account; F—Certification; and G—Address for Return of Certificate) are similar to the final sections of the copyright application and should be completed as discussed in Chapter 19. For further information on supplementary registrations, see Copyright Office Circular R8.

CANCELLATION OF COMPLETED REGISTRATIONS

If, after registration, the Copyright Office learns that a work is not copyrightable, the Copyright Office will commence a procedure that will result in cancellation of the registration. What could cause such an action? Three common reasons are:

1. the work does not constitute copyrightable subject matter. For example, a clothing designer registers her dresses as "three-dimensional soft sculptures." The Copyright Office later determines that the works are useful articles (that is, clothing) and are not registrable;[1]

2. the work does not meet legal or formal requirements. For example, if a work was first published before 1978, and copyright notice was omitted from the deposit materials; or

3. the work does not meet the requirements of the regulations. For example, the check used to pay the fee was written against insufficient funds, or the application and the deposit materials do not match.

The Copyright Office will attempt to correct minor errors, such as the kind normally rectified during the application procedure, by contacting the applicant. If a work has been registered in the wrong class, the Copyright Office will cancel the basic registration in the incorrect class and issue a new registration in the proper class. Prior to canceling any registration, the Copyright Office will provide notice to the registrant and offer an opportunity to respond. Further information on cancellation of completed registrations can be found in 37 *Code of Federal Regulations* section 201.7.

Life After Copyright Cancellation

The cancellation of a copyright registration by the Copyright Office does not necessarily terminate copyright protection. In 1998, a federal court in California granted a preliminary injunction to the owner of a watch face design. The Copyright Office subsequently canceled the registration based upon its determination that the watch face design (the letter "G") was an unprotectible element of a useful object. The court left the preliminary injunction in place, indicating that cancellation simply removed the presumption of copyright validity.[2] The court held that its decision was based on independent findings, and its conclusion was that the watch face was protectible.

DEPOSIT ACCOUNTS

Applicants who deal regularly with the Copyright Office can maintain a deposit account, which means that the applicant does not need to include a check every time an application is mailed or a transfer is filed. Deposit accounts are not charge accounts; there must be sufficient funds in an account before an application will be accepted. The requirements for deposit accounts are as follows:

- the initial deposit must be at least $250;
- all subsequent deposits must be $250 or more;
- there must be at least twelve transactions per year;
- the exact name and number of the deposit account must be in all applications or requests for services; and
- the deposit account holder must maintain a sufficient balance to cover all charges.

The Copyright Office will send holders monthly statements showing deposits, charges, and balances. For more information regarding deposit accounts, see Copyright Office Circular R5. The following letter can be used to establish a deposit account.

Example of Letter to Establish Deposit Account
TO: Department DS
Library of Congress
Washington, DC 20540
Attention: Deposit Accounts

Enclosed is my remittance of $_____ to establish a Deposit Account under the name of _____ _____ whose address is_____, _____ [*telephone   no.*],   attention   of _____ [*give name of the person to whom monthly statements and "no funds" notifications should be sent*].

_____ [signature]

END NOTES

1. Whimsicality, Inc. v. Rubie's Costume Co., 836 F. Supp. 112 (E.D.N.Y. 1993).
2. Gucci Timepieces Am., Inc. v. Yidah Watch Co., 47 U.S.P.Q.2d 1938 (C.D. Cal. 1998).

CHAPTER 22
Copyright Infringement

There are two general categories of copyright infringements: obvious unauthorized uses, for example, duplicating a compact disc or broadcasting a video without permission; and plagiarism, the borrowing of portions of a copyrighted work in the creation of a new work—for example, paraphrasing a work or creating similar characters. In this chapter, the standards and tests for both types of infringements are discussed including:

- elements of copyright infringement;
- principle of access;
- standards for substantial similarity; and
- determining liability for infringement.

ELEMENTS OF INFRINGEMENT

Infringement occurs when a copyrighted work is copied, modified, displayed, or performed without authorization. In order to claim infringement, two elements must be proven:

1. *ownership*—the party claiming infringement must prove ownership of a valid copyright;
2. *copying*—the party claiming infringement must demonstrate that the infringer had access to the work and violated one of the exclusive rights.

Ownership of Copyright

Proving ownership is accomplished by introducing the copyright registration as evidence. The copyright registration establishes prima facie proof of ownership and creates a presumption of copyright validity. In other words, the court will presume that the work is protected under copyright law and that the owner has properly acquired rights to the work. This presumption can be rebutted, as explained in Chapter 23.

Establishing Transfer of Ownership. When an owner of copyright transfers exclusive rights to someone, that person may sue if the rights are infringed. For example, Rufus Thomas, the writer of the song "Walkin' the Dog," transferred his rights in the song to a music publisher, Almo Music. If unauthorized copies are made of "Walkin' the Dog," Almo Music can sue the infringer. However, Almo Music would have to prove ownership of *its* right. That is, Almo Music would have to introduce a recorded document that evidences the transfer from Rufus Thomas. Ownership is often challenged when the work is created by an employee or independent contractor. For more information on works made for hire, see Chapter 13.

JUDGE LEARNED HAND ON COPYRIGHT: A POINT OF HONOR

The purpose of an infringement lawsuit is to provide a remedy for the copyright owner's injury. Without a real injury, for example, lost revenue, the issue of infringement is academic and one for which judges have little patience, as demonstrated by the 1924 case of *Fred Fisher, Inc. v. Dillingham.*[1] In *Fisher,* the owner of the song "Dardanella" sued the owner of "Kahlua." The melodies of the two songs were different, but the plaintiff claimed that the composer of "Kahlua," Jerome Kern, had copied part of the *ostinato* (an eight-note pattern that repeated within the background accompaniment). The *ostinato* was not an essential element of either work, and the owner of "Dardanella" could not prove any injury from the infringement. Judge Hand was annoyed. "This controversy is a mere point of honor of scarcely more than irritation, involving no substantial interest. Except that it raises an interesting point of law, it would be a waste of time for everyone concerned." Judge Hand awarded the plaintiff the minimum amount possible—$250. This case is a reminder that copyright claims should not be filed on principle, but only if there is damage. Similarity of works is important, but only if closely related to proving an injury.

Copying

To prove infringement, the copyright owner must prove that the work was copied. Since it is difficult to find direct evidence of copying, a court will conclude copying has occurred if:

- the defendant had access to the copyrighted work; and
- the defendant's work is substantially similar to the copyrighted work.

ACCESS

Access means that the alleged infringer had a reasonable opportunity to view or hear the copyrighted work. As a general rule, the more popular a work is, the easier it is to prove access. Conversely, if a work was not published, the copyright owner has a harder time proving access. There are various ways to prove access, as shown in the examples provided.

EXAMPLE

In a case involving infringement of the H.R. Pufsnuf characters, the plaintiffs proved that the representatives of a fast-food chain had visited the plaintiff's headquarters and discussed use of the characters in commercials. The presence of representatives at the headquarters demonstrated that the copyrighted characters had been viewed.[2]

EXAMPLE

The copyright owner of the song "He's So Fine" sued former Beatle George Harrison, alleging that Harrison's song "My Sweet Lord" infringed copyright. The plaintiff proved that Harrison had access to "He's So Fine," since the song was on the British pop charts in 1963 (while a song by the Beatles was also on the British charts). The court concluded Harrison had a reasonable opportunity to hear the plaintiff's song.[3]

EXAMPLE

Playboy Enterprises (the publisher of *Playboy* magazine) sued a computer bulletin board operator for permitting the posting and downloading of photographs and other images from *Playboy* magazine. *Since* Playboy distributed 3.4 million copies of the magazine each month, the court presumed that the defendant had reasonable access to the works.[4]

EXAMPLE

In a 1997 case, makers of Beanie Babies sued a company marketing a pig bean bag, known as "Preston the Pig," that was nearly identical to the Beanie Baby known as "Squealor." The similarity between the two was so close as to create a reasonable presumption of access.[5]

When Works Are Identical

If the infringement involves identical copies, such as photographs copied from a magazine, access may be presumed and does not need to be proven. That is because in cases of verbatim copying, it is virtually impossible that two works could have been independently created. It is presumed that the defendant *had* to have had access to the plaintiff's work in order to create an exact duplicate. In situations such as this, the burden is on the defendant, the alleged infringer, to disprove access.

SUBSTANTIAL SIMILARITY

In addition to proving access, the plaintiff must prove that the infringing work is substantially similar to the copyrighted work. Substantial similarity means that the works have similarities that could have resulted only from copying, not from coincidence.

Measuring Substantial Similarity

During the twentieth century, various tests have been adopted for proving works are substantially similar. Most of these tests are derived from the abstractions test devised by Judge Learned Hand and explained in Chapter 3. Regardless of the name of the test, courts are always concerned with three types of similarities:

1. unprotectible similarities—elements that are not protected under copyright;
2. literal similarities—verbatim copying or identical duplication; and
3. nonliteral similarities—paraphrasing, modifications, and other borrowing of expressions.

How does a court analyze an infringement? In one test commonly used in computer software cases, the **abstraction-filtration-comparison** test,[6] the court breaks down the allegedly infringed work into its constituent parts and examines each of these parts for incorporated ideas and elements taken from the public domain. The court sifts out the nonprotectible material and compares the remaining material to determine whether the protectible elements are substantially similar to the defendant's work. When comparing protectible elements, a court examines both literal similarities such as verbatim copying and nonliteral similarities such as paraphrased elements.[7]

Unprotectible Similarities

Unprotectible similarities are those aspects of a work not protected under copyright law such as facts, ideas, common dramatic stock elements, information taken from public documents or other common sources, and material in the public domain.

EXAMPLE

A clothing company copied another company's line of children's sweaters that included leaves, acorns, squirrels, and other fall motifs. The court filtered out those elements that were unprotectible and reviewed the remaining elements as well as the arrangement of the imagery and determined the works were substantially similar.[8]

EXAMPLE

A songwriter used the phrase " I like to gamble, I like to smoke. I like to drink and tell a dirty joke." The defendant wrote a song with dissimilar music containing the phrase "She don't drink. She don't smoke. She can't stand a dirty joke." The court determined that the similarity of such public domain phrases did not amount to substantial similarity.[9]

EXAMPLE

An author wrote a novel about a wealthy Jewish family in San Francisco, borrowing factual material and several short phrases from another book, a social history of Jewish migration to San Francisco. Even though there were similarities between the two books, the novelist did not infringe the historical work because all that was borrowed were short phrases and facts, both unprotectible under copyright law.[10]

EXAMPLE

A dollmaker created a wooden doll modeled after paper dolls. A former employee of the dollmaker created her own line of wooden dolls with different facial expressions. Even though there were similarities, there was no infringement because the only elements of the dolls that were copied (size, shape, and medium) were unprotectible.[11]

For more information on what is not protectible, see Chapter 5.

Arrangements of Public Domain Materials May Be Protectible.   Although items from the public domain are never copyrightable, the arrangement of public domain material may be protectible.

Literal Similarities

After sorting out the unprotectible elements, the remaining protectible similarities are divided into literal and nonliteral similarities. Literal similarities are word-for-word or note-for-note reproductions such as photocopying chapters from a text or using a pop song in a commercial. Sometimes, only snippets or pieces of literal similarities are copied, and in these cases, a court may apply a standard known as "fragmented literal similarity" in which the court examines the portions taken and determines whether they constitute a substantial portion of the plaintiff's work. For example, the taking of one sentence from a work generally will not be considered an infringement. However, when that one sentence is "E.T., phone home," the court will consider that line to be a substantial portion, and the unauthorized reprinting of the sentence on cups and merchandise will amount to an infringement.[12]

Nonliteral Similarities

Many infringements are not exact duplications but are plagiarisms resulting from the creation of new works. These similarities, such as paraphrasings or modifications, are considered nonliteral similarities. In cases of nonliteral similarities, it is not how *much* is taken but whether the defendant has "appropriated the fundamental essence or structure of plaintiff's work."[13] One standard used to assess this infringement is referred to as "comprehensive nonliteral similarity."

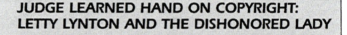

JUDGE LEARNED HAND ON COPYRIGHT: LETTY LYNTON AND THE DISHONORED LADY

The principles of nonliteral similarity were not always obvious to judges, and it was not until 1936 that Judge Learned Hand introduced the idea that an infringement could occur without verbatim copying. In the 1936 case *Sheldon v. Metro Goldwyn Pictures*,[14] the author of the play *Dishonored Lady* sued the producer of the movie *Letty Lynton* for copyright infringement. The plaintiff's work was derived from the true story of a nineteenth-century Scottish woman—a story over which no author could claim a monopoly. The defendant borrowed the plot of the plaintiff's play, but not any of the specific dialogue. The lower court held that there was no infringement, but Judge Hand disagreed and ruled that the play's expression was copied by the film, even though no literal copying of the dialogue occurred. "Speech is only a small part of a dramatist's means of expression . . . the play may often be most effectively pirated by leaving out the speech. . . ." As a result of this decision, courts recognized that nonliteral similarities could amount to copyright infringement.

Following are two cases in which the courts analyzed works with nonliteral similarities.

EXAMPLE

Star Wars v. Battle Star Gallactica. In 1983, the owners of *Star Wars* sued the owners of the television show *Battlestar Gallactica* for copyright infringement.[15] There was no duplication of *Star Wars* dialogue in the television show, but there were many *nonliteral* similarities. In their brief to the court, the owners of *Star Wars* listed thirty-four such nonliteral similarities, for example: the central conflict of each story is a war between the galaxy's democratic and totalitarian forces; a friendly robot, who aids the democratic forces, is severely injured (*Star Wars*) or destroyed (*Battlestar*) by the totalitarian forces; there is a romance between the hero's friend (the cynical fighter pilot) and the daughter of one of the leaders of the democratic forces; and there is a scene in a cantina (*Star Wars*) or casino (*Battlestar*) in which musical entertainment is offered by bizarre, nonhuman creatures. On the basis of the thirty-four nonliteral similarities, the owners of *Star Wars* were able to prove infringement.

EXAMPLE

Two Tales of Slave Ships. The author of a historical novel, *Echo of Lions,* sued the makers of the film *Amistad.*[16] The book and film were based upon actual incidents aboard a slave ship, and the similarities included a narrator who links the black and white communities; a slave who has one child and remains true to his African roots, calling upon his ancestors for help in his legal battle; the destruction of a slave colony concurrent with a court decision; and an ending tied to the Civil War. The court determined that these similarities were too general to be protected, and the mood, pace, and plot (the novel was based around a love story, the movie was not) were dissimilar. On that basis the court refused to halt release of the film.

What About the Material That Is *Not* Taken?

Should a court consider how much of a work was *not* taken by an alleged infringer? One judge stated, "[N]o plagiarist can excuse the wrong by showing how much of his work he did not pirate."[17] It is immaterial if the vast majority of material in a defendant's book is not similar to the plaintiff's book. What matters is the quality of the taking and whether the ordinary observer would find that the similarities could have resulted only from copying.

The Lay Observer Test

When determining substantial similarity, some courts apply a **lay observer** test derived from a ruling by Judge Learned Hand.[18] A court asks, "Would the ordinary observer, when examining both works, consider that the defendant has misappropriated the plaintiff's work?" By using this lay observer test, the court applies a personal "gut level" inquiry, rather than an expert or technical opinion, as to whether an infringement has occurred. For example, when comparing two medical texts on embryology, the court rejected the need for an expert and, instead, applied a lay observer test.[19]

Attorneys apply their own lay observer test when analyzing an infringement case. An attorney may show a copyrighted work and the infringing work to friends or office workers to get their initial opinion on whether they feel that the defendant has misappropriated something from the plaintiff.

When an Expert Is Needed

In some cases, an expert opinion is the key to proving or unraveling a claim of infringement. For example, in one case, experts in musicology were able to demonstrate that the only similarity between two compositions was a recurring three-note sequence found also in the works of Johann Sebastian Bach.[20] The use of an expert is dependent upon the intended audience for the works. For example, in actions involving computer programming infringement, the lay observer simply lacks the necessary expertise to determine similarities or differences between software codes, and an expert is needed.[21]

Higher Standards for Factual Works

Because of the factual nature of works such as maps, charts, and factual compilations, courts often use a higher standard for establishing infringement. When determining infringement for these works, judges require verbatim copying or very similar paraphrasing. The reasoning is there is a limited number of ways to express facts and factual compilations and therefore similarities should be literal. This is sometimes referred to as the merger doctrine, explained in more detail in Chapter 23. For example, two authors may write books about the ingredients and side effects of prescription drugs. There is only a limited number of ways to express this information. Therefore, infringement will occur only if there is verbatim copying (that is, literal similarity).

LIABILITY FOR INFRINGEMENT

An infringer is any person who is liable for an unauthorized use of copyrighted material. The court determines who is legally culpable for the infringing acts. An infringer may not have directly copied but is liable under legal principles that apportion responsibility, for example:

- *Employer-employee liability.* The acts of an employee within the scope of employment duties are attributable to the employer. Therefore, if an employee infringes a book while writing a text for a publishing company, the publishing company may be named as a defendant.
- *Independent contractors.* In the case of an independent contractor who infringes in the course of doing work for a client, both client and contractor may be defendants. For example, an ad agency infringes a photographic copyright when preparing an ad for a car company. The ad is published in a magazine. The car company, the magazine, and the ad agency could be named in the copyright infringement lawsuit.

Infringer's Intent

The intent of the person performing the infringing acts is irrelevant for determining whether an infringement occurred. For example, in a situation involving a museum that prints postcards of a photographer's photos, it does not matter if the museum innocently believes that it had the right to print postcards. The intention of the museum or the printer may be relevant only for determining the remedy for the infringement, that is, the amount of damages or whether attorney fees will be awarded. These principles are explained in Chapter 24.

Setting a Trap for Infringers

How can direct or verbatim copying be proven? Sometimes, the author of a factual work, compilation, or computer program may deliberately place unnecessary or incorrect information into the work (known as "salting the work"). For example, a cartographer may place the name of a fictitious city in the index of a map, and if the same fictitious city appears in the index of the defendant's map, there is proof of direct copying.

Unconscious Copying

Artists are aware that art is always based upon borrowed ideas and expressions. As Judge Hand stated, "Everything registers somewhere in our memories and no one can tell what may evoke it."[22] In other words, a songwriter may write a melody and not recall that it was from another work. Judge Hand sympathetically dubbed such copying as "unconscious." Although the author is still liable for unconscious copying, the sympathetic reference offsets the perception of the defendant and may influence the court's award of damages. Judge Hand's "unconscious copying" was adopted by a federal court sixty years later in a case involving songwriter George Harrison.[23]

Myth: No Liability for Nonprofit Users

Some people incorrectly believe that there is no liability if the infringer is a nonprofit organization. This is not true. Nonprofits are subject to the same liability as any infringer. However, nonprofit status has a bearing on two issues: a defense of fair use and proof of lost profits.

Myth: Attribution Prevents a Claim of Infringement

Attribution (crediting material to its author) is important to preserve academic credibility and may be a factor in determining fair use (see Chapter 7), but it does not prevent a claim of infringement and may even lead to additional claims of the right of publicity or false endorsement (see Chapter 1).

Contributory Infringement

A **contributory infringer** is anyone who, with knowledge or reason to know of infringing activity of another, induces, causes, or contributes to the infringement. A contributory infringer is also anyone who has the right and ability to supervise the infringing activities with a direct financial interest in such activities. The Supreme Court has described a contributory infringer as one who was in a position to control the use of copyrighted works by others and has authorized the use without permission from the copyright owner.

The key elements in determining contributory infringement are:

- the knowledge or reason to know of the infringing activity; and
- the extent to which the party is entangled in the infringement.

The following are some examples of rulings regarding contributory infringement.

EXAMPLE

The Dance Club. A dance club hires bands and deejays and music is performed without a performance rights license. The deejays and bands are infringing the performance rights of the copyright owners of certain songs. The proprietor of the dance club will be liable as a contributory infringer for the infringing activities of hired bands or deejays.[24] The proprietor has a reason to know of the infringing activity, and in addition, the proprietor has a direct financial interest. That is, the dance club proprietor profits directly from the infringing activity. The landlord of the building in which the dance club is located is probably not a contributory infringer because the landlord does not supervise and does not have a reason to know of the infringing activity, and the landlord does not have a direct financial interest in the infringing activity.[25]

EXAMPLE

The Television Broadcast. A television station broadcasts a movie infringing the copyright of a motion picture owner. The television station is a contributory infringer because it supervises and reviews the television movie before it is broadcast, and the station also has a direct financial interest. Note: The result would be different if it were a cable television channel, and not a local TV station, because under a special exemption, a cable television broadcaster who has no control over the content or selection of a television signal *is not* a contributory infringer.[26]

EXAMPLE

The Videotape Duplicator. A person infringes copyright by making multiple copies of a motion picture using a videotape recording machine. This person is an infringer, but the suppliers of the videotape recording machine *are not* contributory infringers. The Supreme Court has ruled that where a device has multiple uses besides infringement, the suppliers of such devices are not contributory infringers. For example, manufacturers of photocopying machines are not considered contributory infringers simply because some persons illegally use the devices to infringe copyright.

EXAMPLE

The Helpful Copy Shop. A copy shop near a university rents required textbooks to customers. Students can illegally copy the necessary chapters without buying the books. The copy shop is a contributory infringer because it induces or materially contributes to the infringing activity. However, an exemption provides that a library or archives *is not* a contributory infringer with respect to the unsupervised use of copy machines located on its premises.[27]

EXAMPLE

The Swap Meet Owner. A swap meet or flea market operator leases space to vendors who sell counterfeit recordings. The operator is a contributory infringer if he or she is aware of the infringing sales and has a financial interest.[28]

EXAMPLE

The Website Owner Who Gives It Away. The operator of a computer bulletin board distributes copyrighted software without charging users. Prior to 1998, the operator was not criminally liable. However, this loophole was closed, and this activity is prohibited regardless of whether the operator receives "commercial gain."[29] See Chapter 11 for more information on computer and Internet uses.

CAN AUTHORS INFRINGE THEIR OWN WORK?

This may seem like an academic question, but it had a very real application for songwriter John Fogerty when he was sued in 1985. Many of the songs written by Fogerty and popularized by his group Creedence Clearwater Revival are owned by Fantasy, a California company. Fantasy sued Fogerty, claiming that one of his newer songs, "The Old Man Down the Road," infringed a 1970 song, "Run Through the Jungle," also written by Fogerty and owned by Fantasy. Fogerty brought his guitar into court, sang both songs for the jury, and demonstrated that the elements common to both songs were unprotectible and common to many rock and roll songs. Fogerty won this novel lawsuit and, in the process, established a standard for the award of attorney fees.[30]

END NOTES

1. 293 F. 145 (S.D.N.Y. 1924).
2. Sid & Marty Krofft Television Prods., Inc. v. McDonald's Corp., 562 F.2d 1157 (9th Cir. 1977).
3. Abkco Music, Inc. v. Harrisongs Music, Ltd., 722 F.2d 988 (2d Cir. 1983).

4. Playboy Enters., Inc. v. Frena, 839 F. Supp. 1552 (D.C. Fla. 1993).

5. Ty, Inc. v. GMA Accessories, Inc. 132 F.3d 1167 (7th Cir. 1997).

6. Computer Assocs., Inc. v. Altai, Inc., 982 F.2d 693 (2d Cir. 1992).

7. Paramount Pictures Corp. v. Carol Publishing Group, 11 F. Supp. 2d 329 (S.D.N.Y. 1998).

8. Knitwaves, Inc. v. Lollytogs, Ltd., 71 F.3d 996 (2d Cir. 1995).

9. Pendleton v. Acuff-Rose Publications, Inc., 225 U.S.P.Q. 935 (M.D. Tenn. 1984).

10. Narrell v. Freeman, 872 F.2d 907 (9th Cir. 1980).

11. Country Kids 'N City Slicks, Inc. v. Sheen, 77 F.3d 1280 (10th Cir. 1996).

12. Universal Studios v. Kamar Indus., Inc., 217 U.S.P.Q. 1162 (S.D. Tex. 1982).

13. Arica Inst. v. Palmer, 970 F.2d 1067 (2d Cir. 1992).

14. 81 F.2d 49 (2d Cir. 1936).

15. Twentieth Century Fox Film Corp. v. MCA, Inc., 715 F.2d 1327 (9th Cir. 1983).

16. *In* Chase-Riboud v. Dreamworks, Inc., 987 F. Supp. 1222 (C.D. Cal. 1997).

17. Churchill Livingstone, Inc. v. Williams & Wilkins, 949 F. Supp. 1045 (S.D.N.Y. 1996).

18. Arnstein v. Porter, 154 F.2d 464 (2d Cir. 1946).

19. Churchill Livingstone, Inc. v. Williams & Wilkins, 949 F. Supp. 1045 (S.D.N.Y. 1996).

20. Ferguson v. National Broadcasting Co., 584 F.2d 111 (5th Cir. 1978).

21. Whelan Assocs. v. Jaslow Dental Lab., 797 F.2d 1222 (3d Cir. 1986), *cert. denied,* 479 U.S. 1031 (1987).

22. Fred Fisher, Inc. v. Dillingham, 293 F. 145 (S.D.N.Y. 1924).

23. Abkco Music, Inc. v. Harrisongs Music, Ltd., 722 F.2d 988 (2d Cir. 1983).

24. Dreamland Ball Room, Inc. v. Shapiro, Bernstein & Co., 36 F.2d 354 (7th Cir. 1929).

25. Deutsch v. Arnold, 98 F.2d 686 (2d Cir. 1938).

26. 17 U.S.C. § 111(a)(3).

27. 17 U.S.C. § 108(f)(1).

28. Fonovisa, Inc. v. Cherry Auction, Inc., 76 F.3d 259 (9th Cir. 1995).

29. 17 U.S.C. § 506(a).

30. Fantasy, Inc. v. Fogerty, 510 U.S. 517 (1994).

FOR MORE INFORMATION

Infringement of Musical Works and Sound Recordings
See Chapter 10.

Software and Internet Infringement
See Chapter 11.

Defenses in a Copyright Infringement Lawsuit
See Chapter 23.

Remedies for Infringement
See Chapter 24.

Resolving Disputes Without Litigation
See Chapter 25.

The Litigation Process
See Chapter 26.

CHAPTER 23
Defenses to Infringement

In this chapter, information is provided about the following defenses to copyright infringement:

- plaintiff is not the copyright owner;
- plaintiff's work is not copyrightable;
- plaintiff did not comply with copyright rules;
- defendant independently created the work;
- defendant did not have access to the plaintiff's work;
- similarities between the two works are not substantial;
- defendant's copying is a fair use;
- defendant's copying is *de minimis*;
- defendant was authorized to use the work;
- defendant's use is permitted under the merger doctrine;
- plaintiff is estopped from suing the defendant;
- plaintiff has unclean hands or has misused copyright;
- plaintiff waited too long to bring the suit (that is, laches and the statute of limitations); and
- defendant believes that the author has been dead more than seventy years.

PLAINTIFF IS NOT THE OWNER OF RIGHTS

If the defendant can prove that the plaintiff does not own the copyright or did not acquire rights under an assignment or an exclusive license, the case will be dismissed. A plaintiff who does not own rights lacks the legal capacity (or "standing") to bring the suit. For example, a software company sued a former employee for copying a program. The employee proved that under the work made for hire doctrine, the software company did not own the copyright. Therefore, the software company lacked standing, and the case was dismissed.[1]

Beware of Frivolous and Fraudulent Defenses

A defense should be asserted only if the defendant has a good faith belief that it is applicable. A defense that is completely without merit, or based upon untrue facts, can destroy the defendant's credibility and result in sanctions or imprisonment stemming from felony perjury.

WORK IS NOT COPYRIGHTABLE

If the defendant can demonstrate that the work is not copyrightable, the infringement claim will be dismissed. A work is not copyrightable if it lacks originality, is not fixed, or does not meet the standards of protectibility described in Chapter 3.

THE PLAINTIFF DID NOT COMPLY WITH COPYRIGHT RULES

If the defendant can show that the plaintiff failed to comply with copyright rules or formalities, the case may be dismissed, or delayed until compliance occurs. For example, a construction company sued a former employee who had copied portions of a brochure. The defendant proved that the construction company had published the work without notice prior to 1989. The court determined that the work was in the public domain, and therefore the copying was permitted.[2]

THE DEFENDANT INDEPENDENTLY CREATED THE WORK

If the defendant can prove that the work was independently created, there is no infringement. The simplest method of proving independent creation is to prove that the defendant's work was created before the plaintiff's work. This can be accomplished by furnishing a certified registration with the earlier date or by witnesses who provide statements under penalty of perjury. Another method of proving independent creation is a "clean room" in which computer programmers are insulated from external sources when they create software programs. A clean room can also counter a claim of access to the plaintiff's work.

You've Got Mail, *Not!*

Mailing a work to oneself is not proof of the date of creation of the work. The postmark does not demonstrate that the material sealed inside was prepared on a certain date. This type of evidence is inconclusive because the envelope may have been mailed empty and unsealed. At a later date the material could have been placed in the postmarked envelope and sealed. It is also possible that the envelope may have been opened and resealed after being postmarked.

THE DEFENDANT DID NOT HAVE ACCESS TO THE PLAINTIFF'S WORK

If the defendant did not have a reasonable opportunity to view or hear the copyrighted work, the infringement claim can be defeated because there was no access. One method to demonstrate a lack of access is to show that the defendant's work was created prior to any alleged access to the plaintiff's work. For example, screenwriters at a movie studio were able to prove they had written the first draft of a screenplay before the plaintiff had even mailed his work to the studio.[3]

Because of concerns about infringement, many entertainment and publishing companies routinely return unsolicited works without opening them.

THE SIMILARITIES BETWEEN THE TWO WORKS ARE NOT SUBSTANTIAL

A defendant must demonstrate that the works are not substantially similar. The defendant should isolate and list all of the similarities. If the only similarities between the works are unprotectible elements, the defendant will prevail. Unprotectible materials are described in Chapters 5 and 22.

THE COPYING IS A FAIR USE

Under a fair use defense, it does not matter if the works are substantially similar because the defendant has a *right* to use the copied materials. In other words, fair use is a legal infringement. Descriptions of fair use standards and examples of fair use cases are provided in Chapter 7.

THE COPYING IS *DE MINIMIS*

If the court determines that the amount copied by the defendant is insubstantial, the copying will be excused as *de minimis*. This is not a fair use defense; it is a defense based solely upon the inconsequential amount of material copied. For example, several photographs appeared briefly in the film *Seven*. The court determined that a lay observer would have been unable to identify them. Therefore, the photos were not infringed because the copying was *de minimis*.[4]

THE DEFENDANT WAS AUTHORIZED TO USE THE WORK

If the defendant can prove that the use is authorized by the copyright owner, the infringement claim is defeated. For example, in a copyright infringement lawsuit, the Microsoft Corporation proved that it had previously acquired a license from Apple Computer to use the works at issue.[5]

THE USE IS PERMITTED UNDER THE MERGER DOCTRINE

If the defendant can demonstrate that there is a limited number of ways to express an idea, the defendant can defeat an infringement claim using the **merger doctrine**. The merger doctrine refers to the fact that the idea and the expression are merged or inseparable. For example, consider the use of the "garbage can" icon to signify the deletion of a computer file. Since there are very few images that concisely express the destruction of a file, it is not an infringement to copy a garbage can icon for use in a screen display. In the case of a map, there may be very few ways to express the symbol for an airport, other than by using a small image of an airplane.

PLAINTIFF IS ESTOPPED FROM SUING THE DEFENDANT

The band, the Grateful Dead, set up special areas at concerts where fans could tape-record the shows. Some of these Grateful Dead bootleg recordings were very high quality, and members of the band often obtained copies. If the Grateful Dead were to suddenly file suit against the fans who tape-recorded the shows, these fans could assert the defense of **estoppel**. Under this defense, the copyright owner cannot contradict behavior upon which the defendant has justifiably relied. There are two elements to estoppel:

1. the plaintiff must know about the defendant's conduct (for example, the Grateful Dead knew about the tape-recording); and
2. the defendant must have a justifiable belief that the infringing conduct is permitted (for example, the Grateful Dead established special areas for tape-recording the shows).

Estoppel, although commonly pleaded, requires a very unique set of facts. For this reason, it is rarely successful.

THE PLAINTIFF HAS DONE SOMETHING WRONG

There is a principle in law that a wrongdoer cannot complain about another person's alleged wrongs. In copyright litigation, this is expressed by two defenses: unclean hands and misuse of copyright.

Unclean Hands

Unclean hands is asserted when the plaintiff has committed a serious act of wrongdoing—so serious that it would be unfair for the court to allow the plaintiff to proceed. The court may determine that the act of wrongdoing outweighs any harm resulting from the infringement. In other words, because the plaintiff has unclean hands, the infringement lawsuit must be dismissed. Some examples of unclean hands could include:

- the plaintiff falsified material facts in an application;
- the plaintiff made material misrepresentations when recording a transfer; or
- the plaintiff demanded a license agreement without a valid claim of copyright.

Misuse of Copyright

Misuse of copyright is a form of unclean hands derived from antitrust and patent laws. Misuse occurs when there is some form of anticompetitive behavior based upon copyright ownership. For example, as a condition of a copyright license, a company is prohibited from marketing its own version of a software program; or a licensee is required to purchase additional (noncopyrighted) products as a condition of licensing the work. Although copyright misuse has been asserted successfully as a response to infringement,[6] there is a split in the federal courts as to whether it is a proper defense. Misuse is sometimes asserted by the defendant as a counterclaim. See Chapter 26 for information on counterclaims.

Obscenity Defense

It is a felony to engage in the business of distributing obscene material in interstate commerce.[7] What happens when an obscene work is infringed? Can a defendant use pornography as a defense, arguing that enforcing the copyright laws would assist in illegal activity? The Fifth[8] and Ninth Circuit[9] Courts of Appeals have ruled that obscenity is not a defense to copyright infringement. However, a federal court in New York City refused to issue an order to seize infringing copies of adult videos because the court determined the works were obscene.[10]

PLAINTIFF WAITED TOO LONG TO BRING THE SUIT

If a copyright owner has waited too long before bringing an infringement lawsuit, the defendant may use either laches or the statute of limitations as a defense. The application of either defense depends upon the amount of time that has passed.

Laches

Laches is a defense that is asserted when the plaintiff has waited an unreasonable amount of time to bring the lawsuit. Even though the statute of limitations (see the next section) has not expired, the defendant contends that the delay is so unreasonable that it would be unfair to permit the plaintiff to proceed with the lawsuit. Judge Learned Hand was one of the first judges to apply the rule of laches to copyright infringement.

JUDGE LEARNED HAND ON COPYRIGHT: I DIDN'T RAISE MY BOY TO BE A SOLDIER

A songwriter claimed the chorus of his song, "You Will Never Know How Much I Really Cared," was infringed by the chorus of another song, "I Didn't Raise My Boy to Be a Soldier." The plaintiff learned of the infringing song in 1914 but waited two years, until after the defendant's song had become popular, to file the lawsuit. Judge Hand ruled that the plaintiff could not receive damages for the period *after* which he learned of the infringement. Otherwise, stated Judge Hand, copyright owners would engage in a "speculative enterprise," waiting for an infringer to accumulate maximum profits and file suit.[11] In other words, a copyright owner has a duty to act within a reasonable period of time.

Statute of Limitations

The plaintiff has three years from the date of the infringement (when the claim "accrued") to file the lawsuit.[12]This is known as the statute of limitations. If the lawsuit is filed after the three-year period, the defendant can have the suit dismissed. If the action is a criminal action, the government has five years to prosecute a claim.[13]

What if an infringement occurs over several years? For example, what if an infringer sold unauthorized graphic prints from 1997 through December 31, 1999. The claim could be brought anytime through 2002. However, if the plaintiff files a claim in 2002, there is disagreement among the federal courts as to what infringements are covered. Some courts believe that *all* previous infringements should be covered (because the infringement is "continuing"). The majority of courts, however, believe that the lawsuit should only relate to infringements that occurred within the three years preceding the filing.

Some courts have held that the time limit for bringing a lawsuit begins when the plaintiff should have *reasonably known* about the claim.[14]This is referred to as "tolling the statute." For example, if a woman did not know that her father was a famous songwriter, she could not have reasonably known that she was entitled to claim copyright in his songs. The three-year period under the statue is "tolled" (does not begin) until she learns about her father.[15]

The Difference Between Laches and the Statute of Limitations

If the statute of limitations permits three years to file a suit, why was the copyright owner penalized in the case involving the song "I Didn't Raise My Boy to Be a Soldier"? Laches is a discretionary defense based upon a judge's sense of fairness. The copyright owner in the "I Didn't Raise My Boy to Be a Soldier" case knew about the infringement, allowed the owner to invest the effort, and only filed the suit after the song had run its course. Judge Hand did not deny *all* damages, but limited the damages based upon a sense of fairness.

The statute of limitations defense, unlike laches, does not provide judicial flexibility. It is a mandatory rule that requires that a case be dismissed if it is filed more than three years after the infringement could be reasonably discovered. There is no discretion for a judge and no right to award partial damages.

DEFENDANT BELIEVES THAT THE AUTHOR HAS BEEN DEAD MORE THAN SEVENTY YEARS

The Copyright Act provides a complete defense to infringement if the defendant has a reasonable belief that the author of the work has been dead for more than seventy years. After a period of ninety-five years from the year of first publication of a work, or a period of one hundred and twenty years from the year of its creation (whichever expires first), anyone can obtain a certified report from the Copyright Office that indicates the author is presumed to be deceased more than seventy years. A defendant's reliance in good faith upon this report is a complete defense to any action for infringement.[16]

END NOTES

1. Avtec Sys. v. Peiffer, 38 U.S.P.Q.2d (4th Cir. 1995).
2. Harris Custom Builders, Inc. v. Hoffmeyer, 92 F.3d 517 (7th Cir. 1996).
3. McGaughey v. Twentieth Century Fox Television, 12 F.3d 62 (5th Cir.1994).
4. Sandoval v. New Line Cinema Corp., 47 U.S.P.Q.2d 121(2d Cir. 1998).
5. Apple Computer, Inc. v. Microsoft Corp., 799 F. Supp. 1006 (N.D. Cal. 1992).
6. DSC Communications Corp. v. DGI Technologies, 81 F.3d 597 (5th Cir. 1996); Lasercomb Am., Inc. v. Reynolds, 911 F.2d 970 (4th Cir. 1990).
7. 18 U.S.C. § 1466.
8. Mitchell Bros. Film Group v. Cinema Adult Theater, 604 F.2d 852 (5th Cir. 1979).
9. Jartech, Inc. v. Clancy, 666 F.2d 403 (9th Cir. 1979).
10. Devil Films, Inc. v. Nectar Video, 49 U.S.P.Q.2d (BNA) 1059 (S.D.N.Y. 1998).
11. Haas v. Leo Feist, Inc., 234 F. 105 (S.D.N.Y. 1916).
12. 17 U.S.C. § 507(b).
13. 17 U.S.C. § 507(a).
14. Taylor v. Meirick, 712 F.2d 1112 (7th Cir. 1983).
15. Stone v. Williams, 891 F.2d 401 (2d Cir. 1989). This case is sometimes referred to as "Stone II" because there were three cases with the same title.
16. 17 U.S.C. § 302(e).

CHAPTER 24
Remedies for Copyright Infringement

This chapter provides information on remedies for copyright infringement including:

- temporary restraining orders, and preliminary and permanent injunctions;
- writs of seizure;
- actual and statutory damages;
- attorney fees and costs; and
- the basis for criminal prosecution.

INSTRUCTION

The Copyright Act offers two categories of remedies for copyright infringement: injunctions and damages.

INJUNCTIONS

An **injunction** is a court order issued to stop the infringing activity. If the infringer fails to abide by the injunction, a court can hold the infringer in contempt of court, resulting in fines or imprisonment. A copyright owner must have a valid registration in order to seek an injunction.[1] There are three types of injunctions:

1. Temporary restraining order (TRO);
2. Preliminary injunction; and
3. Permanent injunction.

Temporary Restraining Order

Initially, the copyright owner may seek a temporary restraining order (TRO). The TRO can be granted *ex parte*, that is, without the court hearing an opposition from the infringer. A TRO may be used in cases of mobile or "fly-by-night" infringers such as T-shirt and video infringers. Some musical groups bring an attorney on tour to serve TROs on T-shirt infringers at each show. The TRO is short in duration and only remains in effect until the court has an opportunity to schedule a hearing for the preliminary injunction.

Preliminary Injunction

The preliminary injunction is issued after a hearing where both parties have an opportunity to present evidence. Often these preliminary injunction hearings are "mini-trials" and require considerable preparation. The court may request that a bond be posted by the copyright owner. The purpose of the bond is to cover any damages suffered by the alleged infringer, in case the court determines that no infringement has occurred.

Standards for Preliminary Injunction.   A court uses two factors when determining whether to grant a preliminary injunction: (1) Is the copyright owner likely to succeed in the lawsuit?, and (2) Will the copyright owner suffer irreparable harm if the injunction is not granted? Normally, if the copyright owner can demonstrate copyright infringement, irreparable harm will be presumed. The preliminary injunction is requested through a **motion for preliminary injunction**. When seeking the motion, the plaintiff will attempt to prove that:

- the plaintiff is likely to succeed because (1) the plaintiff has a valid claim of ownership; (2) the defendant had access to the work; and (3) the defendant's work is substantially similar; and
- the plaintiff is likely to suffer irreparable harm as a result of the infringement.

A plaintiff has a harder time demonstrating irreparable harm if a substantial time period has passed between knowledge of the infringement and seeking an injunction. For example, a court refused to issue a preliminary injunction when the plaintiff waited thirteen months before seeking an injunction.[2] If other claims such as trademark or trade secrecy are joined with the copyright claim, they would also be addressed in the preliminary injunction hearing.

Effect of Preliminary Injunction.   The preliminary injunction lasts until the end of the trial. Since the trial may not occur for a year or more, the outcome of the preliminary injunction hearing has an important strategic effect. Many copyright cases settle after the preliminary injunction. Why should the parties proceed when the court has given them a preview of the trial outcome?

Permanent Injunction

If the defendant wins the case, the preliminary injunction is dissolved and there is no further court order. If the ruling is in favor of the copyright owner, the court issues a permanent injunction, which permanently restrains the infringer.

WRIT OF SEIZURE

Prior to instituting a lawsuit, a copyright owner may be concerned that the infringer will relocate, destroy evidence, or attempt to sell the infringing merchandise. Under such circumstances, the copyright owner may seek a **writ of seizure**—an extraordinary remedy in which the infringing merchandise and manufacturing materials are seized or "impounded." A writ of seizure, like an injunction, can only occur by order of the court. The writ directs the federal marshal to seize and hold infringing merchandise. A writ is usually granted upon payment of a bond by the copyright owner of at least twice the value of the infringing articles. The purpose of the bond is to protect the infringer in case the copyright owner was not infringed.

Under a judicial process known as *ex parte*, the writ may be obtained without consulting with the infringer. That is, upon a sufficient showing of evidence that the infringing activity will be hidden or destroyed, the copyright owner may obtain the writ without allowing the infringer an opportunity to appear and contest the writ in court.[3] However, such writs are granted only for a very short time, usually until a hearing can be scheduled. In the past decade, legal experts have raised questions about the constitutionality of the writ of seizure, and lawyers report that it has become more difficult to obtain the writ *ex parte* without the infringer present to defend his or her position. The writ may also be obtained during the course of the trial or following the trial.

DAMAGES

A copyright owner who prevails in an infringement lawsuit is entitled to a monetary payment known as damages. The copyright owner can receive **actual damages**, which are compensation for the copyright owner's losses and include profits earned by the infringer. If the work was registered prior to the infringement, the copyright owner can be awarded special damages known as **statutory damages**.

Actual Damages

Actual damages (also known as "compensatory damages") are the larger of either:

- the copyright owner's losses, that is, money lost as a result of the infringement; or
- the infringer's profits, that is, money earned by the infringer as a result of the infringement.

In some cases, these two forms of damages can overlap, as explained in the following text.

Lost Profits.   The copyright owner's losses are often difficult to calculate because it is hard to prove lost sales or lost business opportunities. The owner must prove how much money would have been made if the infringement had not occurred. If the copyright owner's estimates are too speculative (that is, the owner overestimates potential sales), a court will not award lost profits. One measure of loss is to examine sales to customers who had previously purchased from the copyright owner and are now purchasing from the infringer. Sometimes a copyright owner is able to pinpoint specific losses. For example, President

Gerald Ford negotiated an agreement to publish a portion of his memoirs in *Time* magazine. When *Nation* magazine, without authorization, published portions of the memoirs prior to *Time*'s scheduled publication, *Time* canceled the agreement. Ford was able to prove that he lost $12,500, which was the amount *Time* owed him, as a result of *Nation*'s infringement.[4]

The Infringer's Profits. The copyright owner can recover more than lost revenue. If the infringer's profits from the infringement exceed the owner's losses, the copyright owner is entitled to the larger amount, that is, the infringer's profits.

EXAMPLE

Sandy Tombs, a jewelry designer, proves a loss of $3,000 in canceled jewelry orders. Junky Jewelry has profits of $10,000 from infringing Sandy's design. Sandy is entitled to $10,000.

In this example, why is Sandy not entitled to $13,000, which is all of her losses and all of Junky's profits? The reason is because her lost profits comprise part of the infringer's earned profits. If she received both, that would be considered a double recovery, which is prohibited.

Since it is difficult to prove a copyright owner's losses, the owner usually concentrates on proving the infringer's profits. The copyright owner is entitled to the infringer's net profit, which is the total or gross revenue minus the infringer's expenses.

EXAMPLE

A T-shirt infringer has gross revenues of $20,000 from its infringing shirts. The infringer proves that its expenses were $5,000 ($3,000 for shirts; $1,000 for silk-screen reproduction costs; and $1,000 for shipping). The net profit would be $15,000.

The copyright owner has the obligation of proving the infringer's gross revenue. This is usually obtained by discovery procedures, witnesses (including expert witnesses), or private investigation. The infringer has the burden of proving deductions. For example, if a jewelry company infringed a design, the jewelry company will have to prove the manufacturing and shipping costs before it can deduct them. Normally, these deductions must be directly attributable to the infringement, for example, purchasing metal for infringing earrings. However, in some cases where the infringer had a reasonable belief that the copying was permitted, a court will permit the deduction of a portion of overhead expenses. For example, in cases of innocent infringement, the defendant may deduct a portion of the rent. If the infringer cannot prove any deductions, the copyright owner is entitled to all of the revenue from the infringing sales. In cases of willful infringement, courts are divided over the defendant's right to deduct overhead expenses in calculating the profit that the plaintiff is entitled to recover. Some courts follow an "incremental" approach, permitting deduction of those costs that can be shown to be directly related to the production of the infringing goods. The Second Circuit follows the principle established by Judge Hand in *Sheldon v. Metro Goldwyn Pictures* (see the following text) that overhead expenses which do not assist in the production of the infringement should not be credited to the infringer.[5]

Apportioning Actual Damages. What if the copyrighted work only comprised a portion of the infringer's work? For example, the infringer borrowed eleven pages of the copyright owner's book and used them in a book of several hundred pages. Should the infringer have to pay all of the profits from his or her book? No. The court may apportion damages based upon a percentage. Where it is difficult to reasonably approximate the proportion, the court may use the assistance of expert testimony.

JUDGE LEARNED HAND ON COPYRIGHT: LETTY LYNTON 2—WHY DOES A FILM MAKE MONEY?

This rule regarding apportionment of damages was established by Judge Learned Hand in the case of *Sheldon v. Metro Goldwyn Pictures*,[6] an earlier version of which was discussed in Chapter 22. In *Sheldon*, a playwright contended that a film, *Letty Lynton*, infringed his play. A court determined there was infringement and awarded all of the profits from the film to the playwright. On appeal, Judge Hand maintained that the success of the motion picture was based upon many factors besides the elements taken from the play. These elements included the public's interest in the stars, the film's advertising, the director, and the set designer. Judge Hand believed that the damages should be apportioned based upon the value of the infringed work in proportion to the rest of the work, and he awarded the copyright owner twenty percent of the film's profits. The Supreme Court affirmed Judge Hand's decision. The logic of the decision was incorporated into the Copyright Act of 1976, which allows an infringer to deduct "the elements of profit attributable to factors other than the copyrighted work."[7]

Statutory Damages

The Copyright Act provides for statutory damages,[8] a payment that is set by law and does not have to be proven. Unless the infringement is categorized as either innocent or willful (see the following text), a court can award between $500 and $20,000 per infringement. A copyright owner who has registered a work prior to the infringement, or within three months of publication, can choose to receive statutory damages instead of actual damages. A copyright owner who has *not* registered a work prior to the infringement, or within three months of publication, must receive actual damages and cannot choose statutory damages.

Statutory Damages and Intent.   Sometimes the intent of the infringer affects the amount of statutory damages. If a court determines that the infringement is innocent, statutory damages can be as little as $200 per infringement, instead of $500. If a court determines that the infringement is willful, statutory damages can be as high as $100,000 per infringement, instead of $20,000.

Willful and Innocent Infringement.   An infringement is willful if committed with a reckless disregard for the copyright owner's rights, for example:

- the copyright owner notifies the infringer to stop infringing, but the infringer continues; or
- the infringer has a regular practice of illegal copying and knew that the work was protected under copyright.

An infringement is innocent if the infringer can demonstrate a good faith belief, based upon reasonable grounds, that the activities were not infringing, for example:

- an infringer had consulted with an attorney who advised that the copying was legal; or
- the infringer copied a work that lacked copyright notice and believed that it was in the public domain.

Lack of knowledge of the law, by itself, does not prove an infringement was innocent. An infringer's intent (that is, willful or innocent) is not relevant for proving infringement, only for awarding damages.

The Innocent Infringer Exception.   A court has the discretion to refuse to award *any* statutory damages if the infringer is a nonprofit public broadcasting company or nonprofit educational facility that reasonably believes the use of a copyrighted work was a fair use.[9]

Calculating Statutory Damages.   Statutory damages are awarded per each work infringed. If several works have been infringed, the statutory damages are multiplied by the number of works. For example, if an infringer makes one hundred copies of one book, there is only one infringement. If the infringer makes ten copies of two books, there are two infringements. Using its discretion, the court calculates the number of infringements and multiplies this by a sum between $500 and $20,000, unless the infringement is considered to be either willful or innocent, as described earlier.

For purposes of statutory damages, all of the parts of a compilation or derivative work are considered one work. For example, if a cartoonist publishes and registers a collection of cartoons, the unauthorized use of four different cartoons from the collection is considered one infringement. However, a series of works, such as separately copyrighted comic strips or television episodes, are separate works. For example, a television station broadcast episodes of several television series (that is, *Who's the Boss?*, *Silver Spoons*, *Hart to Hart*, and *T.J. Hooker*) without authorization. The station argued that each series was a separate work. The court, however, determined that each episode was a separate work and awarded the maximum of $20,000 per infringement for a total of $8.8 million in statutory damages.[10]

Because statutory damages are usually higher than actual damages and because they do not have to be proven, copyright owners usually elect to choose statutory instead of actual damages. Occasionally, there may be an advantage to choosing actual damages.

EXAMPLE

WebFunk sells a customized software program. E-Bucks creates a similar program and sells five copies at $50,000 per copy. A court rules that E-Bucks has infringed. Since only one work was infringed, statutory damages would be an amount between $500 and $20,000 (or as high as $100,000 if the infringement was willful). Actual damages, which are E-Bucks's net profits, probably exceed $100,000. WebFunk would choose actual damages

The decision to choose between statutory and actual damages can be made at any time prior to judgment.

Does a Judge or Jury Determine Statutory Damages?   In 1998, the Supreme Court ruled that the Constitution provides a right to a jury trial on all issues related to an award of statutory damages in a copyright infringement case.[11] Therefore, the parties can elect to have either a judge or a jury determine statutory damages.

IMPOUNDMENT AND DESTRUCTION OF INFRINGING ARTICLES

After a trial, a court may order the destruction of all infringing copies. In addition, the court may order the destruction of all plates, molds, masters, film negatives, or other means by which the infringing copies were reproduced. For example, in the case of a jewelry designer, the court may order the destruction of all infringing earrings and the metal molds used to make these earrings. Instead of ordering destruction, some courts have ordered that the infringing copies be delivered to the copyright owner. The court acquires control over the infringing copies by issuing a writ of seizure, described earlier in this chapter. The Copyright Act provides for seizure any time after a copyright infringement action has been filed.[12]

ATTORNEY FEES AND COSTS

Provided that the copyright owner has registered the work prior to the infringing activity, or within three months of publication, the winning or "prevailing" party can seek attorney fees and costs. Costs are nonattorney expenses incurred in litigation such as filing fees, deposition costs, and witness fees. The award of attorney fees and costs is not mandatory; it is at the discretion of the court.

For many years there was a dual standard regarding attorney fees, which made it easier for a prevailing plaintiff to obtain fees. A prevailing defendant could recover fees only if the case was frivolous and completely without merit. However, in the 1994 case of *Fantasy, Inc. v. Fogerty*,[13] the United States Supreme Court struck down the dual standard and ruled that a defendant and plaintiff must be judged by the same standard when a court awards attorney fees and costs. These fees and costs can be quite expensive. In the *Fogerty* case, the defendant, songwriter John Fogerty, was awarded attorney fees of $1.34 million.

A victorious party does not have to receive a large damages award to receive attorney fees. In one case, a photographer was awarded $1,000 but was also awarded attorney fees because he was victorious proving infringement of his copyright.[14]

CRIMINAL PROSECUTION

Criminal prosecution is a very serious matter because the federal government, not the copyright owner, files a lawsuit against an infringer. If the government wins, the infringer can be sentenced to prison or required to pay a fine or both. The Copyright Act of 1976 was amended so that anyone who willfully infringes a copyright can now be criminally prosecuted,[15] and the government can pursue infringers of any copyrighted work.

Criminal Infringement Standards

An infringer who commits one or more infringements that have a total retail value of more than $1,000 during a 180-day period or who infringes a copyright willfully for "purposes of commercial advantage or private financial gain" can be fined and imprisoned from one to five years, depending upon the total value of the infringements.[16] Repeat violations can result in fines and imprisonment for up to ten years.[17]

Regardless of whether there is financial gain, an infringer may be liable for fines and up to three years in jail if the infringement is ten or more copies of one or more copyrighted works that have a total retail value of $2,500. Repeat offenders may be liable for jail time up to six years.

The government will also prosecute anyone who knowingly and willfully aids in a criminal infringement. The government will not prosecute innocent infringers, that is, persons who had a good faith reason to believe that copying was permitted, although those persons can still be subject to a civil law suit.

Fraudulent Use or Removal of Copyright Notice

A person who fraudulently uses or removes a copyright notice can be fined up to $2,500. In addition, a person who imports for distribution any article with a fraudulent or removed notice can be fined up to $2,500.[18]

Fraudulent Representation in a Copyright Application

Any person who knowingly makes a false statement regarding an important (or "material") fact in a copyright application or in a written statement filed in connection with the application can be liable for a criminal fine of not more than $2,500.[19]

END NOTES

1. Rene Perez & Assoc., Inc. v. Almeida, 39 U.S.P.Q.2d 2010 (S.D. Fla. 1996); *see* 17 U.S.C. § 411(a).
2. Markowitz Jewelry Co. v. Chapal/Zenray, Inc., 988 F. Supp. 404 (S.D.N.Y. 1997).
3. The federal rules for the writ follow the annotations at the end of 17 U.S.C. ß 501.
4. Harper & Row v. Nation Enters., 471 U.S. 539 (1985).
5. Hamil Am., Inc. v. SGS Studio, Inc., 45 U.S.P.Q.2d 1699 (S.D.N.Y. 1998).
6. 106 F.2d 45 (2d Cir. 1939), *aff'd* 309 U.S. 390 (1940).
7. 17 U.S.C. § 911(b).
8. 17 U.S.C. § 504(c).
9. 17 U.S.C. § 504(c)(2).
10. Columbia Pictures Television v. Krypton Broadcasting of Birmingham, Inc., 106 F.3d 284 (9th Cir. 1997).
11. Felner v. Columbia Pictures Television, 523 U.S. 340 (1998).
12. 17 U.S.C. § 503(a).
13. 510 U.S. 517 (1994).
14. Scanlon v. Kessler, 23 F. Supp. 2d 413 (S.D.N.Y. 1998).
15. 17 U.S.C. § 506; 18 U.S.C. § 2319.
16. 17 U.S.C. § 506(a)(1); 18 U.S.C. § 2319.
17. 17 U.S.C. § 506(a)(2).
18. 17 U.S.C. § 506(d).
19. 17 U.S.C. § 506(e).

CHAPTER 25
Resolving a Copyright
Dispute Without Litigation

How does a copyright owner stop an infringer without resorting to litigation? This chapter provides information on:

- drafting a cease and desist letter;
- using alternative dispute resolution procedures; and
- drafting a settlement agreement.

THE CEASE AND DESIST LETTER

The cease and desist letter is the opening shot in the copyright dispute. The copyright owner requests that the infringer stop all infringing activity. Before writing the cease and desist letter, the copyright owner should:

- review copyright ownership;
- identify and investigate the infringers; and
- apply for copyright registration if the work has not been registered.

The first two activities—review of copyright ownership and investigation of the infringers—are discussed in Chapter 26. It is not necessary to have the Certificate of Registration at the time the cease and desist letter is sent. However, the Certificate of Registration has a powerful psychological effect when used in conjunction with a cease and desist letter. For laypersons who are not knowledgeable about copyright law, the Certificate of Registration implies "government certification" of the copyright owner.

If the copyright owner does not have a registration, the recipient of the letter may be aware that a lawsuit cannot be filed—at least until the registration has been acquired. For that reason, the copyright owner may want to consider expediting the registration process, as explained in Chapter 21. If the copyright owner has applied for but not acquired a registration, the cease and desist letter should state that the copyright application is being processed.

Avoiding Passion

The cease and desist letter should have a dispassionate tone. It is important to remember that this letter, like all correspondence preceding a lawsuit, may become an exhibit or addendum to papers filed with the court, where a shrill or overbearing tone is unnecessary.

Using High-Quality Reproductions of the Work

Whether writing a cease and desist letter or filing a copyright complaint, it is important to use high-quality reproductions of the copyrighted work and the infringing work. Fuzzy photographs or poor-quality photocopies make it difficult to discern the copyright owner's claims. In addition, inferior reproductions create an impression that may result in the claim being taken less seriously.

DRAFTING THE CEASE AND DESIST LETTER

The cease and desist letter usually has the following elements:

- an explanation of the copyright owner's rights;
- a description of the infringing activity;
- a request that the infringing activity stop;
- a statement of what will happen if the infringement continues;
- a request for payment (an "accounting") for the infringing activities; and
- a time limit for future action.

Part 1: Explanation of the Copyright Owner's Rights

The opening section of a cease and desist letter describes the rights of the copyright owner.

EXAMPLE

I am the attorney for Bobby Grenadier, a jewelry designer based in San Mateo, California. Ms. Grenadier is the owner of all rights in the jewelry design entitled *Bunny Love #1*. A copy of her copyright registration VA 553-434 is attached. Also attached is a photocopy of Ms. Grenadier's work as registered. Ms. Grenadier's copyright grants her the right to prevent duplication of her work.

Part 2: Description of the Infringing Activity

The second part of a cease and desist letter describes the infringing activity.

EXAMPLE

I have reason to believe that Junky Jewelry may be in violation of United States copyright law. Attached you will find a photograph of an earring purchased at a San Francisco Junky Jewelry store in January 1998. A close examination of this earring indicates that the principal rabbit-shaped piece is an exact duplicate of *Bunny Love #1*. Ms. Grenadier has consulted with an expert in metal casting who confirmed that the Junky Jewelry earring was created from a mold that used *Bunny Love #1* as its source. In fact, in the fashioning of the original design of *Bunny Love #1*, a portion of Ms. Grenadier's fingerprint was incorporated in the design. The same fingerprint is evident on the Junky Jewelry pieces. Please examine the Junky Jewelry earring and consult with your manufacturing source. I feel confident that your investigation will confirm that Ms. Grenadier's work was used as the source for the Junky Jewelry earring.

Part 3: Request That the Infringing Activity Stop

The heart of the cease and desist letter is the request to stop the infringing activity. Attorneys refer to this as the "set up" because it is written notice that further infringements will be considered as willful. A willful infringement can result in larger damages (see Chapter 24).

EXAMPLE

I demand that you cease any further copying, sale, distribution, or use of the Junky Jewelry earring as shown in the attached photograph. Any further infringing activity occurring after the receipt of this letter shall be considered a willful infringement.

Part 4: What Happens If the Activity Does Not Stop

There are two strategies used when drafting the "threat" portion of the cease and desist letter. One strategy is to take a stern or "hardball" approach to the infringer and threaten litigation. Large corporations commonly take this approach. The advantage is that it may frighten a smaller or less powerful infringer. The disadvantage is that it may trigger an action for declaratory relief, described in the following text.

A second approach is to invite the infringer to begin an informal or formal process of resolving the dispute. Litigation is not threatened. The advantage is that it avoids a declaratory relief action and invites a nonlitigious resolution. The disadvantage is that since it is not threatening, the infringer may not take the letter as seriously. Examples of both approaches follow.

EXAMPLE:

Hardball Approach. Ms. Grenadier vigorously protects her copyrights. As your attorney can advise you, infringement of copyright exposes you to extensive liability. Be advised that Title 17 of the United States Code Section 504(c) provides that in the case of willful infringement, a court may award up to the sum of $100,000 in damages for each infringement, as well as full court costs and reasonable attorney fees. If necessary, Ms. Grenadier is prepared to seek temporary restraining orders, injunctions, and other appropriate relief in addition to compensation for damages. Your attorney can undoubtedly advise you as to the relevant details.

EXAMPLE

Nonthreatening Approach. Naturally, it is in the best interests of both parties to avoid litigation. Ms. Grenadier is prepared and willing to consider nonlitigious alternate dispute resolution procedures. I am hopeful that your reasonable investigation will result in a speedy resolution.

Part 5: Request for Payment (an "Accounting")

A request for payment for the infringement is not necessary but is often included in hardball cease and desist letters. If the copyright owner does not request payment in the letter, the request can still be made at a later time.

EXAMPLE

I expect a prompt response from you or your attorney addressing the issues raised in this letter and providing (1) an accounting of all unauthorized copies produced or distributed by you; and (2) payment for all unauthorized copies distributed.

Part 6: Time Limit for Future Action

As with the preceding sections, there are two approaches to the final paragraph of the letter. One strategy is to set a time limit for response. However, if there is a time limit, the copyright owner should be prepared to take action at the end of the time period. If no action is taken, it is unlikely that the infringer will take any further threats seriously. A second strategy is to leave the response period open-ended. If no response is received within two weeks, a follow-up letter will be sent.

EXAMPLE

Hardball Approach. If I do not hear from you within seven days of the date of this letter, I will be compelled to advise Ms. Grenadier to take appropriate legal action to protect her copyrights and to receive just compensation for any damage she has suffered. I look forward to hearing from you or your attorney.

EXAMPLE

Nonthreatening Approach. After you have reviewed this letter, please contact me.

CONSIDERATIONS WHEN SENDING A CEASE AND DESIST LETTER

There are two instances when a copyright owner should reconsider the cease and desist letter:

1. the infringer may destroy evidence or transfer assets; or
2. the infringer may file a declaratory relief action.

Infringer May Destroy Evidence or Transfer Assets

When the copyright owner believes that the infringer may destroy evidence or transfer assets, there is no point in providing a cease and desist letter. Instead, the copyright owner will want to obtain an *ex parte* temporary restraining order or writ of seizure, as explained in Chapter 24. Powerful copyright owners, such as the Disney Company, employ investigators who can discern the likelihood of illegal behavior. As a general rule, a copyright owner should beware of mobile infringers who can move their operation quickly, for example, T-shirt infringers, disk duplicators, and video and tape duplicators.

Declaratory Relief Action

Sometimes, after receiving a cease and desist letter, or after the breakdown of negotiations to settle a dispute, the alleged infringer may file a lawsuit seeking **declaratory relief**. A declaratory relief action is not a lawsuit for money, but a suit in which a court reviews the facts and makes a declaration as to each party's rights.

How can an alleged infringer sue a copyright owner? The Federal Rules of Civil Procedure permit a federal court to "declare the rights of any interested party" involved in an "actual controversy."[1] When a company is notified of a potential lawsuit, that is considered an "actual controversy." The alleged infringer that receives the letter may ask a federal court to make a declaration as to its rights. For example, a company in Florida is accused of infringing but does not believe that the copyright owner located in California has a valid claim. The company does not want to be sued for infringement in California, so it files a declaratory relief action in Florida. This creates a problem for the copyright owner, who must travel to Florida and hire local attorneys or pay for the travel costs of California attorneys.

From the perspective of the copyright owner, there are two disadvantages to a declaratory relief action. First, it is possible that the copyright owner never intended to file a lawsuit, and now the copyright owner has been drawn into litigation. Second, the copyright owner must travel and has lost the "home-court advantage." (Obviously, if the copyright owner and alleged infringer are in the same state, this is not an issue.)

There are two ways for a copyright owner to avoid a declaratory relief action:

1. avoid creating an "actual controversy"; and
2. use a "short-fuse" cease and desist letter.

Avoiding Creating an Actual Controversy. A declaratory relief action can only be filed if an "actual controversy" exists. A controversy exists when the copyright owner threatens to file a lawsuit if the infringement continues. If there is no threat of infringement litigation, there is no actual controversy.[2] It is for this reason that copyright owners may prefer to send a cease and desist letter that does not threaten litigation. In addition, a nonthreatening letter may establish a better environment for alternative dispute resolution.

Using a "Short-Fuse" Cease and Desist Letter. Some copyright owners fax a cease and desist letter to the infringer and attach a copyright infringement complaint, the document that will be filed to commence litigation. The copyright owner threatens to file the lawsuit within a very short period (for example, twenty-four hours) unless the infringement is immediately halted. This time period is usually too short for an infringer to prepare and file a declaratory relief action. The advantage of this strategy is that it is intimidating and avoids declaratory relief. The disadvantage is that the copyright infringement complaint can cost between five hundred and several thousand dollars in attorney fees.

AFTER THE CEASE AND DESIST LETTER

If the infringer does not respond to the letter or denies the infringement, the copyright owner must decide whether to proceed with a lawsuit. If, however, the infringer wants to resolve the dispute, the parties will attempt to negotiate a settlement.

Settlement

A written settlement is necessary to formally resolve the dispute. There are several advantages to a negotiated settlement:

- it saves money because there are no costs for litigation;
- it saves time compared to the two to three years required for litigation; and
- it is a guaranteed payment, unlike a court judgment that must be collected and enforced.

Because of these advantages, a copyright owner may accept less money in settlement than that demanded in a court case. For example, a copyright owner might accept seventy percent instead of one hundred percent, of an infringer's profits as settlement. When negotiating a settlement, both sides must make a realistic assessment of the facts and law. The copyright owner must consider the likelihood of prevailing in a federal court and any resulting award of damages. Sometimes, a copyright owner will forego payment of damages in exchange for the infringer's agreement to halt infringement. In other cases, the copyright owner may agree to permit continued copying provided that the infringer pays a royalty for all past and future sales. This is sometimes referred to as a "reverse license."

A settlement is a contract signed by both parties, usually executed at the time one party pays the other. Some states have requirements regarding settlement agreements and specific language must be included to protect the rights of the parties. An example of a settlement agreement is provided in Appendix F. Sometimes the terms of the settlement are presented in a document that is filed with the court in a form known as a stipulated judgment.

Some Cases Will *Never* Settle.   Although most infringement claims settle prior to litigation, some cases will never settle because the litigants have an ulterior purpose for bringing the suit. For example, some businesses use litigation as a tool to bludgeon competitors. Sometimes the litigants are motivated solely by acrimony. For example, in the case of *Fantasy, Inc. v. Fogerty,* described in Chapters 22 and 24, the two principals, songwriter John Fogerty and the owner of Fantasy, Saul Zaentz, had a history of disputes dating back to when Fantasy acquired rights to Fogerty's musical group, Creedence Clearwater Revival.

ALTERNATIVE DISPUTE RESOLUTION

Instead of a negotiated settlement or a lawsuit, disputes may be resolved through procedures known as alternative dispute resolution (ADR). There are two common forms of ADR:

1. mediation, and
2. arbitration.

Mediation

In mediation, the parties submit their dispute to an impartial mediator who assists the parties in reaching a settlement. Professional mediators are trained to negotiate and are knowledgeable about the relevant law. A mediator does not have the authority to make a binding decision.

- *Advantages:* The parties can discuss their dispute with a knowledgeable neutral negotiator. The costs are low, and the relaxed atmosphere promotes settlement.
- *Disadvantages:* The mediator's determination is not binding, and the parties may not benefit from the rules of discovery or evidence that are used in litigation.

Arbitration

Arbitration is the referral of a dispute to one or more impartial persons for a final determination. Both parties usually agree on the choice of the arbitrator.

Some arbitration agreements allow each party to choose one arbitrator, and these two arbitrators choose a third, comprising a three-member panel. Usually each party submits a document to the arbitrator that sums up each party's position (the arbitration brief).

- *Advantages:* Arbitration saves time and money and is not as formal as litigation.
- *Disadvantages:* The arbitration decision is final and cannot be appealed. The parties may not benefit from the rules of discovery or evidence that are used in litigation, and there may not be a written record of the arbitrator's decision.

Getting to ADR

Arbitration and mediation take place when the parties voluntarily agree to it or are compelled to participate. The parties volunteer to submit to ADR by signing a statement. Organizations such as the American Arbitration Association provide forms (Submission to Dispute Resolution) in which two parties agree on arbitration. Parties are compelled to participate if they have previously signed an agreement that requires ADR. For example, many license agreements have a provision requiring that disagreements must be submitted to ADR. A sample provision is provided at the end of this chapter. Some courts have a mandatory procedure known as Early Neutral Evaluation (ENE) in which an evaluator reviews the facts and advises the parties as to the likely outcome of the lawsuit. This procedure encourages settlement.

Organizations such as the American Arbitration Association or the Volunteer Lawyers for the Arts provide arbitration and mediation services. If the parties have submitted to "binding" arbitration, the arbitrator's decision can be entered as a judgment in a court.

Sample ADR Provision from License Agreement

If a dispute arises between the parties arising under or relating to this Agreement, the parties agree to submit such dispute to arbitration in the state of *[insert state here]* conducted on a confidential basis pursuant to the Commercial Arbitration Rules of the American Arbitration Association. Any decision or award as a result of any such arbitration proceeding shall be in writing and shall provide an explanation for all conclusions of law and fact and shall include the assessment of costs, expenses, and reasonable attorney fees. Any such arbitration shall be conducted by an arbitrator experienced in copyright law and shall include a written record of the arbitration hearing. The parties reserve the right to object to any individual who shall be employed by or affiliated with a competing organization or entity. An award of arbitration may be confirmed in a court of competent jurisdiction.

END NOTES

1. 28 U.S.C. § 2201(a).

2. Progressive Apparel Group v. Anheuser-Busch, Inc., 38 U.S.P.Q.2d 1057 (S.D.N.Y. 1996).

CHAPTER 26
Litigation

This chapter provides information about:

- commencing a lawsuit;
- drafting a copyright complaint;
- responding to a complaint;
- discovery tools; and
- the trial and appellate process.

PLAINTIFF'S PREFILING CHECKLIST

Copyright litigation begins when a plaintiff files a complaint in the federal district court. Prior to filing, the plaintiff should accomplish the following:

- review copyright ownership;
- identify and investigate the defendants;
- acquire evidence of the infringement;
- determine if there are any noncopyright claims;
- determine if cross-claims will be filed against another plaintiff;
- review the statute of limitations;
- determine if an injunction is necessary;
- consider methods of resolving the dispute;
- determine whether to seek a jury trial;
- confirm federal jurisdiction;
- determine proper venue;
- review federal rules of civil procedure and local rules;
- prepare the complaint; and
- prepare civil cover sheet and summons.

Review Copyright Ownership

In order to file a lawsuit, the plaintiff must have a legal capacity (or "standing") to sue the infringer. (Note: for simplicity, the defendant's activities are referred to as "infringing" even though they are alleged and have not been proven.) The plaintiff must be able to prove a copyright ownership interest or a right to receive royalties from the copyright. For example, a co-author must be able to prove that she is the co-creator of the work. An assignee must be able to prove that the copyright has been assigned. The following questions should be answered:

- What is the plaintiff's business form? Is the plaintiff a corporation, partnership, or sole proprietor?
- Has the work been registered with the Copyright Office? If an application has not been filed, the plaintiff should proceed with filing and consider an expedited application as described in Chapter 21.
- What claim does the plaintiff have to the copyright? Was the work created (or co-created) by the plaintiff? If not, how does the plaintiff claim rights?
- Was the copyright assigned or exclusively licensed to the plaintiff? Has this transfer been recorded with the Copyright Office? Chapter 15 provides information about transfers.
- Has the work been published without copyright notice? A lack of notice may cause a loss of copyright. Chapter 17 provides information about omission of notice.

Identify and Investigate Defendants

Even if the defendant has infringed, it may be useless to bring a lawsuit if the defendant has no money or can avoid liability. The plaintiff should:

- research the financial background of the defendant;
- research the corporate background of the defendant. If a company is a subsidiary or affiliate of a parent company, it may be necessary to name the parent as a defendant;
- determine if anyone else is contributing to the infringement (review Chapter 22 for information on contributory infringement);
- determine whether the infringing party has been sued for copyright infringement previously. The fact may not be admissible at trial, but could be useful; and
- determine if there is an agent for service of process. If the defendant is a corporation or limited partnership, state laws require that it provide the identity and address of a person who will accept service of the lawsuit.

The Internet, Westlaw, LEXIS, and private search companies can all provide tools for investigating the corporate status and ownership of various entities. For example, the agent for service can be obtained through online services such as Westlaw and LEXIS that contain records from any Secretary of State. LEXIS and Westlaw also provide detailed financial information about companies. Information about Westlaw and LEXIS is provided in Chapter 16.

Acquire Evidence of the Infringement

The plaintiff in an infringement suit must prove that the defendant had access to the plaintiff's work and that the defendant's work is substantially similar to the plaintiff's work. In addition, the plaintiff must connect the infringement with the infringer. In other words, there must be proof that the infringer manufactured, broadcast, or sold the infringing material. Therefore, the plaintiff must acquire evidence of the infringement prior to commencing litigation. This information is often acquired by purchasing the infringing goods. The plaintiff's attorney should not make the purchase because the attorney may later have to take the stand to discuss the transaction, requiring a second lawyer in the courtroom. When acquiring infringing merchandise:

- pay for the infringing merchandise with check or credit card. The returned canceled check or credit card statement may provide more information about the name of the infringing business or the location of its bank account;
- ask questions at the time of purchase. For example, ask the salesperson if the item is popular, and ask if purchases can be made in bulk (for example, lots of ten or twenty). The answers can be used to cross-examine or contradict the infringer; and
- save all tags and identifying markers, for example, "Imported by Emexco" or "Made in India." These may assist in locating manufacturers and distributors.

Determine If There Are Any Noncopyright Claims

The basis of any lawsuit is the legal claim or "cause of action." A claim for copyright infringement is usually joined with other noncopyright claims. For example, a claim for infringement of software usually is joined with a trade secrecy claim. Infringement of artwork usually involves a copyright and a trademark claim. A plaintiff should:

- determine if additional claims such as trade secrecy, trademark, or other contract, tort, or related claims can be made as a result of the infringing activity;
- list *all* possible defenses to each cause of action. A lawsuit should not be filed until all possible defenses have been considered; and
- perform legal research and review case law and statutes regarding infringement issues. Special copyright rules may apply, thereby eliminating the claim.

Review the Statute of Limitations

A plaintiff has three years from the date of the infringement (when the claim "accrued") to file the lawsuit.[1] If the lawsuit is not filed within this three-year period, the defendant can have the suit dismissed. Therefore, the plaintiff must review the dates of infringement before commencing the lawsuit. For more information on the statute of limitations, see Chapter 23.

Determine If an Injunction Is Necessary

Is the infringement ongoing? Will the defendant halt the infringement pending the outcome of the litigation? If an injunction is required, it may be necessary for the plaintiff to file a request for a preliminary injunction at the time the complaint is filed.

Consider Methods of Resolving the Dispute

There are many advantages to resolving a dispute without litigation. The plaintiff should consider alternative dispute resolution (ADR) prior to filing. After filing, some district courts offer ADR programs or independent evaluations that enable swift resolution.

Determine Whether to Seek a Jury Trial

If the plaintiff wants a jury trial, that request should be made in the complaint and reflected in the civil cover sheet, described later in this chapter.

Confirm Federal Jurisdiction

The plaintiff must confirm that the federal courts have jurisdiction over the claim. The federal courts have exclusive jurisdiction over any lawsuit arising under the copyright statute. Exclusive jurisdiction means that a court has the sole authority to hear a certain type of case. Because of this exclusive jurisdiction, copyright infringement or any matter requiring interpretation and application of the Copyright Act can be brought only in federal court.

What Does It Mean to "Arise Under" Copyright Law?   Certain cases may relate to copyright law, but may not "arise under" the copyright law. For example, a divorce proceeding or a dispute over a will in which copyright ownership is at stake would not be a federal matter. These cases would be brought in state court. A breach of a copyright license is also generally not a matter of federal jurisdiction. For example, a computer company licenses a computer program, but fails to make one of the payments required under the license. The issue is not copyright infringement; it is a breach of the license agreement. Therefore, the federal courts would not have exclusive jurisdiction over this matter.

There are exceptions to this rule. If the breach of the license is so substantial as to justify recission—termination of the agreement with all rights reverting to the nonbreaching party—the federal courts may have jurisdiction. This was the case with the band, the Kingsmen, who never received a royalty payment for the sale of their master recording of "Louie, Louie."[2]

Determine Proper Venue

Venue rules establish the location of the court. The United States is divided into ninety-four districts, each having a federal court. Each state has at least one federal district court. A copyright lawsuit may be brought in the district in which the defendant or the defendant's agent resides or may be found. For example, if an infringer operates a business in Manhattan, the case can be brought in the Southern District of New York.

If the defendant is a corporation, the lawsuit may be brought in any district where the company is:

- incorporated;
- licensed to do business; or
- doing business.

In the interest of justice and for the convenience of parties and witnesses, a judge can order that the lawsuit be transferred to another district court. The statute authorizing copyright venue is 28 *United States Code* section 1400.

Review Federal Rules of Civil Procedure and Local Rules

The Federal Rules of Civil Procedure (FRCP) are the procedural rules that govern the parties in federal litigation. These rules set forth the requirements for the parties when filing papers, appearing in court, or communicating with counsel. These rules are located in title 28 of the *United States Code*.

Each federal district court has its own local rules. Before commencing an action, it is important to acquire a copy of the local rules. For example, the district court may have rules regarding the assignment of the case to a magistrate instead of a district court judge. Some local rules require an initial disclosure system to speed the resolution of the dispute. These rules can be acquired from the clerk of the district court.

Prepare the Complaint

The complaint is the initial document (or pleading) filed with the court; it identifies the parties, establishes jurisdiction, describes the factual basis for the lawsuit, and makes a demand for relief. The drafting of the complaint is explained later in this chapter. The content and format of the complaint are dictated by the Federal Rules of Civil Procedure and by local court rules.

Prepare Civil Cover Sheet and Summons

In addition to the complaint, the defendant is served with a summons and civil cover sheet, both of which are available from the clerk's office of the local federal court. The summons is a one-page document that explains the defendant has been sued and has a certain time limit in which to respond. The civil cover sheet is a one-page form required for use by the court in maintaining statistical records. An example of both are provided later in this chapter.

FILING THE COMPLAINT

A lawsuit is filed when the clerk of the federal court accepts the original complaint and assigns a docket number to the case. The clerk will file a copy of the summons, and the original summons is retained by the plaintiff until after the defendant has been served. All papers filed in the case and correspondence to the court must use this docket number. In order to file the complaint, a fee, usually between $100 and $200, must be paid. The court will waive the fee in the event of hardship.

SERVING THE DEFENDANT

The defendant in the copyright lawsuit receives notice of the lawsuit by service of process, a procedure in which the summons, complaint, and any other required documents are delivered to the defendant. The local rules of many district courts require that alternative dispute resolution documents be furnished to the defendant along with the complaint. Service of process must be performed according to rule 4 of the Federal Rules of Civil Procedure. In order to expedite service and guarantee that it is performed properly, service is commonly performed by a licensed process server. Except for defendants outside the United States, service must occur within 120 days of filing the complaint. After the defendant has been served, the plaintiff must file a Proof of Service with the court.

Report of a Copyright Action

The Copyright Act of 1976 requires that the clerk of the federal court report all copyright actions to the Register of Copyrights. Normally, the federal district clerk's office will prepare the form, but in some instances, the clerk may require the plaintiff to complete the form.

DRAFTING THE COMPLAINT

The complaint is the initial document filed in a lawsuit. It sets forth the basis of the plaintiff's claims and requests remedies. A complaint consists of:

- a caption that identifies the court, the parties, and the docket number;
- a statement of the facts, known as the "allegations";
- a request for relief, known as the "prayer"; and
- a signature (or "verification") by the party preparing the document.

Information and Belief

The plaintiff and the plaintiff's attorney must affirm that all statements contained in the complaint are true. Both the plaintiff and the plaintiff's attorney can be punished or "sanctioned" if facts are concealed or misrepresented. If a plaintiff is not certain about information, that information can be prefaced with the disclaimer it is being provided on "information and belief."

In other words, the plaintiff is informed and believes that a statement or fact is true but cannot swear it is true. For example, if unsure of the residence of a defendant, the plaintiff can state, "Plaintiff is informed and believes, and on that basis alleges, that the defendant is a resident of New Mexico." Another way it is stated is, "On information and belief, the plaintiff alleges that the defendant is a resident of New Mexico."

Basic Rules

Requirements regarding the appearance of a complaint, that is, the size of the margins, page numbering, and other formatting requirements, are set forth in the Federal Rules of Civil Procedure and local rules. These rules must be followed or the clerk will reject the complaint. For example, the local rules will specify how the exhibit is to be attached, whether a tab must be used to indicate the exhibit, and where the exhibit tab is to be located on the page.

The Caption

The contents of the caption are determined by the Federal Rules of Civil Procedure and local rules. Generally the caption contains the name of the court, the names of the parties, name and address of the plaintiff's attorney, and the basis for complaint, that is, the "causes of action." An example of a caption is provided in the sample complaint in Appendix F.

The Jurisdiction Statement

The first paragraph of a copyright complaint usually states the basis for jurisdiction.

EXAMPLE

This court has original jurisdiction under 28 U.S.C. § 1338(a) in that this action arises under the copyright laws of the United States, 17 U.S.C. § 101 *et seq.*

The Venue Statement

The basis for venue is commonly provided after the jurisdiction statement and includes a statement of law and an allegation as to the location of the defendant or the infringing activity.

EXAMPLE

Venue is proper pursuant to 28 U.S.C. § 1400(a). Plaintiff is informed and believes that defendant Final Straw, Inc., is a corporation organized under the laws of the State of California, having its principal place of business in San Francisco, California.

Even though it is not necessary to include the residency of the plaintiff, it is commonly included following the venue statement.

EXAMPLE

Plaintiff S. Murphy is a resident of the City and County of San Francisco, California, and a citizen of the United States.

Plaintiff's Right to the Work and Registration

The plaintiff must introduce the copyrighted work and establish that he or she owns the work, either as a result of creation or transfer. The plaintiff also must demonstrate that the work has been registered or, if not registered, why registration is not required. See Chapter 18 for information on registration.

EXAMPLE

Plaintiff is the creator and owner of an original photographic visual arts work entitled *Pelican Beauty* that contains copyrightable subject matter under the laws of the United States.

Plaintiff complied in all respects with the Copyright Act, 17 U.S.C. § 101 et seq., and all other laws governing copyright and secured the exclusive rights and privileges in copyright to the *Pelican Beauty* visual arts image and received from the Register of Copyrights a Certificate of Registration, dated and identified as follows: January 12, 2000, Class: VA No. 657-980. A copy of the Certificate of Registration is attached to this Complaint as Exhibit A and is incorporated in this Complaint by reference.

Pelican Beauty was first published with notice under plaintiff's authorization in February 2000, in *Back to Nature* magazine. A copy of the publication is attached as Exhibit B and incorporated by reference in this Complaint. Plaintiff has been and still is the sole proprietor of all rights, title, and interest in and to the copyright in *Pelican Beauty*.

Factual Allegations of Infringement

As succinctly as possible, the plaintiff must establish the basis of the infringement.

EXAMPLE

In February 2000, defendant infringed the copyright in *Pelican Beauty* by publishing and selling postcards containing a substantially similar visual arts image entitled *Pretty Pelican*, which plaintiff is informed and believes was copied from *Pelican Beauty*. A copy of defendant's work is attached to this Complaint as Exhibit C and incorporated by reference in this Complaint.

Plaintiff has notified defendant that defendant has infringed the *Pelican Beauty* copyright of plaintiff, and defendant has continued to infringe the copyright.

The Prayer

The prayer is at the end of the complaint and has its own sequential numbering or lettering.

EXAMPLE

Wherefore plaintiff demands that:

(1) Defendant, its agents, and servants be enjoined during the pendency of this action and permanently enjoined from infringing the *Pelican Beauty* photograph in any manner and from publishing, selling, marketing, or otherwise disposing of copies of the work entitled *Pretty Pelican*.

(2) Defendant be required to pay to plaintiff such damages as plaintiff has sustained in consequence of defendant's infringement of copyright and to account for all gains, profits, and advantages derived by defendant by its infringement or such damages as the court shall deem proper within the provisions of the copyright statutes, but not less than $500.

(3) Defendant be required to deliver up to be impounded during the pendency of this action all copies of the work entitled *Pretty Pelican* in its possession or control and to deliver up for destruction all infringing copies and all plates, molds, and other matter for making such infringing copies.

(4) Defendant pay to plaintiff the costs of this action and reasonable attorney fees as allowed by the court.

(5) Plaintiff have such other and further relief as is just.

Jury Demand

If the plaintiff wants a trial by jury rather than by a judge, this must be stated in the complaint.

EXAMPLE

Plaintiff demands trial by jury on all issues triable to a jury.

DEFENDANT'S PREFILING CHECKLIST

Prior to filing the response, the defendant should complete the following activities:

- determine if an insurance policy provides coverage for the lawsuit;
- investigate the plaintiff's claim to copyright ownership;
- review the infringement;
- determine whether to admit or deny the allegations of the complaint;
- review all possible affirmative defenses;
- determine if sales of the infringing merchandise should be halted;
- determine whether to seek a jury trial;
- review federal rules of civil procedure and local rules;
- determine if a responsive pleading other than an answer should be filed;
- prepare the answer; and
- determine if a counterclaim or cross-claim should be filed.

Determine If an Insurance Policy Provides Coverage for the Lawsuit

The defendant's business or homeowner's insurance policy should be reviewed to determine if it provides coverage for the lawsuit. Usually this coverage is derived from a provision in the insurance policy known as an "advertising injury." If the copyright claim is not covered by the insurance policy, one of the related claims in the complaint (for example, theft of trade secrets, trade libel, trademark infringement) may trigger coverage. The insurance company should be notified promptly of the lawsuit.

Investigate the Plaintiff's Claim to Copyright Ownership

In order to file the suit, the plaintiff must have the legal right (or "capacity") to sue the defendant. If the defendant can prove that the plaintiff lacks capacity, or that the defendant is not the proper party to sue, the defendant will avoid liability. To obtain information about the plaintiff and the work, the defendant may have to research Copyright Office records or hire a search firm to prepare a copyright report. The defendant should obtain answers to the following:

- Does the plaintiff have a legitimate claim to ownership of the work?
- Has the work been published without copyright notice? A lack of notice may cause a loss of copyright.
- Does the defendant have any right to the plaintiff's work, for example, because of a contractual or other relationship? Was the work co-created by the defendant?
- Are there any other parties involved in the infringement? If the plaintiff fails to include ("join") another defendant or contributory infringer, that may be a basis for dismissing the complaint.

Review the Infringement

The defendant should review the facts in the complaint with employees or persons who may have knowledge about the facts to determine if anyone affiliated with the defendant had access to the plaintiff's work. In addition, a review should be made to determine if the defendant's work is substantially similar to the plaintiff's work.

- What evidence is there that the defendant infringed, manufactured, broadcast, or sold the copyrighted work?
- If an infringement has occurred, is the defendant the proper party to sue? It is possible that a subsidiary or parent company should have been named, rather than the defendant.
- Is the copyrighted work and the defendant's work substantially similar? Both works must be compared for similarities.

Determine Whether to Admit or Deny the Allegations of the Complaint

The defendant must carefully review the complaint to determine its accuracy. In the defendant's response to the complaint, the defendant responds paragraph by paragraph to the complaint and admits or denies the factual claims.

Review All Possible Affirmative Defenses

When responding to the complaint, the defendant must consider all possible affirmative defenses. An affirmative defense, if proven, can defeat the complaint. Examples of common affirmative defenses are in Chapter 23.

Determine If Sales of the Infringing Merchandise Should Be Halted

It may be advantageous to halt the infringing activity pending the outcome of the litigation. This is both a business and a legal decision. How much sales will be lost? What is the likelihood that the defendant will prevail in the lawsuit? If the sales are not halted, it is likely that the plaintiff will bring a motion for a preliminary injunction.

Some defendants prefer to fight the motion for the preliminary injunction. If the defendant prevails, it means that the court does not believe the plaintiff's case is likely to succeed. Chapter 24 provides information on injunctions.

Determine Whether to Seek a Jury Trial

Even if the plaintiff does not want a jury trial, the defendant can still choose to have a jury by indicating that choice in the answer.

Determine If a Responsive Pleading Other Than an Answer Should Be Filed

The plaintiff's complaint may be attacked for procedural reasons. That is, the plaintiff may have made an error regarding the civil procedure rules and, for that reason, the complaint should be dismissed or modified. Examples of errors in procedure are if the court lacks jurisdiction, venue is improper, a necessary party was not included in the lawsuit, or the complaint is so vague or ambiguous that the defendant is unable to prepare a response. In these situations, rather than filing an answer, the defendant can file a motion to dismiss, a motion for more definite statement, or a motion to strike. Information regarding these motions is provided in rule 12 of the FRCP.

Prepare the Answer

An answer is a pleading that contests the allegations of the complaint. Unless the defendant attacks the complaint on procedural grounds—for example, the defendant argues that service is improper or that the court has no jurisdiction—the defendant must file an answer. In the answer, the defendant admits or denies the allegations and provides a list of defenses. The answer, like the complaint, includes a caption, and is filed with the court. Like the complaint, the answer must contain truthful statements. False or concealed facts can result in sanctions. Unless the court grants an extension, the defendant must file a response to the copyright complaint within twenty days of service. Failure to file an answer can result in an judgment in favor of the plaintiff (known as a "default judgment").

An answer generally consists of two parts: admissions or denials of the allegations in the complaint, and affirmative defenses. The admissions or denials appear in four different ways:

1. defendant denies all allegations of a paragraph;
2. defendant admits all allegations of a paragraph;
3. defendant denies all allegations in a paragraph because the defendant lacks information; and
4. defendant denies some allegations and admits some allegations of a paragraph.

Affirmative defenses are always short—a succinct statement of the defense.

EXAMPLE

First Affirmative Defense: Unclean Hands. Plaintiff is barred from obtaining relief on any of the claims alleged in the Complaint by its unclean hands in taking actions calculated to unfairly deceive the public by falsifying documents filed with the United States Copyright Office.

Determine If a Counterclaim or Cross-Claim Should Be Filed

If the defendant wants to assert a claim against the plaintiff, a counterclaim, which is a separate pleading, must be filed with the answer. A counterclaim is compulsory— that is, it *must* be filed—if it arises out of the transaction or occurrence that is the subject of the complaint. For example, consider the case of a jewelry designer who, after discovering infringement, physically attacks the infringer. Because the attack arose out of the transaction or occurrence, the claim for personal injury against the designer *must* be brought as a counterclaim.

If there are multiple defendants, one defendant may make a claim, known as a cross-claim, against another. For example, if one defendant tricked another into the infringement, that could give rise to a cross-claim. A plaintiff can also cross-claim against another plaintiff.

DISCOVERY

After the complaint and answer are filed, discovery begins. During discovery, the parties acquire facts and evidence relating to the case. Usually the first piece of information sought by the plaintiff during discovery is whether the defendant has an insurance policy that will cover the damages in the complaint. The Federal Rules of Civil Procedure and local court rules establish the procedures for discovery. Local court rules establish regulations regarding discovery procedures and formats. For example, the parties must develop a detailed discovery plan that must conform to rule 26(f) in the FRCP.

If a dispute arises during the exchange of discovery information, the district court will rule on the issue. The four common forms of discovery are:

1. interrogatories—written questions that must be answered in writing (and under oath) within a specified time. Interrogatories are only exchanged among parties to the lawsuit, that is, persons named in the caption of the complaint or counterclaim;
2. production of documents—written requests for documents from parties to the lawsuit;
3. depositions—oral or written testimony of a party or witness, given under oath. A party may depose any person who has information relevant to the lawsuit; and
4. requests for admissions—a request for a party to the lawsuit to admit the truthfulness of a fact or statement.

MOTIONS

A motion is a request for an order of the court. For example, if the venue is inconvenient, one party may make a request for an order for a change of venue. This would be made as a motion for change of venue. If a party objects to a discovery request, a motion to compel may be made requesting an order requiring the party to respond. One of the most common motions made in copyright infringement lawsuits is the **motion for summary judgment**. This a request that the court order a judgment without having a trial because there is no genuine issue as to any material facts. For example, if a defendant admitted copying the plaintiff's work, there may not be an issue of triable fact. There is nothing for a jury to deliberate over because there is no dispute as to liability. Therefore, a judge may determine that a trial is not necessary.

EXPERT WITNESS

Sometimes the nature of the work in a copyright infringement lawsuit requires the opinions or testimony of persons who are experts. For example, in a jewelry case, it may be necessary to use testimony from a person who is an expert in metal casting. Information about the expert witness and the subject matter and substance of the expert's expected testimony is discoverable prior to trial. Normally, interrogatories are used to learn about each party's choice of expert witnesses. Sometimes, expert witnesses are deposed prior to litigation.

TRIAL

During trial, the parties present their facts and evidence to a judge or jury. If either party requests a jury, then **jury instructions** must be prepared. These instructions provide the legal rules that the jury will use in reaching a verdict. For example, a jury instruction may state that access to the plaintiff's work is a required element of copyright infringement. As a result of the final deliberation of the judge or jury, a judgment is issued.

APPEAL

Either party may appeal the final determination of the district court to the appropriate court of appeals. The party bringing the appeal is the appellant; the party responding is the appellee. To initiate an appeal, a **notice of appeal** is filed with the appropriate court of appeals. If justified, either party may seek an expedited appeal. Expedited appeals are sought because emergency relief is necessary to prevent irreparable damage.

On appeal, a panel of judges reviews the trial court record to determine if a legal error occurred. An example of a legal error could be if a judge did not permit the introduction of evidence relevant to the case. An appellate court ruling requires a majority determination of three judges. If the parties are not satisfied with the court of appeals determination, they have two choices. The parties can seek an *en banc* rehearing in which all of the judges in a particular circuit review the case. The other choice is to seek review of the case by the United States Supreme Court. If the United States Supreme Court refuses to hear the case, the determination of the court of appeals is the final ruling in the case.

END NOTES

1. 17 U.S.C. § 507.
2. Peterson v. Highland Music, Inc., 140 F.3d 1313 (9th Cir. 1998).

CHAPTER 27
International
Copyright

This chapter provides information on international copyright protection including information about:

- the Universal Copyright Convention;
- the Berne Convention; and
- the GATT\TRIPS agreement.

WHERE CAN A UNITED STATES COPYRIGHT OWNER SUE FOREIGN INFRINGERS?

Treaty affiliations and national treatment do not establish where a copyright infringement lawsuit can be filed. When an American copyright owner's work is infringed in a foreign nation, the copyright owner can file the lawsuit in the United States *only* if the foreign infringer has substantial economic ties to the United States and qualifies for jurisdiction in the United States. Otherwise, the United States copyright owner will have to hire foreign counsel and pursue the infringer in the foreign nation. However, if the infringement took place in a nation that is a signatory to a treaty such as Berne, the copyright owner will be entitled to the same rights as any citizen of that nation bringing a copyright lawsuit.

INTERNATIONAL COPYRIGHT TREATIES

International copyright protection for United States authors is determined by international copyright treaties. These treaties provide **national treatment** between the United States and a foreign country. National treatment, sometimes referred to as **mutuality,** means that every member nation of a treaty must give a foreign work the same degree of copyright protection that the nation gives to its own citizens. For example, the United States will protect the rights of a French author in the same manner that a United States author is protected; and France will protect the rights of a United States author as it would protect a French author.

The United States is a signatory, that is, a country that has signed the treaty, to three international copyright treaties. With the exception of a few countries, including Afghanistan, Ethiopia, Iran, Iraq, Nepal, North Korea, Oman, Tonga, and Yemen, most nations belong to one of these treaties:

- the Berne Convention;
- the Universal Copyright Convention;
- BAC (the Buenos Aires Convention of 1910); and
- GATT (Uruguay Round General Agreement on Tariffs and Trade).

In addition to these treaties, some nations have **bilateral treaties** with the United States. A bilateral treaty is an agreement by proclamation or treaty solely between the United States and that country in which copyright protection is mutually guaranteed for citizens of both nations.

The Berne Convention

The oldest international copyright treaty is the Berne Convention, organized in 1886 in Berne, Switzerland. Every Berne member nation must give national treatment to the authors of other Berne countries. The Berne Convention is administered by the World Intellectual Property Organization (WIPO) and is distinguished by three elements:

1. the minimum term of copyright protection is life of the author plus fifty years;
2. no formalities such as notice or registration are required for copyright protection; and
3. protection must be granted for certain moral rights. Moral rights protect the professional honor and reputation of an artist by guaranteeing the right to prevent distortion, mutilation, or other modification of the work.

Two elements of the Berne Convention—no formalities and moral rights—were stumbling blocks for United States entry into this international treaty: United States copyright law had historically conditioned copyright protection upon formalities such as notice and registration, and the United States did not recognize moral rights. American copyright owners were eager to benefit from the protections of the Berne Convention and lobbied Congress to modify the Copyright Act. The result was the Berne Convention Implementation Act, a series of amendments commencing in 1989.

EXAMPLE

National Treatment, Da! In 1997, a Russian news agency sued a Russian-language newspaper based in New York.[1] The newspaper had copied portions of news agency articles and headlines and argued that the news agency did not own copyright to the works. Since Russia and the United States were members of the Berne Convention, the news agency was entitled to the same treatment in the federal courts as a United States citizen. The court of appeals ruled that the copyright law of Russia should be interpreted to determine the ownership question. Next, the court of appeals interpreted United States copyright law (the country where the alleged copyright violation occurred) and determined that the newspaper had infringed the works.

The Universal Copyright Convention

The Universal Copyright Convention (UCC) was created in 1952 under the direction of UNESCO, and the United States became a signatory in 1955. For United States authors, there are two important elements to UCC protection:

1. every UCC member nation must give national treatment to the authors of other UCC countries (that is, a foreign work is given the same degree of copyright protection that the UCC nation gives its own citizens); and
2. as long as the copyright owner uses the copyright notice required by the UCC (the symbol ©, name of the owner, and the year), the owner is excused from any other formal requirements by another UCC nation.

The Buenos Aires Convention Of 1910

The Buenos Aires Convention (BAC) was ratified in 1911, and the United States joined in 1914. It is a treaty between the United States and sixteen Central and South American nations. There are actually two separate BAC treaties—one for patents and designs, and the other for copyright. The only formality required for national protection is the use of the term "All Rights Reserved."

Berne and UCC: Notice Requirements. The UCC requires copyright notice, but the Berne Convention does not. Should a United States author continue to use notice? Yes! Some countries (Russia, Uganda, Cambodia, and Laos) belong to the UCC but do not belong to Berne. A United States author's work published without notice will not be protected in these UCC countries. In order to enjoy international protection, a prudent copyright owner should include notice.

GATT

In December 1994, President Clinton signed a treaty known as the Uruguay Round General Agreement on Tariffs and Trade (GATT) that was intended to harmonize international trade. Over one hundred countries signed the GATT agreement. The GATT treaty includes an agreement on Trade-Related Aspects of Intellectual Property (TRIPS). The TRIPS agreement goes into effect gradually, and some developing countries that signed the agreement do not have to comply with the provisions until 2006. The GATT\TRIPS agreements established three important elements:

1. each GATT signatory must abide by substantive provisions of the Berne Convention, that is, these countries can have no formalities (no notice or registration required) and copyright must last for at least life of the author plus fifty years. The GATT agreement has no moral rights requirement;
2. every GATT member country must provide penalties for copyright infringement including injunctions and monetary damages; and

3.   every GATT member country must provide a means for excluding infringing goods at its border (for example, via the United States Customs at the United States border).

In addition, GATT established the World Trade Organization (WTO), an international organization that supervises each country's adoption of GATT rules and penalizes countries that violate GATT rules.

In order to conform to certain provisions of GATT, the United States amended copyright law to permit automatic restoration of copyright for certain foreign works in the public domain in the United States and protected by copyright in the respective GATT country.[2] Information regarding automatic restoration is provided in Appendix H.

END NOTES

1. Itar-Tass Russian News Agency v. Russian Kurier, Inc., 153 F.3d 82 (2d Cir. 1998).
2. 17 U.S.C. § 104A.

FOR MORE INFORMATION

List of Nations and Their Treaty Affiliation with the United States
See Appendix H.

APPENDIX A   COPYRIGHT RESOURCES

Adobe Systems, Inc.
http://www.adobe.com
Source of Adobe Acrobat Reader for reading and printing PDF files.

American Intellectual Property Law Assocation
2001 Jefferson Davis Highway, Suite 203, Arlington, VA 22202
http://www.aipla.org
Links and information regarding intellectual property attorneys.

American Society of Composers, Authors, and Publishers (ASCAP)
One Lincoln Plaza, New York, NY 10023
http://www.ascap.com
Performing rights organization with copyright song database.

American Society of Media Photographers
http://www.asmp.com
Newspaper and magazine photographers.

Association of American Publishers (AAP)
http://www.publishers.org
Trade association for the book publishing industry.

Authors Registry
330 West 42nd Street, 29th Floor, New York, NY 10036
http://www.webcom.com/registry
Directory of authors.

Broadcast Music Incorporated (BMI)
320 West 57th Street, New York, NY 10019
http://bmi.com
Performing rights organization with copyright song database.

BZ Rights & Permissions, Inc.
125 West 72nd Street, New York, NY 10023
http://bzrights.com
Clears rights for copyrighted works.

Campus Custom Publishing (CCP)
4355 D International Blvd., Norcross, GA 30093
http://menus.atlanta.com/ccp/
Provides academic coursepacks and secures copyright clearances.

Copyright Clearance Center (CCC)
222 Rosewood Drive, Danvers, MA 01923
http://www.copyright.com
Clears rights for works for commercial purposes.

Copyright Office
Library of Congress, Washington, DC 20559-6000
http://lcweb.loc.gov/copyright

- Fax-on-Demand (202) 707-2600
- Publications Sections, LM-455, Copyright Office, Library of Congress, Washington, DC 20559
- Licensing Division Section, LM-458, Copyright Office, Library of Congress, Washington, DC 20559, (202) 707-8150

Graphic Artists Guild
90 John Street, #403, New York, NY 10038
http://www.gag.org
Represents rights for graphic artists.

Harry Fox Agency
711 Third Avenue, New York, NY 10017
http://www.harryfox.com
Clears rights for use of music (mechanical licenses).

Intellectual Property Mall
http://www.ipmall.fplc.edu
IP links and information.

International Federation of Reproduction Rights Organisations (IFRRO)
Goethestrasse 49 D - 80336, München, Germany
http://www.copyright.com/ifrro
Facilitates international collective administration of reproduction and related
    copyright rights.

Legal Information Institute
http://www.law.cornell.edu/
Intellectual property links and downloadable copies of statutes and cases.

Legal Star
P.O. Box 415, Williamsville, NY 14221-0415
http://www.legalstar.com
Interactive electronic copyright, trademark, and patent forms.

LEXIS-NEXIS
P.O. Box 933, Dayton, OH 45401-0933
http://www.lexis-nexis.com
Subscription legal research service.

Media Photographers' Copyright Agency
http://www.mpca.com
Organization for newspapers and magazine photographers.

Motion Pictures Licensing Corp (MPLC)
http://www.mplc.com
Grants licenses for public performances of videocassettes and videodiscs.

Nolo Press
950 Parker Street, Berkeley, CA 94710
http://www.nolo.com
Self-help law source with information on copyright, patents, and trademarks.

Patent Office
Assistant Commissioner of Patents, Washington, DC 20231
http://www.uspto.gov/

SESAC
421 West 54th Street, 4th Floor, New York, NY 10036
http://www.sesac.com
Performing rights organization with copyright song database.

Software and Information Industry Association
1730 M Street NW, Washington, DC 20036
http://www.siia.net
Trade organization for software companies and programmers.

Thomson & Thomson
500 E Street, SW, Suite 970, Washington, DC 20024
http://www.thomson-thomson.com
Performs copyright and related searches.

Trademark Office
Assistant Commissioner for Trademarks, 2900 Crystal Drive, Arlington, VA
22202-3515
http://www.uspto.gov

Westlaw
620 Opperman Drive, Eagan, MN 55123
http://www.westpub.com
Subscription legal research service.

Yahoo Intellectual Property Directory
http://www.yahoo.com/Government/Law/Intellectual_Property/
Directory of IP resources on the Internet.

APPENDIX B GLOSSARY OF TERMS

access The reasonable opportunity of the defendant to view or hear the copyrighted work.

actual damages The plaintiff's provable monetary damages resulting from the infringing acts.

anonymous A work written by an author who is not identified on the copies of the work.

answer A written response to the complaint in which the defendant admits or denies the allegations and provides defenses.

architectural work The design of a building as embodied in any tangible medium of expression, including a building, architectural plans, or drawings; it includes the overall form as well as the arrangement and composition of spaces and elements in the design, but does not include individual standard features.

audiovisual works Works that consist of a series of related images that are intrinsically intended to be shown by the use of machines or devices such as projectors, viewers, or electronic equipment, together with accompanying sounds, if any, regardless of the nature of the material objects, such as films or tapes, in which the works are embodied.

author The creator of a copyrightable expression, whether literary, musical, or otherwise; or under work made for hire circumstances, the party that commissions a work or employs the creator.

automated database A body of facts, data, or other information assembled into an organized format suitable for use in a computer and comprising one or more files.

basic registration The primary copyright record made for each version of a particular work.

best edition The edition of a work that the Library of Congress determines to be most suitable for its purposes.

browser A software program that allows a computer user to view the worldwide web.

CD-ROM A disk (similar to compact disks that contain music) that can hold a large amount of digital information. When a CD-ROM or other program contains a combination of software, sounds, pictures, movies, or text, the combination is referred to as multimedia. CD-ROM disks will eventually be replaced by DVD-ROMs, which have a larger storage capacity.

cease and desist letter Correspondence from owner of proprietary work that informs the infringing party of the validity and ownership of the proprietary work, the nature of the infringement, and remedies that are available to the owner, and requests the cessation of all infringing activity.

children A person's immediate offspring, whether legitimate or not, and any children legally adopted by that person.

choreography Composition and arrangement of dance movements.

civil cover sheet A form required at the time of filing of the complaint for use by the court in maintaining certain statistical records.

coin-operated phonorecord player A machine or device employed solely for the performance of nondramatic musical works by means of phonorecords and upon insertion of coins or currency (or their equivalent); in order to qualify for compulsory license, such device must meet requirements of 17 U.S.C. § 116.

collaboration agreement A contract in which joint authors specify the rights, obligations, and percentage of copyright ownership and revenues attributable to each author.

collective work A work, such as a periodical issue, anthology, or encyclopedia, in which a number of contributions, constituting separate and independent works in themselves, are assembled into a collective whole.

common law A system of legal rules derived from the precedents and principles established by court decisions.

common law copyright A system of protection based upon the precedents and principles established by court decisions; affects unpublished, unregistered works created before January 1, 1978; applied by state courts or federal courts interpreting state law.

compilation A work formed by the collection and assembling of preexisting materials or of data that are selected, coordinated, or arranged in such a way that the resulting work as a whole constitutes an original work of authorship. The term *compilation* includes collective works.

complaint The initial document filed in a lawsuit. It sets forth the basis of the plaintiff's claims and requests certain remedies.

complete copy All elements comprising the unit of publication of the best edition of the work, including elements that, if considered separately, would not be copyrightable subject matter or would otherwise be exempt from mandatory deposit requirements.

compulsory license A system established by statute that permits the use of copyrighted works under certain circumstances and provided that certain fixed fees are paid.

computer A machine that processes digital information. A computer usually includes three components: a monitor or some other method of viewing information, a device such as a keyboard or mouse to input data; and a central processing unit that includes a system for storing information such as a floppy or hard disk. The machine components of a computer (disk drive, keyboard, etc.) are referred to as hardware.

computer program   A set of statements or instructions to be used directly or indirectly in a computer in order to bring about a certain result.

contributory infringer   One who, with knowledge or reason to know of infringing activity of another, induces, causes, or materially contributes to the infringement; or one who has the right and ability to supervise the infringing activities and also has a direct financial interest in such activities.

copies   Tangible object (other than phonorecord) in which a work is fixed by any method now known or later developed, and from which the work can be perceived, reproduced, or otherwise communicated, either directly or with the aid of a machine or device; the term *copies* includes the tangible object (other than a phonorecord) in which the work is first fixed.

copyright   The legal right to exclude others for a limited time from copying, selling, performing, displaying, or making derivative versions of a work of authorship.

counterclaim   A claim for relief usually asserted by the defendant against an opposing party, usually the plaintiff.

created   When a work is fixed in a copy or phonorecord for the first time; where a work is prepared over a period of time, the portion of it that has been fixed at any particular time constitutes the work as of that time, and where the work has been prepared in different versions, each version constitutes a separate work.

declaratory relief   A request that the court sort out the rights and legal obligations of the parties in the midst of an actual controversy.

deposition   Oral or written testimony of a party or witness and given under oath.

derivative work   A work based upon one or more preexisting works, such as a translation, musical arrangement, dramatization, fictionalization, motion picture version, sound recording, art reproduction, abridgment, condensation, or any other form in which a work may be recast, transformed, or adapted. A work consisting of editorial revisions, annotations, elaborations, or other modifications that, as a whole, represent an original work of authorship is also a derivative work.

design patent   Legal protection granted for a new, original, and ornamental design for an article of manufacture; protects only the appearance of an article, and not its structure or utilitarian features.

digital transmission   A transmission in whole or in part in a digital or other nonanalog format.

display publicly   To show a copy of a work, either directly or by means of a film, slide, television image, or any other device or process where the public is gathered *or* the work is transmitted or otherwise communicated to the public; in the case of a motion picture or other audiovisual work, the nonsequential showing of individual images.

dramatic works   Narrative presentations (and any accompanying music) that generally use dialogue and stage directions as the basis for a theatrical exhibition.

e-mail "Electronic mail" that is transmitted over a network or over the Internet.

ephemeral recordings Copies or phonorecords of works that are made for purposes of later transmission.

establishment A store, shop, or any similar place of business open to the general public for the primary purpose of selling goods or services in which the majority of the gross square feet of space that is nonresidential is used for that purpose, and in which nondramatic musical works are performed publicly.

estoppel . A defense to infringement in which the defendant prevents the plaintiff from contradicting behavior upon which the defendant has justifiably relied. In order to assert successfully an estoppel defense, the plaintiff must know the facts of the defendant's conduct, and the defendant must have a justifiable belief that the infringing conduct is permitted.

exclusive jurisdiction A court has the sole authority to hear a certain type of case.

exclusive license An agreement to restrict the grant of proprietary rights to one person.

extended renewal term An extension of the renewal term from 28 to 47 years for works registered under the Copyright Act of 1909 that were in their renewal term on January 1, 1978, or that were renewed after January 1, 1978. In 1998, the period was extended for an additional 20 years.

fair use Right to use copyrighted material for limited purposes and without authorization of the author; determined by federal court after weighing several factors including: purpose and character of the use, amount and substantiality of portion borrowed, and effect of the use on the market for the copyrighted material.

financial gain Receipt, or expectation of receipt, of anything of value, including the receipt of other copyrighted works.

first sale doctrine Right of the owner of a lawfully made copy or phonorecord to sell or otherwise dispose of possession of that copy or phonorecord without the authority of the copyright owner.

fixed Embodiment of a work in a tangible medium of expression by or under the authority of the author, which is sufficiently permanent or stable to permit it to be perceived, reproduced, or otherwise communicated for a period of more than transitory duration; in the case of sounds, images, or both, that are being transmitted, a work is "fixed" if a fixation of the work is being made simultaneously with its transmission.

food service (or drinking establishment) A restaurant, inn, bar, tavern, or any other similar place of business in which the public or patrons assemble for the primary purpose of being served food or drink, in which the majority of the gross square feet of space that is nonresidential is used for that purpose, and in which nondramatic musical works are performed publicly.

freeware Copyrighted software that is made available to the public for free.

gross square feet of space of an establishment The entire interior space of that establishment, and any adjoining outdoor space used to serve patrons, whether on a seasonal basis or otherwise.

infringement The unauthorized use of a work protected by copyright; occurs when a party with access to a copyrighted work creates a substantially similar work without permission of the copyright owner and in violation of copyright laws.

injunction A court order directing the defendant to stop certain activities.

instructional text A literary, pictorial, or graphic work prepared for use in day-to-day instructional activities. For example, a textbook would be an instructional text, but a novel used in a literature class would not be an instructional text.

intellectual property Any product of the human mind that is protected under law.

Internet A worldwide network of computers connected by phone lines. The Internet is customized to allow users to see images and text in a graphical environment known as the worldwide web. A computer user with a modem, browser, and online access can access different locations (or websites) by typing in the name of the site (the "domain name" which is usually prefaced with the letters http://www). Anyone can own or establish a website by making an arrangement with an online service. When an Internet user visits a website, the user is actually viewing the contents of another person's or company's computer.

Internet service provider (ISP) A company or institution that provides access to the Internet (for example, America Online or the Microsoft Network).

interrogatories Written questions that must be answered under oath.

joint work A work prepared by two or more authors with the intention that their contributions will be merged into inseparable or interdependent parts of a unitary whole.

judgment The relief awarded by the court as the result of the judge's or jury's verdict.

jury instructions Explanations of the legal rules that the jury shall use in reaching a verdict.

laches A defense to infringement in which the defendant argues that the plaintiff's delay in bringing the lawsuit is so unreasonable that the plaintiff should be barred from proceeding.

lay observer A test for copyright infringement in which a court asks, "Would the ordinary observer, when examining both works, consider that the defendant has misappropriated the plaintiff's work?"

license A contract that grants rights or permission to do something subject to certain conditions.

licensee Person acquiring rights under the license.

licensor Person granting rights, usually the author.

literary works Works, other than audiovisual works, expressed in words, numbers, or other verbal or numerical symbols or indicia, regardless of the nature of the material objects, such as books, periodicals, manuscripts, phonorecords, film, tapes, disks, or cards, in which they are embodied.

mechanical right The right to reproduce a musical work on phonorecords.

merger doctrine When an idea is incapable of being expressed in more than one way, then the idea and expression are inseparable, and it is not an infringement to copy it.

modem A device that allows the computer to send and receive information.

moral rights Rights that protect the professional honor and reputation of an artist by guaranteeing the right to claim or disclaim authorship of a work and the right to prevent, in certain cases, distortion, mutilation, or other modification of the work.

motion A request for an order of the court.

motion for summary judgment A request that the court order a judgment without having a trial because there is no genuine issue as to any material facts.

motion in limine A request made to the court, usually prior to trial, that certain information not be presented to the jury.

motion picture An audiovisual work consisting of a series of related images that, when shown in succession, impart an impression of motion, together with accompanying sounds, if any.

multimedia work A work that combines authorship in two or more media.

multiple file database A collection of separate and distinct groups of data records.

music publisher A company that has acquired a copyright interest in a musical composition and collects revenue, handles business formalities, sues infringers, and looks for new ways to exploit the composition.

musical work A composition incorporating melody, rhythm, and harmonic elements (and accompanying lyrics, if any).

network When computers are connected to other computers by cables or phone lines and information can be exchanged. Computers are often networked in offices and businesses. The term *intranet* refers to a network within a business. Only employees of the business or persons with a special code have access to an intranet.

owner of copyright Person or persons holding title to copyright; either the author or any party to whom the author has licensed or transferred a right under copyright.

pantomime A form of theater expressed by gestures but without words.

patent The legal right to exclude others from using, selling, or making invention or discovery for a limited term.

pendent jurisdiction The authority of the federal courts to hear a matter normally within the jurisdiction of state courts; exists where that matter is combined with a claim that is within the authority of the federal courts.

perform publicly To recite, render, play, dance, or act a work, either directly or by means of any device or process, where the public is gathered *or* the work is transmitted or otherwise communicated to the public; in the case of a motion picture or other audiovisual work, to show its images in any sequence or to make the sounds accompanying it audible.

performing rights society An association or corporation that licenses the public performance of nondramatic musical works on behalf of the copyright owners.

permanent injunction A durable injunction issued after a final judgment on the merits of the case; permanently restrains the defendant from engaging in the infringing activity.

phonorecords Material objects in which sounds, other than those accompanying a motion picture or other audiovisual work, are fixed by any method now known or later developed, and from which the sounds can be perceived, reproduced, or otherwise communicated, either directly or with the aid of a machine or device. The term *phonorecords* includes the material object in which the sounds are first fixed.

pictorial, graphic, and sculptural works Two-dimensional and three-dimensional works of fine, graphic, and applied art, photographs, prints and art reproductions, maps, globes, charts, diagrams, models, and technical drawings, including architectural plans; such works include works of artistic craftsmanship insofar as their form but not their mechanical or utilitarian aspects are concerned; the design of a useful article shall be considered a pictorial, graphic, or sculptural work only if, and only to the extent that, such design incorporates pictorial, graphic, or sculptural features that can be identified separately from, and are capable of existing independently of, the utilitarian aspects of the article.

preemption The authority of the federal government to preclude the states from exercising powers granted to the federal government pursuant to the Constitution.

preliminary injunction An injunction granted after a noticed hearing where the parties have an opportunity to present evidence as to the likelihood of plaintiff's success on the merits and irreparability of the harm to be suffered if the injunction is not granted; lasts until a final judgment has been rendered.

presumption An inference as to the truth or validity of an allegation; a presumption shifts the burden to the other party to disprove or show, with sufficient evidence, the falsity or invalidity of the allegation.

proprietor An individual, corporation, partnership, or other entity, as the case may be, that owns an establishment or a food service or drinking establishment, except that no owner or operator of a radio or television station licensed by the Federal Communications Commission, cable system or satellite carrier, cable or satellite carrier service or programmer, provider of online services or network access or the operator of facilities therefor, telecommunications company, or any other such audio or audiovisual service or programmer now known or as may be developed in the future, commercial subscription music service, or owner or operator of any other transmission service, shall under any circumstances be deemed to be a proprietor.

pseudonymous   A work written by an author identified by a fictitious name.

public domain   Material that is not protected under copyright law and is free for use by the public.

publication   The distribution of copies or phonorecords of a work to the public by sale or other transfer of ownership, or by rental, lease, or lending; the offering to distribute copies or phonorecords to a group of persons for purposes of further distribution, public performance, or public display.

RAM (random access memory)   A computer's temporary storage system.

renewal term   For works registered under the Copyright Act of 1909, it is a 28-year period following the initial 28-year term of copyright protection.

request for admission   A request for a party to the lawsuit to admit the truthfulness of a fact or statement.

rule of doubt   A work is registered even though a reasonable doubt exists at the Copyright Office as to whether the requirements of the Copyright Act have been met or whether the deposit materials constitute protectible subject matter under copyright law; the final determination will be made by a federal court.

secure test   A nonmarketed test administered under supervision at specified centers on specific dates, all copies of which are accounted for and either destroyed or returned to restricted locked storage following each administration. A test is "nonmarketed" if copies are not sold and the test is distributed and used in such a manner that ownership and control of copies remain with the test sponsor or publisher.

serial   A work, such as a newspaper, magazine, newsletter, or journal, issued or intended to be issued in successive parts bearing numerical or chronological designations and intended to be continued indefinitely.

service mark   A mark that is used in the sale or advertising of services in order to identify and distinguish services performed for the benefit of others.

settlement   An agreement between the parties in which the dispute is formally resolved.

shareware   A system of marketing copyrighted software whereby trial copies are made available for free and the user, if he or she wants to keep the program, pays a fee.

shrink-wrap agreement   A license between the manufacturer of a computer software program and a consumer granting certain legal rights and warranties in exchange for the right to use the program; usually triggered by the opening of the shrink-wrap containing the computer software program diskettes or by the return of the software registration or warranty card.

single file database   A database that consists of data records pertaining to a single common subject matter.

software or computer program   A set of instructions in a special code loaded into the computer. Software is used to perform functions and obtain results such as writing a letter, locating a zip code, or modifying a picture. When a new version of a software program is released, it is referred to as an upgrade.

sound recordings   Works that result from the fixation of a series of musical, spoken, or other sounds, but not including the sounds accompanying a motion picture or other audiovisual work, regardless of the nature of the material objects, such as disks, tapes, or other phonorecords, in which they are embodied.

statute of limitations   The time limit during which the plaintiff must file a lawsuit. In copyright, it is three years from the date when the infringing activity occurred (or when the copyright owner could have reasonably known that the infringing activity occurred.)

statutory damages   An award of damages prescribed by statute and not contingent upon proof of the copyright owner's loss or defendant's profits; monetary damages awarded for infringement of any one work in a sum of not less than $500 or more than $20,000, as the court considers just.

substantial similarity   Two works have similarities that could have only resulted from copying, rather than from coincidence, common source derivation, or independent creation.

summons   A document served with the complaint that explains that the defendant has been sued and has a certain time limit in which to respond.

supplementary work   A work prepared by an author for the purpose of introducing, concluding, illustrating, explaining, revising, commenting upon, or assisting in the use of another author's work. Examples would be forewords, afterwards, pictorial illustrations, maps, charts, tables, editorial notes, musical arrangements, answer material for tests, bibliographies, appendixes, and indexes.

temporary restraining order   An injunction, often granted *ex parte*, that is short in duration and only remains in effect until the court has an opportunity to schedule a hearing for the preliminary injunction.

tenancy in common   A legal form of co-ownership of property that grants to each co-owner an independent right to use or license the property, subject to a duty of accounting to the other co-owners for any profits; upon a co-owner's death, that co-owner's share goes to his or her beneficiaries or heirs, but not to other co-owners.

trade secret   Any formula, pattern, device, or compilation of information that is used in one's business and that gives the owner of the secret an opportunity to obtain an advantage over competitors who do not know or use it.

trademark Any word, symbol, design, device, slogan, or combination that identifies and distinguishes goods.

transfer of copyright ownership An assignment, mortgage, exclusive license, transfer by will or intestate succession, or any other change in the ownership of any or all of the exclusive rights in a copyright, whether or not it is limited in time or place of effect, but not including a nonexclusive license.

unclean hands A defense asserted when the plaintiff has committed a serious act of wrongdoing in regard to the lawsuit or the activity precipitating the lawsuit.

unfair competition A collection of common law principles and precedents, many of which are adopted as state laws, that protect against unfair business practices.

useful article An article having an intrinsic utilitarian function that is not merely to portray the appearance of the article or to convey information.

utility patent Patent granted for inventions or discoveries that are categorized as machines, processes, compositions, articles of manufacture, or new uses of any of these.

visually perceptible copy A copy that can be visually observed when it is embodied in a material object, either directly or with the aid of a machine or device.

work made for hire (1) A work prepared by an employee within the scope of employment; or (2) a work specially ordered or commissioned for use as a contribution to a collective work, as a part of a motion picture or other audiovisual work, as a translation, as a supplementary work, as a compilation, as an instructional text, as a test, as answer material for a test, or as an atlas, if the parties expressly agree in a written instrument signed by them that the work shall be considered a work made for hire.

work of authorship Creation of intellectual or artistic effort fixed or embodied in a perceptible form and meeting the statutory standards of copyright protection.

work of visual art Under the Copyright Act of 1976, it is either (1) a painting, drawing, print, or sculpture, existing in a single copy, in a limited edition of 200 copies or fewer that are signed and consecutively numbered by the author, or, in the case of a sculpture, in multiple cast, carved, or fabricated sculptures of 200 or fewer that are consecutively numbered by the author and bear the signature or other identifying mark of the author; or (2) a still photographic image produced for exhibition purposes only, existing in a single copy that is signed by the author, or in a limited edition of 200 copies or fewer that are signed and consecutively numbered by the author.

writ of seizure An order of the court directing the federal marshal to seize and hold infringing merchandise; granted only upon payment of a bond of not less than twice the value of the infringing articles.

APPENDIX C COPYRIGHT OFFICE CIRCULARS AND FORM LETTERS

Following is a list of circulars and form letters furnished by the United States Copyright Office. All of these circulars can be obtained from:

- Publications Sections, LM-455, Copyright Office, Library of Congress, Washington, DC 20559
- Copyright Office website at http://www.loc.gov/copyright
- Copyright Office's fax-on-demand telephone line at (202) 707-2600

United States Copyright Office, Information Circulars

Circular 1 Copyright Basics

Circular 1b Limitations/Information Furnished by Copyright Office

Circular 2 Publications on Copyright

Circular 4 Copyright Fees

Circular 5 How to Open and Maintain a Deposit Account in the U.S. Copyright Office

Circular 6 Access to/Copies of Copyright Records and Deposit

Circular 7d Mandatory Deposit of Copies of Phonorecords

Circular 8 Supplementary Copyright Registration

Circular 9 Work-Made-for-Hire Under the 1976 Copyright Act

Circular 10 Special Handling

Circular 12 Recordations of Transfers and Other Documents

Circular 14 Copyright Registration for Derivative Works

Circular 15 Renewal of Copyright

Circular 21 Reproductions of Copyrighted Works by Educators

Circular 22 How to Investigate the Copyright Status of a Work

Circular 23 Copyright Card Catalog and the Online Files

Circular 31 Ideas, Methods, or Systems

Circular 32 Blank Forms/Other Works Not Protected by Copyright

Circular 34 Copyright Protection NOT Available for Names, Titles

Circular 38a International Copyright Relations of the United States

Circular 38b Highlights of Copyright Amendments Contained in the URAA

Circular 40 Copyright Registration for Works of the Visual Arts

Circular 40a Deposit Requirements in Visual Arts Material

Circular 41 Copyright Claims in Architectural Works

Circular 44 Cartoons and Comic Strips

Circular 45 Motion Pictures including Video Recordings

Circular 50 Musical Compositions

Circular 55 Copyright Registration for Multimedia Works

Circular 56 Copyright for Sound Recordings

Circular 56a Copyright Registration of Musical Compositions

Circular 61 Copyright Registration for Computer Programs

Circular 62 Copyright Registration for Serials on Form SE

Circular 62b Group Registration for Daily Newspapers

Circular 62c Group Registration for Daily Newsletters

Circular 64 Copyright Registration for Secure Tests

Circular 65 Copyright Registration for Automated Databases

Circular 66 Copyright Registration for Online Works

Circular 73 Compulsory License for Making and Distributing Phonorecords

Circular 74 How to Make Compulsory License Royalty Payment

Circular 75 The Licensing Division of the Copyright Office

Circular 100 Federal Statutory Protection for Mask Works

Form Letters and SLs

International Copyright (FL 100)

Pseudonyms (FL 101)

Fair Use (FL 102)

Useful Articles (FL 103)

Music (FL 105)

Poetry (FL 106)

Photographs (FL 107)

Games (FL 108)

Books, Manuscripts, and Speeches (FL 109)

Visual Arts (FL 115)

Dramatic Works: Scripts, Pantomimes, and Choreography (FL 119)

Recipes (FL 122)

Get It Quick Over the Net (SL 10)

Terms for Copyright Protection (SL 15)

APPENDIX D COPYRIGHT FORMS

- Form TX with instructions—for published or unpublished nondramatic literary works
- Form PA with instructions—for published or unpublished works of the performing arts
- Form SR with instructions—for published or unpublished sound recordings
- Form VA with instructions—for published or unpublished works of the visual arts
- Form SE with instructions—for serials (newspapers, magazines, newsletters, annuals, journals, and so on)
- Form SE/Group—for registration of a group of serials
- Form G/DN—for registration of a group of daily newspapers
- Form RE with instructions—for claims to renewal of copyright
- Form GATT—for restored works under the URAA
- Form CA—to correct an error or amplify the information given in a registration
- Form CON—continuation sheet to be used only in conjunction with basic application Forms CA, PA, SE, SR, TX, and VA
- Document Cover Sheet—for use when submitting a document for recordation in the United States Copyright Office
- Form GR/CP—an adjunct application to be used for a group of contributions to periodicals in addition to an application Form TX, PA, or VA

✍ Application Form TX ✍

Detach and read these instructions before completing this form.
Make sure all applicable spaces have been filled in before you return this form.

BASIC INFORMATION

When to Use This Form: Use Form TX for registration of published or unpublished nondramatic literary works, excluding periodicals or serial issues. This class includes a wide variety of works: fiction, nonfiction, poetry, textbooks, reference works, directories, catalogs, advertising copy, compilations of information, and computer programs. For periodicals and serials, use Form SE.

Deposit to Accompany Application: An application for copyright registration must be accompanied by a deposit consisting of copies or phonorecords representing the entire work for which registration is to be made. The following are the general deposit requirements as set forth in the statute:

Unpublished Work: Deposit one complete copy (or phonorecord)
Published Work: Deposit two complete copies (or one phonorecord) of the best edition.
Work First Published Outside the United States: Deposit one complete copy (or phonorecord) of the first foreign edition.
Contribution to a Collective Work: Deposit one complete copy (or phonorecord) of the best edition of the collective work.

The Copyright Notice: Before March 1, 1989, the use of copyright notice was mandatory on all published works, and any work first published before that date should have carried a notice. For works first published on and after March 1, 1989, use of the copyright notice is optional. For more information about copyright notice, see Circular 3, "Copyright Notice."

For Further Information: To speak to an information specialist, call (202) 707-3000 (TTY: (202) 707-6737). Recorded information is available 24 hours a day. Order forms and other publications from the address in space 9 or call the Forms and Publications Hotline at (202) 707-9100. Most circulars (but not forms) are available via fax. Call (202) 707-2600 from a touchtone phone. Access and download circulars, forms, and other information from the Copyright Office Website at http://www.loc.gov/copyright.

LINE-BY-LINE INSTRUCTIONS

Please type or print using black ink. The form is used to produce the certificate.

1 SPACE 1: Title

Title of This Work: Every work submitted for copyright registration must be given a title to identify that particular work. If the copies or phonorecords of the work bear a title or an identifying phrase that could serve as a title, transcribe that wording *completely* and *exactly* on the application. Indexing of the registration and future identification of the work will depend on the information you give here.

Previous or Alternative Titles: Complete this space if there are any additional titles for the work under which someone searching for the registration might be likely to look or under which a document pertaining to the work might be recorded.

Publication as a Contribution: If the work being registered is a contribution to a periodical, serial, or collection, give the title of the contribution in the "Title of This Work" space. Then, in the line headed "Publication as a Contribution," give information about the collective work in which the contribution appeared.

2 SPACE 2: Author(s)

General Instructions: After reading these instructions, decide who are the "authors" of this work for copyright purposes. Then, unless the work is a "collective work," give the requested information about every "author" who contributed any appreciable amount of copyrightable matter to this version of the work. If you need further space, request Continuation Sheets. In the case of a collective work, such as an anthology, collection of essays, or encyclopedia, give information about the author of the collective work as a whole.

Name of Author: The fullest form of the author's name should be given. Unless the work was "made for hire," the individual who actually created the work is its "author." In the case of a work made for hire, the statute provides that "the employer or other person for whom the work was prepared is considered the author."

What is a Work Made for Hire ? A "work made for hire" is defined as (1) "a work prepared by an employee within the scope of his or her employment"; or (2) "a work specially ordered or commissioned for use as a contribution to a collective work, as a part of a motion picture or other audiovisual work, as a translation, as a supplementary work, as a compilation, as an instructional text, as a test, as answer material for a test, or as an atlas, if the parties expressly agree in a written instrument signed by them that the works shall be considered a work made for hire." If you have checked "Yes" to indicate that the work was "made for hire," you must give the full legal name of the employer (or other person for whom the work was prepared). You may also include the name of the employee along with the name of the employer (for example: "Elster Publishing Co., employer for hire of John Ferguson").

Anonymous or Pseudonymous Work: An author's contribution to a work is "anonymous" if that author is not identified on the copies or phonorecords of the work. An author's contribution to a work is "pseudonymous" if that author is identified on the copies or phonorecords under a fictitious name. If the work is "anonymous" you may: (1) leave the line blank; or (2) state "anonymous" on the line; or (3) reveal the author's identity. If the work is "pseudonymous" you may: (1) leave the line blank; or (2) give the pseudonym and identify it as such (for example: "Huntley Haverstock, pseudonym"); or (3) reveal the author's name, making clear which is the real name and which is the pseudonym (for example, "Judith Barton, whose pseudonym is Madeline Elster"). However, the citizenship or domicile of the author **must** be given in all cases.

Dates of Birth and Death: If the author is dead, the statute requires that the year of death be included in the application unless the work is anonymous or pseudonymous. The author's birth date is optional but is useful as a form of identification. Leave this space blank if the author's contribution was a "work made for hire."

Author s Nationality or Domicile: Give the country of which the author is a citizen or the country in which the author is domiciled. Nationality or domicile **must** be given in all cases.

Nature of Authorship: After the words "Nature of Authorship," give a brief general statement of the nature of this particular author's contribution to the work. Examples: "Entire text"; "Co-author of entire text"; "Computer program"; "Editorial revisions"; "Compilation and English translation"; "New text."

SPACE 3: Creation and Publication

General Instructions: Do not confuse "creation" with "publication." Every application for copyright registration must state "the year in which creation of the work was completed." Give the date and nation of first publication only if the work has been published.

Creation: Under the statute, a work is "created" when it is fixed in a copy or phonorecord for the first time. Where a work has been prepared over a period of time, the part of the work existing in fixed form on a particular date constitutes the created work on that date. The date you give here should be the year in which the author completed the particular version for which registration is now being sought, even if other versions exist or if further changes or additions are planned.

Publication: The statute defines "publication" as "the distribution of copies or phonorecords of a work to the public by sale or other transfer of ownership, or by rental, lease, or lending." A work is also "published" if there has been an "offering to distribute copies or phonorecords to a group of persons for purposes of further distribution, public performance, or public display." Give the full date (month, day, year) when, and the country where, publication first occurred. If first publication took place simultaneously in the United States and other countries, it is sufficient to state "U.S.A."

SPACE 4: Claimant(s)

Name(s) and Address(es) of Copyright Claimant(s): Give the name(s) and address(es) of the copyright claimant(s) in this work even if the claimant is the same as the author. Copyright in a work belongs initially to the author of the work (including, in the case of a work made for hire, the employer or other person for whom the work was prepared). The copyright claimant is either the author of the work or a person or organization to whom the copyright initially belonging to the author has been transferred.

Transfer: The statute provides that, if the copyright claimant is not the author, the application for registration must contain "a brief statement of how the claimant obtained ownership of the copyright." If any copyright claimant named in space 4 is not an author named in space 2, give a brief statement explaining how the claimant(s) obtained ownership of the copyright. Examples: "By written contract"; "Transfer of all rights by author"; "Assignment"; "By will." Do not attach transfer documents or other attachments or riders.

SPACE 5: Previous Registration

General Instructions: The questions in space 5 are intended to show whether an earlier registration has been made for this work and, if so, whether there is any basis for a new registration. As a general rule, only one basic copyright registration can be made for the same version of a particular work.

Same Version: If this version is substantially the same as the work covered by a previous registration, a second registration is not generally possible unless: (1) the work has been registered in unpublished form and a second registration is now being sought to cover this first published edition; or (2) someone other than the

author is identified as copyright claimant in the earlier registration, and the author is now seeking registration in his or her own name. If either of these two exceptions apply, check the appropriate box and give the earlier registration number and date. Otherwise, do not submit Form TX. Instead, write the Copyright Office for information about supplementary registration or recordation of transfers of copyright ownership.

Changed Version: If the work has been changed and you are now seeking registration to cover the additions or revisions, check the last box in space 5, give the earlier registration number and date, and complete both parts of space 6 in accordance with the instructions below.

Previous Registration Number and Date: If more than one previous registration has been made for the work, give the number and date of the latest registration.

SPACE 6: Derivative Work or Compilation

General Instructions: Complete space 6 if this work is a "changed version," "compilation," or "derivative work" and if it incorporates one or more earlier works that have already been published or registered for copyright or that have fallen into the public domain. A "compilation" is defined as "a work formed by the collection and assembling of preexisting materials or of data that are selected, coordinated, or arranged in such a way that the resulting work as a whole constitutes an original work of authorship." A "derivative work" is "a work based on one or more preexisting works." Examples of derivative works include translations, fictionalizations, abridgments, condensations, or "any other form in which a work may be recast, transformed, or adapted." Derivative works also include works "consisting of editorial revisions, annotations, or other modifications" if these changes, as a whole, represent an original work of authorship.

Preexisting Material (space 6a): For derivative works, complete this space **and** space 6b. In space 6a identify the preexisting work that has been recast, transformed, or adapted. The preexisting work may be material that has been previously published, previously registered, or that is in the public domain. An example of preexisting material might be: "Russian version of Goncharov's 'Oblomov.'"

Material Added to This Work (space 6b): Give a brief, general statement of the new material covered by the copyright claim for which registration is sought. Derivative work examples include: "Foreword, editing, critical annotations"; "Translation"; "Chapters 11-17." If the work is a **compilation**, describe both the compilation itself and the material that has been compiled. Example: "Compilation of certain 1917 Speeches by Woodrow Wilson." A work may be both a derivative work and compilation, in which case a sample statement might be: "Compilation and additional new material."

SPACE 7,8,9: Fee, Correspondence, Certification, Return Address

Deposit Account: If you maintain a Deposit Account in the Copyright Office, identify it in space 7a. Otherwise leave the space blank and send the fee of $20* with your application and deposit.

Correspondence (space 7b): This space should contain the name, address, area code, telephone number, fax number, and email address (if available) of the person to be consulted if correspondence about this application becomes necessary.

Certification (space 8): The application cannot be accepted unless it bears the date and the **handwritten signature** of the author or other copyright claimant, or of the owner of exclusive right(s), or of the duly authorized agent of author, claimant, or owner of exclusive right(s).

Address for Return of Certificate (space 9): The address box must be completed legibly since the certificate will be returned in a window envelope.

FORM TX
For a Nondramatic Literary Work
UNITED STATES COPYRIGHT OFFICE

REGISTRATION NUMBER

TX   TXU

EFFECTIVE DATE OF REGISTRATION

Month   Day   Year

DO NOT WRITE ABOVE THIS LINE. IF YOU NEED MORE SPACE, USE A SEPARATE CONTINUATION SHEET.

1

TITLE OF THIS WORK ▼

PREVIOUS OR ALTERNATIVE TITLES ▼

PUBLICATION AS A CONTRIBUTION If this work was published as a contribution to a periodical, serial, or collection, give information about the collective work in which the contribution appeared.   Title of Collective Work ▼

If published in a periodical or serial give: Volume ▼   Number ▼   Issue Date ▼   On Pages ▼

2 a

NAME OF AUTHOR ▼

DATES OF BIRTH AND DEATH
Year Born ▼   Year Died ▼

Was this contribution to the work a "work made for hire"?
☐ Yes
☐ No

AUTHOR'S NATIONALITY OR DOMICILE
Name of Country
OR { Citizen of ▶
Domiciled in▶

WAS THIS AUTHOR'S CONTRIBUTION TO THE WORK
Anonymous?   ☐ Yes ☐ No
Pseudonymous? ☐ Yes ☐ No
If the answer to either of these questions is Yes, see detailed instructions.

NATURE OF AUTHORSHIP Briefly describe nature of material created by this author in which copyright is claimed. ▼

NOTE

Under the law, the author of a work made for hire is generally the employer, not the employee (see instructions). For any part of this work that was made for hire check Yes in the space provided, give the employer (or other person for whom the work was prepared) as Author of that part, and leave the space for dates of birth and death blank.

b

NAME OF AUTHOR ▼

DATES OF BIRTH AND DEATH
Year Born ▼   Year Died ▼

Was this contribution to the work a "work made for hire"?
☐ Yes
☐ No

AUTHOR'S NATIONALITY OR DOMICILE
Name of Country
OR { Citizen of ▶
Domiciled in▶

WAS THIS AUTHOR'S CONTRIBUTION TO THE WORK
Anonymous?   ☐ Yes ☐ No
Pseudonymous? ☐ Yes ☐ No
If the answer to either of these questions is Yes, see detailed instructions.

NATURE OF AUTHORSHIP Briefly describe nature of material created by this author in which copyright is claimed. ▼

c

NAME OF AUTHOR ▼

DATES OF BIRTH AND DEATH
Year Born ▼   Year Died ▼

Was this contribution to the work a "work made for hire"?
☐ Yes
☐ No

AUTHOR'S NATIONALITY OR DOMICILE
Name of Country
OR { Citizen of ▶
Domiciled in▶

WAS THIS AUTHOR'S CONTRIBUTION TO THE WORK
Anonymous?   ☐ Yes ☐ No
Pseudonymous? ☐ Yes ☐ No
If the answer to either of these questions is Yes, see detailed instructions.

NATURE OF AUTHORSHIP Briefly describe nature of material created by this author in which copyright is claimed. ▼

3 a

YEAR IN WHICH CREATION OF THIS WORK WAS COMPLETED This information must be given ◀Year in all cases.

b DATE AND NATION OF FIRST PUBLICATION OF THIS PARTICULAR WORK
Complete this information ONLY if this work has been published.
Month ▶   Day▶   Year ▶   ◀ Nation

4

COPYRIGHT CLAIMANT(S) Name and address must be given even if the claimant is the same as the author given in space 2. ▼

TRANSFER If the claimant(s) named here in space 4 is (are) different from the author(s) named in space 2, give a brief statement of how the claimant(s) obtained ownership of the copyright. ▼

See instructions before completing this space.

DO NOT WRITE HERE OFFICE USE ONLY

APPLICATION RECEIVED

ONE DEPOSIT RECEIVED

TWO DEPOSITS RECEIVED

FUNDS RECEIVED

MORE ON BACK ▶ ¥ Complete all applicable spaces (numbers 5-9) on the reverse side of this page.
¥ See detailed instructions.   ¥ Sign the form at line 8.

DO NOT WRITE HERE
Page 1 of _____ pages

EXAMINED BY

FORM TX

CHECKED BY

☐ CORRESPONDENCE
Yes

FOR
COPYRIGHT
OFFICE
USE
ONLY

DO NOT WRITE ABOVE THIS LINE. IF YOU NEED MORE SPACE, USE A SEPARATE CONTINUATION SHEET.

PREVIOUS REGISTRATION Has registration for this work, or for an earlier version of this work, already been made in the Copyright Office?
☐ Yes ☐ No If your answer is "Yes," why is another registration being sought? (Check appropriate box.) ▼
a. ☐ This is the first published edition of a work previously registered in unpublished form.
b. ☐ This is the first application submitted by this author as copyright claimant.
c. ☐ This is a changed version of the work, as shown by space 6 on this application.
If your answer is "Yes," give: **Previous Registration Number** ▼   **Year of Registration** ▼

5

DERIVATIVE WORK OR COMPILATION
Preexisting Material Identify any preexisting work or works that this work is based on or incorporates.▼

Material Added to This Work Give a brief, general statement of the material that has been added to this work and in which copyright is claimed.▼

a
b

6

See instructions
before completing
this space.

DEPOSIT ACCOUNT If the registration fee is to be charged to a Deposit Account established in the Copyright Office, give name and number of Account.
Name ▼   **Account Number** ▼

CORRESPONDENCE Give name and address to which correspondence about this application should be sent.   Name/Address/Apt/City/State/ZIP ▼

Area code and daytime telephone number ▶   Fax number   ▶
Email ▶

a
b

7

CERTIFICATION* I, the undersigned, hereby certify that I am the
Check only one ▶
☐ author
☐ other copyright claimant
☐ owner of exclusive right(s)
☐ authorized agent of _____
of the work identified in this application and that the statements made
by me in this application are correct to the best of my knowledge.
Name of author or other copyright claimant, or owner of exclusive right(s) ▲

8

Typed or printed name and date ▼ If this application gives a date of publication in space 3, do not sign and submit it before that date.

_____ Date ▶ _____

Handwritten signature (X)▼

X _

**Registration filing fees are effective through June 30, 1999. After that date, please write the Copyright Office,
check the Copyright Office Website at http://www.loc.gov/copyright, or call (202) 707-3000 for the latest fee information.**

Mail
certificate
to:

Certificate
will be
mailed in
window
envelope

Name ▼

Number/Street/Apt ▼

City/State/ZIP ▼

YOU MUST:
¥ Complete all necessary spaces
¥ Sign your application in space 8
SEND ALL 3 ELEMENTS
IN THE SAME PACKAGE:
1. Application form
2. Nonrefundable filing fee in check or money order
payable to *Register of Copyrights*
3. Deposit material
MAIL TO:
Library of Congress
Copyright Office
101 Independence Avenue, S.E.
Washington, D.C. 20559-6000

9

*17 U.S.C. /506(e): Any person who knowingly makes a false representation of a material fact in the application for copyright registration provided for by section 409, or in any written statement filed in connection
with the application, shall be fined not more than $2,500.
July 1998   ⟳ PRINTED ON RECYCLED PAPER   ☆U.S. GOVERNMENT PRINTING OFFICE: 1998-

✍ Application Form PA ✍

Detach and read these instructions before completing this form.
Make sure all applicable spaces have been filled in before you return this form.

BASIC INFORMATION

When to Use This Form: Use Form PA for registration of published or unpublished works of the performing arts. This class includes works prepared for the purpose of being "performed" directly before an audience or indirectly "by means of any device or process." Works of the performing arts include: (1) musical works, including any accompanying words; (2) dramatic works, including any accompanying music; (3) pantomimes and choreographic works; and (4) motion pictures and other audiovisual works.

Deposit to Accompany Application: An application for copyright registration must be accompanied by a deposit consisting of copies or phonorecords representing the entire work for which registration is made. The following are the general deposit requirements as set forth in the statute:
Unpublished Work: Deposit one complete copy (or phonorecord).
Published Work: Deposit two complete copies (or phonorecords) of the best edition.
Work First Published Outside the United States: Deposit one complete copy (or phonorecord) of the first foreign edition.
Contribution to a Collective Work: Deposit one complete copy (or phonorecord) of the best edition of the collective work.
Motion Pictures: Deposit *both* of the following: (1) a separate written description of the contents of the motion picture; and (2) for a published work, one complete copy of the best edition of the motion picture; or, for an unpublished work, one complete copy of the motion picture or identifying material. Identifying material may be either an audiorecording of the entire soundtrack or one frame enlargement or similar visual print from each 10-minute segment.

The Copyright Notice: Before March 1, 1989, the use of copyright notice was mandatory on all published works, and any work first published before that date should have carried a notice. For works first published on and after March 1, 1989, use of the copyright notice is optional. For more information about copyright notice, see Circular 3, "Copyright Notice."

For Further Information: To speak to an information specialist, call (202) 707-3000 (TTY: (202) 707-6737). Recorded information is available 24 hours a day. Order forms and other publications from the address in space 9 or call the Forms and Publications Hotline at (202) 707-9100. Most circulars (but not forms) are available via fax. Call (202) 707-2600 from a touchtone phone. Access and download circulars, forms, and other information from the Copyright Office Website at http://www.loc.gov/copyright.

PRIVACY ACT ADVISORY STATEMENT Required by the Privacy Act of 1974 (P.L. 93-579)
    The authority for requesting this information is title 17, U.S.C., secs. 409 and 410. Furnishing the requested information is voluntary. But if the information is not furnished, it may be necessary to delay or refuse registration and you may not be entitled to certain relief, remedies, and benefits provided in chapters 4 and 5 of title 17, U.S.C.
    The principal uses of the requested information are the establishment and maintenance of a public record and the examination of the application for compliance with the registration requirements of the copyright code.
    Other routine uses include public inspection and copying, preparation of public indexes, preparation of public catalogs of copyright registrations, and preparation of search reports upon request.
    NOTE: No other advisory statement will be given in connection with this application. Please keep this statement and refer to it if we communicate with you regarding this application.

LINE-BY-LINE INSTRUCTIONS

Please type or print using black ink. The form is used to produce the certificate.

1 SPACE 1: Title

Title of This Work: Every work submitted for copyright registration must be given a title to identify that particular work. If the copies or phonorecords of the work bear a title (or an identifying phrase that could serve as a title), transcribe that wording *completely* and *exactly* on the application. Indexing of the registration and future identification of the work will depend on the information you give here. If the work you are registering is an entire "collective work" (such as a collection of plays or songs), give the overall title of the collection. If you are registering one or more individual contributions to a collective work, give the title of each contribution, followed by the title of the collection. For an unpublished collection, you may give the titles of the individual works after the collection title.

Previous or Alternative Titles: Complete this space if there are any additional titles for the work under which someone searching for the registration might be likely to look, or under which a document pertaining to the work might be recorded.

Nature of This Work: Briefly describe the general nature or character of the work being registered for copyright. Examples: "Music"; "Song Lyrics"; "Words and Music"; "Drama"; "Musical Play"; "Choreography"; "Pantomime"; "Motion Picture"; "Audiovisual Work."

2 SPACE 2: Author(s)

General Instructions: After reading these instructions, decide who are the "authors" of this work for copyright purposes. Then, unless the work is a "collective work," give the requested information about every "author" who contributed any appreciable amount of copyrightable matter to this version of the work. If you need further space, request additional Continuation Sheets. In the case of a collective work, such as a songbook or a collection of plays, give the information about the author of the collective work as a whole.

Name of Author: The fullest form of the author's name should be given. Unless the work was made "for hire," the individual who actually created the work is its "author." In the case of a work made for hire, the statute provides that "the employer or other person for whom the work was prepared is considered the author."

What is a Work Made for Hire? A "work made for hire" is defined as: (1) "a work prepared by an employee within the scope of his or her employment"; or (2) "a

work specially ordered or commissioned for use as a contribution to a collective work, as a part of a motion picture or other audiovisual work, as a translation, as a supplementary work, as a compilation, as an instructional text, as a test, as answer material for a test, or as an atlas, if the parties expressly agree in a written instrument signed by them that the work shall be considered a work made for hire." If you have checked "Yes" to indicate that the work was "made for hire," you must give the full legal name of the employer (or other person for whom the work was prepared). You may also include the name of the employee along with the name of the employer (for example: "Elster Music Co., employer for hire of John Ferguson").

Anonymous or Pseudonymous Work: An author's contribution to a work is "anonymous" if that author is not identified on the copies or phonorecords of the work. An author's contribution to a work is "pseudonymous" if that author is identified on the copies or phonorecords under a fictitious name. If the work is "anonymous" you may: (1) leave the line blank; or (2) state "anonymous" on the line; or (3) reveal the author's identity. If the work is "pseudonymous" you may: (1) leave the line blank; or (2) give the pseudonym and identify it as such (example: "Huntley Haverstock, pseudonym"); or (3) reveal the author's name, making clear which is the real name and which is the pseudonym (for example: "Judith Barton, whose pseudonym is Madeline Elster"). However, the citizenship or domicile of the author **must** be given in all cases.

Dates of Birth and Death: If the author is dead, the statute requires that the year of death be included in the application unless the work is anonymous or pseudonymous. The author's birth date is optional, but is useful as a form of identification. Leave this space blank if the author's contribution was a "work made for hire."

Author s Nationality or Domicile: Give the country of which the author is a citizen, or the country in which the author is domiciled. Nationality or domicile **must** be given in all cases.

Nature of Authorship: Give a brief general statement of the nature of the particular author's contribution to the work. Examples: "Words"; "Coauthor of Music"; "Words and Music"; "Arrangement"; "Coauthor of Book and Lyrics"; "Dramatization"; "Screen Play"; "Compilation and English Translation"; "Editorial Revisions."

SPACE 3: Creation and Publication

General Instructions: Do not confuse "creation" with "publication." Every application for copyright registration must state "the year in which creation of the work was completed." Give the date and nation of first publication only if the work has been published.

Creation: Under the statute, a work is "created" when it is fixed in a copy or phonorecord for the first time. Where a work has been prepared over a period of time, the part of the work existing in fixed form on a particular date constitutes the created work on that date. The date you give here should be the year in which the author completed the particular version for which registration is now being sought, even if other versions exist or if further changes or additions are planned.

Publication: The statute defines "publication" as "the distribution of copies or phonorecords of a work to the public by sale or other transfer of ownership, or by rental, lease, or lending"; a work is also "published" if there has been an "offering to distribute copies or phonorecords to a group of persons for purposes of further distribution, public performance, or public display." Give the full date (month, day, year) when, and the country where, publication first occurred. If first publication took place simultaneously in the United States and other countries, it is sufficient to state "U.S.A."

SPACE 4: Claimant(s)

Name(s) and Address(es) of Copyright Claimant(s): Give the name(s) and address(es) of the copyright claimant(s) in this work even if the claimant is the same as the author. Copyright in a work belongs initially to the author of the work (including, in the case of a work made for hire, the employer or other person for whom the work was prepared). The copyright claimant is either the author of the work or a person or organization to whom the copyright initially belonging to the author has been transferred.

Transfer: The statute provides that, if the copyright claimant is not the author, the application for registration must contain "a brief statement of how the claimant obtained ownership of the copyright." If any copyright claimant named in space 4 is not an author named in space 2, give a brief statement explaining how the claimant(s) obtained ownership of the copyright. Examples: "By written contract"; "Transfer of all rights by author"; "Assignment"; "By will." Do not attach transfer documents or other attachments or riders.

SPACE 5: Previous Registration

General Instructions: The questions in space 5 are intended to show whether an earlier registration has been made for this work and, if so, whether there is any basis for a new registration. As a general rule, only one basic copyright registration can be made for the same version of a particular work.

Same Version: If this version is substantially the same as the work covered by a previous registration, a second registration is not generally possible unless: (1) the work has been registered in unpublished form and a second registration is now being sought to cover this first published edition; or (2) someone other than the author is identified as copyright claimant in the earlier registration, and the author is now seeking registration in his or her own name. If either of these two exceptions apply, check the appropriate box and give the earlier registration number and date. Otherwise, do not submit Form PA; instead, write the Copyright Office for information about supplementary registration or recordation of transfers of copyright ownership.

Changed Version: If the work has been changed and you are now seeking registration to cover the additions or revisions, check the last box in space 5, give the earlier registration number and date, and complete both parts of space 6 in accordance with the instructions below.

Previous Registration Number and Date: If more than one previous registration has been made for the work, give the number and date of the latest registration.

SPACE 6: Derivative Work or Compilation

General Instructions: Complete space 6 if this work is a "changed version," "compilation," or "derivative work," and if it incorporates one or more earlier works that have already been published or registered for copyright or that have fallen into the public domain. A "compilation" is defined as "a work formed by the collection and assembling of preexisting materials or of data that are selected, coordinated, or arranged in such a way that the resulting work as a whole constitutes an original work of authorship." A "derivative work" is "a work based on one or more preexisting works." Examples of derivative works include musical arrangements, dramatizations, translations, abridgments, condensations, motion picture versions, or "any other form in which a work may be recast, transformed, or adapted." Derivative works also include works "consisting of editorial revisions, annotations, or other modifications" if these changes, as a whole, represent an original work of authorship.

Preexisting Material (space 6a): Complete this space and space 6b for derivative works. In this space identify the preexisting work that has been recast, transformed, or adapted. For example, the preexisting material might be: "French version of Hugo's 'Le Roi s'amuse'." Do not complete this space for compilations.

Material Added to This Work (space 6b): Give a brief, general statement of the additional new material covered by the copyright claim for which registration is sought. In the case of a derivative work, identify this new material. Examples: "Arrangement for piano and orchestra"; "Dramatization for television"; "New film version"; "Revisions throughout; Act III completely new." If the work is a compilation, give a brief, general statement describing both the material that has been compiled and the compilation itself. Example: "Compilation of 19th Century Military Songs."

SPACE 7, 8, 9: Fee, Correspondence, Certification, Return Address

Deposit Account: If you maintain a Deposit Account in the Copyright Office, identify it in space 7a. Otherwise, leave the space blank and send the fee of $20* (see box page 1) with your application and deposit.

Correspondence (space 7b): This space should contain the name, address, area code, telephone number, fax number, and email address (if available) of the person to be consulted if correspondence about this application becomes necessary.

Certification (space 8): The application cannot be accepted unless it bears the date and the **handwritten signature** of the author or other copyright claimant, or of the owner of exclusive right(s), or of the duly authorized agent of the author, claimant, or owner of exclusive right(s).

Address for Return of Certificate (space 9): The address box must be completed legibly since the certificate will be returned in a window envelope.

MORE INFORMATION

How to Register a Recorded Work: If the musical or dramatic work that you are registering has been recorded (as a tape, disk, or cassette), you may choose either copyright application Form PA (Performing Arts) or Form SR (Sound Recordings), depending on the purpose of the registration.

Form PA should be used to register the underlying musical composition or dramatic work. Form SR has been developed specifically to register a "sound recording" as defined by the Copyright Act—a work resulting from the "fixation of a series of sounds," separate and distinct from the underlying musical or dramatic work. Form SR should be used when the copyright claim is limited to the sound recording itself. (In one instance, Form SR may also be used to file for a copyright registration for both kinds of works—see (4) below.) Therefore:

(1) File Form PA if you are seeking to register the musical or dramatic work, not the "sound recording," even though what you deposit for copyright purposes may be in the form of a phonorecord.

(2) File Form PA if you are seeking to register the audio portion of an audiovisual work, such as a motion picture soundtrack; these are considered integral parts of the audiovisual work.

(3) File Form SR if you are seeking to register the "sound recording" itself, that is, the work that results from the fixation of a series of musical, spoken, or other sounds, but not the underlying musical or dramatic work.

(4) File Form SR if you are the copyright claimant for both the underlying musical or dramatic work and the sound recording, *and* you prefer to register both on the same form.

(5) File both forms PA and SR if the copyright claimant for the underlying work and sound recording differ, or you prefer to have separate registration for them.

Copies and Phonorecords : To register for copyright, you are required to deposit "copies" or "phonorecords." These are defined as follows:

Musical compositions may be embodied (fixed) in "copies," objects from which a work can be read or visually perceived, directly or with the aid of a machine or device, such as manuscripts, books, sheet music, film, and videotape. They may also be fixed in "phonorecords," objects embodying fixations of sounds, such as tapes and phonograph disks, commonly known as phonograph records. For example, a song (the work to be registered) can be reproduced in sheet music ("copies") or phonograph records ("phonorecords"), or both.

FORM PA
For a Work of the Performing Arts
UNITED STATES COPYRIGHT OFFICE

REGISTRATION NUMBER

PA   PAU

EFFECTIVE DATE OF REGISTRATION

Month   Day   Year

DO NOT WRITE ABOVE THIS LINE. IF YOU NEED MORE SPACE, USE A SEPARATE CONTINUATION SHEET.

1
TITLE OF THIS WORK ▼

PREVIOUS OR ALTERNATIVE TITLES ▼

NATURE OF THIS WORK ▼See Instructions

2
a NAME OF AUTHOR ▼

DATES OF BIRTH AND DEATH
Year Born ▼   Year Died ▼

Was this contribution to the work a "work made for hire"?
☐ Yes
☐ No

AUTHOR'S NATIONALITY OR DOMICILE
Name of Country
OR { Citizen of ▶
Domiciled in▶

WAS THIS AUTHOR'S CONTRIBUTION TO THE WORK
Anonymous? ☐ Yes ☐ No
Pseudonymous? ☐ Yes ☐ No
If the answer to either of these questions is Yes, see detailed instructions.

NATURE OF AUTHORSHIP Briefly describe nature of material created by this author in which copyright is claimed. ▼

NOTE
Under the law, the author of a work made for hire is generally the employer, not the employee (see instructions). For any part of this work that was made for hire check Yes in the space provided, give the employer (or other person for whom the work was prepared) as Author of that part, and leave the space for dates of birth and death blank.

b NAME OF AUTHOR ▼

DATES OF BIRTH AND DEATH
Year Born ▼   Year Died ▼

Was this contribution to the work a "work made for hire"?
☐ Yes
☐ No

AUTHOR'S NATIONALITY OR DOMICILE
Name of Country
OR { Citizen of ▶
Domiciled in▶

WAS THIS AUTHOR'S CONTRIBUTION TO THE WORK
Anonymous? ☐ Yes ☐ No
Pseudonymous? ☐ Yes ☐ No
If the answer to either of these questions is Yes, see detailed instructions.

NATURE OF AUTHORSHIP Briefly describe nature of material created by this author in which copyright is claimed. ▼

c NAME OF AUTHOR ▼

DATES OF BIRTH AND DEATH
Year Born ▼   Year Died ▼

Was this contribution to the work a "work made for hire"?
☐ Yes
☐ No

AUTHOR'S NATIONALITY OR DOMICILE
Name of Country
OR { Citizen of ▶
Domiciled in▶

WAS THIS AUTHOR'S CONTRIBUTION TO THE WORK
Anonymous? ☐ Yes ☐ No
Pseudonymous? ☐ Yes ☐ No
If the answer to either of these questions is Yes, see detailed instructions.

NATURE OF AUTHORSHIP Briefly describe nature of material created by this author in which copyright is claimed. ▼

3
a YEAR IN WHICH CREATION OF THIS WORK WAS COMPLETED This information must be given ◀Year in all cases.
b DATE AND NATION OF FIRST PUBLICATION OF THIS PARTICULAR WORK
Complete this information ONLY if this work has been published.
Month ▶   Day ▶   Year ▶
◀ Nation

4
COPYRIGHT CLAIMANT(S) Name and address must be given even if the claimant is the same as the author given in space 2. ▼

See instructions before completing this space.

TRANSFER If the claimant(s) named here in space 4 is (are) different from the author(s) named in space 2, give a brief statement of how the claimant(s) obtained ownership of the copyright. ▼

APPLICATION RECEIVED
ONE DEPOSIT RECEIVED
TWO DEPOSITS RECEIVED
FUNDS RECEIVED

DO NOT WRITE HERE OFFICE USE ONLY

MORE ON BACK ▶ ¥ Complete all applicable spaces (numbers 5-9) on the reverse side of this page.
¥ See detailed instructions.   ¥ Sign the form at line 8.

DO NOT WRITE HERE
Page 1 of _____ pages

EXAMINED BY	FORM PA
CHECKED BY	
☐ CORRESPONDENCE Yes	FOR COPYRIGHT OFFICE USE ONLY

DO NOT WRITE ABOVE THIS LINE. IF YOU NEED MORE SPACE, USE A SEPARATE CONTINUATION SHEET.

PREVIOUS REGISTRATION Has registration for this work, or for an earlier version of this work, already been made in the Copyright Office?

☐ Yes ☐ No If your answer is "Yes," why is another registration being sought? (Check appropriate box.) ▼

a. ☐ This is the first published edition of a work previously registered in unpublished form.

b. ☐ This is the first application submitted by this author as copyright claimant.

c. ☐ This is a changed version of the work, as shown by space 6 on this application.

If your answer is "Yes," give: **Previous Registration Number** ▼   **Year of Registration** ▼

5

DERIVATIVE WORK OR COMPILATION Complete both space 6a and 6b for a derivative work; complete only 6b for a compilation.

Preexisting Material Identify any preexisting work or works that this work is based on or incorporates.▼

Material Added to This Work Give a brief, general statement of the material that has been added to this work and in which copyright is claimed.▼

a 6 b

See instructions before completing this space.

DEPOSIT ACCOUNT If the registration fee is to be charged to a Deposit Account established in the Copyright Office, give name and number of Account.

Name ▼   **Account Number** ▼

a 7 b

CORRESPONDENCE Give name and address to which correspondence about this application should be sent. Name/Address/Apt/City/State/ZIP ▼

Area code and daytime telephone number ▶ (   )   Fax number ▶ (   )

Email ▶

CERTIFICATION* I, the undersigned, hereby certify that I am the

Check only one ▶
☐ author
☐ other copyright claimant
☐ owner of exclusive right(s)
☐ authorized agent of

Name of author or other copyright claimant, or owner of exclusive right(s) ▲

of the work identified in this application and that the statements made by me in this application are correct to the best of my knowledge.

8

Typed or printed name and date ▼ If this application gives a date of publication in space 3, do not sign and submit it before that date.

Date ▶

Handwritten signature (X) ▼

x _____

Mail certificate to:	Name ▼	**YOU MUST:** ✔ Complete all necessary spaces ✔ Sign your application in space 8
Certificate will be mailed in window envelope	Number/Street/Apt ▼	**SEND ALL 3 ELEMENTS IN THE SAME PACKAGE:** 1. Application form 2. Nonrefundable filing fee in check or money order payable to *Register of Copyrights* 3. Deposit material
	City/State/ZIP ▼	**MAIL TO:** Library of Congress Copyright Office 101 Independence Avenue, S.E. Washington, D.C. 20559-6000

9

⌾ Application Form SR ⌾

Detach and read these instructions before completing this form.
Make sure all applicable spaces have been filled in before you return this form.

BASIC INFORMATION

When to Use This Form: Use Form SR for copyright registration of published or unpublished sound recordings. It should be used when the copyright claim is limited to the sound recording itself, and it may also be used where the same copyright claimant is seeking simultaneous registration of the underlying musical, dramatic, or literary work embodied in the phonorecord.

With one exception, "sound recordings" are works that result from the fixation of a series of musical, spoken, or other sounds. The exception is for the audio portions of audiovisual works, such as a motion picture soundtrack or an audio cassette accompanying a filmstrip. These are considered a part of the audiovisual work as a whole.

Deposit to Accompany Application: An application for copyright registration of a sound recording must be accompanied by a deposit consisting of phonorecords representing the entire work for which registration is to be made.

Unpublished Work: Deposit one complete phonorecord.

Published Work: Deposit two complete phonorecords of the best edition, together with "any printed or other visually perceptible material" published with the phonorecords.

Work First Published Outside the United States: Deposit one complete phonorecord of the first foreign edition.

Contribution to a Collective Work: Deposit one complete phonorecord of the best edition of the collective work.

The Copyright Notice: For sound recordings first published on or after March 1, 1989, the law provides that a copyright notice in a specified form "may be placed on all publicly distributed phonorecords of the sound recording." Use of the copyright notice is the responsibility of the copyright owner and does not require advance permission from the Copyright Office. The required form of the notice for phonorecords of sound recordings consists of three elements: (1) the symbol "℗" (the letter "P" in a circle); (2) the year of first publication of the sound recording; and (3) the name of the owner of copyright. For example "℗ 1997 XYZ Record Co." The notice is to be "placed on the surface of the phonorecord, or on the label or container, in such manner and location as to give reasonable notice of the claim of copyright." Notice was required under the 1976 Copyright Act. This requirement was eliminated when the United States adhered to the Berne Convention, effective March 1, 1989. Although works published without notice before that date could have entered the public domain in the United States, the Uruguay Round Agreements Act restores copyright in certain foreign works originally published without notice.

For information about notice requirements for works published before March 1, 1989, or other copyright information, write: Library of Congress, Copyright Office, Publications Section, LM-455, 101 Independence Avenue, S.E., Washington, D.C. 20559-6000.

LINE-BY-LINE INSTRUCTIONS

Please type or print neatly using black ink. The form is used to produce the certificate.

1 SPACE 1: Title

Title of This Work: Every work submitted for copyright registration must be given a title that particular work. If the phonorecords or any accompanying printed material bear a title (or an identifying phrase that could serve as a title), transcribe that wording completely and exactly on the application. Indexing of the registration and future identification of the work may depend on the information you give here.

Previous, Alternative, or Contents Titles: Complete this space if there are any previous or alternative titles for the work under which someone searching for the registration might be likely to look, or under which a document pertaining to the work might be recorded. You may also give the individual contents titles, if any, in this space or you may use a Continuation Sheet. Circle the term that describes the titles given.

2 SPACE 2: Author(s)

General Instructions: After reading these instructions, decide who are the "authors" of this work for copyright purposes. Then, unless the work is a "collective work," give the requested information about every "author" who contributed any appreciable amount of copyrightable matter to this version of the work. If you need further space, request additional Continuation Sheets. In the case of a collective work such as a collection of previously published or registered sound recordings, give information about the author of the collective work as a whole. If you are submitting this Form SR to cover the recorded musical, dramatic, or literary work as well as the sound recording itself, it is important for space 2 to include full information about the various authors of all of the material covered by the copyright claim, making clear the nature of each author's contribution.

Name of Author: The fullest form of the author's name should be given. Unless the work was "made for hire," the individual who actually created the work is its "author." In the case of a work made for hire, the statute provides that "the employer or other person for whom the work was prepared is considered the author."

What is a Work Made for Hire ? A "work made for hire" is defined as: (1) "a work prepared by an employee within the scope of his or her employment"; or (2) "a work specially ordered or commissioned for use as a contribution to a collective work, as a part of a motion picture or other audiovisual work, as a translation, as a supplementary work, as a compilation, as an instructional text, as a test, as answer material for a test, or as an atlas, if the parties expressly agree in a written instrument signed by them that the work shall be considered a work made for hire." If you have checked "Yes" to indicate that the work was "made for hire," you must give the full legal name of the employer (or other person for whom the work was prepared). You may also include the name of the employee along with the name of the employer (for example: "Elster Record Co., employer for hire of John Ferguson").

Anonymous or Pseudonymous Work: An author's contribution to a work is "anonymous" if that author is not identified on the copies or phonorecords of the work. An author's contribution to a work is "pseudonymous" if that author is identified on the copies or phonorecords under a fictitious name. If the work is "anonymous" you may: (1) leave the line blank; or (2) state "anonymous" on the line; or (3) reveal the author's identity. If the work is "pseudonymous" you may: (1) leave the line blank; or (2) give the pseudonym and identify it as such (for example: "Huntley Haverstock, pseudonym"); or (3) reveal the author's name, making clear which is the real name and which is the pseudonym (for example: "Judith Barton, whose pseudonym is Madeline Elster"). However, the citizenship or domicile of the author **must** be given in all cases.

Dates of Birth and Death: If the author is dead, the statute requires that the year of death be included in the application unless the work is anonymous or pseudonymous. The author's birth date is optional, but is useful as a form of identification. Leave this space blank if the author's contribution was a "work made for hire."

Author s Nationality or Domicile: Give the country in which the author is a citizen, or the country in which the author is domiciled. Nationality or domicile **must** be given in all cases.

Nature of Authorship: Sound recording authorship is the performance, sound production, or both, that is fixed in the recording deposited for registration. Describe this authorship in space 2 as "sound recording." If the claim also covers the underlying work(s), include the appropriate authorship terms for each author, for example, "words," "music," "arrangement of music," or "text."

Generally, for the claim to cover both the sound recording and the underlying work(s), every author should have contributed to both the sound recording and the underlying work(s). If the claim includes artwork or photographs, include the appropriate term in the statement of authorship.

3 SPACE 3: Creation and Publication

General Instructions: Do not confuse "creation" with "publication." Every application for copyright registration must state "the year in which creation of the work was completed." Give the date and nation of first publication only if the work has been published.

Creation: Under the statute, a work is "created" when it is fixed in a copy or phonorecord for the first time. Where a work has been prepared over a period of time, the part of the work existing in fixed form on a particular date constitutes the created work on that date. The date you give here should be the year in which the author completed the particular version for which registration is now being sought, even if other versions exist or if further changes or additions are planned.

Publication: The statute defines "publication" as "the distribution of copies or phonorecords of a work to the public by sale or other transfer of ownership, or by rental, lease, or lending"; a work is also "published" if there has been an "offering to distribute copies or phonorecords to a group of persons for purposes of further distribution, public performance, or public display." Give the full date (month, date, year) when, and the country where, publication first occurred. If first publication took place simultaneously in the United States and other countries, it is sufficient to state "U.S.A."

4 SPACE 4: Claimant(s)

Name(s) and Address(es) of Copyright Claimant(s): Give the name(s) and address(es) of the copyright claimant(s) in the work even if the claimant is the same as the author. Copyright in a work belongs initially to the author of the work (including, in the case of a work made for hire, the employer or other person for whom the work was prepared). The copyright claimant is either the author of the work or a person or organization to whom the copyright initially belonging to the author has been transferred.

Transfer: The statute provides that, if the copyright claimant is not the author, the application for registration must contain "a brief statement of how the claimant obtained ownership of the copyright." If any copyright claimant named in space 4a is not an author named in space 2, give a brief statement explaining how the claimant(s) obtained ownership of the copyright. Examples: "By written contract"; "Transfer of all rights by author"; "Assignment"; "By will." Do not attach transfer documents or other attachments or riders.

5 SPACE 5: Previous Registration

General Instructions: The questions in space 5 are intended to show whether an earlier registration has been made for this work and, if so, whether there is any basis for a new registration. As a rule, only one basic copyright registration can be made for the same version of a particular work.

Same Version: If this version is substantially the same as the work covered by a previous registration, a second registration is not generally possible when: (1) the work has been registered in unpublished form and a second registration is now being sought to cover this first published edition; or (2) someone other than the author is identified as copyright claimant in the earlier registration and the author is now seeking registration in his or her own name. If either of these two exceptions apply, check the appropriate box and give the earlier registration number and date. Otherwise, do not submit Form SR. Instead, write the Copyright Office for information about supplementary registration or recordation of transfers of copyright ownership.

Changed Version: If the work has been changed, and you are now seeking registration to cover the additions or revisions, check the last box in space 5, give the earlier registration number and date, and complete both parts of space 6 in accordance with the instructions below.

Previous Registration Number and Date: If more than one previous registration has been made for the work, give the number and date of the latest registration.

6 SPACE 6: Derivative Work or Compilation

General Instructions: Complete space 6 if this work is a "changed version," "compilation," or "derivative work," and if it incorporates one or more earlier works that have already been published or registered for copyright, or that have fallen into the public domain, or sound recordings that were fixed before February 15, 1972. A "compilation" is defined as "a work formed by the collection and assembling of preexisting materials or of data that are selected, coordinated, or arranged in such a way that the resulting work as a whole constitutes an original work of authorship." A "derivative work" is "a work based on one or more preexisting works." Examples of derivative works include recordings reissued with substantial editorial revisions or abridgments of the recorded sounds, and recordings republished with new recorded material, or "any other form in which a work may be recast, transformed, or adapted." Derivative works also include works "consisting of editorial revisions, annotations, or other modifications" if these changes, as a whole, represent an original work of authorship.

Preexisting Material (space 6a): Complete this space **and** space 6b for derivative works. In this space identify the preexisting work that has been recast, transformed, or adapted. The preexisting work may be material that has been previously published, previously registered, or that is in the public domain. For example, the preexisting material might be: "1970 recording by Sperryville Symphony of Bach Double Concerto."

Material Added to This Work (space 6b): Give a brief, general statement of the **additional** new material covered by the copyright claim for which registration is sought. In the case of a derivative work, identify this new material. Examples: "Recorded performances on bands 1 and 3"; "Remixed sounds from original multitrack sound sources"; "New words, arrangement, and additional sounds." If the work is a compilation, give a brief, general statement describing both the material that has been compiled **and** the compilation itself. Example: "Compilation of 1938 Recordings by various swing bands."

7,8,9 SPACE 7,8,9: Fee, Correspondence, Certification, Return Address

Deposit Account: If you maintain a Deposit Account in the Copyright Office, identify it in space 7a. Otherwise, leave the space blank and send the filing fee with your application and deposit. (See space 8 on form.)

Correspondence (space 7b): This space should contain the name, address, area code, telephone number, fax number, and email address (if available) of the person to be consulted if correspondence about this application becomes necessary.

Certification (space 8): This application cannot be accepted unless it bears the date and the **handwritten signature** of the author or other copyright claimant, or of the owner of exclusive right(s), or of the duly authorized agent of the author, claimant, or owner of exclusive right(s).

Address for Return of Certificate (space 9): The address box must be completed legibly since the certificate will be returned in a window envelope.

MORE INFORMATION

Works : "Works" are the basic subject matter of copyright; they are what authors create and copyright protects. The statute draws a sharp distinction between the "work" and "any material object in which the work is embodied."

Copies and Phonorecords : These are the two types of material objects in which "works" are embodied. In general, **copies** are objects from which a work can be read or visually perceived, directly or with the aid of a machine or device, such as manuscripts, books, sheet music, film, and videotape. **Phonorecords** are objects embodying fixations of sounds, such as audio tapes and phonograph disks. For example, a song (the "work") can be reproduced in sheet music ("copies") or phonograph disks ("phonorecords"), or both.

Sound Recordings : These are "works," not "copies" or "phonorecords." "Sound recordings" are "works" that result from the fixation of a series of musical, spoken, or other sounds, but not including the sounds accompanying a motion picture or other audiovisual work." Example: When a record company issues a new release, the release will typically involve two distinct "works": the "musical work" that has been recorded, and the "sound recording" as a separate work in itself. The material objects that the record company sends out are "phonorecords": physical reproductions of both the "musical work" and the "sound recording."

Should You File More Than One Application? If your work consists of a recorded musical, dramatic, or literary work and if both that "work" and the sound recording as a separate "work" are eligible for registration, the application form you should file depends on the following:

File Only Form SR if: The copyright claimant is the same for both the musical, dramatic, or literary work and for the sound recording, and you are seeking a single registration to cover both of these "works."

File Only Form PA (or Form TX) if: You are seeking to register only the musical, dramatic, or literary work, not the sound recording. Form PA is appropriate for works of the performing arts; Form TX is for nondramatic literary works.

Separate Applications Should Be Filed on Form PA (or Form TX) and on Form SR if: (1) The copyright claimant for the musical, dramatic, or literary work is different from the copyright claimant for the sound recording; or (2) You prefer to have separate registrations for the musical, dramatic, or literary work and for the sound recording.

FORM SR
For a Sound Recording
UNITED STATES COPYRIGHT OFFICE

REGISTRATION NUMBER

_____

SR _____ SRU _____
EFFECTIVE DATE OF REGISTRATION

_____
Month   Day   Year

DO NOT WRITE ABOVE THIS LINE. IF YOU NEED MORE SPACE, USE A SEPARATE CONTINUATION SHEET.

1 TITLE OF THIS WORK ▼

_____

PREVIOUS, ALTERNATIVE, OR CONTENTS TITLES (CIRCLE ONE) ▼

2 **a** NAME OF AUTHOR ▼

DATES OF BI RTH AND DEATH
Year Born ▼   Year Died ▼

Was this contribution to the work a "work made for hire"?
☐ Yes
☐ No

AUTHOR S NATIONALITY OR DOMICILE
Name of Country
OR { Citizen of ▶_____
Domiciled in ▶_____

WAS THIS AUTHOR S CONTRIBUTION TO THE WORK
Anonymous? ☐ Yes ☐ No
Pseudonymous? ☐ Yes ☐ No

If the answer to either of these questions is Yes, see detailed instructions.

NATURE OF AUTHORSHIP Briefly describe nature of material created by this author in which copyright is claimed. ▼

NOTE

Under the law. the author of a work made for hire is generally the employer, not the employee (see instructions). For any part of this work that was made for hire, check Yes in the space provided, give the employer (or other person for whom the work was prepared) as Author of that part, and leave the space for dates of birth and death blank.

b NAME OF AUTHOR ▼

DATES OF BI RTH AND DEATH
Year Born ▼   Year Died ▼

Was this contribution to the work a "work made for hire"?
☐ Yes
☐ No

AUTHOR S NATIONALITY OR DOMICILE
Name of Country
OR { Citizen of ▶_____
Domiciled in ▶_____

WAS THIS AUTHOR S CONTRIBUTION TO THE WORK
Anonymous? ☐ Yes ☐ No
Pseudonymous? ☐ Yes ☐ No

If the answer to either of these questions is Yes, see detailed instructions.

NATURE OF AUTHORSHIP Briefly describe nature of material created by this author in which copyright is claimed. ▼

c NAME OF AUTHOR ▼

DATES OF BI RTH AND DEATH
Year Born ▼   Year Died ▼

Was this contribution to the work a "work made for hire"?
☐ Yes
☐ No

AUTHOR S NATIONALITY OR DOMICILE
Name of Country
OR { Citizen of ▶_____
Domiciled in ▶_____

WAS THIS AUTHOR S CONTRIBUTION TO THE WORK
Anonymous? ☐ Yes ☐ No
Pseudonymous? ☐ Yes ☐ No

If the answer to either of these questions is Yes, see detailed instructions.

NATURE OF AUTHORSHIP Briefly describe nature of material created by this author in which copyright is claimed. ▼

3 **a** YEAR IN WHICH CREATION OF THIS WORK WAS COMPLETED
_____ ◀ Year This information must be given in all cases.

b DATE AND NATION OF FIRST PUBLICATION OF THIS PARTICULAR WORK
Complete this information ONLY if this work has been published.
Month ▶ _____ Day▶ _____ Year ▶ _____ ◀ Nation

4 **a** COPYRIGHT CLAIMANT(S) Name and address must be given even if the claimant is the same as the author given in space 2. ▼

See instructions before completing this space.

b TRANSFER If the claimant(s) named here in space 4 is (are) different from the author(s) named in space 2, give a brief statement of how the claimant(s) obtained ownership of the copyright. ▼

APPLICATION RECEIVED

ONE DEPOSIT RECEIVED

TWO DEPOSITS RECEIVED

FUNDS RECEIVED

DO NOT WRITE HERE
OFFICE USE ONLY

MORE ON BACK ▶ ¥ Complete all applicable spaces (numbers 5-9) on the reverse side of this page.
¥ See detailed instructions. ¥ Sign the form at line 8.

DO NOT WRITE HERE
Page 1 of _____ pages

EXAMINED BY	FORM SR
CHECKED BY	
CORRESPONDENCE ❑ Yes	FOR COPYRIGHT OFFICE USE ONLY

DO NOT WRITE ABOVE THIS LINE. IF YOU NEED MORE SPACE, USE A SEPARATE CONTINUATION SHEET.

PREVIOUS REGISTRATION Has registration for this work, or for an earlier version of this work, already been made in the Copyright Office?

❑ Yes ❑ No If your answer is "Yes," why is another registration being sought? (Check appropriate box) ▼

a. ❑ This work was previously registered in unpublished form and now has been published for the first time.

b. ❑ This is the first application submitted by this author as copyright claimant.

c. ❑ This is a changed version of the work, as shown by space 6 on this application.

If your answer is "Yes," give: **Previous Registration Number ▼**   **Year of Registration ▼**

5

DERIVATIVE WORK OR COMPILATION

Preexisting Material Identify any preexisting work or works that this work is based on or incorporates.▼

a _____

Material Added to This Work Give a brief, general statement of the material that has been added to this work and in which copyright is claimed.▼

b _____

6

See instructions before completing this space.

DEPOSIT ACCOUNT If the registration fee is to be charged to a Deposit Account established in the Copyright Office, give name and number of Account.

Name ▼   **Account Number ▼**

a _____

CORRESPONDENCE Give name and address to which correspondence about this application should be sent.   Name/Address/Apt/City/State/ZIP ▼

b _____

Area code and daytime telephone number ▶   Fax number ▶

Email ▶

7

CERTIFICATION* I, the undersigned, hereby certify that I am the

Check only one ▼

❑ author

❑ other copyright claimant

❑ owner of exclusive right(s)

❑ authorized agent of _____

Name of author or other copyright claimant, or owner of exclusive right(s) ▲

of the work identified in this application and that the statements made by me in this application are correct to the best of my knowledge.

Typed or printed name and date ▼ If this application gives a date of publication in space 3, do not sign and submit it before that date.

_____ **Date ▶** _____

Handwritten signature ▼

☞ X _

8

The fee is $20.00 effective through June 30, 1999. After that date, please write the Copyright Office, check the Copyright Office Website at http://www.loc.gov/copyright, or call (202) 707-3000 for the latest fee information.

Mail certificate to:

Certificate will be mailed in window envelope

Name ▼

Number/Street/Apt ▼

City/State/ZIP ▼

YOU MUST:
❈ Complete all necessary spaces
❈ Sign your application in space 8

SEND ALL 3 ELEMENTS IN THE SAME PACKAGE:
1. Application form
2. Nonrefundable filing fee in check or money order payable to *Register of Copyrights*
3. Deposit material

MAIL TO:
Library of Congress
Copyright Office
101 Independence Avenue, S.E.
Washington, D.C. 20559-6000

9

*17 U.S.C./506(e): Any person who knowingly makes a false representation of a material fact in the application for copyright registration provided for by section 409, or in any written statement filed in connection with the application, shall be fined not more than $2,500.

September 1997 60,000   ♻ PRINTED ON RECYCLED PAPER   ☆ U.S. GOVERNMENT PRINTING OFFICE: 1997—417-750/60,019

☑ Application Form VA ☑

Detach and read these instructions before completing this form.
Make sure all applicable spaces have been filled in before you return this form.

BASIC INFORMATION

When to Use This Form: Use Form VA for copyright registration of published or unpublished works of the visual arts. This category consists of "pictorial, graphic, or sculptural works," including two-dimensional and three-dimensional works of fine, graphic, and applied art, photographs, prints and art reproductions, maps, globes, charts, technical drawings, diagrams, and models.

What Does Copyright Protect? Copyright in a work of the visual arts protects those pictorial, graphic, or sculptural elements that, either alone or in combination, represent an "original work of authorship." The statute declares: "In no case does copyright protection for an original work of authorship extend to any idea, procedure, process, system, method of operation, concept, principle, or discovery, regardless of the form in which it is described, explained, illustrated, or embodied in such work."

Works of Artistic Craftsmanship and Designs: "Works of artistic craftsmanship" are registrable on Form VA, but the statute makes clear that protection extends to "their form" and not to "their mechanical or utilitarian aspects." The "design of a useful article" is considered copyrightable "only if, and only to the extent that, such design incorporates pictorial, graphic, or sculptural features that can be identified separately from, and are capable of existing independently of, the utilitarian aspects of the article."

Labels and Advertisements: Works prepared for use in connection with the sale or advertisement of goods and services are registrable if they contain "original work of authorship." Use Form VA if the copyrightable material in the work you are registering is mainly pictorial or graphic; use Form TX if it consists mainly of text. **NOTE**: Words and short phrases such as names, titles, and slogans cannot be protected by copyright, and the same is true of standard symbols, emblems, and other commonly used graphic designs that are in the public domain. When used commercially, material of that sort can sometimes be protected under state laws of unfair competition or under the federal trademark laws. For information about trademark registration, write to the Commissioner of Patents and Trademarks, Washington, D.C. 20231.

Architectural Works: Copyright protection extends to the design of buildings created for the use of human beings. Architectural works created on or after December 1, 1990, or that on December 1, 1990, were unconstructed and embodied only in unpublished plans or drawings are eligible. Request Circular 41 for more information. Architectural works and technical drawings cannot be registered on the same application.

Deposit to Accompany Application: An application for copyright registration must be accompanied by a deposit consisting of copies representing the entire work for which registration is to be made.

> **Unpublished Work:** Deposit one complete copy.
> **Published Work:** Deposit two complete copies of the best edition.
> **Work First Published Outside the United States:** Deposit one complete copy of the first foreign edition.
> **Contribution to a Collective Work:** Deposit one complete copy of the best edition of the collective work.

The Copyright Notice: Before March 1, 1989, the use of copyright notice was mandatory on all published works, and any work first published before that date should have carried a notice. For works first published on and after March 1, 1989, use of the copyright notice is optional. For more information about copyright notice, see Circular 3, "Copyright Notice."

For Further Information: To speak to an information specialist, call (202) 707-3000 (TTY: (202) 707-6737). Recorded information is available 24 hours a day. Order forms and other publications from the address in space 9 or call the Forms and Publications Hotline at (202) 707-9100. Most circulars (but not forms) are available via fax. Call (202) 707-2600 from a touchtone phone. Access and download circulars, forms, and other information from the Copyright Office Website at:

http://www.loc.gov/copyright

LINE-BY-LINE INSTRUCTIONS

Please type or print using black ink. The form is used to produce the certificate.

SPACE 1: Title

Title of This Work: Every work submitted for copyright registration must be given a title to identify that particular work. If the copies of the work bear a title (or an identifying phrase that could serve as a title), transcribe that wording *completely* and *exactly* on the application. Indexing of the registration and future identification of the work will depend on the information you give here. For an architectural work that has been constructed, add the date of construction after the title; if unconstructed at this time, add "not yet constructed."

Publication as a Contribution: If the work being registered is a contribution to a periodical, serial, or collection, give the title of the contribution in the "Title of This Work" space. Then, in the line headed "Publication as a Contribution," give information about the collective work in which the contribution appeared.

Nature of This Work: Briefly describe the general nature or character of the pictorial, graphic, or sculptural work being registered for copyright. Examples: "Oil Painting"; "Charcoal Drawing"; "Etching"; "Sculpture"; "Map"; "Photograph"; "Scale Model"; "Lithographic Print"; "Jewelry Design"; "Fabric Design."

Previous or Alternative Titles: Complete this space if there are any additional titles for the work under which someone searching for the registration might be likely to look, or under which a document pertaining to the work might be recorded.

SPACE 2: Author(s)

General Instruction: After reading these instructions, decide who are the "authors" of this work for copyright purposes. Then, unless the work is a "collective work," give the requested information about every "author" who contributed any appreciable amount of copyrightable matter to this version of the work. If you need further space, request Continuation Sheets. In the case of a collective work, such as a catalog of paintings or collection of cartoons by various authors, give information about the author of the collective work as a whole.

Name of Author: The fullest form of the author's name should be given. Unless the work was "made for hire," the individual who actually created the work is its "author." In the case of a work made for hire, the statute provides that "the employer or other person for whom the work was prepared is considered the author."

What is a "Work Made for Hire"? A "work made for hire" is defined as: (1) "a work prepared by an employee within the scope of his or her employment"; or (2) " a work specially ordered or commissioned for use as a contribution to a collective work, as a part of a motion picture or other audiovisual work, as a translation, as a supplementary work, as a compilation, as an instructional text, as a test, as answer material for a test, or as an atlas, if the parties expressly agree in a written instrument signed by them that the work shall be considered a work made for hire." If you have checked "Yes" to indicate that the work was "made for hire," you must give the full legal name of the employer (or other person for whom the work was prepared). You may also include the name of the employee along with the name of the employer (for example: "Elster Publishing Co., employer for hire of John Ferguson").

"Anonymous" or "Pseudonymous" Work: An author's contribution to a work is "anonymous" if that author is not identified on the copies or phonorecords of the work. An author's contribution to a work is "pseudonymous" if that author is identified on the copies or phonorecords under a fictitious name. If the work is "anonymous" you may: (1) leave the line blank; or (2) state "anonymous" on the line; or (3) reveal the author's identity. If the work is "pseudonymous" you may: (1) leave the line blank; or (2) give the pseudonym and identify it as such (for example: "Huntley Haverstock, pseudonym"); or (3) reveal the author's name, making clear which is the real name and which is the pseudonym (for example: "Henry Leek, whose pseudonym is Priam Farrel"). However, the citizenship or domicile of the author **must** be given in all cases.

Dates of Birth and Death: If the author is dead, the statute requires that the year of death be included in the application unless the work is anonymous or pseudonymous. The author's birth date is optional but is useful as a form of identification. Leave this space blank if the author's contribution was a "work made for hire."

Author's Nationality or Domicile: Give the country of which the author is a citizen or the country in which the author is domiciled. Nationality or domicile **must** be given in all cases.

Nature of Authorship: Categories of pictorial, graphic, and sculptural authorship are listed below. Check the box(es) that best describe(s) each author's contribution to the work.

3-Dimensional sculptures: fine art sculptures, toys, dolls, scale models, and sculptural designs applied to useful articles.

2-Dimensional artwork: watercolor and oil paintings; pen and ink drawings; logo illustrations; greeting cards; collages; stencils; patterns; computer graphics; graphics appearing in screen displays; artwork appearing on posters, calendars, games, commercial prints and labels, and packaging, as well as 2-dimensional artwork applied to useful articles, and designs reproduced on textiles, lace, and other fabrics; on wallpaper, carpeting, floor tile, wrapping paper, and clothing.

Reproductions of works of art: reproductions of preexisting artwork made by, for example, lithography, photoengraving, or etching.

Maps: cartographic representations of an area, such as state and county maps, atlases, marine charts, relief maps, and globes.

Photographs: pictorial photographic prints and slides and holograms.

Jewelry designs: 3-dimensional designs applied to rings, pendants, earrings, necklaces, and the like.

Designs on sheetlike materials: designs reproduced on textiles, lace, and other fabrics; wallpaper; carpeting; floor tile; wrapping paper; and clothing.

Technical drawings: diagrams illustrating scientific or technical information in linear form, such as architectural blueprints or mechanical drawings.

Text: textual material that accompanies pictorial, graphic, or sculptural works, such as comic strips, greeting cards, games rules, commercial prints or labels, and maps.

Architectural works: designs of buildings, including the overall form as well as the arrangement and composition of spaces and elements of the design.

NOTE: Any registration for the underlying architectural plans must be applied for on a separate Form VA, checking the box "Technical drawing."

SPACE 3: Creation and Publication

General Instructions: Do not confuse "creation" with "publication." Every application for copyright registration must state "the year in which creation of the work was completed." Give the date and nation of first publication only if the work has been published.

Creation: Under the statute, a work is "created" when it is fixed in a copy or phonorecord for the first time. Where a work has been prepared over a period of time, the part of the work existing in fixed form on a particular date constitutes the created work on that date. The year you give here should be the year in which the author completed the particular version for which registration is now being sought, even if other versions exist or if further changes or additions are planned.

Publication: The statute defines "publication" as "the distribution of copies or phonorecords of a work to the public by sale or other transfer of ownership, or by rental, lease, or lending"; a work is also "published" if there has been an "offering to distribute copies or phonorecords to a group of persons for purposes of further distribution, public performance, or public display." Give the full date (month, day, year) when, and the country where, publication first occurred. If first publication took place simultaneously in the United States and other countries, it is sufficient to state "U.S.A."

SPACE 4: Claimant(s)

Name(s) and Address(es) of Copyright Claimant(s): Give the name(s) and address(es) of the copyright claimant(s) in this work even if the claimant is the same as the author. Copyright in a work belongs initially to the author of the work (including, in the case of a work made for hire, the employer or other person for whom the work was prepared). The copyright claimant is either the author of the work or a person or organization to whom the copyright initially belonging to the author has been transferred.

Transfer: The statute provides that, if the copyright claimant is not the author, the application for registration must contain "a brief statement of how the claimant obtained ownership of the copyright." If any copyright claimant named in space 4 is not an author named in space 2, give a brief statement explaining how the claimant(s) obtained ownership of the copyright. Examples: "By written contract"; "Transfer of all rights by author"; "Assignment"; "By will." Do not attach transfer documents or other attachments or riders.

*Registration filing fees are effective thru June 30, 1999. For the latest fee information, write the Copyright Office, check the Website at http://loc.gov/copyright, or call (202) 707-3000.

SPACE 5: Previous Registration

General Instructions: The questions in space 5 are intended to find out whether an earlier registration has been made for this work and, if so, whether there is any basis for a new registration. As a rule, only one basic copyright registration can be made for the same version of a particular work.

Same Version: If this version is substantially the same as the work covered by a previous registration, a second registration is not generally possible unless: (1) the work has been registered in unpublished form and a second registration is now being sought to cover this first published edition; or (2) someone other than the author is identified as a copyright claimant in the earlier registration, and the author is now seeking registration in his or her own name. If either of these two exceptions apply, check the appropriate box and give the earlier registration number and date. Otherwise, do not submit Form VA; instead, write the Copyright Office for information about supplementary registration or recordation of transfers of copyright ownership.

Changed Version: If the work has been changed and you are now seeking registration to cover the additions or revisions, check the last box in space 5, give the earlier registration number and date, and complete both parts of space 6 in accordance with the instruction below.

Previous Registration Number and Date: If more than one previous registration has been made for the work, give the number and date of the latest registration.

SPACE 6: Derivative Work or Compilation

General Instructions: Complete space 6 if this work is a "changed version," "compilation," or "derivative work," and if it incorporates one or more earlier works that have already been published or registered for copyright, or that have fallen into the public domain. A "compilation" is defined as "a work formed by the collection and assembling of preexisting materials or of data that are selected, coordinated, or arranged in such a way that the resulting work as a whole constitutes an original work of authorship." A "derivative work" is "a work based on one or more preexisting works." Examples of derivative works include reproductions of works of art, sculptures based on drawings, lithographs based on paintings, maps based on previously published sources, or "any other form in which a work may be recast, transformed, or adapted." Derivative works also include works "consisting of editorial revisions, annotations, or other modifications" if these changes, as a whole, represent an original work of authorship.

Preexisting Material (space 6a): Complete this space and space 6b for derivative works. In this space identify the preexisting work that has been recast, transformed, or adapted. Examples of preexisting material might be "Grunewald Altarpiece" or "19th century quilt design." Do not complete this space for compilations.

Material Added to This Work (space 6b): Give a brief, general statement of the **additional** new material covered by the copyright claim for which registration is sought. In the case of a derivative work, identify this new material. Examples: "Adaptation of design and additional artistic work"; "Reproduction of painting by photolithography"; "Additional cartographic material"; "Compilation of photographs." If the work is a compilation, give a brief, general statement describing both the material that has been compiled **and** the compilation itself. Example: "Compilation of 19th century political cartoons."

SPACE 7,8,9: Fee, Correspondence, Certification, Return Address

Deposit Account: If you maintain a Deposit Account in the Copyright Office, identify it in space 7a. Otherwise, leave the space blank and send the $20* (see box this page) fee with your application and deposit.

Correspondence (space 7b): This space should contain the name, address, area code, telephone number, email address, and fax number (if available) of the person to be consulted if correspondence about this application becomes necessary.

Certification (space 8): The application cannot be accepted unless it bears the date and the **handwritten signature** of the author or other copyright claimant, or of the owner of exclusive right(s), or of the duly authorized agent of the author, claimant, or owner of exclusive right(s).

Address for Return of Certificate (space 9): The address box must be completed legibly since the certificate will be returned in a window envelope.

FEE CHANGES

Registration filing fees are effective through June 30, 1999. For information on the fee changes, write the Copyright Office, check http://www.loc.gov/copyright, or call (202) 707-3000. Beginning as early as January 1, 2000, the Copyright Office may impose a service charge when insufficient fees are received.

FORM VA
For a Work of the Visual Arts
UNITED STATES COPYRIGHT OFFICE

REGISTRATION NUMBER

_____

VA _____ VAU _____
EFFECTIVE DATE OF REGISTRATION

_____

Month _____ Day _____ Year _____

DO NOT WRITE ABOVE THIS LINE. IF YOU NEED MORE SPACE, USE A SEPARATE CONTINUATION SHEET.

1

TITLE OF THIS WORK ▼

NATURE OF THIS WORK ▼ See instructions

PREVIOUS OR ALTERNATIVE TITLES ▼

Publication as a Contribution If this work was published as a contribution to a periodical, serial, or collection, give information about the collective work in which the contribution appeared.   **Title of Collective Work ▼**

If published in a periodical or serial give: Volume ▼   Number ▼   Issue Date ▼   On Pages ▼

2

a

NAME OF AUTHOR ▼

DATES OF BIRTH AND DEATH
Year Born ▼   Year Died ▼

NOTE

Under the law, the "author" of a "work made for hire" is generally the employer, not the employee (see instructions). For any part of this work that was "made for hire" check "Yes" in the space provided, give the employer (or other person for whom the work was prepared) as "Author" of that part, and leave the space for dates of birth and death blank.

Was this contribution to the work a "work made for hire"?
   Yes
   No

Author?s Nationality or Domicile
Name of Country
OR { Citizen of ▶ _____
    Domiciled in ▶ _____

Was This Author?s Contribution to the Work
Anonymous? Yes No
Pseudonymous? Yes No
If the answer to either of these questions is "Yes," see detailed instructions.

NATURE OF AUTHORSHIP Check appropriate box(es). **See instructions**
   3-Dimensional sculpture   Map   Technical drawing
   2-Dimensional artwork   Photograph   Text
   Reproduction of work of art Jewelry design   Architectural work

b

NAME OF AUTHOR ▼

DATES OF BIRTH AND DEATH
Year Born ▼   Year Died ▼

Was this contribution to the work a "work made for hire"?
   Yes
   No

Author?s Nationality or Domicile
Name of Country
OR { Citizen of ▶ _____
    Domiciled in ▶ _____

Was This Author?s Contribution to the Work
Anonymous? Yes No
Pseudonymous? Yes No
If the answer to either of these questions is "Yes," see detailed instructions.

NATURE OF AUTHORSHIP Check appropriate box(es). **See instructions**
   3-Dimensional sculpture   Map   Technical drawing
   2-Dimensional artwork   Photograph   Text
   Reproduction of work of art Jewelry design   Architectural work

3

a Year in Which Creation of This Work Was Completed
This information must be given ◀Year In all cases.

b Date and Nation of First Publication of This Particular Work
Complete this information ONLY if this work has been published.
Month ▶ _____ Day▶ _____ Year▶ _____   ◀ Nation

4

See instructions before completing this space.

COPYRIGHT CLAIMANT(S) Name and address must be given even if the claimant is the same as the author given in space 2. ▼

Transfer If the claimant(s) named here in space 4 is (are) different from the author(s) named in space 2, give a brief statement of how the claimant(s) obtained ownership of the copyright. ▼

DO NOT WRITE HERE OFFICE USE ONLY

APPLICATION RECEIVED

ONE DEPOSIT RECEIVED

TWO DEPOSITS RECEIVED

FUNDS RECEIVED

MORE ON BACK ▶ • Complete all applicable spaces (numbers 5-9) on the reverse side of this page.
• See detailed instructions.   • Sign the form at line 8.

DO NOT WRITE HERE
Page 1 of _____ pages

```
                                            EXAMINED BY _____          FORM VA

                                            CHECKED BY _____

                                                CORRESPONDENCE                    FOR
                                                Yes                               COPYRIGHT
                                                                                  OFFICE
                                                                                  USE
                                                                                  ONLY
```

DO NOT WRITE ABOVE THIS LINE. IF YOU NEED MORE SPACE, USE A SEPARATE CONTINUATION SHEET.

PREVIOUS REGISTRATION Has registration for this work, or for an earlier version of this work, already been made in the Copyright Office? **5**
    Yes   No If your answer is "Yes," why is another registration being sought? (Check appropriate box.) ▼

a. This is the first published edition of a work previously registered in unpublished form.

b. This is the first application submitted by this author as copyright claimant.

c. This is a changed version of the work, as shown by space 6 on this application.

If your answer is "Yes," give: **Previous Registration Number ▼**   **Year of Registration ▼**

DERIVATIVE WORK OR COMPILATION Complete both space 6a and 6b for a derivative work; complete only 6b for a compilation. **6**
a. Preexisting Material Identify any preexisting work or works that this work is based on or incorporates. ▼

_____ **a**
See instructions
before completing
_____ this space.

b. Material Added to This Work Give a brief, general statement of the material that has been added to this work and in which copyright is claimed. ▼

_____ **b**

DEPOSIT ACCOUNT If the registration fee is to be charged to a Deposit Account established in the Copyright Office, give name and number of Account. **7**
Name ▼   **Account Number ▼**

_____ **a**

CORRESPONDENCE Give name and address to which correspondence about this application should be sent.   Name/Address/Apt/City/State/ZIP ▼

_____ **b**

Area code and daytime telephone number ▶ (   )   Fax number ▶ (   )

Email ▶

CERTIFICATION* I, the undersigned, hereby certify that I am the **8**

                     check only one ▶   author

                                 other copyright claimant

                                 owner of exclusive right(s)

                                 authorized agent of _____
                                         Name of author or other copyright claimant, or owner of exclusive right(s) ▲

of the work identified in this application and that the statements made by me in this application are correct to the best of my knowledge.

Typed or printed name and date ▼ If this application gives a date of publication in space 3, do not sign and submit it before that date.

                                                Date ▶

Handwritten signature (X) ▼

X _____

Mail   Name ▼   **YOU MUST:**   *Regis-**9**
certificate   • Complete all necessary spaces tration
to: • Sign your application in space 8 filing
           Number/Street/Apt ▼   **SEND ALL 3 ELEMENTS**   fees
Certificate   **IN THE SAME PACKAGE:** are ef-
will be   1. Application form   fective
mailed in   City/State/ZIP ▼   2. Nonrefundable $20* filing fee in check or through
window   money order payable to *Register of Copyrights* June 30, 1999. For
envelope   3. Deposit material   the latest fee infor-
                                            MAIL TO: mation, write the
                                            Library of Congress Copyright Office,
                                            Copyright Office   check the Copyright
                                            101 Independence Avenue, S.E. Office Website at
                                            Washington, D.C. 20559-6000 http://www.loc.gov/
                                                    copyright, or call
                                                    (202) 707-3000.

*17 U.S.C. § 506(e): Any person who knowingly makes a false representation of a material fact in the application for copyright registration provided for by section 409, or in any written statement filed in connection with the application, shall be fined not more than $2,500.

July 1998—125,000   ⊛ PRINTED ON RECYCLED PAPER   ☆U.S. GOVERNMENT PRINTING OFFICE: 1998-432-381/80,014
WEB REV: July 1998

◨ Filling Out Application Form SE

Detach and read these instructions before completing this form.
Make sure all applicable spaces have been filled in before you return this form.

BASIC INFORMATION

When To Use This Form: Use a separate Form SE for registration of each individual issue of a serial, Class SE. A serial is defined as a work issued or intended to be issued in successive parts bearing numerical or chronological designations and intended to be continued indefinitely. This class includes a variety of works; periodicals; newspapers; annuals; the journals, proceedings, transactions, etc., of societies. Do not use Form SE to register an individual contribution to a serial. Request Form TX for such contributions.

Deposit to Accompany Application: An application for copyright registration must be accompanied by a deposit consisting of copies or phonorecords representing the entire work for which registration is to be made. The following are the general deposit requirements as set forth in the statute:

> **Unpublished Work:** Deposit one complete copy (or phonorecord).

> **Published Work:** Deposit two complete copies (or one phonorecord) of the best edition.

> **Work First Published Outside the United States:** Deposit one complete copy or phonorecord) of the first foreign edition.

Mailing Requirements: It is important that you send the application, the deposit copy or copies, and the $20 fee together in the same envelope or package. The Copyright Office cannot process them unless they are received together. Send to: *Register of Copyrights, Library of Congress, Washington, D. C. 20559.*

The Copyright Notice: For works first published on or after March 1, 1989, the law provides that a copyright notice in a specified form "may be placed on all publicly distributed copies from which the work can be visually perceived." Use of the copyright notice is the responsibility of the copyright owner and does not require advance permission from the Copyright Office. The required form of the notice for copies generally consists of three elements: (1) the symbol "©," or the word "Copyright," or the abbreviation "Copr."; (2) the year of first publication; and (3) the name of the owner of copyright. For example: "© 1993 Jane Cole." The notice is to be affixed to the copies "in such manner and location as to give reasonable notice of the claim of copyright." Works first published prior to March 1, 1989, must carry the notice or risk loss of copyright protection.

For information about notice requirements for works published before March 1, 1989, or other copyright information, write: Information Section, LM-401, Copyright Office, Library of Congress, Washington, D.C. 20559.

PRIVACY ACT ADVISORY STATEMENT Required by the Privacy Act of 1974 (P.L. 93-579)
The authority for requesting this information is title 17, U.S.C. secs. 409 and 410. Furnishing the requested information is voluntary. But if the information is not furnished, it may be necessary to delay or refuse registration and you may not be entitled to certain relief, remedies, and benefits provided in chapters 4 and 5 of title 17, U.S.C.
The principal uses of the requested information are the establishment and maintenance of a public record and the examination of the application for compliance with legal requirements.
Other routine uses include public inspection and copying, preparation of public indexes, preparation of public catalogs of copyright registrations, and preparation of search reports upon request.
NOTE: No other advisory statement will be given in connection with this application. Please keep this statement and refer to it if we communicate with you regarding this application.

LINE-BY-LINE INSTRUCTIONS

Please type or print using black ink.

1 SPACE 1: Title

Title of This Serial: Every work submitted for copyright registration must be given a title to identify that particular work. If the copies or phonorecords of the work bear a title (or an identifying phrase that could serve as a title), copy that wording *completely* and *exactly* on the application. Give the volume and number of the periodical issue for which you are seeking registration. The "Date on Copies" in space 1 should be the date appearing on the actual copies (for example: "June 1981," " Winter 1981"). Indexing of the registration and future identification of the work will depend on the information you give here.

Previous or Alternative Titles: Complete this space only if there are any additional titles for the serial under which someone searching for the registration might be likely to look or under which a document pertaining to the work might be recorded.

2 SPACE 2: Author(s)

General Instructions: After reading these instructions, decide who are the "authors" of this work for copyright purposes. In the case of a serial issue, the organization which directs the creation of the serial issue as a whole is generally considered the author of the "collective work" (see "Nature of Authorship") whether it employs a staff or uses the efforts of volunteers. Where, however, an individual is independently responsible for the serial issue, name that person as author of the "collective work."

Name of Author: The fullest form of the author's name should be given. In the case of a "work made for hire," the statute provides that "the employer or other person for whom the work was prepared is considered the author." If this issue is a "work made for hire," the author's name will be the full legal name of the hiring organization, corporation, or individual. The title of the periodical should not ordinarily be listed as "author" because the title itself does not usually correspond to a legal entity capable of authorship. When an individual creates an issue of a serial independently and not as an "employee" of an organization or corporation, that individual should be listed as the "author."

Author's Nationality or Domicile: Give the country of which the author is a citizen, or the country in which the author is domiciled. Nationality or domicile **must** be given in all cases. The citizenship of an organization formed under United States Federal or state law should be stated as "U.S.A."

What is a "Work Made for Hire"? A "work made for hire" is defined as (1) "a work prepared by an employee within the scope of his or her employment"; or (2) "a work specially ordered or commissioned for use as a contribution to a collective work, as a part of a motion picture or other audiovisual work, as a translation, as a supplementary work, as a compilation, as an instructional text, as a test, as answer material for a test, or as an atlas, if the parties expressly agree in a written instrument signed by them that the work shall be considered a work made for hire." An organization that uses the efforts of volunteers in the creation of a "collective work" (see "Nature of Authorship") may also be considered the author of a "work made for hire" even though those volunteers were not specifically paid by the organization. In the case of a "work made for hire," give the full legal name of the employer and check "Yes" to indicate that the work was made for hire. You may also include the name of the employee along with the name of the employer (for example: "Elster Publishing Co., employer for hire of John Ferguson").

"Anonymous" or "Pseudonymous" Work: Leave this space blank if the serial is a "work made for hire." An author's contribution to a work is "anonymous" if that author is not identified on the copies or phonorecords of the work. An author's contribution to a work is "pseudonymous" if that author is identified on the copies or phonorecords under a fictitious name. If the work is "anonymous" you may: (1) leave the line blank; or (2) state "anonymous" on the line; or (3) reveal the author's identity. If the work is "pseudonymous" you may: (1) leave the line blank; or (2) give the pseudonym and identify it as such (for example: "Huntley Haverstock, pseudonym"); or (3) reveal the author's name, making clear which is the real name and which is the pseudonym (for example: "Judith Barton, whose pseudonym is Madeline Elster"). However, the citizenship or domicile of the author **must** be given in all cases.

Dates of Birth and Death: Leave this space blank if the author's contribution was a "work made for hire." If the author is dead, the statute requires that the year of death be included in the application unless the work is anonymous or pseudonymous. The author's birth date is optional but is useful as a form of identification.

Nature of Authorship: Give a brief statement of the nature of the particular author's contribution to the work. If an organization directed, controlled, and supervised the creation of the serial issue as a whole, check the box "collective work." The term "collective work" means that the author is responsible for compilation and editorial revision and may also be responsible for certain individual contributions to the serial issue. Further examples of "Authorship" which may apply both to organizational and to individual authors are "Entire text"; "Entire text and/or illustrations"; "Editorial revision, compilation, plus additional new material."

3 SPACE 3: Creation and Publication

General Instructions: Do not confuse "creation" with "publication." Every application for copyright registration must state "the year in which creation of the work was completed." Give the date and nation of first publication only if the work has been published.

Creation: Under the statute, a work is "created" when it is fixed in a copy or phonorecord for the first time. Where a work has been prepared over a period of time, the part of the work existing in fixed form on a particular date constitutes the created work on that date. The date you give here should be the year in which this particular issue was completed.

Publication: The statute defines "publication" as "the distribution of copies or phonorecords of a work to the public by sale or other transfer of ownership or by rental, lease, or lending"; a work is also "published" if there has been an "offering to distribute copies or phonorecords to a group of persons for purposes of further distribution, public performance, or public display." Give the full date (month, day, year) when, and the country where, publication of this particular issue first occurred. If first publication took place simultaneously in the United States and other countries, it is sufficient to state "U.S.A."

4 SPACE 4: Claimant(s)

Name(s) and Address(es) of Copyright Claimant(s): This space must be completed. Give the name(s) and address(es) of the copyright claimant(s) of this work even if the claimant is the same as the author named in space 2. Copyright in a work belongs initially to the author of the work (including, in the case of a work made for hire, the employer or other person for whom the work was prepared). The copyright claimant is either the author of the work or a person or organization to whom the copyright initially belonging to the author has been transferred.

Transfer: The statute provides that, if the copyright claimant is not the author, the application for registration must contain "a brief statement of how the claimant obtained ownership of the copyright." If any copyright claimant named in space 4 is not an author named in space 2, give a brief statement explaining how the claimant(s) obtained ownership of the copyright. Examples: "By written contract"; "Transfer of all rights by author"; "Assignment"; "By will." Do not attach transfer documents or other attachments or riders.

5 SPACE 5: Previous Registration

General Instructions: This space rarely applies to serials. Complete space 5 if this particular issue has been registered earlier or if it contains a substantial amount of material that has been previously registered. Do not complete this space if the previous registrations are simply those made for earlier issues.

Previous Registration:
a. Check this box if this issue has been registered in unpublished form and a second registration is now sought to cover the first published edition.
b. Check this box if someone other than the author is identified as copyright claimant in the earlier registration and the author is now seeking registration in his or her own name. If the work in question is a contribution to a collective work as opposed to the issue as a whole, file Form TX, not Form SE.
c. Check this box (and complete space 6) if this particular issue or a substantial portion of the material in it has been previously registered and you are now seeking registration for the additions and revisions which appear in this issue for the first time.

Previous Registration Number and Date: Complete this line if you checked one of the boxes above. If more than one previous registration has been made for the issue or for material in it, give only the number and year date for the latest registration.

6 SPACE 6: Derivative Work or Compilation

General Instructions: Complete space 6 if this issue is a "changed version," "compilation," or "derivative work" that incorporates one or more earlier works that have already been published or registered for copyright or that have fallen into the public domain. Do not complete space 6 for an issue consisting of entirely new material appearing for the first time such as a new issue of a continuing serial. A "compilation" is defined as "a work formed by the collection and assembling of preexisting materials or of data that are selected, coordinated, or arranged in such a way that the resulting work as a whole constitutes an original work of authorship." A "derivative work" is "a work based on one or more preexisting works." Examples of derivative works include translations, fictionalizations, abridgments, condensations, or "any other form in which a work may be recast, transformed, or adapted." Derivative works also include works "consisting of editorial revisions, annotations, or other modifications" if these changes, as a whole, represent an original work of authorship.

Preexisting Material (space 6a): For derivative works, complete this space and space 6b. In space 6a identify the preexisting work that has been recast, transformed, adapted, or updated. Example: "1978 Morgan Co. Sales Catalog." Do not complete space 6a for compilations.

Material Added to This Work (space 6b): Give a brief, general statement of the new material covered by the copyright claim for which registration is sought. **Derivative work** examples include: "Editorial revisions and additions to the Catalog"; "Translation"; "Additional material." If a periodical issue is a **compilation**, describe both the compilation itself and the material that has been compiled. Examples: "Compilation of previously published journal articles"; "Compilation of previously published data." An issue may be both a derivative work and a compilation, in which case a sample statement might be: "Compilation of [describe] and additional new material."

7 SPACE 7: Manufacturing Provisions

Due to the expiration of the Manufacturing Clause of the copyright law on June 30, 1986, this space has been deleted.

8 SPACE 8: Reproduction for Use of Blind or Physically Handicapped Individuals

General Instructions: One of the major programs of the Library of Congress is to provide Braille editions and special recordings of works for the exclusive use of the blind and physically handicapped. In an effort to simplify and speed up the copyright licensing procedures that are a necessary part of this program, section 710 of the copyright statute provides for the establishment of a voluntary licensing system to be tied in with copyright registration. Copyright Office regulations provide that you may grant a license for such reproduction and distribution solely for the use of persons who are certified by competent authority as unable to read normal printed material as a result of physical limitations. The license is entirely voluntary, nonexclusive, and may be terminated upon 90 days notice.

How to Grant the License: If you wish to grant it, check one of the three boxes in space 8. Your check in one of these boxes together with your signature in space 10 will mean that the Library of Congress can proceed to reproduce and distribute under the license without further paperwork. For further information, write for Circular 63.

9,10,11 SPACE 9,10,11: Fee, Correspondence, Certification, Return Address

Fee: The Copyright Office has the authority to adjust fees at 5-year intervals, based on changes in the Consumer Price Index. The next adjustment is due in 1996. Please contact the Copyright Office after July 1995 to determine the actual fee schedule.

Deposit Account: If you maintain a Deposit Account in the Copyright Office, identify it in space 9. Otherwise leave the space blank and send the fee of $20 with your application and deposit.

Correspondence (space 9): This space should contain the name, address, area code, and telephone number of the person to be consulted if correspondence about this application becomes necessary.

Certification (space 10): The application cannot be accepted unless it bears the date and the **handwritten signature** of the author or other copyright claimant, or of the owner of exclusive right(s), or of the duly authorized agent of the author, claimant, or owner of exclusive right(s).

Address for Return of Certificate (space 11): The address box must be completed legibly since the certificate will be returned in a window envelope.

FORM SE
For a Serial
UNITED STATES COPYRIGHT OFFICE

REGISTRATION NUMBER

U

EFFECTIVE DATE OF REGISTRATION

Month	Day	Year

DO NOT WRITE ABOVE THIS LINE. IF YOU NEED MORE SPACE, USE A SEPARATE CONTINUATION SHEET.

1

TITLE OF THIS SERIAL ▼

Volume ▼	Number ▼	Date on Copies ▼	Frequency of Publication ▼

PREVIOUS OR ALTERNATIVE TITLES ▼

2

a

NAME OF AUTHOR ▼

DATES OF BIRTH AND DEATH
Year Born ▼   Year Died ▼

Was this contribution to the work a "work made for hire"?
☐ Yes
☐ No

AUTHOR'S NATIONALITY OR DOMICILE
Name of Country
OR { Citizen of ▶_____
Domiciled in▶_____

WAS THIS AUTHOR'S CONTRIBUTION TO THE WORK
Anonymous? ☐ Yes ☐ No
Pseudonymous? ☐ Yes ☐ No
If the answer to either of these questions is Yes, see detailed instructions.

NATURE OF AUTHORSHIP Briefly describe nature of material created by this author in which copyright is claimed. ▼
☐ Collective Work   Other:

NOTE

Under the law, the author of a work made for hire is generally the employer, not the employee (see instructions). For any part of this work that was made for hire check Yes in the space provided, give the employer (or other person for whom the work was prepared) as Author of that part, and leave the space for dates of birth and death blank.

b

NAME OF AUTHOR ▼

DATES OF BIRTH AND DEATH
Year Born ▼   Year Died ▼

Was this contribution to the work a "work made for hire"?
☐ Yes
☐ No

AUTHOR'S NATIONALITY OR DOMICILE
Name of Country
OR { Citizen of ▶_____
Domiciled in▶_____

WAS THIS AUTHOR'S CONTRIBUTION TO THE WORK
Anonymous? ☐ Yes ☐ No
Pseudonymous? ☐ Yes ☐ No
If the answer to either of these questions is Yes, see detailed instructions.

NATURE OF AUTHORSHIP Briefly describe nature of material created by this author in which copyright is claimed. ▼
☐ Collective Work   Other:

c

NAME OF AUTHOR ▼

DATES OF BIRTH AND DEATH
Year Born ▼   Year Died ▼

Was this contribution to the work a "work made for hire"?
☐ Yes
☐ No

AUTHOR'S NATIONALITY OR DOMICILE
Name of Country
OR { Citizen of ▶_____
Domiciled in▶_____

WAS THIS AUTHOR'S CONTRIBUTION TO THE WORK
Anonymous? ☐ Yes ☐ No
Pseudonymous? ☐ Yes ☐ No
If the answer to either of these questions is Yes, see detailed instructions.

NATURE OF AUTHORSHIP Briefly describe nature of material created by this author in which copyright is claimed. ▼
☐ Collective Work   Other:

3

a
YEAR IN WHICH CREATION OF THIS ISSUE WAS COMPLETED This information must be given ◀ Year in all cases.

b
DATE AND NATION OF FIRST PUBLICATION OF THIS PARTICULAR ISSUE Complete this information ONLY if this work has been published. Month ▶ _____ Day ▶ _____ Year ▶ _____ ◀ Nation

4

COPYRIGHT CLAIMANT(S) Name and address must be given even if the claimant is the same as the author given in space 2. ▼

TRANSFER If the claimant(s) named here in space 4 is (are) different from the author(s) named in space 2, give a brief statement of how the claimant(s) obtained ownership of the copyright. ▼

See instructions before completing this space.

DO NOT WRITE HERE OFFICE USE ONLY

APPLICATION RECEIVED

ONE DEPOSIT RECEIVED

TWO DEPOSITS RECEIVED

REMITTANCE NUMBER AND DATE

MORE ON BACK ▶   ¥ Complete all applicable spaces (numbers 5-11) on the reverse side of this page.
¥ See detailed instructions.   ¥ Sign the form at line 10.

DO NOT WRITE HERE
Page 1 of _____ pages

EXAMINED BY	FORM SE
CHECKED BY	
CORRESPONDENCE ☐ Yes	FOR COPYRIGHT OFFICE USE ONLY

DO NOT WRITE ABOVE THIS LINE. IF YOU NEED MORE SPACE, USE A SEPARATE CONTINUATION SHEET.

PREVIOUS REGISTRATION Has registration for this issue, or for an earlier version of this particular issue, already been made in the Copyright Office?

☐ Yes ☐ No If your answer is "Yes," why is another registration being sought? (Check appropriate box) ▼

a. ☐ This is the first published edition of an issue previously registered in unpublished form.

b. ☐ This is the first application submitted by this author as copyright claimant.

c. ☐ This is a changed version of this issue, as shown by space 6 on this application.

If your answer is "Yes," give: **Previous Registration Number** ▼   **Year of Registration** ▼

5

DERIVATIVE WORK OR COMPILATION Complete both space 6a and 6b for a derivative work; complete only 6b for a compilation.

a. Preexisting Material Identify any preexisting work or works that this work is based on or incorporates.▼

b. Material Added to This Work Give a brief, general statement of the material that has been added to this work and in which copyright is claimed.▼

6

See instructions before completing this space.

—space deleted—

7

REPRODUCTION FOR USE OF BLIND OR PHYSICALLY HANDICAPPED INDIVIDUALS A signature on this form at space 10 and a check in one of the boxes here in space 8 constitutes a non-exclusive grant of permission to the Library of Congress to reproduce and distribute solely for the blind and physically handicapped and under the conditions and limitations prescribed by the regulations of the Copyright Office: (1) copies of the work identified in space 1 of this application in Braille (or similar tactile symbols); or (2) phonorecords embodying a fixation of a reading of that work; or (3) both.

a ☐ Copies and Phonorecords   b ☐ Copies Only   c ☐ Phonorecords Only

8

See instructions.

DEPOSIT ACCOUNT If the registration fee is to be charged to a Deposit Account established in the Copyright Office, give name and number of Account.

Name ▼   **Account Number** ▼

9

CORRESPONDENCE Give name and address to which correspondence about this application should be sent.   Name/Address/Apt/City/State/ZIP ▼

Area Code and Telephone Number ▶

Be sure to give your daytime phone ◀ number

CERTIFICATION* I, the undersigned, hereby certify that I am the

Check only one ▶

☐ author

☐ other copyright claimant

☐ owner of exclusive right(s)

☐ authorized agent of _____

of the work identified in this application and that the statements made by me in this application are correct to the best of my knowledge.

Name of author or other copyright claimant, or owner of exclusive right(s) ▲

10

Typed or printed name and date ▼ If this application gives a date of publication in space 3, do not sign and submit it before that date.

_____ date ▶ _____

☞ **Handwritten signature (X)**▼

MAIL CERTIFI-CATE TO

Certificate will be mailed in window envelope

Name ▼

Number/Street/Apartment Number ▼

City/State/ZIP ▼

YOU MUST:
¥ Complete all necessary spaces
¥ Sign your application in space 10

SEND ALL 3 ELEMENTS IN THE SAME PACKAGE:
1. Application form
2. Nonrefundable $20 filing fee in check or money order payable to *Register of Copyrights*
3. Deposit material

MAIL TO:
Register of Copyrights
Library of Congress
Washington, D.C. 20559-6000

11

*17 U.S.C. / 506(e): Any person who knowingly makes a false representation of a material fact in the application for copyright registration provided for by section 409, or in any written statement filed in connection with the application, shall be fined not more than $2,500.

April 1993 100,000

☆ U.S. GOVERNMENT PRINTING OFFICE: 1993-342-581/60,511

Form SE/GROUP

BASIC INFORMATION

Read these instructions before completing this form.
Make sure all applicable spaces have been filled in before you return this form.

When to Use This Form: All the following conditions must be met in order to use this form. If any one of the conditions does not apply, you must register the issues separately using Form SE or Short Form SE.
1. You must have given a complimentary subscription for two copies of the serial to the Library of Congress, confirmed by letter to:

Library of Congress
Group Periodicals Registration
Washington, D.C. 20540-4161

Subscription copies must be mailed separately to the same address.
2. The claim must be in the collective works.
3. The works must be essentially all new collective works or issues.
4. Each issue must be a work made for hire.
5. The author(s) and claimant(s) must be the same person(s) or organization(s) for all the issues.
6. Each issue must have been created no more than 1 year prior to publication.
7. All issues in the group must have been published within the same calendar year.

For copyright purposes, serials are defined as works issued or intended to be issued in successive parts bearing numerical or chronological designations and intended to be continued indefinitely. The classification "serial" includes periodicals, newspapers, magazines, bulletins, newsletters, annuals, journals, proceedings of societies, and other similar works.

Which Issues May Be Included in a Group Registration: You may register two or more issues of a serial published at intervals of 1 week or longer under the same continuing title, provided that the issues were published within a 90-day period during the same calendar year.

Deposit to Accompany Application: Send one copy of each issue included in the group registration with the application and fee.

Fee: A nonrefundable filing fee of $10.00 FOR EACH ISSUE LISTED ON FORM SE/GROUP must be sent with the application or charged to an active deposit account in the Copyright Office. **The fee is effective through June 30, 1999. For information on the fee changes, please write the Copyright Office, check the Copyright Office Website at http://www.loc.gov/copyright, or call (202) 707-3000 for the latest fee information.** There is a minimum fee of $20.00 for Form SE/Group. Make checks payable to **Register of Copyrights.**
Special handling is not available for Form SE/Group.

Mailing Instructions: Send the application, deposit copies, and fee together in the same package to: Library of Congress, Copyright Office, 101 Independence Ave., S.E., Washington, D.C. 20559-6000.

International Standard Serial Number (ISSN): ISSN is an internationally accepted code for the identification of serial publications. If a published serial has not been assigned an ISSN, application forms and additional information may be obtained from: Library of Congress, National Serials Data Program, 101 Independence Ave., S.E., Washington, D.C. 20540-4160. Do not contact the Copyright Office for ISSNs.

Collective Work: The term "collective work" refers to a work, such as a serial issue, in which a number of contributions are assembled into a collective whole. A claim in the "collective work" extends to all copyrightable authorship created by employees of the author, as well as any independent contributions in which the claimant has acquired ownership of the copyright.

Publication: The statute defines "publication" as "the distribution of copies or phonorecords of a work to the public by sale or other transfer of ownership, or by rental, lease, or lending." A work is also "published" if there has been an "offering to distribute copies or phonorecords to a group of persons for purposes of further distribution, public performance, or public display."

Creation: A work is "created" when it is fixed in a copy (or phonorecord) for the first time. For a serial, the year in which the collective work was completed is the creation date.

Work Made for Hire: A "work made for hire" is defined as: (1) a work prepared by an employee within the scope of his or her employment; or (2) a work specially ordered or commissioned for certain uses (including use as a contribution to a collective work), if the parties expressly agree in a written instrument signed by them that the work shall be considered a work made for hire. The employer is the author of a work made for hire.

The Copyright Notice: Generally, for works published prior to March 1, 1989, a copyright notice was required. For more information about copyright notice, see Circular 3, "Copyright Notice."
To obtain Circular 3, call the Copyright Office Forms Hotline at (202) 707-9100 or write: Library of Congress, Copyright Office, Publications Section, LM-455, 101 Independence Ave., S.E., Washington, D.C. 20559-6000. Or obtain the circular via Fax-on-Demand at (202) 707-2600 or the Internet at http://www.loc.gov/copyright.

LINE-BY-LINE INSTRUCTIONS

SPACE 1: Title and Date of Publication

Give the complete title of the serial, followed by the International Standard Serial Number (ISSN), if available. List the issues in the order of publication. For each issue, give the volume, number, and issue date appearing on the copies, followed by the complete date of publication, including month, day, and year. If you have not previously registered this identical title under Section 408 of the Copyright Act, please indicate by checking the box.

SPACE 2: Author and Copyright Claimant

Give the fullest form of the author and claimant's name and mailing address. If there are joint authors and claimants, give the names and addresses of all the author/claimants. If the work is not of U.S. origin, add the citizenship or domicile of the author/claimant, or the nation of publication.

Certification: The application cannot be accepted unless it bears the handwritten signature of the copyright claimant or the duly authorized agent of the copyright claimant.

Person to Contact for Correspondence About This Claim: Give the name and telephone number, including area code, of the person to whom any correspondence concerning this claim should be addressed. Give the address only if it is different from the address for mailing of the certificate.

Deposit Account: If the filing fee is to be charged against a deposit account in the Copyright Office, give the name and number of the account in this space. Otherwise, leave the space blank and forward the filing fee with your application and deposit.

Mailing Address of Certificate: This address must be complete and legible since the certificate will be mailed in a window envelope.
(Information continues on reverse ▶)

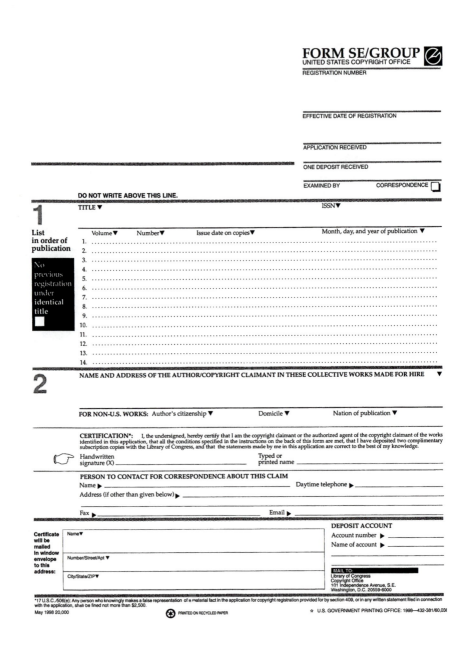

FORM SE/GROUP
UNITED STATES COPYRIGHT OFFICE

REGISTRATION NUMBER

EFFECTIVE DATE OF REGISTRATION

APPLICATION RECEIVED

ONE DEPOSIT RECEIVED

EXAMINED BY   CORRESPONDENCE ☐

DO NOT WRITE ABOVE THIS LINE.

1

List in order of publication

No previous registration under identical title ☐

TITLE ▼   ISSN▼

Volume ▼	Number▼	Issue date on copies▼	Month, day, and year of publication ▼
1.			
2.			
3.			
4.			
5.			
6.			
7.			
8.			
9.			
10.			
11.			
12.			
13.			
14.			

2

NAME AND ADDRESS OF THE AUTHOR/COPYRIGHT CLAIMANT IN THESE COLLECTIVE WORKS MADE FOR HIRE ▼

FOR NON-U.S. WORKS: Author's citizenship ▼   Domicile ▼   Nation of publication ▼

CERTIFICATION*: I, the undersigned, hereby certify that I am the copyright claimant or the authorized agent of the copyright claimant of the works identified in this application, that all the conditions specified in the instructions on the back of this form are met, that I have deposited two complimentary subscription copies with the Library of Congress, and that the statements made by me in this application are correct to the best of my knowledge.

Handwritten signature (X) _____

Typed or printed name _____

PERSON TO CONTACT FOR CORRESPONDENCE ABOUT THIS CLAIM

Name ▶ _____   Daytime telephone ▶ _____

Address (if other than given below) ▶ _____

Fax ▶ _____   Email ▶ _____

Certificate will be mailed in window envelope to this address:

Name▼

Number/Street/Apt ▼

City/State/ZIP▼

DEPOSIT ACCOUNT

Account number ▶ _____

Name of account ▶ _____

MAIL TO:
Library of Congress
Copyright Office
101 Independence Avenue, S.E.
Washington, D.C. 20559-6000

*17 U.S.C./506(e): Any person who knowingly makes a false representation of a material fact in the application for copyright registration provided for by section 409, or in any written statement filed in connection with the application, shall be fined not more than $2,500.

May 1998 20,000   ♻ PRINTED ON RECYCLED PAPER   ☆ U.S. GOVERNMENT PRINTING OFFICE: 1998—432-381/60,03(

Ⓔ Form Group/Daily Newspapers

BASIC INFORMATION

Read these instructions before completing this form.
Make sure all applicable spaces have been filled in
before you return this form.

When to Use This Form: All the following conditions must be met in order to use this form. If any one of the conditions does not apply, you must use Form SE. Incorrect use of this form will result in a delay in your registration.
1. The work must be a daily newspaper.
2. The claim must include all issue dates within the calendar month within the same year.
3. The applicant must submit a complete month's issues in microfilm form.
4. Each issue must essentially be an all-new collective work.
5. The work must be a work made for hire.
6. The author(s) and claimant(s) must be the same person(s) or organization(s).
7. The application must be filed within 3 months after the last publication date included in the group.

Deposit to Accompany Application: This application must be accompanied by a deposit of a positive, 35mm silver-halide microfilm that includes all issue dates within a calendar month for the specific title that was published as the last (final) edition.

Fee: The nonrefundable filing fee for registration of a group of newspapers is $40.00. Unless you maintain a Deposit Account in the Copyright Office, the $40.00 fee in the form of a check, money order, or bank draft must accompany your application form and copies. Do not send cash or currency. Make your remittance payable to: **Register of Copyrights** . Remittances must be payable immediately through a U.S. institution in U.S. dollars. Remittances may be in the form of International Money Order only if it is immediately redeemable in U.S. dollars. Special Handling is not available for the group registration of daily newspapers.
NOTE: The Copyright Office has the authority to adjust fees at 5-year intervals, based on changes in the Consumer Price Index. The next adjustment is due in 1995. Please contact the Copyright Office after July 1995 to determine the actual fee schedule.

Mailing Procedures: It is important that you send the application, the deposit, and the $40.00 fee together in the same envelope or package to: Register of Copyrights, Library of Congress, Washington, D.C. 20559.

Reproduction for Use by Blind
or Physically Handicapped Individuals: A signature on this form and a check in one of the boxes in space 3 (on verso of page) constitute a nonexclusive grant of permission to the Library of Congress to reproduce and distribute solely for the blind and physically handicapped under the conditions and limitations prescribed by the regulations of the Copyright Office: (1) copies of the work identified in space 1 of this application in Braille (or similar tactile symbols); or (2) phonorecords embodying a fixation of a reading of that work; or (3) both.

Collective Work: The term "collective work" refers to a work , such as a serial issue, in which a number of contributions are assembled into a collective whole. A claim in the "collective work" extends to all copyrightable authorship created by employees of the author, as well as any independent contributions in which the claimant has acquired ownership of the copyright.

Publication: The Copyright Law defines "publication" as "the distribution of copies or phonorecords of a work to the public by sale or other transfer of ownership, or by rental, lease, or lending." A work is also "published" if there has been an "offering to distribute copies or phonorecords to a group of persons for purposes of further distribution, public performance, or public display."

Work Made for Hire: A "work made for hire" is defined as: (1) a work prepared by an employee within the scope of his or her employment; or (2) a work specially ordered or commissioned for certain uses (including use as a contribution to a collective work), if the parties expressly agree in a written instrument signed by them that the work shall be considered a work made for hire. The employer is the author of a work made for hire.

Newspaper: As defined by the Newspaper Section of the Serials and Government Publications Division of the Library of Congress, works classified as newspapers are serials mainly designed to be a primary source of written information on current events, either local, national, or international in scope. Newspapers contain a broad range of news on all subjects and activities and are not limited to any specific subject matter. Newspapers are intended either for the general public or for a particular group.

─SPACE-BY-SPACE INSTRUCTIONS─

1 **SPACE 1: Title**

Space 1 must identify the work being registered by giving the complete title of the newspaper, the month and year printed on the copies, the number of issues in the group, the city and state, the edition, and, if known, the ISSN number.

2 **SPACE 2: Author and Copyright Claimant**

Give the fullest form of the author and claimant's name. If there are joint authors and owners, give the names of all the author/owners. (It is assumed that the authors and claimant are the same, that the work is made for hire, and that the claim is in the collective work.)

3 **SPACE 3: Date of Publication**

Give the exact date on which publication of the first and last issues in this group took place. The full date, including month, day, and year must be given.

Certification: The application cannot be accepted unless it bears the handwritten signature of the copyright claimant or the duly authorized agent of the copyright claimant.

Person to Contact for Correspondence
About This Claim: Give the name and telephone number, including area code, of the person to whom any correspondence concerning this claim should be addressed. Give the address only if it is different from the address for the mailing of the certificate.

Deposit Account: If the filing fee is to be charged against a Deposit Account in the Copyright Office, give the name and number of the account in this space. Otherwise, leave the space blank and forward the $40.00 filing fee with your application and deposit.

Mailing Address of Certificate: This address must be complete and legible because the certificate will be mailed in a window envelope.

FORM G/DN

For Group/Daily Newspapers
UNITED STATES COPYRIGHT OFFICE

REGISTRATION NUMBER

EFFECTIVE DATE OF REGISTRATION
(Assigned by Copyright Office)

Month	Day	Year

APPLICATION RECEIVED

ONE MICROFILM DEPOSIT RECEIVED

EXAMINED BY   CORRESPONDENCE

DO NOT WRITE ABOVE THIS LINE.

1 TITLE OF THIS NEWSPAPER AS IT APPEARS ON THE COPIES ▼   City/State▼

Month and year date on copies ▼   Number of issues in this group ▼   ISSN▼   Edition▼

2 NAME AND ADDRESS OF THE AUTHOR/COPYRIGHT CLAIMANT IN THESE COLLECTIVE WORKS MADE FOR HIRE

3 DATE OF PUBLICATION OF THE FIRST AND LAST ISSUES IN THIS GROUP
Month▼   Day▼   Year▼

(First) _____

(Last) _____

REPRODUCTION FOR USE OF BLIND OR PHYSICALLY HANDICAPPED INDIVIDUALS

a☐ Copies and Phonorecords
b☐ Copies Only
c☐ Phonorecords Only

CERTIFICATION*:   I, the undersigned, hereby certify that I am the copyright claimant or the authorized agent of the copyright claimant of the works identified in this application, that all the conditions specified in the instructions on the back of this form are met, and that the statements made by me in this application are correct to the best of my knowledge.

Handwritten
signature (X) _____   Typed or printed
name of signer _____

PERSON TO CONTACT FOR CORRESPONDENCE ABOUT THIS CLAIM

Name ▶ _____

Daytime telephone number ▶ _____

Address (if other than given below) ▶ _____

DEPOSIT ACCOUNT

Account number ▶ _____

Name of account ▶ _____

MAIL CERTIFI-CATE TO

Certificate will be mailed in window envelope

Name▼

Number/Street/Apartment Number▼

City/State/ZIP▼

YOU MUST:
¥ Complete all necessary spaces
¥ Sign your application

SEND ALL 3 ELEMENTS IN THE SAME PACKAGE:
1. Application form
2. Nonrefundable $40.00 filing fee in check, money order, or bank draft payable to *Register of Copyrights*
3. Deposit material

MAIL TO:
Register of Copyrights
Library of Congress
Washington, D.C. 20559

The Copyright Office has the authority to adjust fees at 5-year intervals, based on changes in the Consumer Price Index. The next adjustment is due in 1995. Please contact the Copyright Office after July 1995 to determine the actual fee schedule.

*17 U.S.C. §506(e): Any person who knowingly makes a false representation of a material fact in the application for copyright registration provided for by section 409, or in any written statement filed in connection with the application, shall be fined not more than $2,500.

August 1992 20,000   ☆ U.S. GOVERNMENT PRINTING OFFICE: 1992—312-432/60,005

☑Filling Out Application Form RE

Detach and read these instructions before completing this form.
Make sure all applicable spaces have been filled in before you return this form.

BASIC INFORMATION

How to Register a Renewal Claim:

First: Study the information on this page and make sure you know the answers to two questions:
(1) What is the renewal filing period in your case?
(2) Who can claim the renewal?

Second: Read through the specific instructions for filling out Form RE. Before starting to complete the form, make sure that the copyright is now eligible for renewal, that you are authorized to file a renewal claim, and that you have all of the information about the copyright you will need.

Third: Complete all applicable spaces on Form RE, following the line-by-line instructions. Use typewriter or print the information in black ink.

Fourth: Detach this sheet and send your completed Form RE to: Register of Copyrights, Library of Congress, Washington, D.C. 20559-6000. Unless you have a Deposit Account in the Copyright Office, your application must be accompanied by a check or money order for $20, payable to: *Register of Copyrights*. Do not send copies, phonorecords, or supporting documents with your renewal application unless specifically requested to do so by the Copyright Office.

What Is Renewal of Copyright?

For works copyrighted before January 1, 1978, the copyright law provides a first term of copyright protection lasting 28 years. These works were required to be renewed within strict time limits in order to obtain a second term of copyright protection lasting 47 years. If copyright was originally secured before January 1, 1964, and was not renewed at the proper time, copyright protection expired permanently at the end of the 28th year and could not be renewed.

Public Law 102-307, enacted June 26, 1992, amended the copyright law to extend automatically the term of copyrights secured between January 1, 1964, and December 31, 1977, to a further term of 47 years. This recent legislation makes renewal registration optional. The first term of copyright protection expires on December 31st of the 28th year of the original term of the copyright and the 47-year renewal term automatically vests in the party entitled to claim renewal as of that date.

Some Basic Points About Renewal:

(1) A work is eligible for renewal registration at the beginning of the 28th year of the first term of copyright.
(2) There is no requirement to make a renewal filing in order to extend the original 28-year copyright term to the full term of 75 years; however, there are some benefits from making a renewal registration during the 28th year of the original term. (For more information, write to the Copyright Office for Circular 15.)
(3) Only certain persons who fall into specific categories named in the law can claim renewal.
(4) For works originally copyrighted on or after January 1, 1978, the copyright law has eliminated all renewal requirements and established a single copyright term and different methods for computing the duration of a copyright. For further information, write the Copyright Office for Circular 15a, "Duration of Copyright."

Renewal Filing Period:

The amended copyright statute provides that, in order to register a renewal copyright, the renewal application and fee must be received in the Copyright Office
—within the last (28th) calendar year before the expiration of the original term of copyright or
—at any time during the renewed and extended term of 47 years.

To determine the filing period for renewal in your case:
(1) First, find out the date of original copyright for the work. (In the case of works originally registered in unpublished form, the date of copyright is the date of registration; for published works, copyright begins on the date of first publication.)
(2) Then add 28 years to the year the work was originally copyrighted.
Your answer will be the calendar year during which the copyright will become eligible for renewal. Example: A work originally copyrighted on April 19, 1968, will be eligible for renewal in the calendar year 1996.

To renew a copyright during the original copyright term, the renewal application and fee must be received in the Copyright Office within 1 year prior to the expiration of the original copyright. All terms of the original copyright run through the end of the 28th calendar year making the period for renewal registration during the original term from December 31st of the 27th year of the copyright through December 31st of the following year.

Who May Claim Renewal:

Renewal copyright may be claimed only by those persons specified in the law. Except in the case of four specific types of works, the law gives the right to claim renewal to the individual author of the work, regardless of who owned the copyright during the original term. If the author is dead, the statute gives the right to claim renewal to certain of the author's beneficiaries (widow and children, executors, or next of kin, depending on the circumstances). The present owner (proprietor) of the copyright is entitled to claim renewal only in four specified cases as explained in more detail on the reverse of this page.

For Further Information, write to: Publications Section, LM-455, Copyright Office, Library of Congress, Washington, D.C. 20559-6000 and request Circular 96 202.20, "Deposit of Copies and Phonorecords for Copyright Registration"; Circular 96 202.21, "Deposit of Identifying Material Instead of Copies"; Circular 96 202.17, "Renewals"; and Circular 15, "Renewal of Copyright." Or obtain Circular 15 via fax by calling 202-707-2600 from any touchtone phone and keying in your fax number and the document number of the item(s) you want. If you do not know the document number of the item(s) you want, you may request that an index be faxed to you.

You may also call the Forms Hotline 24 hours a day, 7 days a week, and leave your request for forms and circulars as a recorded message. In addition, forms and circulars are available over Internet via the World Wide Web at http://lcweb.loc.gov/copyright and via gopher to marvel.loc.gov (port 70) at the anonymous ftp site.

To speak with an information specialist, call (202) 707-3000 or TTY: (202) 707-6737, Monday -Friday, 8:30 a.m.-5 p.m., Eastern Time, except Federal holidays.

PRIVACY ACT ADVISORY STATEMENT Required by the Privacy Act of 1974 (Public Law 93-579)	BUT IF THE INFORMATION IS NOT FURNISHED:	OTHER ROUTINE USES:
	¥ It may be necessary to delay or refuse renewal registration	¥ Public inspection and copying
AUTHORITY FOR REQUESTING THIS INFORMATION:	¥ If renewal registration is not made before expiration of the	¥ Preparation of public indexes
¥ Title 17, U.S.C., Sec. 304	original copyright term, ownership of the renewal term may be affected	¥ Preparation of public catalogs of copyright registrations
		¥ Preparation of search reports upon request
FURNISHING THE REQUESTED INFORMATION IS:	PRINCIPAL USES OF REQUESTED INFORMATION:	NOTE:
¥ Voluntary	¥ Establishment and maintenance of a public record	¥ No other advisory statement will be given you in connection with this application
	¥ Examination of the application for compliance with legal requirements	¥ Please keep this statement and refer to it if we communicate with you regarding this application

LINE-BY-LINE INSTRUCTIONS

Please type or print neatly using black ink. The form is used to produce the certificate.

1 SPACE 1: Renewal Claimant(s)

General Instructions: In order for this application to result in a valid renewal, space 1 must identify one or more of the persons who are entitled to renew the copyright under the statute. Give the full name and address of each claimant, with a statement of the basis of each claim, using the wording given in these instructions.

For registration in the 28th year of the original copyright term, the renewal claimant is the individual(s) or entity who is entitled to claim renewal copyright on the date filed.

For registration after the 28th year of the original copyright term, the renewal claimant is the individual(s) or entity who is entitled to claim renewal copyright on December 31st of the 28th year.

Persons Entitled to Renew:

A. The following persons may claim renewal in all types of works except those enumerated in Paragraph B below:

1. The author, if living. State the claim as: *the author*

2. The widow, widower, and/or children of the author, if the author is not living. State the claim as:

    the widow (widower) of the author ....
    (Name of author)

    and/or the child (children) of the deceased author ....
    (Name of author)

3. The author's executor(s), if the author left a will and if there is no surviving widow, widower, or child. State the claim as:

    the executor(s) of the author ....
    (Name of author)

4. The next of kin of the author, if the author left no will and if there is no surviving widow, widower, or child. State the claim as:

    the next of kin of the deceased author .... *there being no will.*
    (Name of author)

B. In the case of the following four types of works, the proprietor (owner of the copyright at the time of renewal registration) may claim renewal:

1. Posthumous work (a work published after the author's death as to which no copyright assignment or other contract for exploitation has occurred during the author's lifetime). State the claim as: *proprietor of copyright in a posthumous work.*

2. Periodical, cyclopedic, or other composite work. State the claim as: *proprietor of copyright in a composite work.*

3. "Work copyrighted by a corporate body otherwise than as assignee or licensee of the individual author." State the claim as: *proprietor of copyright in a work copyrighted by a corporate body otherwise than as assignee or licensee of the individual author.* (This type of claim is considered appropriate in relatively few cases.)

4. Work copyrighted by an employer for whom such work was made for hire. State the claim as: *proprietor of copyright in a work made for hire.*

2 SPACE 2: Work Renewed

General Instructions: This space is to identify the particular work being renewed. The information given here should agree with that appearing in the certificate of original registration.

Title: Give the full title of the work, together with any subtitles or descriptive wording included with the title in the original registration. In the case of a musical composition, give the specific instrumentation of the work.

Renewable Matter: Copyright in a new version of a previously published or copyrighted work (such as an arrangement, translation, dramatization, compilation, or work republished with new matter) covers only the additions, changes, or other new material appearing for the first time in that version. If this work was a new version, state in general the new matter upon which copyright was claimed.

Contribution to Periodical, Serial, or other Composite Work: Separate renewal registration is possible for a work published as a contribution to a periodical, serial, or other composite work, whether the contribution was copyrighted independently or as part of the larger work in which it appeared. Each contribution published in a separate issue ordinarily requires a separate renewal registration. However, the law provides an alternative, permitting groups of periodical contributions by the same individual author to be combined under a single renewal application and fee in certain cases.

If this renewal application covers a single contribution, give all of the requested information in space 2. If you are seeking to renew a group of contributions, include a reference such as "See space 5" in space 2 and give the requested information about all of the contributions in space 5.

3 SPACE 3: Author(s)

General Instructions: The copyright secured in a new version of a work is independent of any copyright protection in material published earlier. The only "authors" of a new version are those who contributed copyrightable matter to it. Thus, for renewal purposes, the person who wrote the original version on which the new work is based cannot be regarded as an "author" of the new version, unless that person also contributed to the new matter.

Authors of Renewable Matter: Give the full names of all authors who contributed copyrightable matter to this particular version of the work.

4 SPACE 4: Facts of Original Registration

General Instructions: Each item in space 4 should agree with the information appearing in the original registration for the work. If the work being renewed is a single contribution to a periodical or composite work that was not separately registered, give information about the particular issue in which the contribution appeared. You may leave this space blank if you are completing space 5.

Original Registration Number: Give the full registration number, which appears in the upper right hand corner of the front of the certificate of registration.

Original Copyright Claimant: Give the name in which ownership of the copyright was claimed in the original registration.

Date of Publication or Registration: Give only one date. If the original registration gave a publication date, it should be transcribed here; otherwise the registration was for an unpublished work, and the date of registration should be given. See following Note.

5 SPACE 5: Group Renewals

General Instructions: A renewal registration using a single application and $20 fee can be made for a group of works if all of the following statutory conditions are met: (1) all of the works were written by the same author, who is named in space 3 and who is or was an individual (not an employer for hire); (2) all of the works were first published as contributions to periodicals (including newspapers) and were copyrighted on their first publication either through separate copyright notice and registration or by virtue of a general copyright notice in the periodical issue as a whole; (3) the renewal claimant or claimants and the basis of claim or claims, as stated in space 1, are the same for all of the works; (4) the renewal application and fee are received not less than 27 years after the 31st day of December of the calendar year in which all of the works were first published (See following Note); and (5) the renewal application identifies each work separately, including the periodical containing it and the date of first publication.

Note: During the 28th year of the original term and during the extended 47-year renewal term, renewal registration may be made for a single work or a group of works without having made an original registration. This option requires the filing of a renewal application Form RE accompanied by a Form RE Addendum, a copy of the work as first published or appropriate identifying material in accordance with the requirements of 37 CFR 202.17, and a $20 filing fee.

Time Limits for Group Renewals: To be renewed as a group, all of the contributions must have been first published during the same calendar year. For example, suppose six contributions by the same author were published on April 1, 1968, July 1, 1968, November 1, 1968, February 1, 1969, July 1, 1969, and March 1, 1970. The three 1968 copyrights can be combined and renewed at any time during 1996, and the two 1969 copyrights can be renewed as a group during 1997, but the 1970 copyright must be renewed by itself, in 1998.

Identification of Each Work: Give all of the requested information for each contribution. The registration number should be that for the contribution itself if it was separately registered, and the registration number for the periodical issue if it was not.

6,7,8 SPACE 6,7,8: Fee, Correspondence, Certification, Return Address

Deposit Account: If you maintain a Deposit Account in the Copyright Office, identify it in space 6. Otherwise, leave the space blank and send the fee of $20 with your application and deposit.

Correspondence: This space should contain the name, address, area code, telephone number, and fax number (if available) of the person to be consulted if correspondence about this application becomes necessary.

Certification (Space 7): The renewal application is not acceptable unless it bears the date and the handwritten signature of the renewal claimant or the duly authorized agent of the renewal claimant.

Address for Return of Certificate (Space 8): The address box must be completed legibly, since the certificate will be returned in a window envelope.

FORM RE

For Renewal of a Work
UNITED STATES COPYRIGHT OFFICE

REGISTRATION NUMBER

_____

EFFECTIVE DATE OF RENEWAL REGISTRATION

_____

| Month | Day | Year |

DO NOT WRITE ABOVE THIS LINE. IF YOU NEED MORE SPACE, USE A SEPARATE CONTINUATION SHEET (FORM RE/CON).

RENEWAL CLAIMANT(S), ADDRESS(ES), AND STATEMENT OF CLAIM   ▼(See Instructions)

1
Name ....
Address ....
Claiming as ....
(Use appropriate statement from instructions)

2
Name ....
Address ....
Claiming as ....

3
Name ....
Address ....
Claiming as ....

TITLE OF WORK IN WHICH RENEWAL IS CLAIMED   ▼

RENEWABLE MATTER ▼

PUBLICATION AS A CONTRIBUTION If this work was published as a contribution to a periodical, serial, or other composite work, give information about the collective work in which the contribution appeared.   **Title of Collective Work ▼**

If published in a periodical or serial give: **Volume ▼**   **Number ▼**   **Issue Date ▼**

AUTHOR(S) OF RENEWABLE MATTER   ▼

ORIGINAL REGISTRATION NUMBER ▼ ORIGINAL COPYRIGHT CLAIMANT ▼

ORIGINAL DATE OF COPYRIGHT

If the original registration for this work was made in published form, give: | If the original registration for this work was made in unpublished form, give:
DATE OF PUBLICATION: _____   OR   DATE OF REGISTRATION: _____
(Month)   (Day)   (Year)   (Month)   (Day)   (Year)

MORE ON BACK ▶   ¥ Complete all applicable spaces (numbers 5-8) on the reverse side of this page.   **DO NOT WRITE HERE**
                     ¥ See detailed instructions.   ¥ Sign the form at space 7.   Page 1 of _____ pages

DO NOT WRITE ABOVE THIS LINE. IF YOU NEED MORE SPACE, USE A SEPARATE CONTINUATION SHEET (FORM RE/CON).

RENEWAL FOR GROUP OF WORKS BY SAME AUTHOR: To make a single registration for a group of works by the same individual author published as contributions to periodicals (see instructions), give full information about each contribution. If more space is needed, request continuation sheet (Form RE/CON).

1

Title of Contribution: ....

Title of Periodical: .... Vol: .... No: .... Issue Date: ....

Date of Publication: .... Registration Number: ....
          (Month)   (Day)   (Year)

2

Title of Contribution: ....

Title of Periodical: .... Vol: .... No: .... Issue Date: ....

Date of Publication: .... Registration Number: ....
          (Month)   (Day)   (Year)

3

Title of Contribution: ....

Title of Periodical: .... Vol: .... No: .... Issue Date: ....

Date of Publication: .... Registration Number: ....
          (Month)   (Day)   (Year)

4

Title of Contribution: ....

Title of Periodical: .... Vol: .... No: .... Issue Date: ....

Date of Publication: .... Registration Number: ....
          (Month)   (Day)   (Year)

DEPOSIT ACCOUNT: If the registration fee is to be charged to a Deposit Account established in the Copyright Office, give name and number of Account.

Name _____

Account Number _____

Area code and daytime telephone number ▶ _____

CORRESPONDENCE: Give name and address to which correspondence about this application should be sent.

Name _____

Address _____
                                            (Apt)

_____
(City)   (State)   (ZIP)

Fax number ▶

CERTIFICATION* I, the undersigned, hereby certify that I am the: (Check one)
❑ renewal claimant   ❑ duly authorized agent of _____
                                               (Name of renewal claimant) ▲
of the work identified in this application and that the statements made by me in this application are correct to the best of my knowledge.

Typed or printed name ▼   Date ▼

☞   Handwritten signature (X)▼

MAIL CERTIFI- CATE TO

Name ▼

Certificate will be mailed in window envelope

Number/Street/Apt ▼

City/State/ZIP ▼

*17 U.S.C./506(e): Any person who knowingly makes a false representation of a material fact in the application for copyright registration provided for by section 409, or in any written statement filed in connection with the application, shall be fined not more than $2,500.

April 1996 30,000   ♻ PRINTED ON RECYCLED PAPER   ☆ U.S. GOVERNMENT PRINTING OFFICE: 1996-405-104/20,045

✒ Filling Out Application Form GATT

Detach and read these instructions before completing this form.
Make sure all applicable spaces have been filled in before you return this form.

FINAL 9/21/95

────── BASIC INFORMATION ──────

When to use this form: Use Form GATT on or after January 1, 1996, to register a copyright claim in a work in which U.S. copyright was restored under the 1994 Uruguay Round Agreements Act (URAA).

This form is appropriate to register a single work or a series of works published under a single title in multiple episodes, installments, or issues **during the same calendar year.** The author(s) for each work in the series must be the same, and the owner(s) of U.S. copyright for each work in the series must be the same. Note: The author and the owner of U.S. copyright do not have to be the same party.

Restoration of copyright: Works from any source country eligible under the URAA may be subject to automatic copyright restoration. However, to be so restored, a work must meet the following requirements:

1. The work is not in the public domain in its source country through expiration of the term of protection.

2. The work is in the public domain in the United States due to
   a. noncompliance with U.S. copyright formalities;
   b. lack of subject matter protection in the case of sound recordings fixed before February 15, 1972; or
   c. lack of national eligibility.

3. The work has at least one author (or rightholder in the case of sound recordings) who was, at the time the work was created, a national or domiciliary of an eligible country.

4. If published, the work was first published in an eligible country and was not published in the United States during the 30-day period following publication in the eligible country.

Note about *architectural works*: Restoration of U.S. copyright for architectural works is available only to architectural works published or constructed on or after December 1, 1990.

Definitions:

Eligible country: A nation, other than the United States, that is a member of the Berne Convention, or a member of the World Trade Organization, or is subject to a presidential proclamation restoring the U.S. copyright to works of that nation on the basis of reciprocal treatment.

Source country of a restored work: A nation other than the United States.

For an unpublished work, the source country is the eligible country of which the author is a national or domiciliary. If a restored work has more than one author, the source country is the country of which the majority of foreign authors are nationals or domiciliaries. If the majority of authors are not foreign, the source country is the nation other than the United States that has the most significant contacts with the work.

For a published work, the source country is the eligible country in which the work was first published. If the restored work was published simultaneously in two or more eligible countries, the source country is the eligible country that has the most significant contacts with the work.

Owner of U.S. copyright : A claim in a restored work may be registered only in the name of the owner(s) of the U.S. copyright, that is, in the name of the owner(s) of all U.S. rights in that work. A licensee or other owner of only certain exclusive rights in a work is not permitted to register a claim in a restored work in his name.

Requirements for registration: Send a completed Form GATT, plus a deposit of the work(s) to be registered, and the $20.00 filing fee together in one package addressed to:
URAA/GATT NIEs and Registrations
Southwest Station P.O. Box 72400
Washington, D.C. 20024 U.S.A.

For **delivery instructions for film prints** (16 or 35 mm), contact the Performing Arts Section of the Examining Division at (202)707-6040 or fax (202)707-1236.

Application Form:

Complete Form GATT legibly in black ink or type. Photocopies of the form are permitted if reproduced on good quality 8 1/2 by 11-inch white paper and printed head to head so that page two is on the back of page one.

Deposit:

Unpublished Sound Recordings: Send one phonorecord that best represents the copyrightable content of the work in which U.S. rights are restored and for which registration is being made, for example, audio tape, vinyl disc, or compact disc.

Published works: Send one copy that best represents the copyrightable content of each work in which U.S. rights are restored and for which registration is being made, in the following order of preference:

1. The work as first published;
2. A reprint or re-release of the work as first published;
3. A photocopy or identical reproduction of the work as first published;
4. A revised version containing a substantial amount of the copyrightable content of the restored work as first published, **together with** a written statement of the percentage of the restored work appearing in the revised version.

Exceptions: Please note the following exceptions to the deposit policy.

Previously registered works : No deposit needed for works previously registered in the U.S. Copyright Office.

Three-dimensional works of the visual arts: One or more photographs, preferably in color.

Machine-readable works : For works embodied only in machine-readable format,
   a. One machine-readable copy plus a descriptive statement* or
   b. Representative excerpts of the work, such as printouts or, if the work is an audiovisual work, a videotape.

* A descriptive statement for a machine-readable work is a separate written statement giving the title of the work, nature of the work (for example, computer program, database, videogame, etc.), plus a brief description of the purpose or subject matter of the work.

Fee: The $20.00 filing fee may be paid in any of the following ways:

Checks, money orders, or bank drafts made payable to the Register of Copyrights and redeemable without service or exchange fees through a U.S. institution, must be payable in U.S. dollars, and must be imprinted with American Banking Association routing numbers. Currency, international money orders, and postal money orders that are negotiable only at a post office are **not** acceptable.

Copyright Office deposit account: This is an account into which an applicant deposits money in advance for use in paying copyright fees. For information on deposit accounts, request Circular 5, "How to Open and Maintain a Deposit Account in the Copyright Office."

Credit cards (for use **only** in filings under the URAA): The Copyright Office will accept VISA, MasterCard, and American Express credit cards. Debit cards are **not** acceptable.

To charge the filing fee on a credit card, include **in a separate letter** the type of card, name of individual or firm as it appears on the card, the account number, expiration date, the total amount, and the signature of the card holder authorizing the Office to charge the fee to the account. DO NOT GIVE CREDIT CARD INFORMATION ANYWHERE ON THE APPLICATION FORM ITSELF.

For Further Information:
To request application forms or information about registration for works under URAA, contact:

Publications Section, LM 455
Copyright Office
Library of Congress
Washington, D.C. 20559-6000

Phone: (202) 707-3000
Fax: (202) 707-3698 (Forms and circulars will not be faxed, but sent by postal mail).

For online information (Internet):
For the World Wide Web use
http://lcweb.loc.gov/copyright.
Telnet or gopher to **marvel.loc.gov**
or the numeric address 140.147.248.7 (log in as "marvel").

LINE-BY-LINE INSTRUCTIONS
Please type or print using black ink.

1 SPACE 1: Title

a. Give the full title of this work as it appears on the copy or phonorecord, followed by an English translation if appropriate.

For a series of works published under a single title in episodes, installments, or issues, give the single title as it appears on the copy of each issue, followed by the total number of issues included in this registration. **Example:** Title: "La Vie (52 issues)." English translation: "Life."

b. Description of Work: Check the box (or boxes) that best describes this work.

2 SPACE 2: Author(s)

Name at least one eligible author as determined by the applicable law of the source country. To list more than two authors, use a continuation sheet Form GATT/CON. For a published series, the author(s) must be the same for all episodes, installments, or issues.

For each author listed, give the nationality and domicile of that author at the time the work was created.

If the author is deceased, give the year of death.

3 SPACE 3: Year and Nation of Publication

Give the year and nation in which the work or series was first published.

4 SPACE 4: Owner(s) of U.S. Copyright

a. Give the name and address of the current owner(s). For a series of works published under a single title, the owner(s) of the U.S. copyright must be the same for all episodes, installments, or issues.

b. Transfer of Copyright: If the author(s) named at space 2 is not the current owner(s) of U.S. copyright, describe how the copyright was transferred. **Examples:** "assignment of all U.S. rights," "by contract," or "by will."

5 SPACE 5: Limitation of Copyright, when less than entire work is subject to registration

If the situation described in 1. or 2. below applies, complete this space giving a brief general description of what is being registered.
1. The restored U.S. copyright in part of this work is owned by another party. **Example:** If the owner named in space 4 owns the rights in the text of a book but the illustrations are owned by someone else, state "text."
2. The work is derived from or based on an earlier work. **Examples:** If the work being registered is a screenplay based on a novel, state "screenplay." If the work is a revised edition of a textbook and contains some new text, state "revisions and additional text."

6 SPACE 6: Registration Number and Year for Previous U.S. Registration

If this work was previously registered with the U.S. Copyright Office give the registration number and the year of registration, if known.
Examples: "Flemish Poets" Ai 345-123, 1970
"Concerto for Flute" Eu 123-456, 1963.

7 SPACE 7: Deposit Account, Correspondence

a. Deposit Account: Give the name and number of an existing deposit account. Do NOT give credit card information in this space or anywhere on the application form. Give credit card information in a separate letter.

b. Correspondence: Give the name, address, and telephone and fax numbers of the person to contact.

8 SPACE 8: Certification

The author or owner of U.S. copyright or the authorized agent must sign in ink.

9 SPACE 9: Mailing Address

Give the name and address of the party to whom the certificate of registration will be mailed. Information in this box must be legible (black ink or type) to assure delivery to proper address.

FORM GATT
For a Restored Work
UNITED STATES COPYRIGHT OFFICE

REGISTRATION NUMBER

REGISTRATION NUMBER

| TX | PA | VA | SR | SRU |

EFFECTIVE DATE OF REGISTRATION

Month _____ Day _____ Year _____

DO NOT WRITE ABOVE THIS LINE. IF YOU NEED MORE SPACE, USE FORM GATT/CON.

1

a TITLE:

English translation:

b DESCRIPTION OF THE WORK: *(Check one or more)*
- ☐ literary work
- ☐ musical work, including any accompanying words
- ☐ dramatic work, including any accompanying music
- ☐ pantomime or choreographic work
- ☐ pictorial, graphic, or sculptural work
- ☐ motion picture or other audiovisual work
- ☐ architectural work
- ☐ sound recording, created in _____ (year)

2

a AUTHOR(S):
Name:

Citizenship (when work was created):
Domicile (when work was created):
Date of death:

b Name:

Citizenship (when work was created):
Domicile (when work was created):
Date of death:

3 YEAR AND NATION OF PUBLICATION: (if work was published, give the year and nation in which it was first published.)
Year:

Nation:

4

a OWNER(S) OF U.S. COPYRIGHT:
Name:

Address:

b Means by which copyright ownership was transferred
(if owner is not the author):

DO NOT WRITE HERE
OFFICE USE ONLY

APPLICATION RECEIVED

DEPOSIT RECEIVED

FUNDS RECEIVED

EXAMINED BY

FORM GATT

CHECKED BY

☐ CORRESPONDENCE
☐ Yes

FOR
COPYRIGHT
OFFICE
USE
ONLY

DO NOT WRITE ABOVE THIS LINE. IF YOU NEED MORE SPACE, USE FORM GATT/CON.

LIMITATION OF COPYRIGHT: If the registration does not extend to the entire work, describe the material that is covered by the registration:
(see instructions)

5

PREVIOUS REGISTRATION: If this work was ever registered in the U.S. Copyright Office, give the registration number and year if known:

6

DEPOSIT ACCOUNT If the registration fee is to be charged to a deposit account established in the Copyright Office, give the name and number of that account. **Do not give credit card information on this form.**
Name ▼   Account Number ▼

7

CORRESPONDENCE Give the name and address to which correspondence about this application should be sent.   ☐ Same as space 4a.
                                                                                                                                              ☐ Same as space 9.

Area or Country Code and Telephone Number ▶   Fax Number ▶

CERTIFICATION* I, the undersigned, hereby certify that I am the: (Check one)
☐ Author
☐ Owner of U. S. copyright
☐ Agent of _____
(Name of author or owner of U.S. copyright)
of the work identified in this application and that the statements made by me in this application are correct to the best of my knowledge.

8

Typed or printed name: Date:

Handwritten signature (X) ▼

**MAIL
CERTIFICATE
TO**

Name ▼

**Certificate
will be
mailed in a
window
envelope**

Number/Street/Apt ▼

City/State/ZIP/Nation▼

YOU MUST:
♦ Complete all necessary spaces
♦ Sign your application in space 8
SEND ALL 3 ELEMENTS
IN THE SAME PACKAGE:
1. Application form
2. Nonrefundable filing fee
   (See instructions)
   payable to *Register of Copyrights*
3. Deposit
MAIL TO:
URAA/GATT NIEs and Registrations
Southwest Station P.O. Box 72400
Washington, D.C. 20024 U.S.A.

9

*17 U.S.C./506(e): Any person who knowingly makes a false representation of a material fact in the application for copyright registration provided for by section 409, or in any written statement filed in connection with the application, shall be fined not more than $2,500.

September 1995 100,000   ✪ PRINTED ON RECYCLED PAPER   ☆U.S. COPYRIGHT OFFICE WWW: March 1998

✐ Application Form CA ✐

Detach and read these instructions before completing this form.
Make sure all applicable spaces have been filled in before you return this form.

▬▬▬▬▬▬▬▬▬▬▬ ▬ BASIC INFORMATION ▬▬▬▬▬▬▬▬▬▬▬▬

Use Form CA When:
* An earlier registration has been completed in the Copyright Office; and
* Some of the facts given in that registration are incorrect or incomplete; and
* You want to place the correct or complete facts on record.

Purpose of Supplementary Copyright Registration:
As a rule, only one basic copyright registration can be made for the same work. To take care of cases where information in the basic registration turns out to be incorrect or incomplete, section 408(d) of the copyright law provides for "the filing of an application for supplementary registration, to correct an error in a copyright registration or to amplify the information given in a registration."

Who May File:
Once basic registration has been made for a work, any author or other copyright claimant or owner of any exclusive right in the work or the duly authorized agent of any such author, other claimant, or owner who wishes to correct or amplify the information given in the basic registration may submit Form CA.

Please Note:
Do not use Form CA to correct errors in statements on the copies or phonorecords of the work in question or to reflect changes in the content of the work. If the work has been changed substantially, you should consider making an entirely new registration for the revised version to cover the additions or revisions.

Do not use Form CA as a substitute for renewal registration. Renewal of copyright cannot be accomplished by using Form CA. For information on renewal of copyright, request Circular 15, "Renewal of Copyright," from the Copyright Office. Do not use Form CA to correct an error regarding publication when the work was registered as an unpublished work.

Do not use Form CA as a substitute for recording a transfer of copyright or other document pertaining to rights under a copyright. Recording a document under section 205 of the statute gives all persons constructive notice of the facts stated in the document and may have other important consequences in cases of infringement or conflicting transfers. Supplementary registration does not have that legal effect.

For information on recording a document, request Circular 12, "Recordation of Transfers and Other Documents," from the Copyright Office. To record a document in the Copyright Office, request the Document Cover Sheet.

How to Apply for Supplementary Registration:
First: Study the information on this page to make sure that filing an application on Form CA is the best procedure to follow in your case.
Second: Read the back of this page for specific instructions on filling out Form CA. Before starting to complete the form, make sure that you have all the necessary detailed information from the certificate of the basic registration.

Third: Complete all applicable spaces on the form following the line-by-line instructions on the back of this page. Use a typewriter, or print the information in black ink.
Fourth: Detach this sheet and send your completed Form CA along with a **photocopy** of the front and back of the certificate of registration being amended to:

> Library of Congress
> Copyright Office
> 101 Independence Avenue, S.E.
> Washington, D.C. 20559-6000

Unless you have a Deposit Account in the Copyright Office, your application must be accompanied by a nonrefundable filing fee in the form of a check or money order for $20* payable to: *Register of Copyrights.* Do not send copies, phonorecords, or supporting documents other than the photocopied certificate with your application. They cannot be made part of the record of a supplementary registration.

What Happens When a Supplementary Registration Is Made?
When a supplementary registration is completed, the Copyright Office will assign it a new registration number in the appropriate registration category and will issue a certificate of supplementary registration under that number. The basic registration will not be cancelled. The two registrations will stand in the Copyright Office records. The supplementary registration will have the effect of calling the public's attention to a possible error or omission in the basic registration and of placing the correct facts or the additional information on official record.

> *** NOTE:** Registration filing fees are effective through June 30, 1999. For information on the fee changes, please write the Copyright Office, check the Copyright Office Website at http://www.loc.gov/copyright, or call (202) 707-3000 for the latest fee information.

For Further Information
* **Internet:** Circulars, application forms, announcements, regulations, and other related materials are available at http://www.loc.gov/copyright.
* **Fax:** Circulars are available from Fax-on-Demand at (202) 707-2600.
* **Telephone:** For information about copyright, call the Public Information Office at (202) 707 3000. Recorded information is available 24 hours a day. Or, if you know which application forms and circulars you want, call the Forms and Publications Hotline at (202) 707-9100 24 hours a day.
* **Regular Mail:** Write to:

> Library of Congress
> Copyright Office
> Public Information Office
> 101 Independence Avenue, S.E.
> Washington, D.C. 20599-6000

LINE-BY-LINE INSTRUCTIONS

Please type or print neatly using black ink. The certificate of registration is created by copying your CA application form.

SPACE A: Identification of Basic Registration

General Instructions: The information in this part identifies the basic registration that will be corrected or amplified. Even if the purpose of filing Form CA is to change one of these items, each item must agree exactly with the information as it already appears in the basic registration, that is, as it appears in the registration you wish to correct. Do not give any new information in this part.

Title of Work: Give the title as it appears in the basic registration.

Registration Number: Give the registration number (the series of numbers preceded by one or more letters) that appears in the upper right-hand corner of the certificate of registration. Give only one basic registration number since one CA form may correct or amend only one basic registration.

Registration Date: Give the year when the basic registration was completed.

Name(s) of Author(s) and Copyright Claimant(s): Give all the names as they appear in the basic registration.

SPACE B: Correction

General Instructions: Complete this part **only** if information in the basic registration **was incorrect at the time that basic registration was made.** Leave this part blank and complete Part C instead if your purpose is to add, update, or clarify information rather than to rectify an actual error.

Location and Nature of Incorrect Information: Give the line number and the heading or description of the space in the basic registration where the error occurs. Example: Line number 2…Citizenship of author.

Incorrect Information as It Appears in Basic Registration: Transcribe the incorrect statement exactly as it appears in the basic registration, even if you have already given this information in Part A.

Corrected Information: Give the statement as it should have appeared in the application of the basic registration.

Explanation of Correction: You may need to add an explanation to clarify this correction.

SPACE C: Amplification

General Instructions: Complete this part if you want to provide any of the following: (1) information that was omitted at the time of basic registration; (2) changes in facts other than ownership but including changes such as title or address of claimant that have occurred since the basic registration; or (3) explanations clarifying information in the basic registration.

Location and Nature of Information to be Amplified: Give the line number and the heading or description of the space in the basic registration where the information to be amplified appears.

Amplified Information: Give a statement of the additional, updated, or explanatory information as clearly and succinctly as possible. You should add an explanation of the amplification if it is necessary.

 SPACES D,E,F,G: Continuation, Fee, Certification, Return Address

Continuation (Part D): Use this space if you do not have enough room in Parts B or C.

Deposit Account and Mailing Instructions (Part E): If you maintain a Deposit Account in the Copyright Office, identify it in Part E. Otherwise, you will need to send the nonrefundable filing fee* with your form. The space headed "Correspondence" should contain the name, address, telephone number with area code, and fax and email numbers, if available, of the person to be consulted if correspondence about the form becomes necessary.

Certification (Part F): The application is not acceptable unless it bears the handwritten signature of the author, or other copyright claimant, or of the owner of exclusive right(s), or of the duly authorized agent of such author, claimant, or owner.

Address for Return of Certificate (Part G): The address box must be completed legibly, since a reproduced image of that space will appear in the window of the mailing envelope. *See **NOTE** on previous page.

■FORM CA

For Supplementary Registration
UNITED STATES COPYRIGHT OFFICE

REGISTRATION NUMBER

TX	TXU	PA	PAU	VA	VAU	SR	SRU	RE

EFFECTIVE DATE OF SUPPLEMENTARY REGISTRATION

Month   Day   Year

DO NOT WRITE ABOVE THIS LINE. IF YOU NEED MORE SPACE, USE A SEPARATE CONTINUATION SHEET.

A

Title of Work ▼

Registration Number of the Basic Registration ▼

Year of Basic Registration ▼

Name(s) of Author(s) ▼

Name(s) of Copyright Claimant(s) ▼

B

Location and Nature of Incorrect Information in Basic Registration ▼

Line Number _____ Line Heading or Description _____

Incorrect Information as It Appears in Basic Registration ▼

Corrected Information ▼

Explanation of Correction ▼

C

Location and Nature of Information in Basic Registration to be Amplified ▼

Line Number _____ Line Heading or Description _____

Amplified Information and Explanation of Information ▼

MORE ON BACK ▶   ¥ Complete all applicable spaces (D-G) on the reverse side of this page.
    ¥ See detailed instructions.   ¥ Sign the form at Space F.

DO NOT WRITE HERE

Page 1 of _____ pages

FORM CA RECEIVED	**FORM CA**
FUNDS RECEIVED DATE	
EXAMINED BY	FOR COPYRIGHT OFFICE USE ONLY
CORRESPONDENCE ❑	
REFERENCE TO THIS REGISTRATION ADDED TO BASIC REGISTRATION ❑ YES ❑ NO	

DO NOT WRITE ABOVE THIS LINE. IF YOU NEED MORE SPACE, USE A SEPARATE CONTINUATION SHEET.

Continuation of: ❑ Part B or ❑ Part C

D

Correspondence: Give name and address to which correspondence about this application should be sent.

E

Phone (____)_____ Fax (____)_____ Email _____

Deposit Account: If the registration fee is to be charged to a Deposit Account established in the Copyright Office, give name and number of Account.

Name _____

Account Number _____

Certification* I, the undersigned, hereby certify that I am the: (Check only one)

❑ author ❑ owner of exclusive right(s)
❑ other copyright claimant ❑ duly authorized agent of _____
Name of author or other copyright claimant, or owner of exclusive right(s) ▲

of the work identified in this application and that the statements made by me in this application are correct to the best of my knowledge.

Typed or printed name ▼ _____ Date ▼ _____

Handwritten signature (X) ▼ _____

F

☞

Certificate will be mailed in window envelope to this address:	Name ▼	YOU MUST: ❥ Complete all necessary spaces ❥ Sign your application in Space F	*Registration filing fees are effective through June 30 1999. For the latest fee information, write the Copyright Office, check the Copyright Office Website at http:// www.loc.gov/copyright, or call (202) 707-3000.
	Number/Street/Apt ▼	SEND ALL ELEMENTS IN THE SAME PACKAGE: 1. Application form 2. Nonrefundable filing fee in check or money order payable to *Register of Copyrights*	
	City/State/ZIP ▼	MAIL TO: Library of Congress Copyright Office 101 Independence Avenue, S.E. Washington, D.C. 20559-6000	

G

*17 U.S.C. / 506(e): Any person who knowingly makes a false representation of a material fact in the application for copyright registration provided for by section 409, or in any written statement filed in connection with the application, shall be fined not more than $2,500.

December 1998 15,000 ♲ PRINTED ON RECYCLED PAPER

☆ U.S. GOVERNMENT PRINTING OFFICE: 1998-454-879/80,048

CONTINUATION SHEET
FOR APPLICATION FORMS

- This Continuation Sheet is used in conjunction with Forms CA, PA, SE, SR, TX, and VA **only**. Indicate which basic form you are continuing in the space in the upper right-hand corner.

- If at all possible, try to fit the information called for into the spaces provided on the basic form.

- If you do not have space enough for all the information you need to give on the basic form, use this Continuation Sheet and submit it with the basic form.

- If you submit this Continuation Sheet, clip (do not tape or staple) it to the basic form and fold the two together before submitting them.

- **Part A of this sheet is intended to identify the basic application.**
  Part B is a continuation of Space 2 on the basic application.
  Part C (on the reverse side of this sheet) is for the continuation of Spaces 1, 4, or 6 on the basic application.

DO NOT WRITE ABOVE THIS LINE. FOR COPYRIGHT OFFICE USE ONLY

■ **FORM** ____ /CON
UNITED STATES COPYRIGHT OFFICE

REGISTRATION NUMBER

PA PAU SE SEG SEU SR SRU TX TXU VA VAU

EFFECTIVE DATE OF REGISTRATION

(Month)   (Day)   (Year)
CONTINUATION SHEET RECEIVED

Page _____ of _____ pages

A
Identification of Application

IDENTIFICATION OF CONTINUATION SHEET: This sheet is a continuation of the application for copyright registration on the basic form submitted for the following work:
- TITLE: (Give the title as given under the heading "Title of this Work" in Space 1 of the basic form.)

- NAME(S) AND ADDRESS(ES) OF COPYRIGHT CLAIMANT(S) : (Give the name and address of at least one copyright claimant as given in Space 4 of the basic form.)

B
Continuation of Space 2

d

NAME OF AUTHOR ▼

DATES OF BIRTH AND DEATH
Year Born▼   Year Died▼

Was this contribution to the work a "work made for hire"?

AUTHOR?S NATIONALITY OR DOMICILE
Name of Country

☐ Yes
☐ No

OR { Citizen of ▶ _____
     { Domiciled in ▶ _____

WAS THIS AUTHOR?S CONTRIBUTION TO THE WORK
Anonymous? ☐ Yes ☐ No   If the answer to either of these questions is "Yes" see detailed
Pseudonymous? ☐ Yes ☐ No   instructions.

NATURE OF AUTHORSHIP Briefly describe nature of the material created by the author in which copyright is claimed. ▼

e

NAME OF AUTHOR ▼

DATES OF BIRTH AND DEATH
Year Born▼   Year Died▼

Was this contribution to the work a "work made for hire"?

AUTHOR?S NATIONALITY OR DOMICILE
Name of Country

☐ Yes
☐ No

OR { Citizen of ▶ _____
     { Domiciled in ▶ _____

WAS THIS AUTHOR?S CONTRIBUTION TO THE WORK
Anonymous? ☐ Yes ☐ No   If the answer to either of these questions is "Yes" see detailed
Pseudonymous? ☐ Yes ☐ No   instructions.

NATURE OF AUTHORSHIP Briefly describe nature of the material created by the author in which copyright is claimed. ▼

f

NAME OF AUTHOR ▼

DATES OF BIRTH AND DEATH
Year Born▼   Year Died▼

Was this contribution to the work a "work made for hire"?

AUTHOR?S NATIONALITY OR DOMICILE
Name of Country

☐ Yes
☐ No

OR { Citizen of ▶ _____
     { Domiciled in ▶ _____

WAS THIS AUTHOR?S CONTRIBUTION TO THE WORK
Anonymous? ☐ Yes ☐ No   If the answer to either of these questions is "Yes" see detailed
Pseudonymous? ☐ Yes ☐ No   instructions.

NATURE OF AUTHORSHIP Briefly describe nature of the material created by the author in which copyright is claimed. ▼

Use the reverse side of this sheet if you need more space for continuation of Spaces 1, 4, or 6 of the basic form.

CONTINUATION OF (Check which):   ☐ Space 1   ☐ Space 4   ☐ Space 6

C

**Continuation
of other
Spaces**

**MAIL
TO**

Name ▼

**Certificate
will be
mailed in
window
envelope**

Number/Street/Apt ▼

City/State/ZIP ▼

YOU MUST:
• Complete all necessary spaces
• Sign your application

SEND ALL 3 ELEMENTS
IN THE SAME PACKAGE:

1. Application form
2. Nonrefundable $20 filing fee
in check or money order
payable to *Register of Copyrights*

MAIL TO:
Register of Copyrights
Library of Congress
Washington, D.C. 20559-6000

D

**Address for
return of
certificate**

August 1995–150,000

☆U.S.COPYRIGHT OFFICE WWW FORM: 1995

Document Cover Sheet

Read these instructions carefully before completing this form. Make sure all applicable spaces have been properly filled in before you return this form. Otherwise, the form cannot be used.

BASIC INFORMATION

When to Use This Form: Use the Document Cover Sheet when you are submitting a document for recordation in the U.S. Copyright Office.
Mailing Requirements: It is important that you send **two** copies of the Document Cover Sheet, any additional sheets, the document, and the fee together in the same envelope or package. The Copyright Office cannot process them unless they are received together. Send to: *Library of Congress, Copyright Office, Documents Recordation Section, LM-462, 101 Independence Avenue, S.E., Washington, D.C. 20559-6000.*

Two copies of this Document Cover Sheet should be submitted with each document. Cover sheets should be typed or printed and should contain the information requested so the Copyright Office can process the document and return it. Be sure to complete the return address space. The Copyright Office will process the document based on the information in the document. Therefore, parties and titles should be clearly identified in the document or an attachment to it. Information for indexing will not be taken from the Document Cover Sheet. To be recordable, a document must satisfy the recordation requirements of the copyright code and Copyright Office regulations.

The person(s) submitting a document with a cover sheet is (are) solely responsible for verifying the correctness of the cover sheet and the sufficiency of the document. Recording a document submitted with or without a cover sheet does not constitute a determination by the Copyright Office of the document's validity or effect. Only a court may make such determinations.

Any cover sheets submitted will be recorded with the document as part of the official recordation.

SPACE-BY-SPACE INSTRUCTIONS

 SPACE 1: Name of Party or Parties to the Document
List up to the first three (3) parties to this document.

 SPACE 2: Date of Execution
Give the date the accompanying document (not this Cover Sheet) was executed and/or became effective.

SPACE 3: Completeness of Document
Check a box. All documents recorded under section 205 of the copyright code must be complete by their own terms in order to be recordable. Examples of section 205 documents include transfers of copyright ownerships and other documents pertaining to a copyright, such as exclusive and nonexclusive licenses, contracts, mortgages, powers of attorney, certificates of change of corporate name or title, wills, and decrees of distribution.

SPACE 4: Description of Document
Check a box that describes the document.

SPACE 5: Title of First Work
List the title of the first work included in the document.

 SPACE 6: Number of Titles in Document
The total number of titles determines the recordation fee.* The fee for a document of any length containing one title is $20. Additional titles are $10 for each group of 10 or fewer. In the case of multiple title documents, titles that are repeated in documents will be counted as a single title, except where the document lists different issues, volumes, chapters, or installments following the title. Each such entry will be regarded as a separate title and will be indexed separately and counted separately for purposes of computing the recordation fee. The Copyright Office will verify title counts.

 SPACE 7: Amount of Fee*
Calculate the fee from the information given in Space 6.

SPACE 8: Fee Enclosed
Check a box. If a Copyright Office Deposit Account is to be charged, give the Copyright Office Deposit Account number and name.

SPACE 9: Affirmation
This space must be completed by all applicants. The party to the document submitting it for recordation or his/her authorized agent should sign the affirmation and authorization contained in this space. This affirmation and authorization is not a substitute for the certification required for documents containing a photocopy signature. (See Certification, Space 10.) The affirmation must be signed even if you are signing Space 10.

 SPACE 10: Certification
Complete this section only if submitting photocopied documents in lieu of a document bearing the actual signature.
Certification: Any transfer of copyright ownership or other document pertaining to a copyright (section 205) may be recorded in the Copyright Office if the document bears the actual signature of the person or persons who executed (signed) the documents. If a photocopy of the original signed document is submitted, it must be accompanied by a sworn or official certification. A sworn certification signed by at least one of the parties to the document or their authorized representative (who is identified as such) at Space 10 will satisfy that requirement. **Copies of documents on file in a federal, state, or local government office must be accompanied by an official certification.**
If you sign Space 10, you must also have signed Space 9.

FEE CHANGES
Registration filing fees are effective through June 30, 1999. For information on the fee changes, write the Copyright Office, check http://www.loc.gov/copyright, or call (202) 707-3000. Beginning as early as January 1, 2000, the Copyright Office may impose a service charge when insufficient fees are received.

DOCUMENT COVER SHEET
For Recordation of Documents
UNITED STATES COPYRIGHT OFFICE

DATE OF RECORDATION
(Assigned by Copyright Office)

Month	Day	Year

Volume _____ Page _____

Volume _____ Page _____

FUNDS RECEIVED _____

Do not write above this line.

To the Register of Copyrights:

Please record the accompanying original document or copy thereof.

FOR OFFICE USE ONLY

1 Name of the party or parties to the document spelled as they appear in the document (List up to the first three)

_____
_____
_____

2 Date of execution and/or effective date of the accompanying document

(month)	(day)	(year)

3 Completeness of document
❑ Document is complete by its own terms.
❑ Document is not complete. Record "as is."

4 Description of document
❑ Transfer of Copyright
❑ Security Interest
❑ Change of Name of Owner
❑ Termination of Transfer(s) [Section 304]
❑ Shareware
❑ Life, Identity, Death Statement [Section 302]
❑ Transfer of Mask Works
❑ Other _____

5 Title of first work as given in the document _____

6 Total number of titles in document _____

7 Amount of fee calculated
$ _____

8 Fee enclosed
❑ Check
❑ Money Order

❑ Fee authorized to be charged to :
Copyright Office
Deposit Account number _____
Account name _____

9 Affirmation: I hereby affirm to the Copyright Office that the information given on this form is a true and correct representation of the accompanying document. This affirmation will not suffice as a certification of a photocopy signature on the document.
(Affirmation *must* be signed even if you are also signing Space 10.)

Signature _____

Date _____

Phone Number _____ Fax Number _____

10 Certification: Complete this certification in addition to the Affirmation if a photocopy of the original signed document is substituted for a document bearing the actual signature.
NOTE: This space *may not* be used for an official certification.
   I certify under penalty of perjury under the laws of the United States of America that the accompanying document is a true copy of the original document.

Signature _____

Duly Authorized Agent of: _____

Date _____

Recordation will be mailed in window envelope to this address:

Name▼ _____

Number/Street/Apt▼ _____

City/State/ZIP▼ _____

YOU MUST:
¥ Complete all necessary spaces
¥ Sign your Cover Sheet in Space 9
SEND ALL 3 ELEMENTS TOGETHER:
1. Two copies of the Document Cover Sheet
2. Check or money order payable to *Register of Copyrights*
3. Document
MAIL TO:
Library of Congress
Copyright Office
Documents Recordation Section, LM-462
101 Independence Avenue, S.E.
Washington, D.C. 20559-6000

*Knowingly and willfully falsifying material facts on this form may result in criminal liability. 18 U.S.C./1001.
December 1998 5,000   PRINTED ON RECYCLED PAPER

☆U.S. GOVERNMENT PRINTING OFFICE: 1998-454-879/80,049

Filling Out Adjunct Application Form GR/CP

Detach and read these instructions before completing this form.
Make sure all applicable spaces have been filled in before you return this form.

BASIC INFORMATION

When to Use This Form: Form GR/CP is the appropriate adjunct application form to use when you are submitting a basic application on Form TX, Form PA, or Form VA for a group of works that qualify for a single registration under section 408(c)(2) of the copyright statute.

This Form:
- Can be used solely as an adjunct to a basic application for copyright registration.
- Is not acceptable unless submitted together with Form TX, Form PA, or Form VA.
- Is acceptable only if the group of works listed on it all qualify for a single copyright registration under 17 U.S.C. § 408 (c)(2).

When Does a Group of Works Qualify for a Single Registration Under 17 U.S.C. §408 (c)(2)? For all works first published on or after March 1, 1989, a single copyright registration for a group of works can be made if all of the following conditions are met:

(1) All of the works are by the same author, who is an individual (not an employer for hire); and

(2) All of the works were first published as contributions to periodicals (including newspapers) within a 12-month period; and

(3) All of the works have the same copyright claimant; and

(4) One copy of the entire periodical issue or newspaper section in which each contribution was first published; or a photocopy of the contribution itself; or a photocopy of the entire page containing the contribution; or the entire page containing the contribution cut or torn from the collective work; or the contribution cut or torn from the collective work; or photographs or photographic slides of the contribution or entire page containing the contribution as long as all contents of the contributions are clear and legible are (is) deposited with the application; and

(5) The application identifies each contribution separately, including the periodical containing it and the date of its first publication.

NOTE: For contributions that were first published prior to March 1, 1989, in addition to the conditions listed above, each contribution as first published must have borne a separate copyright notice, and the name of the owner of copyright in the work (or an abbreviation or alternative designation of the owner) must have been the same in each notice.

How to Apply for Group Registration:

First: Study the information on this page to make sure that all of the works you want to register together as a group qualify for a single registration.

Second: Read through the **Procedure for Group Registration** in the next column. Decide which form you should use for the basic registration (Form TX for nondramatic literary works; Form PA for musical, dramatic, and other works of the performing arts; or Form VA for pictorial and graphic works). Be sure that you have all of the information you need before you start filling out both the basic and the adjunct application forms.

Third: Complete the basic application form, following the detailed instructions accompanying it **and the special instructions on the reverse of this page.**

Fourth: Complete the adjunct application on Form GR/CP and mail it, together with the basic application form and the required copy of each contribution, to: Register of Copyrights
Library of Congress
Washington, D.C. 20559-6000
Unless you have a Deposit Account in the Copyright Office, your application and copies must be accompanied by a check or money order for $20, payable to *Register of Copyrights.*

Procedure for Group Registration

Two Application Forms Must Be Filed
When you apply for a single registration to cover a group of contributions to periodicals, you must submit two application forms:
(1) A basic application on either Form TX, Form PA, or Form VA. It must contain all of the information required for copyright registration except the titles and information concerning publication of the contributions.
(2) An adjunct application on Form GR/CP. The purpose of this form is to provide separate identification for each of the contributions and to give information about their first publication, as required by the statute.

Which Basic Application Form To Use
The basic application form you choose to submit should be determined by the nature of the contributions you are registering. As long as they meet the statutory qualifications for group registration (outlined above), the contributions can be registered together even if they are entirely different in nature, type, or content. However, you must choose which of three forms is generally the most appropriate on which to submit your basic application:

Form TX: for nondramatic literary works consisting primarily of text. Examples are fiction, verse, articles, news stories, features, essays, reviews, editorials, columns, quizzes, puzzles, and advertising copy.
Form PA: for works of the performing arts. Examples are music, drama, choreography, and pantomimes.
Form VA: for works of the visual arts. Examples are photographs, drawings, paintings, prints, art reproductions, cartoons, comic strips, charts, diagrams, maps, pictorial ornamentation, and pictorial or graphic material published as advertising.

If your contributions differ in nature, choose the form most suitable for the majority of them.

Registration Fee for Group Registration
The fee for registration of a group of contributions to periodicals is $20, no matter how many contributions are listed on Form GR/CP. Unless you maintain a Deposit Account in the Copyright Office, the registration fee must accompany your application forms and copies. Make your remittance payable to: *Register of Copyrights.*

What Copies Should Be Deposited for Group Registration?
The application forms you file for group registration must be accompanied by one complete copy of each published contribution listed on Form GR/CP. The deposit may consist of the entire issue of the periodical containing the contribution. Or, if the contribution was first published in a newspaper, the deposit may consist of the entire section in which the contribution appeared. Tear sheets or proof copies are also acceptable for deposit. Additional acceptable deposits for a GR/CP registration include a photocopy of the contribution itself; a photocopy of the entire page containing the contribution; the entire page containing the contribution cut or torn from the collective work; the contribution cut or torn from the collective work; and photographs or photographic slides of the contribution or entire page containing the contribution as long as all contents of the contributions are clear and legible.

NOTE: Since these deposit alternatives differ from the current regulations, the Office will automatically grant special relief upon receipt. There is no need for the applicant to request such relief in writing. This is being done to facilitate registration pending a change in the regulations.

Copyright Notice Requirements
For published works, the law provides that a copyright notice in a specified form "may be placed on all publicly distributed copies from which the work can be visually perceived." The required form of the notice generally consists of three elements: (1) the symbol "©," or the word

continued ▶

"Copyright," or the abbreviation "Copr."; (2) the year of first publication of the work; and (3) the name of the owner of copyright in the work, or an abbreviation or alternative form of the name. For example: "© 1995 Samuel Craig."

Works published prior to March 1, 1989, **must** carry a notice of copyright or risk loss of copyright protection. Furthermore, among the conditions for group registration of contributions to periodicals for works first **published prior to March 1, 1989,** the statute establishes two requirements involving the copyright notice:

(1) Each of the contributions as first published must have borne a separate copyright notice; and

(2) "The name of the owner of copyright in the work, or an abbreviation by which the name can be recognized, or a generally known alternative designation of the owner" must have been the same in each notice.

Works first published after March 1, 1989, need not meet the two above requirements.

> NOTE: The advantage of group registration is that it allows any number of works published within a 12-month period to be registered "on the basis of a single deposit, application, and registration fee." On the other hand, group registration may also have disadvantages under certain circumstances. If infringement of a published work begins before the work has been registered, the copyright owner can still obtain the ordinary remedies for copyright infringement (including injunctions, actual damages and profits, and impounding and disposition of infringing articles). However, in that situation—where the copyright in a published work is infringed before registration is made—the owner cannot obtain special remedies (statutory damages and attorney's fees) unless registration was made within 3 months after first publication of the work.

HOW TO FILL OUT THE BASIC APPLICATION FORM WHEN APPLYING FOR GROUP REGISTRATION

In general, the instructions for filling out the basic application (Form TX, Form PA, or Form VA) apply to group registrations. In addition, please observe the following specific instructions:

1 SPACE 1: Title

Do not give information concerning any of the contributions in space 1 of the basic application. Instead, in the block headed "Title of this Work," state: "See Form GR/CP, attached." Leave the other blocks in space 1 blank.

2 SPACE 2: Author

Give the name and other information concerning the author of all of the contributions listed in Form GR/CP. To qualify for group registration, all of the contributions must have been written by the same individual author.

3 SPACE 3: Creation and Publication

In the block calling for the year of creation, give the year of creation of the last of the contributions to be completed. Leave the block calling for the date and nation of first publication blank.

4 SPACE 4: Claimant

Give all of the requested information, which must be the same for all of the contributions listed on Form GR/CP.

OTHER SPACES:

Complete all of the applicable spaces and be sure that the form is signed in the certification space.

HOW TO FILL OUT FORM GR/CP

Please type or print using black ink.

A PART A: Identification of Application

• **Identification of Basic Application:** Indicate, by checking one of the boxes, which of the basic application forms (Form TX, Form PA, or Form VA) you are filing for registration.

• **Identification of Author and Claimant:** Give the name of the individual author exactly as it appears in line 2 of the basic application, and give the name of the copyright claimant exactly as it appears in line 4. These must be the same for all of the contributions listed in Part B of Form GR/CP.

B PART B: Registration for Group of Contributions

• **General Instructions:** Under the statute, a group of contributions to periodicals will qualify for a single registration only if the application "identifies each work separately, including the periodical containing it and its date of first publication." Part B of the Form GR/CP provides enough lines to list 19 separate contributions; if you need more space, use additional Forms GR/CP. If possible, list the contributions in the order of their publication, giving the earliest first. Number each line consecutively.

• **Important:** All of the contributions listed on Form GR/CP must have been published within a single 12-month period. This does not mean that all of the contributions must have been published during the same calendar year, but it does mean that, to be grouped in a single application, the earliest and latest contributions must not have been published more than 12 months apart. Example: Contributions published on April 1, 1978, July 1, 1978, and March 1, 1979, could be grouped together, but a contribution published on April 15, 1979, could not be registered with them as part of the group.

• **Title of Contribution:** Each contribution must be given a title that is capable of identifying that particular work and of distinguishing it from others. If the contribution as published in the periodical bears a title (or an identifying phrase that could serve as a title), transcribe its wording completely and exactly.

• **Identification of Periodical:** Give the overall title of the periodical in which the contribution was first published, together with the volume and issue number (if any) and the issue date.

• **Pages:** Give the number of the page of the periodical issue on which the contribution appeared. If the contribution covered more than one page, give the inclusive pages, if possible.

• **First Publication:** The statute defines "publication" as "the distribution of copies or phonorecords of a work to the public by sale or other transfer of ownership, or by rental, lease, or lending"; a work is also "published" if there has been an "offering to distribute copies or phonorecords to a group of persons for purposes of further distribution, public performance, or public display." Give the full date (month, day, and year) when, and the country where, publication of the periodical issue containing the contribution first occurred. If first publication took place simultaneously in the United States and other countries, it is sufficient to state "U.S.A."

ADJUNCT APPLICATION
for Copyright Registration for a
Group of Contributions to Periodicals

- Use this adjunct form only if you are making a single registration for a group of contributions to periodicals, and you are also filing a basic application on Form TX, Form PA, or Form VA. Follow the instructions, attached.

- Number each line in Part B consecutively. Use additional Forms GR/CP if you need more space.

- Submit this adjunct form with the basic application form. Clip (do not tape or staple) and fold all sheets together before submittin g them.

FORM GR/CP ■
For a Group of Contributions to Periodicals
UNITED STATES COPYRIGHT OFFICE

REGISTRATION NUMBER

TX	PA	VA

EFFECTIVE DATE OF REGISTRATION

(Month)	(Day)	(Year)

FORM GR/CP RECEIVED

Page _____ of _____ pages

DO NOT WRITE ABOVE THIS LINE. FOR COPYRIGHT OFFICE USE ONLY

A

Identification
of
Application

IDENTIFICATION OF BASIC APPLICATION:
• This application for copyright registration for a group of contributions to periodicals is submitted as an adjunct to an application filed on: (Check which)

☐ Form TX   ☐ Form PA   ☐ Form VA

IDENTIFICATION OF AUTHOR AND CLAIMANT: (Give the name of the author and the name of the copyright claimant in all of the contributions listed in Part B of this form. The names should be the same as the names given in spaces 2 and 4 of the basic application.)

Name of Author _____

Name of Copyright Claimant _____

B

Registration
for Group of
Contributions

COPYRIGHT REGISTRATION FOR A GROUP OF CONTRIBUTIONS TO PERIODICALS: (To make a single registration for a group of works by the same individual author, all first published as contributions to periodicals within a 12-month period (see instructions), give full information about each contribution. If more space is needed, use additional Forms GR/CP.)

☐ Title of Contribution _____
Title of Periodical _____ Vol.____ No._____ Issue Date _____ Pages _____
Date of First Publication _____ Nation of First Publication _____
      (Month)   (Day)   (Year)   (Country)

☐ Title of Contribution _____
Title of Periodical _____ Vol.____ No._____ Issue Date _____ Pages _____
Date of First Publication _____ Nation of First Publication _____
      (Month)   (Day)   (Year)   (Country)

☐ Title of Contribution _____
Title of Periodical _____ Vol.____ No._____ Issue Date _____ Pages _____
Date of First Publication _____ Nation of First Publication _____
      (Month)   (Day)   (Year)   (Country)

☐ Title of Contribution _____
Title of Periodical _____ Vol.____ No._____ Issue Date _____ Pages _____
Date of First Publication _____ Nation of First Publication _____
      (Month)   (Day)   (Year)   (Country)

☐ Title of Contribution _____
Title of Periodical _____ Vol.____ No._____ Issue Date _____ Pages _____
Date of First Publication _____ Nation of First Publication _____
      (Month)   (Day)   (Year)   (Country)

☐ Title of Contribution _____
Title of Periodical _____ Vol.____ No._____ Issue Date _____ Pages _____
Date of First Publication _____ Nation of First Publication _____
      (Month)   (Day)   (Year)   (Country)

☐ Title of Contribution _____
Title of Periodical _____ Vol.____ No._____ Issue Date _____ Pages _____
Date of First Publication _____ Nation of First Publication _____
      (Month)   (Day)   (Year)   (Country)

FORM GR/CP

B

Continued

Title of Contribution _____
Title of Periodical _____ Vol.___ No.____ Issue Date _____ Pages _____
Date of First Publication _____ Nation of First Publication _____
(Month) (Day) (Year) (Country)

Title of Contribution _____
Title of Periodical _____ Vol.___ No.____ Issue Date _____ Pages _____
Date of First Publication _____ Nation of First Publication _____
(Month) (Day) (Year) (Country)

Title of Contribution _____
Title of Periodical _____ Vol.___ No.____ Issue Date _____ Pages _____
Date of First Publication _____ Nation of First Publication _____
(Month) (Day) (Year) (Country)

Title of Contribution _____
Title of Periodical _____ Vol.___ No.____ Issue Date _____ Pages _____
Date of First Publication _____ Nation of First Publication _____
(Month) (Day) (Year) (Country)

Title of Contribution _____
Title of Periodical _____ Vol.___ No.____ Issue Date _____ Pages _____
Date of First Publication _____ Nation of First Publication _____
(Month) (Day) (Year) (Country)

Title of Contribution _____
Title of Periodical _____ Vol.___ No.____ Issue Date _____ Pages _____
Date of First Publication _____ Nation of First Publication _____
(Month) (Day) (Year) (Country)

Title of Contribution _____
Title of Periodical _____ Vol.___ No.____ Issue Date _____ Pages _____
Date of First Publication _____ Nation of First Publication _____
(Month) (Day) (Year) (Country)

Title of Contribution _____
Title of Periodical _____ Vol.___ No.____ Issue Date _____ Pages _____
Date of First Publication _____ Nation of First Publication _____
(Month) (Day) (Year) (Country)

Title of Contribution _____
Title of Periodical _____ Vol.___ No.____ Issue Date _____ Pages _____
Date of First Publication _____ Nation of First Publication _____
(Month) (Day) (Year) (Country)

Title of Contribution _____
Title of Periodical _____ Vol.___ No.____ Issue Date _____ Pages _____
Date of First Publication _____ Nation of First Publication _____
(Month) (Day) (Year) (Country)

Title of Contribution _____
Title of Periodical _____ Vol.___ No.____ Issue Date _____ Pages _____
Date of First Publication _____ Nation of First Publication _____
(Month) (Day) (Year) (Country)

Title of Contribution _____
Title of Periodical _____ Vol.___ No.____ Issue Date _____ Pages _____
Date of First Publication _____ Nation of First Publication _____
(Month) (Day) (Year) (Country)

☆U.S. COPYRIGHT OFFICE WWW FORM: 1995: 387-237/44

APPENDIX E   COPYRIGHT AGREEMENTS

ASSIGNMENT OF COPYRIGHT

Assignment (Short Form)

I, [*name of assignor*], assignor of [*name of work*], in consideration of [*amount of payment*] and other valuable consideration, paid by [*name of assignee*], assignee, hereby assign to assignee, his heirs, and assigns, all my right title and interest in and to the copyright to [*name of work*] and all renewals and extensions of said copyright that may be secured under the laws of the United States of America and any other countries, as such may now or hereafter be in effect.

[*Signature of assignor*]

On this day of ___, before me, _____, the undersigned Notary Public, personally appeared _____ and proved to me based on satisfactory evidence to be the person(s) who executed this instrument.

WITNESS my hand and official seal.

_____

Notary Public

Assignment (Long Form)

[*Name and address of assignor*] ("Assignor") is the owner of all copyright in the work tentatively titled and referred to as [*name of work*] (the "Property"), a copy of which is attached to this agreement. [*Name of assignee*] ("Assignee") desires to own all rights in the property.

THEREFORE, for valuable consideration of [*amount of payment*] and other consideration, the receipt and sufficiency of which are acknowledged, Assignor hereby assigns to Assignee, its successors, and assigns, all right, title, and interest in the Property, including all copyrights and registrations. Assignee shall have the right to register the copyright to the Property in its own name and shall have the exclusive right to dispose of the work in any manner whatsoever. Assignor warrants that assignor is the legal owner of all right, title, and interest in the Property, that the rights have not been previously licensed, pledged, assigned, or encumbered, and that this assignment does not infringe on the rights of any person. Assignor agrees to cooperate with Assignee and to execute and deliver all papers as may be necessary to vest all rights to the Property. This includes cooperation with the recordation of the assignment in the United States Copyright Office.

[Assignor's signature and date]

I am the spouse of Assignor and acknowledge that I have read and understand this Agreement. I am aware that my spouse's interest in the Property is assigned, including any community property interest or other equitable property interest that I may have in it. I consent to the assignment, and agree that my interest, if any, in the Property is subject to the provisions of this Agreement. I will take no action to hinder the Agreement or the underlying assignment of rights.

[Spouse signature]

[Notary Public]

WORK MADE FOR HIRE AGREEMENT

Following is an example of a work made for hire agreement. Often such agreements are simply referred to as "work for hire" agreements. This type of agreement is not necessary for works created by an employee, although many employment contracts contain language regarding works made for hire. If the work that is the subject of this agreement does not fall within one of the enumerated categories, this agreement will not create a work made for hire. This agreement contains standard contract provisions used in copyright agreements.

Work Made for Hire Agreement

This Agreement is made between CompuCo, Inc. ("CompuCo") and Joan Doolittle ("Artist"). CompuCo desires to commission the Artist to create eight (8) illustrations (collectively referred to as the "Work") as supplementary works for use in an instructional manual for the computer program, Holiday Break. The Work consists of a series of black and white camera-ready pen and ink illustrations of the following holiday themes: New Year's, Valentine's Day, Easter, President's Day, Independence Day, Halloween, Thanksgiving, and Christmas. Artist agrees that CompuCo shall acquire all rights in the Work, including but not limited to copyright in the Work as a "work made for hire" as that term is defined in the Copyright Act of 1976. Artist agrees to complete the Work according to the following schedule:

Preliminary sketches	Six months from date of execution of this agreement
Final drawings	Nine months from date of execution of this agreement

CompuCo shall not be required to publish the Work, and whenever it does, CompuCo, as owner of copyright, may add or delete from the Work and may or may not credit Artist as illustrator. Successors and assigns of CompuCo shall have the same rights in the Work. Artist warrants that Artist is the sole creator of the work and that it is original, unpublished, and contains no plagiarized, defamatory, or otherwise unlawful materials or will invade the rights of privacy or publicity of any third parties.

Artist agrees to indemnify and hold CompuCo harmless from any loss of liability, including reasonable attorney fees arising out of any breach or alleged breach of these warranties. This Agreement shall be governed by the laws of the state of California. If any dispute arises under or relating to this Agreement, the prevailing party shall be entitled to its reasonable attorney fees. This is the complete understanding between the parties and cannot be modified without an agreement in writing signed by the parties.

[*Signatures of the parties*]

LICENSE AGREEMENT

There are many variations on license agreements, and each agreement has aspects that are appropriate to a particular industry. For example, music licensing is often quite complex, and payments may be triggered by many types of sales and performances. Software licensing is also complex and may require knowledge of international and antitrust law. License agreements are usually longer than assignments and include common contract clauses such as provisions for resolving disputes. This is because under a license, the author retains ownership and must deal with issues that arise in the ongoing license arrangement. Under an assignment, the author gives up all rights and is only concerned with receiving payments. Below is an example of a basic license agreement for an artist whose works will be reprinted on T-shirts. Under this agreement, the artist retains the right to license the image for other uses besides upper body wear (T-shirts, and sweatshirts, and so on).

Exclusive T-Shirt (Merchandise) License Agreement

Introduction. This Merchandise License Agreement (the "Agreement") is made between [*licensor's name*], a [*type and state of business, for example, a California corporation*] of [*licensor's address*], (referred to as "Licensor"), and [*licensee's name*], a [*type and state of business, for example, a California corporation*] with its principal address at [*licensee's address*] (referred to as "Licensee"). Licensor and Licensee shall be collectively referred to as "the parties." Licensor is the owner of copyright to an image tentatively referred to as the "[*name of image*]," a copy of which is attached to this agreement. Licensee desires to license certain rights in order to make and sell licensed products, specifically upper body wear, including but not limited to T-shirts and sweatshirts, incorporating the image. Therefore the parties agree as follows:

I. The Property. The "Property" refers to the image embodied in U.S. Copyright No. [*If the work is registered, include the copyright number; otherwise simply describe the work. Note: a work does not have to be registered in order to be licensed*].

II. Grant of Rights.

A. Licensed Products. Licensor grants to Licensee an exclusive nonassignable, nontransferable license to use the Property solely in association with the manufacture, sale, use, promotion, or distribution of certain clothing products incorporating the Property and more specifically described in Exhibit A (the "Licensed Products").

B. Reservation of Rights. Licensor expressly reserves all rights other than those being conveyed or granted in this Agreement.

III. Territory. The rights granted to Licensee are limited to the areas specified in Exhibit A (the "Territory").

IV. Term. This Agreement shall commence upon the Effective Date as specified in Exhibit A and shall extend for a period of two years (the "Initial Term"). Following the Initial Term, this agreement may be renewed by Licensee under the same terms and conditions for five consecutive two-year periods (the "Renewal Terms") provided that Licensee provides written notice of its intention to renew this agreement within 30 days prior to expiration of the current term.

V. Payment.

  A. Advance Against Royalties. As a nonrefundable advance against royalties (the "Advance",) Licensee agrees to pay to Licensor upon execution of this Agreement the sum specified in Exhibit A.

  B. Royalties. All royalties ("Royalties") provided for under this Agreement shall accrue when the respective items are sold, shipped, distributed, billed, or paid for, whichever occurs first. Royalties shall also be paid by the Licensee to Licensor on all items, even if not billed (including but not limited to introductory offers, samples, promotions, or distributions) to individuals or companies that are affiliated with, associated with, or subsidiaries of Licensee. "Net Sales" are defined as Licensee's gross sales (i.e., the gross invoice amount billed customers) less quantity discounts and returns actually credited. A quantity discount is a discount made at the time of shipment. No deductions shall be made for cash or other discounts, for commissions, for uncollectible accounts, or for fees or expenses of any kind that may be incurred by the Licensee in connection with the Royalty payments. Licensee agrees to pay the Royalty, as specified in Exhibit A, for all Net Sales of the Licensed Products ("Licensed Product Royalty.").

  C. Payments and Statements to Licensor. Within 30 days after the end of each calendar quarter (the "Royalty Period"), an accurate statement of Net Sales of Licensed Products along with any royalty payments or sublicensing revenues due to Licensor shall be provided to Licensor, regardless of whether any Licensed Products were sold during the Royalty Period. All payments shall be paid in United States currency drawn on a United States bank. The acceptance by Licensor of any of the statements furnished or royalties paid shall not preclude Licensor questioning the correctness at any time of any payments or statements.

  D. Audit. Licensee shall keep accurate books of account and records covering all transactions relating to the license granted in this Agreement, and Licensor or its duly authorized representatives shall have the right, upon five days prior written notice, and during normal business hours, to inspect and audit Licensee's records relating to the Property licensed under this Agreement. Licensor shall bear the cost of such inspection and audit, unless the results indicate an underpayment greater than $1,000 for any six-month period.

E. **Late Payment.** Time is of the essence with respect to all payments to be made by Licensee under this Agreement.

VI. Licensor Warranties. Licensor warrants that [*he/she/it*] has the power and authority to enter into this Agreement and has no knowledge as to any third-party claims regarding the proprietary rights in the Property that would interfere with the rights granted under this Agreement.

VII. Indemnification by Licensor. Licensor shall indemnify Licensee and hold Licensee harmless from any damages and liabilities (including reasonable attorneys' fees and costs) arising from any breach of Licensor's warranties as defined in Licensor's Warranties in Section VI provided: (a) such claim, if sustained, would prevent Licensee from marketing the Licensed Products or the Property; (b) such claim arises solely out of the Property as disclosed to the Licensee, and not out of any change in the Property made by Licensee or a vendor, or by reason of an off-the-shelf component or by reason of any claim for trademark infringement; (c) Licensee gives Licensor prompt written notice of any such claim; (d) such indemnity shall only be applicable in the event of a final decision by a court of competent jurisdiction from which no right to appeal exists; and (e) that the maximum amount due from Licensor to Licensee under this paragraph shall not exceed the amounts due to Licensor under the Payment Section from the date that Licensor notifies Licensee of the existence of such a claim.

VIII. Licensee Warranties. Licensee warrants that it will use its best commercial efforts to market the Licensed Products and that their sale and marketing shall be in conformance with all applicable laws and regulations, including but not limited to all intellectual property laws. The provisions of this Section shall survive any termination.

IX. Indemnification by Licensee. Licensee shall indemnify Licensor and hold Licensor harmless from any damages and liabilities (including reasonable attorneys' fees and costs) (a) arising from any breach of Licensee's warranties and representations as defined in Licensee Warranties in Section VIII, and (b) arising out of any alleged defects or failures to perform of the Licensed Products or any use of the Licensed Products.

X. Proprietary Rights.

A. Intellectual Property Protection. Licensor may, but is not obligated to, seek in its own name and at its own expense appropriate trademark or copyright protection for the Property, and Licensor makes no warranty with respect to the validity of any trademark or copyright that may be granted.

B. Compliance with Laws. The license granted in this Agreement is conditioned on Licensee's compliance with the provisions of the intellectual property laws of the United States and any foreign country in the Territory. All copies of the Licensed Product as well as all promotional material shall bear appropriate proprietary notices.

C. Infringement Against Third Parties. In the event that either party learns of imitations or infringements of the Property or Licensed Products, that party shall notify the other in writing of the infringements or imitations. Licensor shall have the right to commence lawsuits against third persons arising from infringement of the Property or Licensed Products. In the event that Licensor does not commence a lawsuit against an alleged infringer within 60 days of notification by Licensee, Licensee may commence a lawsuit against the third party. Prior to filing suit, Licensee shall obtain the written consent of Licensor to do so and such consent shall not be unreasonably withheld. Licensor will cooperate fully and in good faith with Licensee for the purpose of securing and preserving Licensee's rights to the Property. Any recovery (including but not limited to a judgment, settlement, or licensing agreement included as resolution of an infringement dispute) shall be divided equally between the parties after deduction and payment of reasonable attorneys' fees to the party bringing the lawsuit.

XI. Exploitation. Licensee agrees to commence manufacture, distribution, and sale of the Licensed Products in commercially reasonable quantities within the time period specified in Exhibit A. This is a material provision of this Agreement.

XII. Samples and Quality Control. Licensee shall submit 10 production samples of the Licensed Product to Licensor to ensure that the product meets Licensor's quality standards. In the event that Licensor fails to object in writing within 10 business days after the date of receipt, the Licensed Product shall be deemed to be acceptable. At least once during each calendar year, Licensee shall submit two production samples of each Licensed Product for review. The quality standards applied by Licensor shall be no more rigorous than the quality standards applied by Licensee to similar products.

XIII. Confidentiality. The parties acknowledge that each may be furnished or have access to confidential information that relates to each other's business (the "Information"). The parties agree to preserve and protect the confidentiality of the Information.

XIV. Termination. This Agreement terminates at the end of two years (the "Initial Term") unless renewed by Licensee under the terms and conditions as provided in the Term Section of this Agreement.

    A. Licensor's Right to Terminate. Licensor shall have the right to terminate this Agreement for the following reasons:

    B. Licensee fails to pay Royalties when due or fails to accurately report Net Sales, as defined in the Payment Section of this Agreement, and such failure is not cured within 30 days after written notice from the nonbreaching party;

    C. Licensee fails to introduce the product to market by [*supply date*] or to offer the Licensed Products in commercially reasonable quantities during any preceding year;

    D. Licensee fails to maintain confidentiality regarding Licensor's trade secrets and other Information;

    E. Licensee assigns or sublicenses in violation of the Agreement; or

    F. Licensee fails to maintain or obtain product liability insurance as required by the provisions of this Agreement.

    G. Effect of Termination. Upon termination of this Agreement, all Royalty obligations as established in the Payments Section shall immediately become due. After the termination of this license, all rights granted to Licensee under this Agreement shall revert to Licensor, and Licensee will refrain from further manufacturing, copying, marketing, distribution, or use of any Licensed Product or other product that incorporates the Property. Within 30 days after termination, Licensee shall deliver to Licensor a statement indicating the number and description of the Licensed Products that it had on hand or is in the process of manufacturing as of the termination date. Licensee may dispose of the Licensed Products covered by this Agreement for a period of three months after termination except that Licensee shall have no such right in the event this agreement is terminated according to the Licensor's Right to Terminate, above. At the end of the post-termination sale period, Licensee shall furnish a royalty payment and statement as required under the Payment Section. Upon termination, Licensee shall deliver to Licensor all tooling and molds used in the manufacture of the Licensed Products. Licensor shall bear the costs of shipping for the tooling and molds.

XV. Miscellaneous.

A. Survival. The obligations of Sections (V through X) and XIII shall survive any termination of this Agreement.

B. Attorneys' Fees and Expenses. The prevailing party shall have the right to collect from the other party its reasonable costs and necessary disbursements and attorneys' fees incurred in enforcing this Agreement.

C. Arbitration. If a dispute arises under or relating to this Agreement, the parties agree to submit such dispute to binding arbitration in the state of [insert licensor's state of residence] or another location mutually agreeable to the parties. The arbitration shall be conducted on a confidential basis pursuant to the Commercial Arbitration Rules of the American Arbitration Association. Any decision or award as a result of any such arbitration proceeding shall be in writing and shall provide an explanation for all conclusions of law and fact and shall include the assessment of costs, expenses, and reasonable attorneys' fees. Any such arbitration shall be conducted by an arbitrator experienced in [indicate technical expertise desired] and in invention licensing law and shall include a written record of the arbitration hearing. The parties reserve the right to object to any individual who shall be employed by or affiliated with a competing organization or entity. An award of arbitration may be confirmed in a court of competent jurisdiction.

D. Governing Law. This Agreement shall be governed in accordance with the laws of the state of [insert state of residence].

E. Jurisdiction. The parties consent to the exclusive jurisdiction and venue of the federal and state courts located in [insert county and state of residence] in any action arising out of or relating to this Agreement and waive any other venue to which either party might be entitled by domicile or otherwise.

F. Waiver. The failure to exercise any right provided in this Agreement shall not be a waiver of prior or subsequent rights.

G. Invalidity. If any provision of this Agreement is invalid under applicable statute or rule of law, it is to be considered omitted and the remaining provisions of this Agreement shall in no way be affected.

H. Entire Understanding. This Agreement expresses the complete understanding of the parties and supersedes all prior representations, agreements, and understandings, whether written or oral. This Agreement may not be altered except by a written document signed by both parties.

I. Attachments and Exhibits. The parties agree and acknowledge that all attachments, exhibits, and schedules referred to in this Agreement are incorporated in this Agreement by reference.

J. Notices. Any notice or communication required or permitted to be given under this Agreement shall be sufficiently given when received by certified mail, or sent by facsimile transmission or overnight courier.

K. No Joint Venture. Nothing contained in this Agreement shall be construed to place the parties in the relationship of agent, employee, franchisee, officer, partners, or joint venturers. Neither party may create or assume any obligation on behalf of the other.

L. Assignability. Licensee may not assign or transfer its rights or obligations pursuant to this Agreement without the prior written consent of Licensor. However, no consent is required for an assignment or transfer that occurs: (a) to an entity in which Licensee owns more than fifty percent of the assets; or (b) as part of a transfer of all or substantially all of the assets of Licensee to any party. Any assignment or transfer in violation of this Section shall be void.

Exhibit A

License Terms

The Properties

U.S. Copyright No. _____ (or description of work or attach a copy of work)

Licensed Products

[*List products, for example, "T-shirts and sweatshirts"*]

Effective Date

[*Date when agreement will go into effect, usually date of all signatures*]

Territory

[*List countries, regions, or states in which licensee can sell licensed products, for example, "United States, Canada, and Mexico"*]

Advance

[*Amount of advance*]

Licensed Product Royalty Rate

_% of wholesale price of Licensed Product or _% of retail price if sold directly to consumers [*list percentages*]

Date for Commencement of Sale

[*Date when sales must commence*]

APPENDIX F   SAMPLE COMPLAINT AND SETTLEMENT AGREEMENT

SAMPLE COPYRIGHT COMPLAINT: *GRENADIER V. JUNKY JEWELRY*

The sample complaint details an infringement of a copyrighted earring (Bunny Love #1). Like many copyright cases, the complaint includes several claims: copyright infringement; violation of the Lanham Act § 43(a); and common law unfair competition (the latter two claims are derived from trademark law).

The sample complaint contains some embellishments that are not required but which add to the strength of the case. For example, there is a short statement about the plaintiff's status as a jewelry designer. Although not required, it adds a legitimacy to the claim and demonstrates that a person's livelihood is at stake.

In addition, the complaint includes information about the fashion accessories business. It is advisable to include a short statement about the specific trade because a court may not be aware of how works are copied or how works are distributed.

Bailey W. Rumpole, Esq.
Cal. State Bar. No. 18774
One Market Plaza, 20th Floor
San Francisco, California 94105
(415) 777-4977

Attorney for Plaintiff, Bobby Grenadier

THE UNITED STATES DISTRICT COURT FOR THE NORTHERN DISTRICT OF CALIFORNIA

BOBBY GRENADIER, an individual,	Complaint for Copyright Infringement; Lanham Act § 43(a); and Common Law Unfair Competition
Plaintiff,	
v.	
JUNKY JEWELRY, a California corporation,	
Defendant.	

JURISDICTION

1. Jurisdiction for the copyright claims is based upon the Copyright Act, 28 U.S.C. § 1338(a). Jurisdiction for claims under the Lanham Act is based upon 15 U.S.C. § 1125(a). Jurisdiction over all related common law claims is based upon the provisions of 15 U.S.C. § 1338(b).

VENUE

2. Venue is proper pursuant to 28 U.S.C. § 1400(a) and 28 U.S.C. § 1391(c).

The Parties

3. Plaintiff BOBBY GRENADIER is an individual residing in San Mateo County, California, within the Northern District of California and referred to in this Complaint as "GRENADIER."

4. JUNKY JEWELRY is a California corporation with its principal place of business in Los Angeles, California, and referred to in this complaint as "JUNKY JEWELRY."

FIRST CAUSE OF ACTION

(Copyright Infringement)

5. GRENADIER is a professional jewelry designer whose work has been offered for sale at Nordstrom, Barneys, Macy's, the Guggenheim Museum Gift Shop, and other retail outlets.

6. GRENADIER is the owner of copyright of a jewelry design entitled *Bunny Love #1*. GRENADIER received from the Register of Copyrights a certificate of registration for *Bunny Love #1* identified as follows: Registration No. VA 555-444, dated April 1, 1993, a true copy of which is attached to this Complaint as Exhibit A and incorporated in this Complaint by reference.

7. *Bunny Love #1* was first published and distributed to the public sometime in December 1998.

8. All copies of *Bunny Love #1* were published and distributed in compliance with the Copyright Act of 1976. At all times mentioned in this Complaint, GRENADIER has been and is the sole proprietor of all right, title, and interest in and to the copyright in *Bunny Love #1*.

9. GRENADIER's jewelry design work is marketed within a specialized area of the fashion industry commonly known as the "fashion accessories" market. The fashion accessories market includes jewelry, watches, belts, scarves, and other fashion items.

10. A photograph of GRENADIER's *Bunny Love #1* was featured in *Women's Wear Daily* sometime on or about January 1996, a copy of which is attached as Exhibit B and incorporated in this Complaint by reference.

11. GRENADIER's jewelry design work is prepared for the retail market as follows: First, an original of the jewelry design is prepared out of a wax material. The wax material is then cast into a bronze master mold. A multiple mold is then made from the bronze master. From the multiple mold, production pieces are created. Production pieces are then joined, merged, or attached to other metal pieces to form distinctive jewelry items such as earrings and bracelets.

12. Plaintiff is informed and believes that defendant JUNKY JEWELRY operates retail outlets throughout California under the trade name *Junky Jewelry*.

13. Plaintiff is informed and believes that defendant JUNKY JEWELRY infringed the copyright in *Bunny Love #1* by distributing, advertising for sale, and selling an earring (a photocopy of which is attached as Exhibit C and incorporated by reference and referred to in this Complaint as Earring #1).

14. Plaintiff is informed and believes that Earring #1 is copied from and is substantially similar, if not identical, to *Bunny Love #1* so as to infringe GRENADIER's copyright in *Bunny Love #1*.

15. Plaintiff has notified defendant JUNKY JEWELRY that Earring #1 infringes plaintiff's copyright and JUNKY JEWELRY continues to infringe plaintiff's copyright by offering this item for sale.

16. As a proximate result of the acts alleged above, GRENADIER has and will in the future incur damages in an amount that is not presently ascertainable. Plaintiff shall seek leave of this court to amend this Complaint when the extent of plaintiff's damages can be fully calculated.

17. Defendant's infringement of GRENADIER's copyrighted works has caused, and unless enjoined will continue to cause, plaintiff irreparable harm.

SECOND CAUSE OF ACTION

(False Designation—Lanham Act § 43(a))

Plaintiff alleges and incorporates herein each preceding paragraph of the Complaint as if set forth herein in full.

18. This is a claim for federal unfair competition arising under section 43(a) of the Federal Trademark Act of 1946, as amended (15 U.S.C. § 1125(a)).

19. As established in preceding paragraphs of this complaint, GRENADIER has achieved a national reputation as a professional jewelry designer.

20. GRENADIER has achieved a distinctive and consistent style created by the total image and appearance of her jewelry designs. The total image and appearance of her jewelry products is nonfunctional and results from a specific and unique design sensibility, technique, and texture.

21. GRENADIER's unique style of jewelry design functions to designate and distinguish her jewelry from that of other jewelry designers.

22. GRENADIER is informed and believes that the predominant bunny-shaped piece used in Earring #1 was created by using *Bunny Love #1* as the basis for a mold from which defendant's pieces were cast.

23. GRENADIER is informed and believes that actual confusion has arisen as to the source of the jewelry item Earring #1, in that consumers mistakenly believe that GRENADIER is either the source of or affiliated with, connected to, or associated with the makers and sellers of Earring #1.

24. Such consumer confusion and the likelihood of further consumer confusion causes irreparable damage to GRENADIER and deceives the public, as purchasers will be confused as to whether GRENADIER is the origin of, affiliated with, or endorses or sponsors these unauthorized reproductions of her works.

25. The conduct of defendant as herein alleged has damaged GRENADIER and will, unless restrained, further impair, if not destroy, plaintiff's protectible trade dress and good will.

26. Defendant's duplication by direct casting and sale and distribution of these unauthorized reproductions in connection with their goods has caused, and unless enjoined will continue to cause, plaintiff irreparable harm.

27. As a proximate result of the acts alleged above, GRENADIER has and will in the future incur damages in an amount that is not presently ascertainable. Plaintiff shall seek leave of this court to amend this Complaint when the extent of plaintiff's damages can be fully calculated.

THIRD CAUSE OF ACTION

(Common Law Unfair Competition)

Plaintiff alleges and incorporates herein each preceding paragraph of the Complaint as if set forth herein in full.

28. By virtue of defendant's activities as alleged above, defendant's acts constitute unfair competition.

29. Defendant's acts of common law unfair competition have caused, and unless enjoined will continue to cause, plaintiff irreparable harm.

30. As a proximate result of the acts alleged above, GRENADIER has and will in the future incur damages in an amount that is not presently ascertainable. Plaintiff shall seek leave of this court to amend this Complaint when the extent of plaintiff's damages can be fully calculated.

WHEREFORE plaintiff prays for judgment as follows:

a. Permanently enjoining defendant, its officers, agents, employees, and those persons in active concert or participation with each or any of them from directly or indirectly infringing GRENADIER's copyright in *Bunny Love #1*.

b. As to the first cause of action for copyright infringement, awarding plaintiff such damages in an amount according to proof suffered as a result of defendant's infringement of her copyright.

c. As to the second cause of action for false designation, awarding plaintiff such damages in an amount according to proof.

d. As to the third cause of action for common law unfair competition, awarding plaintiff such damages in an amount according to proof.

e. Directing defendant to account for all profits derived by defendant from its infringement of plaintiff's copyrights and directing that defendant pay over to plaintiff the amount of such revenues.

f. Ordering defendant to deliver for impoundment during the pendency of this action all copies of the infringing works (in any form or medium) in its possession or under its control and to deliver for destruction all infringing copies and all original plates, molds, devices, or other matter for making such infringing copies.

Together with the cost and disbursement of this action and such other and further relief as this Court may deem just and proper.

Dated: _____   _____

BAILEY W. RUMPOLE, Attorney
for Plaintiff
One Market Plaza, 20th Floor
San Francisco, California 94105

SAMPLE SETTLEMENT AGREEMENT

This settlement agreement includes a provision required under California law (Section 5). It is bold-faced because the California Civil Code requires that this provision be highlighted and distinguishable from the rest of the text in the agreement.

CONFIDENTIAL SETTLEMENT AGREEMENT

Bobby Grenadier—Junky Jewelry

This Settlement Agreement and Mutual Release (the "Agreement") is made effective as of the date of signature below by and between Bobby Grenadier and Junky Jewelry, a California corporation.

A dispute has arisen between Grenadier and Junky Jewelry regarding Grenadier's copyright and related claims. The parties desire to settle the matter and, therefore, in consideration of the terms and covenants set forth below, agree as follows:

1. Junky Jewelry agrees to pay the sum of $12,000 in settlement of this action upon Grenadier's signing of the Agreement.

2. Junky Jewelry warrants and represents that: (1) Junky Jewelry did not acquire more than 30,000 units of the item referred to as the Junky Jewelry Earring; (2) upon its sale or other method of disposal of its remaining inventory of the Junky Jewelry Earring (estimated currently at 18,000 copies), Junky Jewelry shall not acquire or sell any further copies of the Junky Jewelry Earring; and (3) Junky Jewelry shall, upon execution of this Agreement by Grenadier, furnish to Grenadier the name and address of its source for the Junky Jewelry Earring.

3. Grenadier, for herself and for her agents, attorneys, successors, and predecessors, hereby releases Junky Jewelry and its officers, directors, managers,

partners, attorneys, agents, servants, employees, customers, suppliers, stockholders, heirs, insurers, executors, administrators, successors, assigns, and affiliates from any and all actions, causes of action, demands, damages, costs, expenses (including attorney fees), liabilities, or other losses known or unknown arising out of this dispute that have occurred prior to the date of this Agreement.

4. Junky Jewelry, for itself and for its agents, attorneys, successors, and predecessors, hereby releases Grenadier and her attorneys, agents, servants, employees, customers, suppliers, heirs, insurers, executors, administrators, successors, assigns, and affiliates from any and all counterclaims, claims, liabilities, demands, damages, costs, expenses (including attorney fees), liabilities, or other losses known or unknown arising out of or related to the dispute that have occurred prior to the date of this Agreement.

5. This Agreement constitutes a compromise. It is not an admission of liability by either party. For purposes of the claims referenced in this Agreement, the parties expressly waive the provisions and benefits of Section 1542 of the California Civil Code (or any similar provision of any law of any jurisdiction that may apply), which section reads as follows:

A general release does not extend to claims which the creditor does not know or suspect to exist in his favor at the time of executing the release, which if known by him must have materially affected his settlement with the debtor.

6. Each of the parties acknowledge they have been advised by an attorney and that they have full authority to execute this agreement in the capacities for which they have signed below.

7. In the event that any portion of this Agreement is found invalid, that portion may be severed from this Agreement and shall not affect the validity of the remainder of the Agreement. In the event of any dispute arising under this Agreement, the prevailing party shall be entitled to attorney fees. This Agreement shall be governed by the laws of the State of California and expresses the complete understanding of the parties and supersedes all prior proposals and representations. No portion of this Agreement shall be construed against the drafter.

AGREED AND CONSENTED TO

BOBBY GRENADIER

Dated: _____ _____

JUNKY JEWELRY INC.,

Dated: _____ By: [*name of person signing*]

Its: [*title of person signing*]

APPENDIX G   COPYRIGHT FEES

New statutory fees	Fee
Registration of a claim in literary materials other than serials (Form TX)	$30
Registration of a claim in a serial (Form SE)	$30
Registration of a claim in a work of the performing arts, including sound recordings and audiovisual works (Form PA, Form SR)	$30
Registration of a claim in a work of the visual arts (Form VA)	$30
Registration of a claim in a group of contributions to periodicals (GRCP)	$30
Registration of a renewal claim (Form RE) ■ Claim without Addendum ■ Claim with Addendum	 $45 $60
Registration of a correction or amplification to a claim (Form CA)	$65
Providing an additional certificate of registration	$25
Any other certification (per hour)	$65
Search—report prepared from official records (per hour)	$65
Search—locating Copyright Office records (per hour)	$65
Recordation of document (single title)	$50
■ Additional titles (per group of 10 titles)	$15

Announcement of new special fees § 708(a)(10) effective July 1, 1999	
Registration of a claim in a group of serials (Form SE/Group)	$10/issue— $30 minimum
Registration of a claim in a group of daily newspapers, including qualified newsletters (Form G/DN)	$55
Registration of a restored copyright (Form GATT)	$30
Registration of a claim in a group of restored works (Form GATT/Group)	$10/claim— $30 minimum

APPENDIX H   INTERNATIONAL COPYRIGHT

17 U.S.C. § 104. SUBJECT MATTER OF COPYRIGHT: NATIONAL ORIGIN

(a) Unpublished works. The works specified by sections 102 and 103, while unpublished, are subject to protection under this title without regard to the nationality or domicile of the author.

(b) Published works. The works specified by sections 102 and 103, when published, are subject to protection under this title if—

(1) on the date of first publication, one or more of the authors is a national or domiciliary of the United States, or is a national, domiciliary, or sovereign authority of a treaty party, or is a stateless person, wherever that person may be domiciled; or

(2) the work is first published in the United States or in a foreign nation that, on the date of first publication, is a treaty party; or

(3) the work is a sound recording that was first fixed in a treaty party; or

(4) the work is a pictorial, graphic, or sculptural work that is incorporated in a building or other structure, or an architectural work that is embodied in a building and the building or structure is located in the United States or a treaty party; or

(5) the work is first published by the United Nations or any of its specialized agencies, or by the Organization of American States; or

(6) the work comes within the scope of a Presidential proclamation. Whenever the President finds that a particular foreign nation extends, to works by authors who are nationals or domiciliaries of the United States or to works that are first published in the United States, copyright protection on substantially the same basis as that on which the foreign nation extends protection to works of its own nationals and domiciliaries and works first published in that nation, the President may by proclamation extend protection under this title to works of which one or more of the authors is, on the date of first publication, a national, domiciliary, or sovereign authority of that nation, or which was first published in that nation. The President may revise, suspend, or revoke any such proclamation or impose any conditions or limitations on protection under a proclamation.

For purposes of paragraph (2), a work that is published in the United States or a treaty party within 30 days after publication in a foreign nation that is not a treaty party shall be considered to be first published in the United States or such treaty party, as the case may be.

(c) Effect of Berne Convention. No right or interest in a work eligible for protection under this title may be claimed by virtue of, or in reliance upon, the provisions of the Berne Convention, or the adherence of the United States thereto. Any rights in a work eligible for protection under this title that derive from this title, other Federal or State statutes, or the common law, shall not be expanded or reduced by virtue of, or in reliance upon, the provisions of the Berne Convention, or the adherence of the United States thereto.

(d) Effect of phonograms treaties. [Caution: This subsection takes effect upon the entry into force of the WIPO Performances and Phonograms Treaty with respect to the United States, as provided by § 105(b)(2) of Act Oct. 28, 1998, P.L. 105-304, which appears as 17 U.S.C.S. § 101.] Notwithstanding the provisions of subsection (b), no works other than sound recordings shall be eligible for protection under this title solely by virtue of the adherence of the United States to the Geneva Phonograms Convention or the WIPO Performances and Phonograms Treaty.

NATIONS AND THEIR COPYRIGHT RELATIONS WITH THE UNITED STATES

Following is a listing of nations and their treaty affiliation with the United States. The term *none* is used to signify that the country has no treaty affiliation with the United States. The term *unclear* is used to signify a nation that became independent since 1943 and that has not established copyright relations with the United States but may be honoring obligations incurred under its former political status.

Nation	Treaty Affiliation	Nation	Treaty Affiliation
Afghanistan	None	Belgium	Berne, UCC,
Albania	Berne		GATT
Algeria	UCC	Belize	UCC, GATT
Andorra	UCC	Benin (formerly	Berne, GATT
Angola	Unclear	Dahomey)	
Antigua and	GATT	Bhutan	None
Barbuda		Bolivia	BAC, UCC,
Argentina	Bilateral, UCC,		GATT
	Berne, GATT	Bosnia and	Berne, UCC
Armenia	None	Herzegovina	
Australia	Bilateral, Berne,	Botswana	GATT
	UCC, GATT	Brazil	BAC, Berne,
Austria	Bilateral, Berne,		UCC, GATT
	UCC, GATT	Brunei	GATT
Bahamas	Berne, UCC	Darussalam	
Bahrain	GATT	Bulgaria	Berne, UCC
Bangladesh	UCC, GATT	Burkina Faso	Berne, GATT
Barbados	Berne, UCC,	(formerly Upper	
	GATT	Volta)	
Belarus	UCC	Burma (see	
Belau	Unclear	Myanmar, Union	
		of)	

Nation	Treaty Affiliation	Nation	Treaty Affiliation
Burundi	GATT	Egypt	Berne, GATT
Cambodia	UCC	El Salvador	Bilateral, UCC, GATT
Cameroon	Berne, UCC, GATT	Equatorial Guinea	Unclear
Canada	Bilateral, Berne, UCC, GATT	Estonia	Berne
Cape Verde	Unclear	Ethiopia	None
Central African Republic	Berne, GATT	European Community	GATT
Chad	Berne	Fiji	Berne, UCC, GATT
Chile	Bilateral, BAC, Berne, UCC, GATT	Finland	Berne, UCC, GATT
China	Bilateral, Berne, UCC	France	Bilateral, Berne, UCC, GATT
Colombia	BAC, Berne, UCC, GATT	Gabon	Berne, GATT
Comoros	Unclear	Gambia, The	Berne
Congo	Berne	Georgia	Berne
Costa Rica	Bilateral, BAC, Berne, UCC, GATT	Germany	Bilateral, UCC, GATT
		Ghana	Berne, UCC, GATT
Cote d'Ivoire (Ivory Coast)	Berne, GATT	Greece	Bilateral, UCC, GATT
Croatia	Berne, UCC	Grenada	GATT
Cuba	Bilateral, UCC, GATT	Guatemala	BAC, UCC, GATT
Cyprus	Berne, UCC, GATT	Guinea	Berne, UCC, GATT
Czechoslovakia	Bilateral	Guinea-Bissau	Berne, GATT
Czech Republic	Berne, UCC, GATT	Guyana	Berne, GATT
Dahomey (see Benin)		Haiti	
		Holy See (see Vatican City)	
Denmark	Bilateral, Berne, UCC, GATT	Honduras	BAC, Berne
		Hong Kong	GATT
Djibouti	GATT	Hungary	Bilateral, Berne, UCC, GATT
Dominica	GATT		
Dominican Republic	BAC, UCC, GATT	Iceland	Berne, UCC, GATT
Ecuador	BAC, Berne, UCC, GATT	India	Bilateral, Berne, UCC, GATT

Nation	Treaty Affiliation	Nation	Treaty Affiliation
Indonesia	Bilateral, GATT	Madagascar	Berne, GATT
Iran	None	(Malagasy	
Iraq	None	Republic)	
Ireland	Berne, UCC, GATT	Malawi	UCC, GATT
		Malaysia	Berne, GATT
Israel	Bilateral, Berne, UCC, GATT	Maldives	GATT
		Mali	Berne, GATT
Italy	Bilateral, Berne, UCC, GATT	Malta	Berne, UCC, GATT
Ivory Coast (see		Mauritania	Berne, GATT
Cote d'Ivoire)		Mauritius	Berne, UCC,
Jamaica	Berne, GATT		GATT
Japan	Berne, UCC, GATT	Mexico	Bilateral, BAC, Berne, UCC, GATT
Jordan	Unclear		
Kazakhstan	UCC	Moldova	Berne
Kenya	Berne, UCC, GATT	Monaco	Berne, UCC, GATT
Kiribati	Unclear	Mongolia	None
Korea (North)	Unclear	Morocco	Berne, UCC, GATT
Democratic			
People's		Mozambique	GATT
Republic of		Myanmar, Union	GATT
Korea		of (formerly	
Koreah (South)	UCC, GATT	Burma)	
Republic of		Namibia	Berne, GATT
Korea		Nauru	Unclear
Kuwait	GATT	Nepal	None
Laos	UCC	Netherlands	Bilateral, Berne, UCC, GATT
Latvia	Berne		
Lebanon	Berne, GATT	New Zealand	Bilateral, Berne, UCC, GATT
Lesotho	Berne, GATT		
Liberia	Berne, UCC	Nicaragua	BAC, UCC, GATT
Libya	Berne		
Liechtenstein	Berne, UCC, GATT	Niger	Berne, UCC
		Nigeria	UCC, GATT
Lithuania	Berne	Norway	Bilateral, Berne, UCC, GATT
Luxembourg	Berne, UCC, GATT		
		Oman	None
Macau	GATT	Pakistan	Berne, UCC, GATT
Macedonia (formerly Yugoslav Republic)	Berne		

Nation	Treaty Affiliation	Nation	Treaty Affiliation
Panama	BAC, UCC	Soviet Union	
Papua New Guinea	Unclear	(see Russian Federation)	
Paraguay	BAC, Berne, UCC, GATT	Spain	Berne, UCC, GATT
Peru	BAC, Berne, UCC, GATT	Sri Lanka	Berne, UCC, GATT
Philippines	Bilateral, Berne, UCC, GATT	Sudan	Unclear
		Suriname	Berne, GATT
Poland	Berne, UCC, GATT	Swaziland	GATT
		Sweden	Berne, UCC, GATT
Portugal	Bilateral, Berne, UCC, GATT	Switzerland	Berne, UCC, GATT
Qatar	GATT		
Romania	Bilateral GATT	Syria	Unclear
Russian Federation	Berne, UCC	Tajikistan	UCC
		Tanzania	Berne, GATT
Rwanda	Berne, UCC	Thailand	Bilateral, Berne, GATT
Saint Christopher (Saint Kitts) and Nevis	Berne, GATT	Togo	Berne, GATT
		Tonga	None
Saint Lucia	Berne, GATT	Trinidad and Tobago	Berne, UCC, GATT
Saint Vincent and the Grenadines	UCC, GATT	Tunisia	Berne, UCC, GATT
San Marino	None	Turkey	Berne, GATT
Sao Tom, and Principe	Unclear	Tuvalu	Unclear
Saudi Arabia	UCC	Uganda	GATT
Senegal	Berne, UCC, GATT	Ukraine	UCC, Berne
		United Arab Emirates	None
Seychelles	Unclear		
Sierra Leone	GATT	United Kingdom	Bilateral, Berne, UCC, GATT
Singapore	Bilateral, GATT		
Slovakia	Berne, UCC, GATT	Upper Volta (see Burkina Faso)	
Slovenia	Berne, UCC, GATT	Uruguay	BAC, Berne, UCC, GATT
Solomon Islands	Unclear	Vanuatu	Unclear
Somalia	Unclear	Vatican City	Berne, UCC
South Africa	Bilateral, Berne, GATT	Venezuela	Berne, UCC, GATT
		Vietnam	Unclear
		Western Samoa	Unclear

Nation	Treaty Affiliation	Nation	Treaty Affiliation
Yemen (Aden)	Unclear	Zaire	Berne
Yemen (San'a)	None	Zambia	Berne, UCC, GATT
Yugoslavia	Berne, UCC		
		Zimbabwe	Berne, GATT

RESTORATION OF COPYRIGHT—GATT

Eligible copyright are restored automatically if they meet *all* of the following requirements:

- the work is in the public domain in the United States because the author failed to follow certain formalities (such as a failure to renew as explained in Chapter 14);
- at the time the work was created, at least one author must have been a national or domiciliary of an "eligible country." (An eligible country is a country, other than the United States, that is a member of the Berne Convention, the World Trade Organization (WTO), or is subject to a presidential proclamation that extends restored copyright protection to that country);
- if published, the work must have first been published in an eligible country (and must not have been published in the United States within thirty days following its first publication); and
- Copyright protection still exists in the country where the work was created (the "eligible country").

If an author or the author's estate wants to enforce rights against a person who relied on the public domain status of the work to reproduce it ("reliance parties"), then the author of a restored work must have filed a Notice of Intent to Enforce (NIE) with the Copyright Office before 1998 and must have sent an NIE to "reliance parties." This notice informs the reliance parties that the work is being restored and to halt future reproductions. For more information, consult Circular 38b. An example of the NIE is provided in the following text and can also be downloaded from the Copyright Office website.

Filing the NIE

The owner of a restored work may file an NIE directly with a reliance party at any time after the date of restoration. A reliance party has a twelve-month grace period to sell off previously manufactured stock. This period begins when the reliance party receives the NIE. The *United States Code*, title 17, section 104A (d)(3), contains special rules with respect to certain derivative works created before December 8, 1994, based on underlying restored works, such as the translation of a restored work or a motion picture based on a restored book or a play. Such derivative works may continue to be exploited by a reliance party if the reliance party pays the owner of the restored copyright reasonable compensation.

The NIE must include a certification statement indicating that the information given is correct to the best of the filer's knowledge. The fee for filing an NIE is $30 for a notice covering one work. For a notice covering multiple works, the fee is $30, plus $1 for each additional work covered beyond the first work. (For example, the fee for an NIE covering three works would be $32.) The fee includes the cost of an acknowledgment of recordation, which will be mailed to the filer after the Copyright Office records the NIE. The fee is not refundable and should be made payable to the Register of Copyrights. It should be paid by check, money order, or bank draft.

Notice of Intent to Enforce Copyright

1. Title:_____
   (If this work does not have a title, state "No title.") OR Brief description of work (for untitled works only):_____
   _____

2. English translation of title (if applicable):_____
   _____

3. Alternative title(s) (if any):_____
   _____

4. Type of work:_____
   _____
   (e.g., painting, sculpture, music, motion picture, sound recording, book)

5. Name of author(s):_____

6. Source country:_____

7. Approximate year of publication: _____

8. Additional identifying information:_____
   _____
   (e.g., for movies: director, leading actors, screenwriter, animator; for photographs: subject matter; for books: editor, publisher, contributors, subject matter)

9. Name of copyright owner:_____
   (Statements may be filed in the name of the owner of the restored copyright or the owner of an exclusive right therein.)

10. If you are not the owner of all rights, specify the rights you own:_____

(e.g., the right to reproduce/distribute/publicly display/publicly perform the work or to prepare a derivative work based on the work)

11. Address at which copyright owner may be contacted:

_____

_____

_____

(Give the complete address, including the country, and an "attention" line, or "in care of" name, if necessary.)

12. Telephone number of owner: _____

13. Telefax number of owner:_____

14. Certification and Signature: I hereby certify that, for each of the work(s) listed above, I am the copyright owner, or the owner of an exclusive right, or the owner's authorized agent, the agency relationship having been constituted in a writing signed by the owner before the filing of this notice, and that the information given herein is true and correct to the best of my knowledge.

Signature:_____

Name (printed or typed):_____

As agent for (if applicable):_____

Date:_____

Index